ALMOST
Budaörs
Budapest
Debrecen
HUNGARY
Gerendas
Lake Balaton
Szeged
Joseph J. Gelleny
Abaliget
Pécs
Danube R.
Drava R.
Papuk Mtns
YUGOSLAVIA

Cover Design: Third Wave Communications
Book Design ©Peter A. Graziano Limited
Editor- Barbara Kerr

Distribution by-
Blake Book Distribution
467 Fralicks Beach Road
Port Perry, Ontario
Canada L9L 1B6
905.985.8686

Canadian Cataloguing in Publication Data
Gelleny, Joseph J., 1923-
Almost

Includes bibliographical references and index
ISBN 0-9687062-2-3 (bound) ISBN 0-9687062-1-5 (pbk.)

1. Gelleny, Joseph J., 1923- . 2. World War, 1939-1945 - Personal narratives, Canadian. 3. World War, 1939-1945 - Underground movements - Hungary. 4. Great Britain. Special Operation Executive - Biography. 5. World War, 1939-1945 - Secret service - Great Britain. 6. World War, 1939-1945 - Prisoners and prisons. I. Hodgson, Lynn-Philip. II. Longfield, Alan. III. Title.

D811.G44 2000 940.54'8641'092 C00-932114-4

Design and Production
Silvio Mattacchione and Co.
Peter A. Graziano Limited
Printed in Canada by Friesens Corp.

Table of Contents

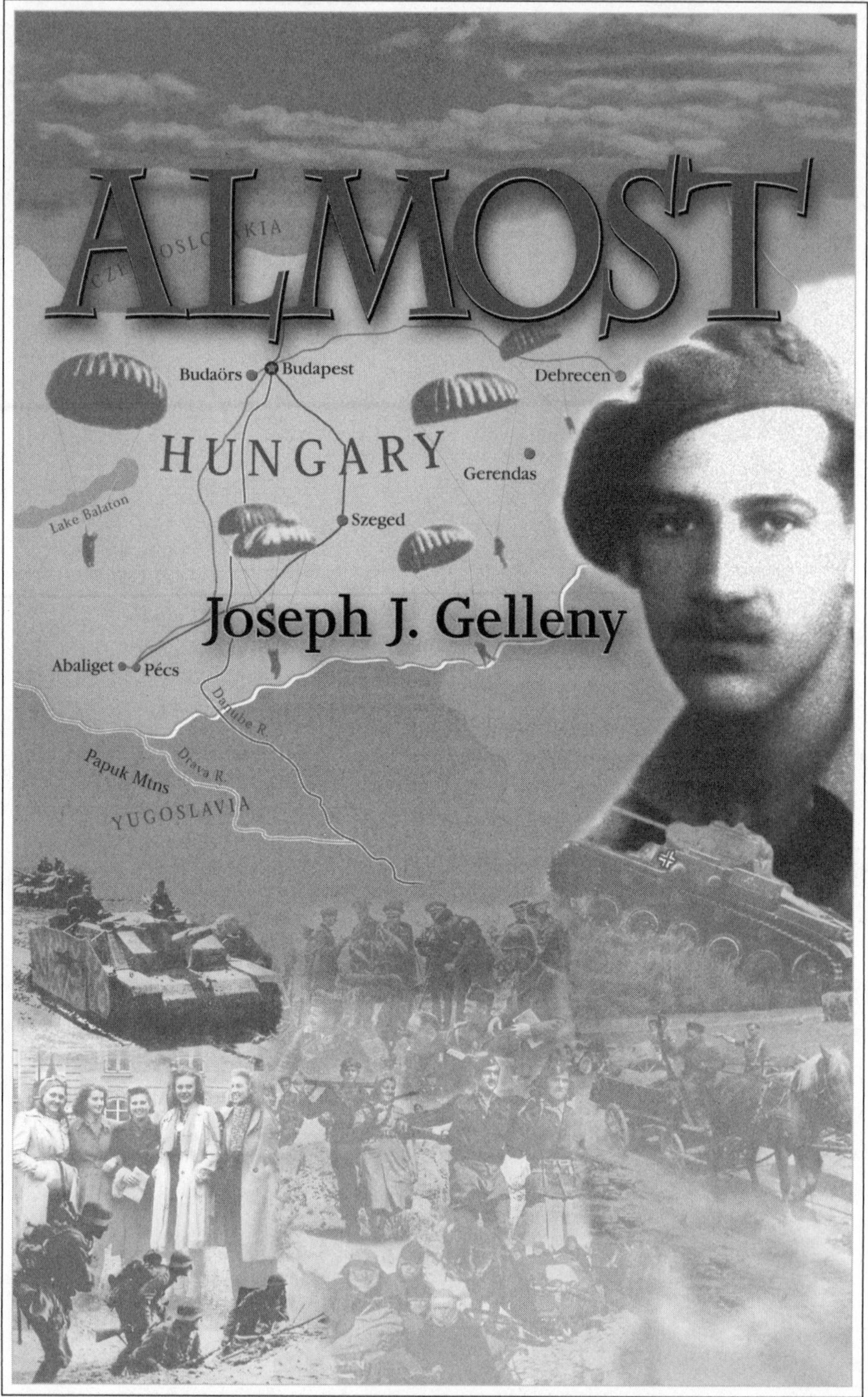
ALMOST
Budaörs
Budapest
Debrecen
HUNGARY
Gerendas
Lake Balaton
Szeged
Joseph J. Gelleny
Abaliget
Pécs
Danube R.
Drava R.
Papuk Mtns
YUGOSLAVIA

Acknowledgements

To the Russian Colonel
who gave me my freedom, and the American and British
officers who joined our freedom, walk from Budaörs to the
U. S. Legation in Debrecen;

To our Russian guide, Boris,
who accompanied us on our journey with his burp gun, and
the Hungarians who helped us along the way;

To Captain Jan Wolzleiger, and the Poles
who aided our escape from Zugliget, and to the Magyars,
both civilian and military, who protected, fed sheltered, and
cheered us;

To Horst Meyer and Krista Ferrier Meyer
for their assistance with the German spelling and Grammar;

To the Jewish people of Budapest
who assisted us and who suffered so terribly;

To Colonel Garzuly, Andras Hegedus,
Karola Koschwitz, Zoltan Perisich, and Matyas Pirithy for
your dedication, magnificent courage and unstinting
acts of kindness;

To Blokie, who was always there with me;
and,

To Mr. Raoul, Raoul Wallenberg,
for demonstrating incredible bravery and selfless
humanitarianism in the face of evil.

Thank you.
Joseph J. Gelleny
October, 2000

Helen Mossey just prior to her wedding day

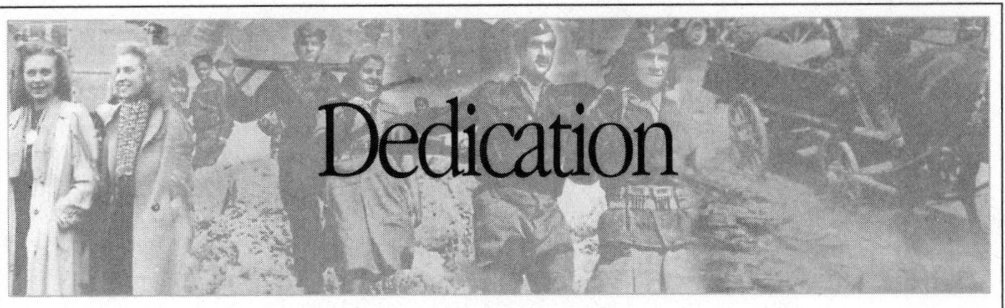

Dedication

To my dear, late wife, Helen,
for her continuous encouragement to write this book;

To my children, Jim, Lorne and Sharon
for their persistent urging;

To my dear friend, Dr. (Major) John Coates,
for his support and invaluable assistance;

To my grandchildren,
Andrew, Ashley, Elissa, Emily Rose, Heather, Jeff, Jim, Justin,
Libby, and Ryan;

To everyone who reads my story,
particularly students, who may be encouraged to read more
about Camp X and Canada's important role in
World War Two;

To all the men and women
in my story whose valour and personal sacrifice shall always
serve as examples of selfless courage in defence
of democracy;

And finally, to my colleagues:
Writer, Alan Paul Longfield; Research Associate, Lynn-Philip
Hodgson; and Editor, Barbara Kerr, my sincere thanks for
bringing Almost to life.

Joseph J. Gelleny, Author
Aurora, Ontario, Canada
October, 2000

The Allied Forces began their orderly evacuation from French soil at Dunkirk, unaware of the ramifications of this setback. Sensing the volatility of the times, Prime Minister Winston Churchill mandated the British War Cabinet to create a special new organization, the SOE (Special Operations Executive).

Churchill declared that the SOE would co-ordinate all activities of subversion and sabotage against the Axis enemy. Putting this operation into practice meant establishing Special Training Schools in strategically placed locations throughout the world where men and women would be trained as Secret Agents.

Churchill then called upon his old friend from Canada, William Stephenson, to create the British Security Co-Ordination with the responsibility of supplying agents for the Balkans as well as for North and South America. In late 1941, Stephenson found the perfect spot for one of his camps, safely distant from the war zone, in the small farm town of Whitby, Ontario, in his native Canada. It was called STS 103 (Special Training School - 103). Here volunteers from Canada and the U.S. were trained for the secret war which would be played out in the Nazi occupied countries.

The RAF were called in to assist, aircraft being one means by which these brave young men and women were dispatched. After the agents had completed their training and had been assigned their missions, the RAF would take over. Special Duties Squadrons #102 and #138 were formed in August of 1941 flying out of Tempsford, north of London, and later #161 Squadron began operation out of Tangmere, Sussex. Other flights originated out of Bari, Italy.

Whitney, Hudson, Halifax, and Wellington bombers and DC 3 airplanes were specially converted with 'Joe Holes' built into the floor allowing for easy and quick release of the agents when successfully positioned over their targets; in the case of quick landing and take off on the coast of France, the smaller Lysanders were used.

My friend, Joe Gelleny, asked me to write the foreward to his book. His story is of the secret and silent operations in occupied Europe which he successfully carried out and survived. Not everyone who applied was accepted for this duty. The men and women who served as agents had to be very intelligent and conscientious, and had to possess the courage to be ready to die for their country. I had the honour and privilege to fly these brave men and women to their destinations and missions. I observed their faces when the time came to leave the plane, either on the ground in enemy territory, or as they were about to jump through the open hole in the fuselage floor.

With these few lines, I pay my respect to the brave men and women with their never ending determination to serve their country.

Preface

On this inspirational note, Hungary was virtually abandoned to 'resist the pressure' of a virulently pro-Nazi Arrow Cross government backed by a massive German army of occupation. The British government might have just as well have wished the Hungarians "Happy Easter" as Nazi legions goose-stepped and the SS took absolute control of the country with a carefully orchestrated, repressive reign of terror.

> **By resisting German pressure, Hungary will make a valuable contribution to the forthcoming victory of the United Nations.**
> **British War Cabinet, Communiqué March 20, 1944.**

The outcomes were inevitable. The first was the human catastrophe of the Hungarian Holocaust. Then, with the surrender of all German occupying forces on February 13, 1945, came the Russian rape of Hungary and many bleak years of Soviet domination. How could these things have happened?

At the end of the First World War, the victorious Allies imposed the Treaties of Versailles (1919) and Trianon (1920) upon the defeated Triple Alliance: Germany, the non-existent Austro-Hungarian Empire, and Italy. Instigated by France, with the connivance of Hungary's former ally, Austria, and supported by Romania and Serbia, Hungary's harshest punishment was to be meted out under the terms of Trianon on June 4, 1920. Nearly two thirds of her land was annexed, taking away one half of her total population or one third of her Magyar-speaking people. The humiliation of this once proud nation was not finished. Trianon decreed that up to ninety percent of the country's abundant natural resources, heavy industries, railways, and infrastructure be seized and redistributed among the 'victors.' The Allied strategy was pragmatic. Hungary would be perpetually isolated from Germany and reduced to a pre-industrial medieval state incapable of mobilising an effective army. Humbled, on the brink of economic collapse and social chaos, Hungary was a fertile breeding ground for revolutionary anarchy.

In 1919, Hungary had a foretaste

of its future under the short-lived government of Communist President Bela Kun. Admiral Miklós Horthy, an authentic war hero and staunch anti-Communist of the aristocratic old guard, raised a small army to march on Budapest and oust the Marxist pretender. Astride his white horse, Horthy led his force into the capital city from which Kun had hurriedly fled merely hours earlier. Parliament immediately declared the restoration of the monarchy by appointing Admiral Horthy as Regent, or royal placeholder, on March 1, 1920. Horthy, unwilling to return to the days of the Austrian confederacy, effectively slammed the door on the possibility of a return to the Hapsburg era, by exiling King Charles IV, the heir to the throne.

Hungary was facing economic ruin. As in Germany, astronomically high levels of inflation and joblessness were rampant. Payment of the Versailles' exorbitant war retributions, combined with the seizure of its lands and prime industries, had devastated the economy. Horthy's moderate rule was in imminent danger of imploding. In a bizarre operation to reclaim a large portion of the nation's wealth, a group of Hungarian officers successfully raided the rich coffers of the Hungarian Embassy in Vienna under the friendly eyes of Viennese police officials.

Under Regent Horthy, Hungary was a kingdom without a crown. Having staunched the Bolshevist threat, Horthy retreated from public view until 1933 when a fast-rising anti-Bolshevik German National Socialist leader, Adolf Hitler, offered to return some of the annexed Hungarian lands. In exchange, Hungary would agree to remain neutral, in the likely event of war. Admiral Horthy, the conservative aristocrat, consented. He thought that, in so doing, he would insulate Hungary against invasion. In reality, he had made a disastrously shortsighted deal with a person whom he quickly came to personally despise, Adolf Hitler, the Nazi *Führer*. Hitler was suspicious of Admiral Horthy's intentions and resolved to keep a close watch on Hungary.

By 1940, Hitler's lightning-quick *blitzkreig* victories had restored Ruthenia and Transylvania to Hungary as promised. However, with the fall of Poland, Hungary was encircled by Hitler's conquest states. Miklós Horthy was to defy Adolf Hitler by courageously providing refuge to 100,000 Polish soldiers and airmen, with great personal benefits to me, as I will relate later in my story.

Hitler called in his markers; on June 22, 1941, massive German forces of close to three million troops smashed across the Soviet frontiers. *Fall Barbarossa* or Case Barbarossa had taken Stalin by complete surprise. Horthy was obliged to provide the *Führer* with two armies of Hungarian troops who were poorly equipped and ill prepared for a brutal war of attrition on the Russian Front. The invasion was stalemated in December on the outskirts of Moscow by an early and desperately cold Russian winter. Horthy, realising that he had led Hungary into a deal with the devil, Adolf Hitler, looked about for a credible spokesman to negotiate a secret agreement with the Allies. His choice was Nicholas Kallay, a wealthy, pro-British politician. Kallay was appointed Prime Minister. Hitler's Intelligence Services needed little time to see that Kallay's agenda was devoted to seeking a pact with London. In response, Hitler ordered his senior staff cadre to prepare a contingency plan for invasion to prevent Hungary's defection. This operation was called Case Margarethe 1.

Ferenc Szállási, a home-grown Nazi and the chief of the Arrow Cross Party, adopted a potent brew of ultra right wing 'Hungary for Hungarians' rhetoric to agitate and spread his venomous anti-Semitic propaganda. Horthy spurned Szállási's excesses as he himself strove to maintain a distant, minimalist relationship with Hitler while keeping the German 'advisors' in Hungary under his control. Hungary's Jews were afforded rights and protection under the law and, as such, were the envy of most others in Nazi occupied Europe where the full horror of the Final Solution was in sway. American Journalist, Anne O'Hare McCormick, wrote at the time, "It must count in the score of Hungary that until the Germans took control, it was the last refuge in Central Europe for the Jews able to escape from Germany, Austria, Poland and Romania. As long as they exercised any authority in their own house, the Hungarians tried to protect the Jews, while the Jewish collectivity was permitted to exist with its property rights intact against the day of Hitler's defeat."[1]

However, this was not to last. Since 1942, with Horthy's tacit approval, Kallay had attempted top-secret overtures through diplomatic channels in Lisbon, Berne, Stockholm, and Istanbul, to convince the Allies of Hungary's desire to declare its neutrality. There was even a proposal for a landing of Allied forces in southern Hungary, near the Yugoslavian border, thus stalling Russia's land-grabbing advances. The Allies were not buying it. They saw Horthy/Kallay as opportunists, trying to wiggle Hungary out of another war, on the losing side. Yet, Romania would finesse a slick 'turnabout', in August 1944, by joining the Russians against Germany. Furthermore, an attack by Britain and America against their ally, Russia, staged in Yugoslavia through Hungary, was out of the question. Deals had been made. Central and Eastern Europe were locked into the post-war Soviet sphere of influence.

[1] *New York Times, July 15, 1944*

On March 19, 1944, Hitler had had enough of Hungary's clandestine manoeuvring and Case Margarethe 1 was launched; the invading German forces met little Hungarian resistance.

As you will read, I personally sent two sets of wireless radio (W/T) messages to Allied HQ at Bari, Italy, and Istanbul, in October 1944, to alert the authorities of Admiral Horthy's forthcoming broadcast to declare an armistice. I immediately received confirmation that my transmissions were received. On October 15, 1944, Regent Horthy made his radio proclamation.[2] Predictably, Adolf Hitler was outraged. The *Führer's* devotedly loyal, odd job specialist, Otto 'Scarface' Skorzeny, seized Regent Horthy in an *SS* operation code-named 'Mickey Mouse'; Horthy was interned in Bavaria. Kallay took refuge in the Turkish Embassy in Budapest but surrendered to the *SS* in November 1944. He survived Mauthausen concentration camp and died after the war, in exile. Berlin installed the fanatical Arrow Cross leader, Major Ferenc Szállási, as their puppet head of state.[3]

For the next four months, Szállási presided over the horrors of the Nazi apocalypse in Hungary. Szállási's *Nyilasok* (sometimes referred to in Hungarian as *Nyilasi*) state police force, which was patterned after the *Gestapo*, was relentless in executing the murderous will of its Hungarian and German masters. After withstanding a monumental Soviet siege for fifty-one days, Budapest fell to Russian forces on February 13, 1945. Bela Kun's beloved Red Star again ascended. The past, it is said, is prologue....

[2] *The complete text of Horthy's address is provided in the Appendices.*

[3] *Miklós Horthy was freed in 1945 by U.S. troops, appeared as a witness at the Nuremberg war crimes trials (1946) and was cleared of all charges. He settled in Portugal, and published his memoirs before he died in 1956. His remains were re-interred in his homeland. Ferenc Szállási was executed as a war criminal.*

Foreword

The following story, *Almost*, is true. Although these events took place more than a half-century ago, I have reconstructed them from my extensive typed notes, which I have accumulated over the last thirty-five years while the names, locations and particulars were still fresh in my mind. Conversations are, to the best of my ability, accurately and faithfully reproduced.

Although I have made every effort to ensure fidelity to every aspect of the story, some names and conversations involving a few of the minor characters have been intentionally condensed or modified for the sake of brevity. My dear friend and SOE Mission DIBBLER leader, Dr. (Major) John Coates,[1] has been of invaluable assistance, where my memory was faulty.

[1] *Dr. John Coates held the rank of Captain, during his time as commanding officer of SOE Mission* DIBBLER. *He was promoted to Major for his work in finding and compensating our Hungarian friends after the war.*

Introduction

I was born on February 5, 1923 in Gerendas, a village of 1,000 inhabitants, which has changed little since the days of the Austro-Hungarian Empire. Gerendas is in southeast Hungary, Bekés Township, near Békéscaba, not far from the Romanian border.

When my father, John Gelleny, returned from the war in 1918, he had a dream. He and Uncle Joe, his brother, would go into the farming business. The war was over, food was scarce, and people obviously needed to eat. Dad and Joe would feed the local populace. They reasoned that the carnage of the Great War, followed by the drift of young and able veterans into the industrialised towns, had seriously depleted the pool of experienced labour that was required to work the traditional family farms. Surplus land abounded and could be rented more cheaply than it could be purchased. Dad and Uncle Joe were convinced that they could become the Township's major food suppliers if they could attract the cream of the workers by providing good wages and opportunities for advancement. They planned to use the most advanced methods of cultivation, putting them years ahead of their competitors. Farming, as an industry, was the agricultural wave of the future. Meanwhile, the world was on the brink of financial collapse. Dad and Joe scraped together their savings and set about to realise their plan.

In spite of their efforts, the early profits were meagre to non-existent after leases, salaries, and their overhead costs for equipment and seeds were deducted. Worse, inflation was skyrocketing out of control and the banks that were still in business were charging extortionate interest rates and calling in loans daily. Dad and Joe had expected the start-up would be challenging, but after months of effort and investment, the company books showed no glimmer of hope for an end to the oceans of red ink. Still, they persisted, somehow managing to pay their creditors on time. The positive outcome for me personally was that Dad met my mother in one of the villages where he was renting a tract of land.

I have few recollections of my early days in Gerendas, other than a sense of childhood contentment. Dad and Uncle Joe seemed to have no time to enjoy themselves, as they struggled with the myriad setbacks and complexities of running a business on little experience and even less capital. Brows furrowed as deeply as the fields they worked, they met nightly, holding solemn, grown-ups only, kitchen table deliberations about their increasingly bleak prospects. These depressing discussions were sometimes enlivened with passionate political debates among relatives and assorted neighbours on the merits of Hungary's alliance with Austria and Germany in the First World War, and the ruinous effects of the peace settlements.

My early education took place in a one-room schoolhouse, which was partitioned into two areas: Primary, and Junior/Intermediate. I was an attentive student who took my assignments with at least a degree of seriousness. I enjoyed all sports and was often chosen as team captain. Except for the occasional sharp rap with a cane ruler on my fingertips for talking out of turn, I was a model student, discounting the one time I was almost expelled.

A few of the older boys had decided to play a prank on our teacher, Miss K., a stern and humourless woman who always wore black as a memorial to a lover, killed in The Great War, or so it was rumoured. A very large wood-fired pot-bellied stove located at the back of the room heated the schoolhouse. My desk was close to the stove. On a particularly bitter winter day, one of the upper grade lads, whose job it was to refuel the wood stove at lunchtime, boasted that he had 'plastered' the stove's entire surface with the juice of several large crushed garlic buds. He then stoked it with hardwood logs. The ringing of the hand bell brought us in, after lunch, cherry-faced and stamping the snow from our boots "like a herd of wild elephants." Miss K. gruffly called for order as we scuttled to our desks, and afternoon classes commenced in absolute silence. I was working on row after row of formidable addition questions, with carrying, in my mathematics exercise book, when I began to sweat. Turning around, I saw that the stove's belly was glowing almost as red as our faces. A peculiarly pungent aroma was emanating from the vicinity. It was exactly like the stories that my father told of gas attacks at the Front as the fumes wafted over our heads and descended, although no one keeled over dead. Instead, the results were fits of coughing, gasping, teary eyes, and then, near-pandemonium in our normally orderly learning community. We barged out into the raw afternoon, without coats, hacking and giggling, "like a pack of animals," as Miss K. later remonstrated. After a thorough airing, we were summoned inside by a very angry Miss K., to commence the inquisition. She was short of stature but as she cruised up and down the aisles, brandishing her trusty cane ruler, she dominated us like an Olympian goddess. While she prowled, she kept up a stream of invective on the lax morality of modern youth. Then, she stopped at my desk.

"Gelleny! Stand up!" she commanded.

As I was nearest to the scene of the crime, she had selected me as the prime suspect. Everyone else knew that the perpetrator was her star pupil, smugly conceited Geigy. I asserted my innocence, denying any involvement. It was not that I was afraid of the consequences of 'ratting out' Geigy, the culprit; rather, I believed that Dad was right when he said an honourable person must 'own up' and be willing to accept the consequences of his own errors and misdeeds.

I knew that I was "in for it." At the very least, I would be soundly beaten on the rump with the dreaded rubber strap, sent to the corner to stand on one leg for an hour, and strapped again if she caught me lounging on both feet. It was certain that I would be barred from all lunchtime sports, and kept indoors to wash the blackboards, sharpen the pencils, fill the inkwells, and load the wood box, not to mention hours of punishment 'lines.' The village grapevine was lethal when it came to passing along bad news; there was no way to prevent the reports of my heinous act of sabotage from reaching my parents' ears. Whatever punishments might be inflicted, facing Mom and Dad would be the hardest.

The little woman was fulminating, in full flight; flecks of foam flew from her mouth as she scolded me. When she began to compare my criminal disregard for the welfare of my schoolmates and refusal to admit my guilt, to the shortcomings of some Hungarian youth in the War, (I believe she meant those who had returned home), I had heard enough. That was a direct insult to my beloved Dad. I gathered my notebooks and was clearing out my desk in preparation for the inevitable expulsion, when a small female voice spoke out.

"Ma'am, this is unfair. It wasn't Gelleny at all. It was Geigy. I can smell it all over him!"

Geigy had indeed neglected to wash off the evidence. Thus, sweet justice was served. I was exonerated and fell immediately and madly in love with my redeeming angel for all of the next month. Miss K. called on the district school inspector to deal with Geigy's parents. It must have been an interesting discussion, as Geigy never did return to our school. I heard years later that he had a successful law practice in Saskatoon. Moreover, to her credit, Miss K. even apologised and wept for her slurs against our veterans.

The market-farming business was going deeply in debt. Dad and Uncle Joe had been unable to turn a profit. Nowadays, they could have sought protection from their debtors by declaring bankruptcy. But, it was 1929, the Great Depression was underway, and such remedies did not exist, at least for entrepreneurs with big ambitions, out in "the sticks." Accordingly, Dad and Uncle Joe sold the equipment to pay off their debts and Dad made arrangements with an agent in Békéscaba for the house to be put up for sale. John Gelleny's family would be emigrating in two stages to Saskatchewan, Canada, where Dad believed he could make a go of wheat farming. Uncle Joe and his wife Maria decided to stay in Hungary.

Dad would go to Canada, establish a homestead, and, when he had saved enough money, send for Mom, John, Steve, Rose, and me. Uncle Oszlacs, who was settled in Ontario, had made other plans: to divert us from the prairies to Welland, in southwestern Ontario. Uncle Oszlacs met Dad at Toronto Union Station and convinced him to retrieve his luggage and transfer to the Welland train. In Welland, Dad soon found a job and was able to make a substantial down payment on the family's tickets with the travel agent. Mom and we kids arrived at Easter, 1931.

The City of Welland, then a semi-rural town, is situated at the heart of Ontario's premier fruit growing belt, on the busy Welland Ship Canal, a mere fifteen-minute drive from Niagara Falls. My two older cousins, Uncle Oszlacs' boys, took an interest in showing me the local sights and attractions.

English as a Second Language instruction for newcomers was non-existent in my public school. The educational wisdom of the day seems to have been based upon the theory that a beginner would pick up enough oral, 'working' English through total immersion, i.e. in the rough and tumble of the schoolyard. Further refinement would seep into the pores, in the classroom. If only the parents and teachers had overheard some of the choice gems that I was absorbing from their little dears! My 'foreign' accent led to some ridicule and teasing. During my first week at school, I made several embarrassing gaffes, which, in retrospect, seem amusing. That is, with one notable exception. I made a major blunder when I was purposely misdirected by another Geigy-type into the Girls' Washroom where the grade eight girls were changing for gym class. The gym teacher chased me out in a fury. I wanted desperately to crawl into a very deep pit, as the screams and shrieks of outrage flew. For that mishap, I was berated unmercifully, and threatened with suspension, until my two cousins, Uncle Oszlacs' boys, stepped in to deflect some of the flak. They laid out my day to day personal survival guide. Uncle O's boys even intervened to appease the gym teacher and the vice-principal.

Aided by my cousins' 'street smarts', my good grades in mathematics, and my growing athletic abilities, over time the teasing and bullying tapered off; I was becoming accepted as 'one of the boys.' In spite of my mathematical talents, which seemed to be attractive to girls, I barely managed to be promoted that year. I undertook a personal mission to 'catch up' in reading, spelling and grammar over the summer, all of which paid off when I made the Principal's Honour Roll the following year. My initiative evidently impressed Dad who made me responsible for delivering his monthly payment to Mr. Garner's travel agency downtown, until the family's tickets were paid in full.

At Welland High School, my friend, Mike, who was an amateur radio enthusiast, or 'ham', was pleased that I showed an interest in his hobby. As did most of his colleagues, then as now, Mike jerry-rigged his short-wave radio set from spare and surplus parts and pieces that he could trade, scavenge, or scrounge. In his bedroom late at night, I would listen, awestruck, to the staccato patterns of Morse Code dots and dashes, as the high frequency radio waves from Venezuela or Bermuda bounced earthward to our earphones, midst the crackling and hissing of the ionosphere. Sensing a convert to the exclusive club, Mike patiently taught me the elements of Morse code and even let me send a few simple messages on his key. My knowledge of Wireless Telegraphy (W/T) was at best primitive, but would serve me later as a helpful 'leg up'.

My fourth year at Welland High School was memorable for two reasons: I met Hank Toews, and Dad and Mother separated. Hank had come from Niagara-on-the-Lake to attend a Welland High School dance. We struck up a conversation in the gym and soon were *kibitzing* and daring each other to ask the best-looking girls to dance. He said he was convinced that Welland's girls were prettier and more fun than the home-grown crop. The trick was to hold onto to them, for more than just one spin on the floor. If things worked out, we would treat our 'dates' to a banana split special at the local hangout and walk them home, like gentlemen.

Hank and I thought that it would also be a good idea to check out the bright lights of Toronto and hitchhiked there and back several times. Through our gallivanting and adventures, we became very close and became experts at navigating the big city by means of its 'red rocket' electric streetcars. With my parents' break-up, Hank and I decided to move to Toronto where we found an inexpensive rooming house on Spadina Avenue, with a good restaurant close by, and near an excellent high school, 'Central Tech', Central Technical School at Bathurst and Harbord Streets, in which we enrolled.

One of my other best friends, 'Beanie' was the envy of the other guys at Welland High. He owned a mint condition, black, 1930 Chevy roadster, which he maintained religiously. He was the only kid I ever met whose nickname fit him so perfectly that everyone, including his widowed Mom, called him Beanie. Beanie and I had stayed in touch after I moved away from Welland. He was responsible in a way for my meeting and later marrying, Helen.

Beanie pulled up in front of my home on a sunny, warm Sunday morning early in June 1938. With one blast of the Chevy's aaooogah horn, I tore out the front door. We set out, high-spirited knights of the road, to visit Beanie's cousin, Aida, in Toronto. Aida proved to be cute, friendly, and smart; we hit it off right away. Aida was keen to go for a drive in Beanie's machine and suggested that we visit her cousin, Helen Mossey, just outside of the Town of Weston, a small Toronto suburb.

Aida was crammed between the gear shift column and me. She was in control of the deluxe dashboard radio, which she tuned to a CBC 'delayed broadcast', featuring the Mart Kenny Orchestra, right from the famous Mart Kenny Ranch. We breezed westward along Wilson Avenue past the city limits at Jane Street, singing along with "Begin the Beguine". We sailed through Weston, into the countryside, which is now prime industrial land. I was just beginning to wonder if we were on our way to Welland when Aida excitedly called for Beanie to slow down and turn into a narrow laneway which wound its way up to an immaculate, brick farmhouse.

I let Aida out and she ran up the drive up to the door. Seconds later, she was back.

"Come on, you two. We're invited in for crumpets and tea. The family name is Mossey. Mind your P's and Q's! Don't embarrass me. They're classy folks...my mother's relatives!"

Beanie and I griped, making excuses.

"Do we have to?"

"Just bring us some food."

We were hot and hungry from the drive and really wanted to go in, but it was a teenage boy ritual to protest. During the trip, Aida had raved about Mrs. Mossey's fabulous baking and had casually remarked that the daughter, Helen, was not too hard on the eyes.

"Helen's going to think you're a couple of dopes."

"Okay, okay, Aida. We're coming. Hold on!" I examined myself in the rear-view mirror and smoothed my hair, which had been mussed by the wind, and caught up with Beanie and Aida.

It happened in the living room, as Aida was introducing our gracious hostess, Mrs. Mossey. From across the room, our eyes met and I was instantaneously, totally love-struck. She blushed; my head pounded and my knees turned to jelly. It was a truly magical, defining moment in my life. I knew that this beautiful, blushing, Helen, the most ethereal and charming female whom I had ever seen in my life was the woman I would marry. Fortunately, as she later confessed, she thought so, too.

Miraculously, I was suddenly transformed into a model well-mannered Sunday gentleman caller. Helen's mother, Mrs. Mossey, brought in a large tray loaded with freshly baked Lithuanian buns and fresh butter then returned to the kitchen to finish making the cocoa. Helen sat demurely on the loveseat opposite me, in splendid isolation. Suddenly, Mr. Mossey popped his head into the room. Beanie and I stood politely while Helen introduced us. We sat down in an awkward silence. Sensing the magnetic force field between us, he broke the stillness by inquiring politely about my background. I gulped, glancing at Helen, for a sign, for inspiration. She was blushing, idly tracing the pattern on the upholstery with an elegant, slim fingertip. Beanie grinned and winked wickedly, relishing my discomfort; Aida had the decency to excuse herself to lend Mrs. Mossey a hand in the kitchen.

"Well, sir, I've just about completed high school and plan on going to university when I've put aside enough money for my tuition."

"What are you interested in studying, son, when you go?"

"Engineering, sir, probably chemical. That interests me quite a lot. The Guidance Counsellor at Central Technical thinks I'll have no trouble at all getting something in a related field…to ch-chemistry, that is."

"Poppa" as he became known to me, was a kind and gentle man, who was obviously adept at sorting out dodgy males with designs on his lovely daughter.

Beanie's smirk was driving me crazy. He knew I was trying to make 'the big impression', and that I had never darkened the door of the Guidance Office at Welland High, nor, in all likelihood, Central Tech.

Poppa excused himself, leaving Aida and me to chat with Helen and Momma. By three o'clock, Aida announced that she was due home by four-thirty for a family dinner. We thanked our hosts and drove back to the city. Aida broke the silence: "Well, Joe, congratulations, you sure impressed the Mosseys. Hardly any male member of the species ever gets invited back."

"I didn't hear any invitation."

"Of course you didn't, dear. You were too far gone, or flustered. I thought the two of you were going to disintegrate and burst into flames right there. Poof! Wow, Hepburn and Tracy, look out! But you have to make the next move. Here's Helen's telephone number. It's long distance from Toronto, but soon you're going to be a working man with money to burn, right?"

"Where did you get that?"

"Where do you think? From Momma, of course! She didn't see the fangs or hair on the back on your hands, so you've made it onto the approved list. Of course, it's up to Helen to decide where it goes from here."

"Thanks, Aida, you're a pal. I'll call."

"Be patient. You are going to have to wait. She's still at school and needs time to figure things out. No pressure or she'll flit away. I'd say that you're definitely on her list, but I also know you have some competition."

I plucked up my courage and telephoned the following Monday evening; luckily, Helen answered. Somehow, I managed to blurt out my wish to see her again, very soon, if possible. She broke off to speak to Momma. When she came back on the line, she said that I was invited to come over on Saturday night.

I boarded the streetcar in Weston and went to the end of the line, then walked the mile to her home. Momma welcomed me warmly then left us alone in the living room. Poppa as usual was upstairs. Helen, of course, was radiant. We chatted and giggled about the Sunday visit while we listened to her favourite Vera Lynn records. Poppa, she said, usually grilled male visitors, which embarrassed them, though she loved him dearly.

Helen said she was interested in hearing about my early days in Hungary and Welland. No sooner had I mentioned 'Gerendas' than Momma popped her head in to inquire if we were hungry. Helen smiled, "Momma, Joe said Hun – gar - y!"

Momma had prepared a marvellous spread of sandwiches and fancy cakes, set out invitingly on the dining room table. Momma and Poppa looked in on us and by ten o'clock, when I had thoroughly exhausted the topics of Father's farming and Hank and Welland High, it was time to walk back to catch the last streetcar to Toronto. I realised how very perceptive Aida's advice about being patient and 'playing the waiting game' had been. Helen and I had a future together. Of that, I was certain. Exactly when that would be, I had no idea.

As soon as I completed the courses in Industrial Chemistry at Central Tech, I was hired by Anaconda Brass, on the Lakeshore in New Toronto, where I planned to settle in and make my contribution to Canada's war effort. I was a kid, earning good money, and the plant manager assured me that I had very good prospects for a career in the industry.

A degree in engineering at university was a possibility, but service overseas or anywhere else was not. I could use the excuse that Dad's disillusionment had rubbed off, but in truth, I was enjoying my financial freedom, and having one whale of a good time. My job was in an industry that had been declared essential to Canada's war *matériel* production, which gave me a patriotic sense of involvement with the grand plan. I figured that Canada was not about to be invaded by the Nazis, so I had no urge to exchange my fat paycheques and contented lifestyle for boot camp. Furthermore, the plant was brimming with attractive, single young women, ready and willing for an innocent evening of laughs, dancing, and clubbing during the week when Helen was studying. But my outlook on world events would soon change, and I volunteered for service with the Canadian Army, as I will describe in the story. Hank Toews went to Canada Packers where he manufactured Vitamin E for the armed services.

Helen and I talked for hours on the telephone, went to movies and dances, and kissed when we thought no one was watching. It was all extremely romantic and thoroughly chaste, even after I had joined the Army and SOE. I was granted an occasional twenty-four hour weekend pass during my ten weeks at Camp X, which I divided equally between visiting Dad in Welland and seeing Helen.

Our final date before I boarded the *Queen Elizabeth* was a formal dance at Casa Loma in Toronto. Forbidden to refer to SOE, I explained that the Army was transferring me overseas to GKW - God Knows Where. Helen laughingly accepted that and we promised to write, often. Soon after my departure, Helen went to work with the British Air Commission (BAC) in Washington D.C.; she wrote frequently and faithfully, even when she received notification that I was missing in action.

Upon my return, we resumed our relationship, but, before we could get married, I was determined to further my education as I had promised Dad and Poppa. The engineering faculties at the University of Toronto, Queen's, and McGill Universities were already overflowing with veterans taking advantage of the Veterans' Loan Act (VLA) tuition plan. Hank and I made inquiries south of the border. We were accepted at Fort Wayne, Indiana and were barely able to scrape up the funds needed to cover our first year's tuition in the Faculty of Applied Sciences. Once there, we found accommodation, landed part-time jobs, and were soon calling ourselves adopted Hoosiers.

Upon entering my second year, the VLA agreed to reimburse me for the first year and would pay for the balance of my courses. Hank had greater financial problems, as he was not VLA qualified, but we graduated together, Bachelors of Science, in Civil and Chemical Engineering.

We had often talked in Indiana about forming a business to capitalise on the wealth of opportunities opening in Canada. We determined, by the process of elimination, that housing was the real growth industry. The demand for decent, affordable homes, particularly bungalows, would exceed the supply for years, we reckoned. We thought it would be smart for one or both of us to take a course in business administration, however expensive it might be. We were delighted when the VLA informed us both that our grade averages qualified us for one year's tuition in the Master of Business Administration program, at the University of Toronto. Hank and I located a Toronto lawyer who was willing to draw up the papers of incorporation for little more than the cost of his expenses, and SGT, our company, was a reality. With more nerve than capital, we plunged headlong into the booming construction industry. We both enrolled at the University of Toronto's Graduate School, but it was soon clear that SGT required our undivided attention if it were to succeed in the hotly competitive house construction business.

We struggled and we took risks, and our little enterprise turned a small profit. It was time to propose marriage to Helen, or risk losing her. Helen suggested that it would be prudent to test the marital waters with Momma and Poppa. Poppa convened a brief 'man to man' in the parlour. Satisfied with my financial prospects, he gave his blessing, sealed with a handshake. Ecstatically, I raced into the kitchen and proposed. Helen accepted, and Momma beamed in approval. The wedding was set for Saturday, September 6, 1947, at 2:00 p.m., at Weston United Church. Once the invitations were sent and replies started coming back, Helen and I were on cloud nine in anticipation.

Such a glorious day: sunny and warm, but tolerable for wearing formal attire. Every detail had been thoroughly planned and reviewed, checked, and triple-checked. The florist had been delayed but carried out her assignment with distinction; the floral displays were magnificent. Check. The photographer had arrived and set up on schedule. Check. The six ushers, and my best man, Hank Toews, were resplendent in their tuxedos, complete with white boutonnieres. Check. Hank had produced the ring, twice, at my insistence. Check. The minister, Reverend Kitchen, had met briefly with Hank and me in his study. Hank had remembered to slip him the envelope. Double check. Helen's family had finalised all of the arrangements for the reception at the lovely Old Mill, on Bloor Street West, weeks ago. Check. Now, the pews were nearly filled. Check.

'There's Dad with all the Welland crew!' Check.

I glanced at my wristwatch… lights, action, …one fifty-five on the dot. With a dramatic flourish, the organist sounded an introductory chord, and nodded to the soloist. Check. When the soloist had completed her offering, the Reverend stood in serene anticipation at the altar, to await the arrival of the bridal party. Check.

Vic, Helen's brother, approached Hank and whispered. Hank uttered three fateful words, under his breath:

"Well, find her!"

"What was that, Hank?"

"Um, Helen's not here yet, Joe."

"Nonsense. Tell Vic to please take the other guys and look outside. She's probably getting out of the limo right now in the parking lot."

"I did and she isn't! Hold on, I'll be back."

Hank and Vic were standing at the rear of the church, conversing, shaking their heads. One look at their faces and I knew.

Hank came forward.

"Helen's really missing, Joe," he confided.

Neither Helen nor Emily, her sister and bridesmaid, could be found in the vestibule, on the front steps, powder room, or in the parking lot. Two oh five, and counting.

"Vic says no one ordered a limo," Hank added. Then, at the top of his form as groomsman, he signalled to the organist, who launched into a bravura recital of all time wedding favourites.

"We'll find her, Joe," he confided. "Don't panic. Someone has to be bringing her. It must be the traffic, or something else, completely… logical."

I wasn't listening. This was to have been the happiest day of our lives; instead, I had been jilted, left standing, abandoned at the altar, in front of two hundred guests, who were craning to the rear, for some sign of the blissful bride-to-be.

What had in the world had I said, or done? What dark secret had she uncovered, at the last minute, to give her second thoughts? Worse, what if something awful had happened to my beloved? Or maybe she had run away with that goofy, spoiled rich kid Alex, from her school, the one with a crush on her as big as all outdoors. We had talked briefly last night when I called to check on some of the names for my toast. She had seemed relaxed and even joked about the last minute rush at her place.

Poppa, who had a game leg, was sitting at the front with Momma. They were deeply in conference with

Vic.

I pulled Hank aside. "Listen. I want you to go into the Minister's office and telephone the Mossey home. If she's not there, call the cops."

"She'll be here Joe. She'll be here."

I was devastated. *'Mission interrupted, or aborted? Was I to be married, or only almost?'*

Chapter 1
Inside Camp X

I somehow had to escape this nightmare. Thwack! Again, the rubber truncheon struck my raw soles, my toes curling with the excruciating pain. I wavered in and out of consciousness, struggling to distance myself from the waves of agony. A disembodied image of my beautiful, blushing Helen, floated tantalisingly close. She arose from the loveseat in her front parlour and smiled, as she blew me a kiss. Her image flickered unsteadily, then faded, slowly dissolving, like the closing frames in a silent movie.

"Helen? Who is Helen?" The interpreter's grating voice jarred me back to reality. I was seated on a wooden chair in a large, dimly lit prison interrogation room in Pécs, Hungary, my hands tightly tied behind the chair. My soles were on fire and my shoulders were being wrenched from their sockets. As my body recoiled in reaction to the blows, the ropes dug ever more deeply into my wrists. "Who is this Helen, damn you, your controller?"

"What?"

"Helen. You called out 'Helen.'"

"My mother" I gasped, "Helen's my mother."

"Our little Englishman is saying he wants his mother, Colonel!" He spit 'little Englishman' in Hungarian to the hazy, blue-clad figure lounging against the wall.

'Colonel? Colonel Bogey? No, no! Focus, Joe. That's the smiling executioner, Colonel Ference Csongor, Hungarian Second Bureau. To my right is the interpreter, Imre, he of the bulging frog eyes. My torturer, Gregor, is waiting anxiously, eager to get back to work.'

Csongor snapped in Hungarian, "Inform him he hasn't a chance in hell of seeing anyone again, unless he co-operates, beginning immediately!"

I understood every word, but didn't let on. If the three of them twigged that I was fluent in Magyar, they would presume that I had to be Hungarian and, logically, a traitor and spy. I would be tortured for days, perhaps weeks, until I begged them to kill me, then tortured more and finally, slowly garrotted to death, on a meathook. My deception was a safety valve, allowing me to hear each question twice, once in Hungarian and again through the interpreter, thus giving me a precious second or two to compose my thoughts before speaking.

"What is your purpose here, British? It is an easy question. Answer!"

"First Lieutenant Joseph Gordon. I am a British officer and I am here only to help the Hungarian people."

Swack! The truncheon struck this time with such force that my chair slid backward on the wood floor.

I blinked in an attempt to clear the sweat from my eyes. I was barely able to make out the blurred features of the frog-eyed interpreter's face; his rancid breath was making my head swim. I was starting to hallucinate again. "M'am, I swear I did not put garlic on the schoolroom stove! Please do not hit me again."

"This bastard's raving, sir! First he wants his mommy; now he's plain crazy."

"He's faking. The questioning will continue." The Colonel paused momentarily as though lost in thought. "Imre, move over please, to let Gregor give him another treatment."

The hulking truncheon man tapped his cudgel tentatively on my feet, like a carpenter preparing to drive home a nail. I gasped in agony. He raised his right arm, to deliver a rain of blows. This time, I would be crippled, like my Camp X classmate, a strapping big Yugoslav, who had volunteered to be the subject for a demonstration. After only four light blows, we had to carry him, semi-conscious, to the Camp's infirmary. He was immobilised there for a week and eventually, dropped out of the training program.

"I said, answer! Do not" – smack - "I repeat, do not" – whack - "take us for fools! Who sent you here? Why do you have a wireless radio? What is your mission?"

Frog Eyes' face swam in front of me. I think I heard Colonel Csongor tell them to stop, to take a rest. He ordered Gregor to untie my wrists, although I was unable to feel the difference. My arms dangled lifelessly at my sides. My legs were still tightly bound, straight out in front of me. My feet were on fire. I tried desperately to imagine myself in another place, a place where there were fresh, warm breezes, cold water, sunshine and friends, just friends, and fun…

I was at Lake Erie, with Beanie. It was the 4th of July weekend, the big American holiday. Tourists from New York State had practically taken over the town. Beanie and I were talking up two older girls from Buffalo, as we stood casually ankle deep in the refreshingly cool water. Beanie was trying unsuccessfully to convince them to meet us in the evening for a drive to Niagara Falls.

They were twins, seventeen, and their parents were watching us, like hawks, from their folding striped canvas chairs. We were definitely on the same wavelength, we had identical favourites: fries with gravy and cherry cola, big band music, and we all listened to the same radio station from Chicago when we were doing our homework. The harder Beanie pitched his proposal, the more Barbara and Beth giggled and blushed. Both were teen queens, and amazingly well endowed, an attribute that was emphasised by their skimpy one-piece matching pink bathing suits.

"Niagara Falls? Are you kidding? We've seen it a million times!"

"It's so boring!"

Strike two! I stepped in to pinch hit. "But the Canadian side is better, and there's lot's more to do over here. Have you ever been to the Wax Museum? It's amazing!"

They looked at me with their baby-blues as if I was trying to sell them the Rainbow Bridge. Finally, Barbara spoke, " Okay, we might sort of be interested, I guess."

Now it was Beanie's turn. They didn't believe that he owned a car. He pointed to Black Beauty, shimmering in the blazing afternoon sun in the distant parking lot.

"What, did you steal it?," asked Beth sarcastically.

"No, no, it's mine. Really! I can prove it!" Beanie was off, loping barefoot across the hot sand toward his prized chariot.

"Hey Beanie, you forgot…!" but he didn't look back.

We watched as he reached into his pocket of his swimming trunks for the key. He turned to face us and threw up his hands sheepishly. I knew the key was in the pocket of his jeans, which were lying in a heap with mine on the beach.

Beth and Barbara were having convulsions as Beanie strode manfully to retrieve his wallet and key chain.

"Don't give up, kids! Watch this!" he stated reassuringly. He returned to the car and unlocked the driver's door with a flourish.

By this time, I had gathered our clothes as the girls and I were drawn closer to the unfolding drama. Beanie rolled down the windows and was starting the car. It turned over vigorously, but without catching. He tried again. It made sounds like a coffee grinder, and stopped, dead. Beanie was smashing the dashboard with the flat of his hand, urging his stallion to life, but to no avail. It was now making impotent clicking sounds.

'Vapour lock…or flooded.'

"Flooded, folks. Just wait five, and all that jive, then foot down to the floor and vroom!" he shouted. He looked confident and under control, but I knew he was sweating bricks.

Beth and Barbara held a brief, private conference, then Barbara walked over to parley with their parents. The fate of our dream double date was at stake. Barbara returned and uttered the magic words, "So, okay, Joe, if he gets it going, pick us up tonight at seven at the entrance of our hotel, to meet Mom and Dad. We have to be home by ten, sharp. House rules. Don't be late. See you!" The two leggy princesses drifted serenely away.

Black Beauty had rumbled to life. When I sat down on the passenger side, Beanie was tapping the fur-covered rim of the steering wheel in time with a jive tune on the radio. "Great work, Joe boy! So, what hotel?" he queried. Fort Erie was Hotel City.

"Ah, gees, I f-f-f-forgot to ask…."

When I regained consciousness, my hands had again been tied tightly behind the wooden chair, on which I was seated. Through a haze, I could see that my trousers had been removed; my skivvies were all that remained of my dignity. My humiliation turned to horror. My groin was hot-wired to a hand-cranked electrical generator. Anyone could get hold of the damn things. My buddy Mike at Welland High had taken one out of an old telephone to use as a backup power supply for his short wave radio. On a dare, I had held the two wires while he gave it a crank. I had yelped so loudly that his cat took off out of the room. The physician at Beaulieu had told us that our synapses would go on overload and shut down the pain pathways, if we could handle the first jolts. I screamed as the lightning bolt struck my genitals. Gregor grinned and turned the magneto handle harder. My body reacted, bending backward in a reflexive arc of agony: no sign of the merciful neural shutdown. I slumped, overcome by the pain and exhaustion. If he turned the crank once more, I hoped I would black out before my privates exploded.

Another question, in Hungarian, drifted out of the haze. I couldn't make any sense of it.

'Think, Joe…something, anything that will take you far away, out of this place. How in hell did I end up here?'

…The beefy sergeant seated at his desk filled the entrance to the big barn. He motioned me over to him. The eerie lighting behind him in the over-heated atmosphere of the Horse Palace, mixed with the pungent aroma of the old stable's usual residents, made my head swim with a confused sense of other-worldliness.

"Whatcha lookin' for there, sonny?"

"I came to, um, join up,

Sergeant, Sir!"

"First rule, sonny. See these?" He pointed to the brevet on his left shoulder.

"Yes, sir".

"Well, take a look at 'em real close. What do they mean?"

"They, ah, mean that you are a sergeant, Sir." I was the number one fan of *Johnny Canuck* comic books and knew my army insignia.

"Wrong, sonny. They mean that I am a plain, no 'Sir', sergeant. A bleeding, big as life, never ever called 'Sir', sergeant. Period."

"Period, Sir?"

He smashed his fist on the rickety table. "I am a bloody sergeant, sonny, and sergeants are never called, blessed or cursed as 'Sir'! *Capisco*?" He sat down heavily.

"Yes, indeed, Sergeant, Sir!"

That was my second error in what would shortly become a lengthy list.

"Yes, Sergeant! Yes, Sergeant! That's it, in bleeding totality: Sergeant. Got it, sonny?"

He appeared to be exhausted from the ordeal. Following a moment of silence, he lowered his voice, as though he were a policeman comforting a lost child and asked,

"Where're ya from, anyway?"

"Right here, Sergeant!"

"So, you were born on a bed of straw and raised on oats and hay, right here, in the bloody Horse Palace?"

'Strike three. I'm going to be drummed out for basic idiocy, before I can even get past the door!' The oppressive steam heat, coupled with the overpowering scent of manure had seeped into my head, and shrivelled my brain to the size of a sun-dried pea.

"Let me put it this way, then. Tell me this: where were you, at the very moment you or your mother decided to bring or send your royal Canadian butt down here and offer it in service of the bloody King?"

I thought King George VI a fine man, a noble monarch and not in the least likely to have done anything in his life to deserve this slight. Perhaps Sergeant was a Tory and meant the present Liberal Prime Minister, Mr. Mackenzie King. I thought it was better not to go any further. I also thought it was better not to mention that my mother had nothing to do with my decision. My resolve was stiffened, so to speak, the previous Saturday night at the usually dependable, pick-up spot, the Silver Rail Tavern. My friends and I had blown our week's wages without a single, encouraging, "Thank you. I'd just adore another gin and tonic. I'm from Sudbury, visiting my sick aunt. Where're you from?" Meanwhile, the youngest and prettiest women on whom we had spent our last nickel, were scooping up every goof in khaki, as fast as the uniforms bellied up to the bar.

My job at Anaconda Brass was semi-classified metallurgical testing; though interesting, well paid and war-related, it did not provide the sort of excitement that I wanted. Although Hitler hadn't threatened to invade Canada, I was impatient to try something more adventurous and gallant, as befitting a red-blooded fan of *Johnny Canuck*. Helen Mossey and I were close, but engagement was a long way off. I decided to do my duty and find some excitement, as well.

"Toronto, Sergeant. I lived in Welland, before Toronto. But b-b-b-born in Hungary."

"Born in Hungary? Hungary? Bloody Hungary, you say?"

Maybe he pictured my native land, the abode of Dracula, afloat in a sea of gore, or, perhaps Hungarians were on general principle, prohibited from active duty in Canada's army. I hastened to add "But I am true blue, patriotic red-blooded Canadian, Sergeant."

"You forgot 'white'; Red, blue *and* white. Good bloody thing you're not an American. They'd probably shoot ya.

"Peppery, hot Hungarian goulash, and a man's wine that's meant for drinkin', not sippin' like that French drizzle. I ought to know. Married one."

"Do you mean, French, Sergeant? I asked, tentatively.

"Magyar, sonny, and Jewish, to boot. She's a hot-blooded, holy terror who can cook, make love, and dance a mean Czardas all at the same time. Knock the socks off anyone half her age. Hails from Pest. The old Danube wasn't too blue, when I saw it in '25, on the honeymoon. Kind of muddy then and likely bloody red by now."

I wondered if he had a morbid fascination for the vital bodily fluid. Then, his tone became reflective, even intimate. "What's your hometown, only for interest's sake, you mind. It's not going on the form."

"Gerendas,...near Romania, Sergeant."

"Good farm land there. Not much else, eh? Father's a farmer, I'd guess?"

I wondered if I would have to tell him the long sad tale of Dad's misadventures in the crop marketing business, but fortunately, he continued.

"What's your name, lad? Last, middle and first, spell them."

I was beginning to lose track of my purpose for coming here. At this rate, it seemed that the Canadian Army would be fortunate to sign up one recruit per hour.

"Okay, 'Gelleny'". He used the Hungarian pronunciation. "You related to Magyar nobility?"

"Somewhere, way back, I guess so, Sergeant."

"Old aristocrats, good fightin' stock…just what it's going to take to kick the livin' daylights out of that Nazi clown, Herr Schickelgruber, eh?"

I agreed wholeheartedly, knowing that Schickelgruber was Adolf Hitler's birth name.

"Well, Joseph J. Gelleny, you just head right over to that line on your far right." He indicated a queue of monumental length. "And take this bloody form with ya. It'll speed things up a smidge when they see that I've screened ya. You've done good, Gelleny. Should be clear sailing ahead, unless the Doc finds out you've got the clap, TB, flat dogs or can't read the third row." He scribbled something on his clipboard with a brown Eberhard Faber HB and tore off a form, which he handed to me.

"Thank you, Sergeant." I saluted.

He smiled and patted my shoulder. "Hurry over there now, Joszi, or you'll be here 'til the horses come home!"

On February 23, 1943, I, Joseph (Joszi) J. Gelleny, twenty years and eighteen days of age had come of my own free will to the Canadian National Exhibition grounds to volunteer for service in the Royal Canadian Army. Outside the Horse Palace, the brutally icy winds off Lake Ontario were threatening to topple and blow away the vast flapping tent city that had been erected overnight to serve as a staging area for some 20,000 soldiers, who were waiting to be shipped overseas. I wondered if I had seen some of them frolicking their last frolic at 'The Rail', on Saturday night.

I joined the line as Sergeant Bloody had instructed. A staff sergeant was making his way down the line, calling out grimly, "Papers only in this line!" I surmised that he wasn't selling the *Toronto Star* or *Evening Telegram* and piped up, "I have, Sergeant!"

I handed him my 'bloody' paper, which he scrutinised as if it were a Martian passport. "Gelleny! Irish, eh? Good. Don't move!" He walked away, without waiting for confirmation or denial. I was next accosted by a fuzzy-cheeked non-com[1] whose nameplate was imprinted, *Corporal Patrick Paterson*. Corporal Paterson escorted me to an antique wooden school desk and chair, and handed me a lengthy questionnaire, which, he directed, was to be "…filled out abso-bloody-lutely completely, with no blank spaces, no blanks left, none at all." I wondered if I wrote in the boxes in Magyar, whether it would matter, as long as I completed all sec-

[1] *A non-commissioned or non-officer rank*

tions. The stubby army issue HB pencil, with eraser, that he supplied was so deeply pocked with tooth marks as to have perhaps been a true relic of Dr. Einstein's cosmic pondering. When the forms were *abso-bloody-lutely* completed, and verified blank-free, I was afforded the unique experience of a thorough physical, Royal Canadian Army recruitment style.

The doctor seemed singularly interested in the reactions of a large white dog with ice-blue eyes and of questionable ancestry, age, and temperament, which eyed me from beneath the table, with that innate suspicion peculiar to Dogdom. It was apparent that the animal had been thoroughly trained to assist the medic in grading the effects of chilled, stainless steel implements when inserted into all of the orifices of the human body. Its tail wagged a semaphore of bliss with each of my convulsive shudders. The doctor/dog special relationship continued as I dutifully coughed, expectorated, and touched my toes. The dog stared at me expectantly while the good doctor prodded, poked, and peered.

"Nice dog, doctor."

"Comes in every day. I have no idea from where. It might live in the stalls, for all I know. Turn to the right and cough. Ever feel dizzy, faint, or nauseous?"

"No, doctor."

"Nurse Brandon, come over here please! Bowels work regularly?"

"As clockwork, Doctor."

As he was distracting me, Nurse Brandon punctured my arm and filled a test-tube with my blood.

"Hmm, good sign…Didn't faint. Here, take this cup and go behind the screen. When you're finished, leave it on the table, on top of this. Don't dribble. Nurse Brandon here hates it when the forms are soaked." She nodded emphatically, in affirmation. He scribbled something medically meaningful on a slip of paper. As I was proceeding to do my duty, he called, "Pee in it. That simpleton before you…." His voice trailed off.

Obviously not amused, Nurse broke her silence. "We'll forward *his* results to Naval recruitment. Should fit in with them perfectly."

With this, the dog lost interest in me entirely, snorted, and pitched its head onto its outstretched paws.

I stepped out of the enclosure. Nurse announced "You'll receive our decision in a week, Gelleny. Kindly fasten yourself before you move along."

On my way out, I had to pass by Sergeant Bloody Cerebus, the guardian of the Palace gates; magisterial now in bifocals; he glanced up from *Major Hoople's Boarding House* in the *Evening Telly's* comic section to wave me by, "You're in, unless you're diabetic or have VD. Good bloody luck, Hungary!"

A week later, I received my first-in-a-lifetime registered letter. In a rites-of-passage father to son conversation, Dad had confided to me that an envelope without a King George VI stamp was from the government, thus, 'sure as shooting official', which meant trouble. This letter stated that the Minister of Defence commanded me to report to base camp in Brampton, Ontario, a farm equipment-manufacturing town, west of Toronto. From Union Station, I enjoyed the pleasant and leisurely milk run across the fertile belt of Ontario's landscape.

From the Brampton station, an old Dodge cab drove me up to the main gate of the Base. As I was over-tipping the driver, he offered me some tidbits of taxi driver wisdom. "Thanks, son! Have a good time and here's some advice. You can take it or leave it."

"Sure, well, okay." *'Take or leave what?'*

"Well, you might find the folks in town a little...reserved...not hostile by any stretch, for the first while. We're new at this army business, and some of the folks are finding it hard to adjust to the newcomers. Some of our young lads aren't at all shy to let you know that they're not exactly thrilled when their girlfriends get excited by the sight of a uniform. Look out for trouble in the pubs and duck if you find it! They's good people, mind. Cheerio, now!"

'Far be it from me, quiet little Joseph Gelleny of Welland, Ontario, to get myself into that kind of a pickle!'

Brampton was an almost painless introduction to army life. Although I didn't learn very much, and did a lot of marching, I took advantage of the track and gym, to lose some of my civilian fat. I never experienced a problem with town roughnecks and felt completely at ease wherever I wandered. Perhaps the sight of me in uniform just didn't cause the female heart to flutter. Our sergeant was a bully; my new friend John and I bought him an occasional beer in the mess, so he tended to ignore our awkward-squad clowning on the parade square. We met some very nice young girls whom we took to the movies and the arena to watch the local hockey and lacrosse teams. Brampton usually won at both, which was always cause for exuberantly noisy and beery partying in the local drinking establishments.

I had been in Brampton for a few weeks when the Sergeant summoned me to accompany him to the Commandant's Office. The CO announced curtly that I had been ordered to report to the Royal Canadian Corps of Signals, in Kingston, Ontario. My background as an amateur short wave ham radio enthusiast, which I had documented and underlined twice, on my application, had obviously been taken seriously! If only they realised how little I actually knew! This was the break I had hoped for!

My enthusiasm changed quickly to disappointment. The first weeks of my Royal Canadian Corps of Signals experience were a crashing bore. By comparison, Brampton's boot camp was like combat training with live ammunition. We learned very little about 'signals' but did a lot of lining up, eyes right, cross-country running, and close-order drills. Fortunately, I had been pre-selected for training to become qualified as a Type 57 and 58 portable radio operator. These nifty units were the last word in battlefield wireless communications, designed to be toted around on the operator's back. We learned the almost holy ritual whereby the short whip antenna was 'loaded' with an electrical charge, to sensitise it so that the radio could send and receive signals. I also discovered how much fun it was during parade manoeuvres to reach out stealthily and touch the guy's antenna in front, causing his radio to go off the air and lose contact with the much bigger Type 19 home base radio, without the poor slob's knowledge. This little trick was of course expressly forbidden. The novelty quickly wore off for John and I, when, during a particularly important inspection parade, the leader marched our squad, quick time, into the barracks wall. I was desperate for more training as a field radio operator, to become an ace Morse code operator, but this was not to be, in Kingston.

My eagerness to be more actively involved in 'the thick of it', prompted me to put in a request for transfer to the paratroops. This request was not refused, but it was deferred because of my questionable vision. As well, my amateur radio experience was considered too valuable, I was told, to waste with the airborne brigade. This was not a winning situation. I wanted advanced radio training, which I couldn't receive, and a transfer to airborne would squander my almost non-existent radio experience. A friendly officer, who was experienced in navigating the unimaginable quagmire of army bureaucracy, suggested that I apply for a transfer to the Royal Canadian Artillery. Once accepted by the R. C. A., he assured me, I could transfer directly into the paratroops. He did not explain this conundrum, but I was keen to try it.

Camp Pettawawa, a two hour drive from the capital city of Ottawa, Ontario, was a well-run installation where I was almost immediately immersed in artillery-related lectures and field exercises which were devoted to the care and feeding of the full range of Canadian Army's heavy weapons arsenal. I enjoyed the trigonometry required to 'sight in' the howitzers and other field pieces, but after a time it became monotonous, as we rarely fired these monsters. Unfortunately, when we actually did shoot live rounds, our officers did not bother to caution us to cover our ears, which, I am certain, contributed to my present hearing loss. I was confident, however, that I was on my way to achieving my goal of joining one of the *élite* Canadian airborne regiments.

Fate was to enter in an unforeseen way when someone much higher up noticed the check mark on my original application, where I had indicated native-like fluency in my first language, Hungarian. *'Thank you, Corporal Patrick Paterson!'* I was interviewed first in English and then Hungarian, and advised to strongly consider a voluntary transfer to the British Army. I asked whether it might lead to parachute training. The interviewer responded that was a distinct possibility; I would be recommended for admission to Special Operations Executive. I had no idea whatsoever what 'special ops' actually meant, but was thrilled to have been offered a chance to jump. My mind raced; would I be trained as a diplomatic courier, a Commando, or hope of hopes, a secret agent, like Richard Hannay in *The Thirty-Nine Steps*? Regardless, in all likelihood, I would experience something more intriguing than close order drills, short arm inspections, stupid radio tricks or making the occasional crater in a field. Perhaps, I might even be sent to fight the war in Europe, before it was all over. Within seconds, I decided that SOE was definitely worth a go, and agreed.

Captain Arthur (Art) Bushell, who would play a significant role in my education as a secret agent at Camp X, where he held the rank of Adjutant-Quarter-Master, was a crackerjack Canadian officer with the authority to represent both the Canadian and British Armies. He interviewed me extensively, and outlined the specific conditions under which I would serve in Special Operations Executive, or SOE, as it was known. The terms of my service with SOE were as follows:

1. I would at all times be in the Canadian Army with Canadian Army pay at the rank I had attained while on loan to the British Army, including Parachute pay and officer's rank with commensurate pay (assuming that I passed all of the exams and met all requirements).

2. Any rank I obtained while on loan to the British Army and SOE would coincidentally be my rank in the Canadian Army with Canadian rate of pay from the time such rank was obtained. I obtained the rank of First Lieutenant in the British Army, for which I have written proof, but I have struggled to have it acknowledged. The best I have obtained from England to date is that I was an

[2] *In 1946, the Canadian Parliament passed* The Special Operators *(sic)* War Service Benefits Act, *which conferred the rank of sergeant on all SOE Canadian recruits regardless of whether or not they served behind enemy lines. Originally this bill as I understood it was to apply only to those recruits who were recruited from civilian life into the SOE and was* **not** *intended to apply to those who were transferred from within the military forces.*

Acting Second Lieutenant.[2]

3. The Royal Canadian Mounted Police and British Secret Intelligence Services (SIS) would conduct thorough background inquiries into all members of my family. Art asked if there was any personal information of a confidential nature, which I should disclose voluntarily, to avoid embarrassing my family and myself. I could think of nothing.

To my knowledge, I am the only Canadian non-Communist of Hungarian descent to have been recruited by SOE. I was simply a name on a page, with the *Other Languages Spoken* section checked and filled in. The leader of the Canadian Communist Party, Tim Buck, co-operated with the RCMP and British Security Co-ordination in forwarding the names of possible recruits from the Party's membership lists. However, my family had never been associated with Mr. Buck's Canadian Marxists. Buck had been uncooperative at first because Hitler and Stalin had signed a ten-year non-aggression pact in August 1939. This all changed after June 22, 1942, when Adolf Hitler treacherously unleashed Case Barbarossa, the swift and brutal *blitzkreig* invasion of Russia. With Eastern Europe under Nazi domination, the need for ethnic SOE agent-trainees escalated. Unlike the USA, Canada was fertile ground for recruitment of anti-Nazi eastern Europeans, some of whom were openly members of the legally constituted Canadian Communist Party.

My notification of acceptance was not long in arriving and I was ordered to present myself at the Horse Palace in Toronto, where my friend, the Bloody Sergeant, had been replaced with a mere stripling of a lean lance corporal. From there, my group of recruits was taken in the back of a military transport truck directly along Kingston Road and easterly on Highway 2 to Thornton Road, then south to Camp X on Lake Ontario.

Special Training School No. 103 Camp X

The guard raised the levered gate to admit us to Special Operations Executive Special Training School No.103, (STS No.103), on June 2, 1943. The first member of staff to greet us was the Camp Adjutant, Captain Arthur Bushell, who introduced our Commandant, Lieutenant-Colonel Skilbeck. This was Whitby, Ontario's mysterious Camp X, on the secluded shores of Lake Ontario in rural Ontario County, thirty-five km east of Toronto. It was the first top secret, joint British and Canadian Intelligence operation, established by Winnipeg-born William Stephenson, *(Intrepid)*, chief of British Security Co-ordination (BSC). British Prime Minister Winston Churchill had appointed Stephenson as Chief of Britain's MI-5, MI-6, and Political Warfare Executive (PWE) operations in the Western Hemisphere. Camp X was *Intrepid's* brilliant gambit, which would assist the Allies in checkmating Hitler's planned endgame: a one thousand-year Nazi Reich. The Camp had begun operations almost exactly one and one-half years before my arrival, opening on December 6, 1941.

The location was of immense strategic importance and tactical value, with its relative isolation and its proximity to New York State. A forty-eight km trip by motor launch across Lake Ontario ferried major American military and political visitors, in absolute secrecy, to the Camp. Northeast of Camp X, the City of Oshawa's airfield provided secure, rapid access for VIP's, as well as operational and logistical air services. Visitors who could not be accommodated at Camp X were comfortably lodged at the Oshawa House. Oshawa, home of General Motors Canada, provided a wealthy and hospitable patron in the person of Colonel R. Samuel 'Sam' McLaughlin. Colonel Sam, the legendary Founder, and Chairman of GMC, picked up the Camp's monthly liquor tab, which, records show, was substantial. Sam also made Parkwood, his magnificent McLauglin estate home, available as a secure, exclusive retreat for the Camp Commandants' most *élite* visitors.

Camp X from the air 1956

Parkwood is now a first-class attraction for visitors, an upscale site for wedding receptions and gracious entertaining, as well as a lucrative motion picture location. Entering it today, one can readily imagine the graceful mansion's fireplaces ablaze and white-gloved servers unobtrusively offering the finest French brandies on silver trays, and Havana cigars from scented humidors, with the finest, single malt scotch whiskies arrayed in crystal decanters on the sideboard. In a quiet den, one can only imagine what might have transpired when *Intrepid*, General William J. 'Wild Bill'

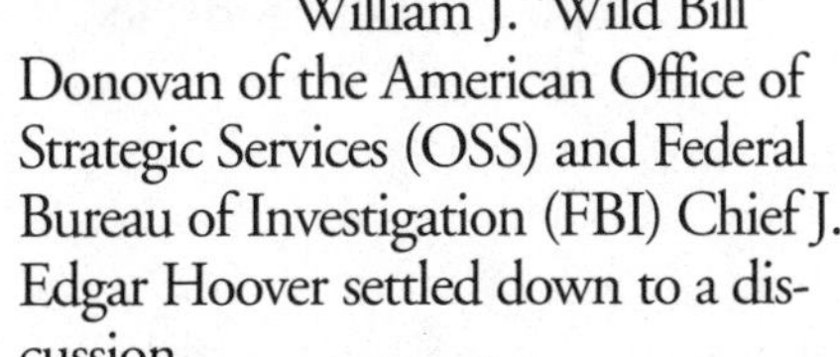

Donovan of the American Office of Strategic Services (OSS) and Federal Bureau of Investigation (FBI) Chief J. Edgar Hoover settled down to a discussion.

Yet, so well-guarded a secret was Camp X that the Canadian Prime Minister, Mackenzie King, was kept in the dark about its existence for several months. Given British Intelligence's watchword, 'Need to Know', it has been suggested that this was done to prevent a disastrous breach of security if the PM were ever to be ambushed during Question

Period in the House of Commons, an explanation woefully lacking the ring of either truth or logic.

Camp X became operational at exactly 6:00 p.m., on a cold and snowy December 6, 1941, only hours before the Japanese assault on Pearl Harbour. Private Arthur 'Mac' McDonald, Royal Canadian Corps of Engineers, has verified the exact date and moment, for very good reason. Mac arrived in the back of an open Army truck from the Horse Palace at that time, and was immediately assigned duty at the gate as the first BSC Camp guard. Coincidentally, STS 103 would serve as the inspiration, working model and template for the fledgling American intelligence service, The Office of Strategic Services (OSS), born of necessity when the Japanese attack shattered America's official neutrality. Buffalo-native OSS General Donovan, was so impressed with the Camp's methods that he ordered the OSS training manual be based on the SOE syllabus. Through *Intrepid*, General Donovan arranged to have OSS senior personnel observe and participate in all aspects of the training at Camp X. It stands clearly documented that Camp X was the spiritual birthplace of the OSS, which was to become the Central Intelligence Agency (CIA), post WWII, under Allen Dulles.

The purchase of the magnificent 275-acre (Lots 17 and 18, broken front concession) lakefront farm property was executed by *Intrepid*, William Stephenson, through the British Security Co-ordination's Manhattan office in the name of Rural Realty Company Ltd., September 1941. Its historic owners were the Sinclair family, whose United Empire Loyalist ancestors had been granted the land by King George III, 140 years previously. BSC personnel casually referred to the gently rolling farmland with its magnificent lake-view vista, as 'The Farm.' Intrigued, OSS adopted this as the code name for their first wartime training centre in Maryland (RTU-11). To this day, 'The Farm' refers to CIA headquarters in Langley, Virginia.

Because of the tight security surrounding STS 103, most local residents were only vaguely aware of its existence, much less its purpose. To some of the more curious, the massive rhombic antenna array on the waterfront was passed off as an experimental CBC radio transmitter. Others surmised that the Camp was the site of a top-secret explosives research and testing laboratory. Lacking any specific information, it was then, and will always be known to most people simply as Camp X, the '*unknown*'.

To the Canadian Military District Number 2, it was project 'J' and to the RCMP, who provided security liaison services, it was and is still identified by the National Defence File Number S 25-1-1. Trainees and staff preferred the 'garden variety' names: 'The Farm', Camp X, or simply, 'the Camp.' [3]

My Commandant was Lieutenant-Colonel Cuthbert Skilbeck. His Adjutant was Captain (Major, in 1944) Art Bushell, who had interviewed and screened me on behalf of SOE. Lieutenant-Colonel Skilbeck had been Chief Instructor until just before my arrival when he succeeded Lieutenant-Colonel R.M. 'Bill' Brooker as Commandant. Also on the senior staff were Captain Hamish Pelham Burn, Chief Instructor, Explosives, our demolition expert, and Bill Ross Smith, an Australian-American. All were British Army except for Art Bushell and Smith. I respected and greatly admired all of these men.

Major William Fairbairn

It is well worth mentioning the legendary Major (later Lieutenant-Colonel) William Ewart Fairbairn, although he had departed as Chief Training Instructor before my time. Major William Fairbairn, co-inventor of the famous (or infamous) double-edged *Fairbairn-Sikes* 'Commando' dagger was apparently a deceptively quiet, fifty-something, cultured English gentleman who had developed and perfected his signature work, called *Silent Killing*, while serving as Chief Instructor with the Shanghai Municipal Constabulary. Based upon the most deadly of the Asian martial arts, which were unknown to most Westerners at that time, *Silent Killing* rapidly became the defining STS training piece. Every agent-trainee had to learn to use these thirty or more deadly techniques flawlessly. We joked that we could do them in our sleep. We always approached this hand-to-hand training with relish in the hope that we would be able to show off our virtuosity in 'taking down' by throwing, but not injuring, our instructor. That this never hap-

[3] *For the most authoritative and authentic history of this unique SOE/BSC base, including its organisation, training operations and radio communications complex, told through exclusive interviews with officials, staff and agents, I highly recommend the richly-illustrated,* Inside-Camp X, *by Lynn-Philip Hodgson, 1999.*

pened with Chief Instructor Major Fairbairn, or his successors, I am quite certain. William Ewart Fairbairn's reputation has remained unchallenged as the pre-eminent, non-Asian disciple of his era, in this lethal and essential part of the secret agent's tradecraft.

On a more mundane and personal note, Military District 2, through arrangements made with the Canadian Government, managed the Camp's payroll. My pay was deposited regularly at the bank and branch of my choice, throughout my SOE service.

At Camp X, my training for covert action behind enemy lines began almost when I came through the gate. It was drilled into us from the outset that it was our duty to become experts in clandestine and guerrilla warfare. Our basic training began with physical fitness, which involved hundreds of kilometres of running, scaling walls, and dodging around, over and through obstacle courses. Camp X was a school in motion. We ran everywhere, all of the time. We competed against each other and the staff in all endurance tests. As a lanky and fit twenty year old non-smoker, I had no problem keeping up with everyone and actually came in first most of the time; I was often able to outdo the instructors. More

The art of silent killing

advanced exercises included small arms courses and drills, and unarmed combat involving disarming, immobilising and killing the enemy *mano à mano, à la* Fairbairn.

We learned how to carry concealed plastic Semtech (RDX, cyclonite or *plastique*) explosive and how to apply it to blow up buildings, train tracks, bridges, and munitions stockpiles, as well as military equipment. Semtech, a Czechoslovakian invention, was completely inert and safe to handle, unlike TNT or nitroglycerine. Our instructor insisted that one could shoot a bullet through it without setting it off. I decided to test this for myself, by placing a chunk on a rock in a field, spread out like plasticene, and shooting at it from a safe distance with my revolver. Then I walked up to inspect it, to make sure of my aim; the RDX was shredded, but otherwise intact. SOE instructors would sometimes toss gobs of RDX at one another to impress new recruits. It could be coloured to match the target object, moulded like putty and would stick to almost any surface. We learned that RDX could only be set off with a special detonator that could be wrapped inside it and connected by a wire to the hand-held firing device. My instructor handed me a small, ball-like wad of the stuff and told me to chew it like a stick of gum. I bit into it gingerly, expecting that the top of my head would blow off. It had the consistency of road tar. When it was 'well worked' he said,

"Now Joe, I want you to explode it!"

"Sir, may I take it out of my mouth first?"

He gave me a withering look and suggested that I take it into the field and blow up a large sheet of metal, left to rust by a farmer. I took the soggy goop from my mouth, squashed it around the detonator, and pressed it onto the metallic surface. Then, from about twenty yards away, I pressed the firing button. With a deafening *whump*, the sheet metal rose, arcing majestically, then shattered mid-air, spraying lethal fragments of white hot shrapnel, clods of earth and a billow of charcoal-grey smoke. When I walked back to inspect my handiwork, the only evidence was a shallow, smoking crater in the superheated Ontario County topsoil. I was temporarily deaf for ten minutes, but could hear him remark, "Well done, Joe. Next time, it could be the tracks on a Tiger." He meant a German Tiger tank, a fearsome fighting machine that was imitated, but never duplicated, although the Russian T-34 came close.

"Big Bang" Camp X style with RDX (Semtech)

We were taught that small, strategically placed quantities of this amazing material could yield highly destructive results with surgical precision. It was especially useful for demolishing railway tracks. We practised by placing charges on the Canadian Pacific Rail line tracks immediately north of the Camp. Although we never armed and fired any charges on these rail lines, the passing train crews who spotted us must have been alarmed to see anarchists or Axis saboteurs skulking in the shadows. Despite, or perhaps in defiance of the instructors' best advice, zealous recruits on training manoeuvres sometimes intentionally set off oversized charges. Massive explosions that literally shook downtown Whitby or Oshawa inevitably resulted in a deluge of telephone calls and queries to the Police, the Mayors' offices, and the newspapers, about these unexpected 'bumps in the night.' Merchants, who were greeted in the morning with the shattered remains of their plate glass windows on the sidewalks, would rightfully lodge a formal complaint with the police. The Bell Telephone Company worked closely with the local chiefs of police and the Camp Commandant's office in maintaining civic calm, with reassuring misinformation. Suffice to

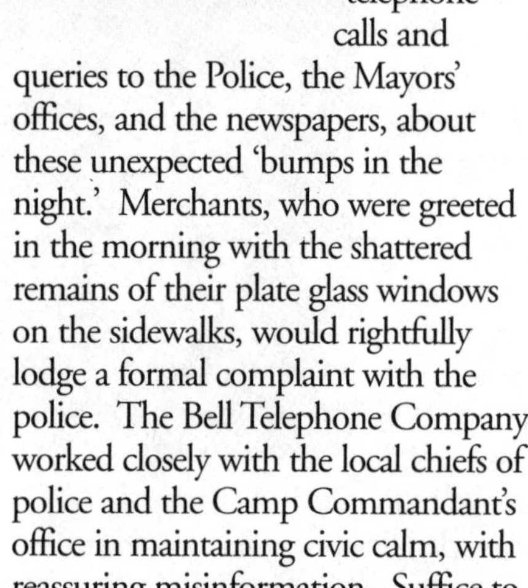

say that there was an arrangement set up whereby Whitby and Oshawa newspaper editors could contact the Commandant, through a designated Bell operator, to seek clearance and authorisation before going to press with a cover story which explained these mysterious happenings. When circumstances warranted, the Commandant would send out Camp Adjutant Art Bushell, who handled these queries with great tact and skill. I can't imagine how Art came up with explanations to satisfy the ruffled citizenry without compromising official secrecy, but he always managed to do so. It must have been 'a poser' for the insurance adjusters to have to settle these claims, without a particle of accurate information. Years later, it was revealed that the explosives storage 'magazine' at Camp X, if detonated, contained enough *materiel* to blow up Whitby and most of western Oshawa.

Intrepid's genius for organisation and co-ordination of security operations and facilities was fully evident in the revolutionary design of STS 103. Camp X opened as an operational SOE training installation in December 1941. SIS urgently required a secure, reliable, high-speed communications link between Great Britain and North and Latin America, for strategic, tactical and political purposes. Appointed by Winston Churchill as Chief of British Intelligence (SIS) west of the Atlantic Ocean, William Stephenson had a reputation as an extraordinarily shrewd and innovative businessman-inventor. These qualities, along with a broad spectrum of accomplishments in the rapidly-developing field of communications, particularly high-frequency wireless technology, gave *Intrepid* privileged access to a vital pool of talented academics, research scientists, engineers, industrial and corporate chiefs, as well as senior government mandarins and the most influential politicians. Stephenson's initial relations with FBI Chief, John Edgar Hoover, had been cordial; BSC co-operated with the FBI in joint counter-espionage roundup operations, and Hoover granted Stephenson's New York office use of FBI radio facilities.

Ever suspicious, Hoover offered *Intrepid* continued use of existing American land and underwater cable communication lines, if, in exchange, Stephenson would grant the FBI access to the top-secret, British Security Co-ordination code system. *Intrepid* declined and Hoover rescinded his offer. Undeterred, Stephenson pursued other options. BSC would build a proprietary, high frequency, short wave communications system on Canadian soil. Stephenson's inventive genius had earned him lucrative patents in wireless communications; he would not have to rely on a testy ally, or fault-prone, underwater cable and landlines, which by their nature, were insecure and highly susceptible to sabotage by Germany's 'friends' in the USA, the Bund.

A number of possible locations throughout Canada were selected for evaluation, including Ottawa, the capital city. Technical support was obtained through *Intrepid's* myriad connections in the private and public sectors, including Bell Telephone Canada, Ontario Hydro, Canadian National and Canadian Pacific Railway Companies. The criteria used for short-listing possible sites were at once highly technical and basic. The location had to be in a remote area with a topography that afforded unobstructed pathways for ultra high-frequency radio signals. Powerful transmitters could send and receive signals at very great distances, across the Atlantic Ocean, by 'skipping' radio waves off the ionosphere, the negatively-charged layer of the upper atmosphere, particularly at night time, as my friend, Mike, in Welland, had explained.

"It's like bouncing a tennis ball off a cement ceiling. It's basic physics. If you know the angle at which it hit the ceiling, you know where it's coming down. Same generally with radio waves" Mike had said.

Each possible site was tested thoroughly and rejected by *Intrepid's* short wave radio 'boffins'.

What about Camp X? Its shoreline was remote, secure, completely barren, and free of any obstacles. The trials conducted there with portable transmitting equipment were promising.

"The signals came in from England, across Lake Ontario and hit here like a ton of bricks", said Bill Hardcastle, one of the small band of gifted amateur short wave radio enthusiasts recruited in Toronto by BSC's Tommy Drew-Brook. The Whitby site not only met, but also exceeded, all of the technical requirements.

By June 1942, Mr. Drew-Brook had recruited top tier Canadian amateur operator/builders such as Bill Hardcastle, Hughey Durant and Bernie Sandbrook. Other BSC operatives scoured Canada and the United States for radio equipment and components, which arrived in unmarked crates for assembly in the Camp's earthen floored radio hut. Under the leadership of the brilliant Benjamin De Forrest (Pat) Bayly, a University of Toronto Professor of Electrical Engineering, a miracle began to take shape. There were no instructions included with these devices; batteries and talent were very definitely required!

"One piece," chuckled Bill Hardcastle, "did have a photograph of the installation taped inside the crate. That was a bit of a help." For the most part, the equipment had come from the corporate and private sector in Canada and the U.S.A., including home-rigged ham radios and a very advanced 10kW transmitter from a radio station in Philadelphia.

"Money was no object, either in the recruitment of specialists like Bernie and me, or in obtaining radio parts," Hardcastle emphasised. "Some of the equipment was taken by BSC agents in co-operation with the RCMP and Americans on the flimsy basis that they were so powerful as to be a clear and present threat to national security! The owners were always very well paid, though," he added with a grin.

Bill, Bernie, and Hughey were so talented that they built the apparatus from notepad sketches, with the help of a few photographs and sheer intuition.

"It worked flawlessly the first time we fired it up!" remarked Bill, proudly.

Within a few short weeks, these few, dedicated amateur radio operators had been formed into a formidable team which produced a short wave radio and wireless teletype installation equal to the very best professionally-built telecommunications and cipher encryption systems in Britain and the United States.

"The Colonel, Pat Bayly, was the best," said Bill.

Three massive, diamond-shaped webs of wires had been strung up between hydro poles, selected and installed by Ontario Hydro, across the lakefront and *Hydra* was officially in business. Bill Hardcastle said that *Hydra* was chosen as the installation's code name, to signify its many-faceted capabilities (*triple diversity receiver* was the term he used); with its three rhombic antennas, it was indeed multi-headed, like the *Hydra* monster of Greek myth.

I didn't receive training on *Hydra*. When I was qualifying in wireless radio telecommunications (W/T) and Morse code at the General Code and Cipher School, Bletchley Park, in England, the epicentre of British wartime short-wave communications, my signals were, however, sometimes patched through *Hydra*.

The SOE programs and staff at Camp X were uniformly first-rate. We all were in top condition mentally and physically, eager to test our skills in the 'real' world, to prepare for our missions. An agent-trainee was taught to disarm a man quietly and efficiently without endangering his own life or his comrades'. He was taught to shoot from the hip, able to selectively kill or to wound an enemy.

During the ten week Camp X training stint, we were familiarised with the SOE agents' trade craft which would become the staples of our survival toolkit, but also the basis of countless popular spy thrillers and films. We learned:

- How to camouflage your appearance in a foreign country to avoid capture. Clothing, gait, hair length, style, and colour can be easily altered.
- How to manufacture false docu-

ments such as passports and police travel permits for oneself and others. This was extremely chancy and likely to be fatal if detected. It was extremely useful knowledge that would be invaluable to me in Budapest, Hungary. We didn't try to counterfeit money. That was the speciality of BSC's Station M (for *magic*) forgers, scattered in secret locations around Toronto.

• How to hide money in your clothing to avoid detection. Money so hidden saved the lives of my comrades John, Mike, Andrew, and me. Money was vital in a foreign country especially if in prison or a PoW camp and during an escape it was absolutely essential, as my story will relate.

• A very brief explanation was given on ciphers and their concealment to make them appear innocent, which was hard to do because the Germans taught the same craft to their agents. The distinction of a cipher from a code was explained. A cipher conceals a message in symbols, which appear to be meaningless, but with the code, a message is revealed.

Camp life was only remotely akin to my experience with the Signal Corps, infinitely more challenging and interesting with mindless regimentation reduced to zero. The days were chock full with stimulating activities. We were up at six in the morning, showered, shaved, bed made, dressed, and eating a hearty breakfast in the mess hall by 6:30 a.m. We Hungarian-Canadian recruits ate all of our meals at the Camp together. Much of the morning was occupied with excellent lectures in the main hall. Emblazoned over the door was the secret agent's axiom:

Know yourself; Know your weapons; Know your enemy!

We were expected to achieve and maintain the highest personal level of physical fitness. We practised jumping from a thirty-metre wooden tower, to prepare for parachute training and scaled high walls, hand over hand, with ropes. At last, I was progressing toward my dream of qualifying for the coveted airborne insignia.

Officers would join us for breakfast, crack jokes, and sketch out the day's upcoming activities before we met in the lecture hall for our daily briefing. The Chief Instructor might say, over bacon and eggs and toast that we were going be dropped off at Rice Lake, near Peterborough. "Well, lads, what should you be thinking of taking along with you?"

One of my classmates suggested, "I'd take a sandwich and a pretty woman who can read a compass and map, Sir!"

That was thought a "… jolly good idea, but picnics are against the Regs, as luck would have it." (SOE Regulations). We sprinted to the day's briefing with contour maps of the terrain to be visited displayed on easels, then up to Rice Lake north-east of the

Camp, by army truck, to be dropped off with a compass and final instructions. "Use your wits, avoid getting picked-up, no hitch-hiking and return to Camp in time for dinner."

We usually could manage to 'liberate' a smuggled sandwich from the kitchen, but my friend's other item was academic. One memorable adventure was the great Camp X egg hunt. We were given rudimentary instructions and then sent off to a remote part of the property to raid a chicken coop, complete with live chickens and sentries. The winners were those who returned with one or more unbroken fresh eggs, without having upset the roost, thereby ending up in the guardhouse. One might think this as ridiculous as parading around a city with a camera in a German uniform, trying to be arrested, which I did, as I will later relate. Nevertheless, it proved a very practical part of our survival training that was invaluable to me when I was in Yugoslavia and later, Hungary. It also reinforced the Instructors' constant theme that planning and stealth were far more valuable tools in a life or death situation than mindless bravado.

Our Chief Instructor, Explosives, Small Arms and Aeronautical, was Captain Hamish Pelham Burn, a tall, aristocratic Highland Scot, who habitually wore a kilt. Captain Pelham Burn was typical of the calibre of SOE officers at the Camp, a thoroughly professional and highly intelligent leader with a zest for adventure, innovation and the destruction of the Third Reich. Pelham Burn's amusing reflection on the potential of a combination of Scots and Hungarians being let loose to give Hitler his "due" is recorded in Andy Durovecz' (Daniels) memoir, *My Secret Mission.*[4]

The Camp authorities were very careful not to involve us in simulations that could deprive the local residents of essentials. We might easily have been instructed to raid Farmer Smith's hen house, but eggs were rationed, expensive, and nutritious. Canadians were sacrificing a great deal under the enforced wartime rationing program and as Camp recruits, we were very well provided for.

Overnight exercises were also designed to test our mettle and ability to 'live off the land', forcing us to bivouac like *couriers de bois*, and put into practice the survival skills which we had been taught. We slept on beds of hand-cut pine branches. We were never issued a sidearm on these outings, but did sometimes carry the famous double-edged *Fairbairn-Sykes* Commando dagger, which was used to skin rabbits for roasting on hand-carved spits. In Ontario County, rabbits were abundant and easily trapped. The meat was quite edible, much like chicken.

[4] My Secret Mission, *Andrew Durovecz, Lugus Publications, 1996*

The difference in Camp life from my Canadian army experience was most apparent in the evenings. After supper, which was always well prepared, appetising, and accompanied by wine and beer, we were encouraged to get together in the main hall, to shoot the bull, play cards, and generally wind down, unless, of course, we had night manoeuvres. We never discussed the instructors or their idiosyncrasies at this time as we felt it would be unprofessional and furthermore were suspicious that the room itself was 'bugged!' If one of our mates was upset by an instructor having dressed him down harshly - a rare occurrence - these discussions were always held out-of-doors. We tried to help our colleague understand why he had been 'chewed out' and offered suggestions to help him make things right. With the luxury of hindsight and the knowledge that the STS syllabus was exceedingly prescriptive, I would not be at all surprised if these events were staged, to test our ability to function as a team. We were model soldiers: little griping, co-operative and keen to try all new challenges. There were no restrictions on our access to or consumption of alcohol of any type, thanks to Colonel McLaughlin. Yet, I never witnessed any incidents where members of my group acted 'silly bugger', at these *soirées*. I believe it is probable that SOE was interested in observing our conduct under the influence of demon rum, but we behaved ourselves.

Captain Hamish Pelham Burn's speciality was the Tiger Moth/flour bag-bombing manoeuvre. The Tiger Moth aircraft was a sturdy, slow, dual control, open cockpit biplane used for basic flight training of fighter pilots by the Commonwealth Air Training Program Schools. Oshawa Airport was one such centre. Pelham Burn would soar at low altitude over the fields, like a magnificent man in his flying machine, while we were out on exercises, and attempt to drop sacks filled with flour on us. This unorthodox activity, he explained, simulated conditions in enemy occupied territory where we could be spotted from the air and would teach us to always be vigilant. We took it all as great fun and didn't mind the occasional 'dust up', when he scored a near miss. [5]

The antiquated but excellent Tiger Moth trainer was designed for short field take-off, which Captain Pelham Burn ably demonstrated. In Europe, I quickly learned to respect the twin-engine DC3 Dakota, one of the most reliable Allied workhorse aircraft which was used for air transport, and to parachute agents and supplies into occupied countries. It could land and take off nimbly, whether on grass, asphalt, or a field of wheat stubble, as

[5] *Captain Hamish Pelham Burn and Lynn-Philip Hodgson have been in indirect contact via e-mail, during the writing of this book. According to Lynn, the Captain intended the flour sack 'bombings' as a caper, but with a serious intent. Hodgson and Longfield will have much more to say on this and other unusual and hitherto unknown pieces of Camp X lore, in a forthcoming book in this* Inside-Camp X *series.*

I would find out.

Full-scale dress rehearsals in covert activities were carried out in Toronto and Oshawa. This was not a *Boys' Own* adventure on which we were being prepared to embark. We were in training to become secret agents, experts in clandestine warfare, who would be risking our lives, operating covertly inside enemy territory. The German intelligence services were extremely sophisticated, thorough, and unrelenting in hunting down and exposing enemy subversives. The *Gestapo* (Secret State Police) and SD (Security Service) employed brutally effective physical and psychological interrogation techniques, including drugs, which were often, but not always, successful in 'breaking' agents. The SOE record tells of heroic men and women, including many Canadians, who withstood the most barbaric forms of torture without divulging any information. The *Abwehr*, German military intelligence service, was less medieval, but was also to be feared as their 'failures' were inevitably turned over to the SD and *Gestapo* interrogation specialists. We were exposed to some of these tools and methods, which included the rubber truncheon, the hand-cranked electrical generator, and extreme forms of psychological grilling. Whether broken, or resistant, the end usually came by summary execution: hanging, firing squad, garrotte, or eventual death in a concentration camp.

We were trained to live by our wits, in any circumstance. On one occasion, I was briefed and dropped off in Toronto, dressed in the uniform of a German soldier. My assignment was to take photographs of war *materiel* production factories. If picked up by the Toronto police, I was expected to be able to talk my way out, without having to resort to calling the SOE number in my wallet. I passed. A variation was to create a disturbance at a restricted site such as an arms factory and avoid being nicked by the constabulary.

It was routine to be dropped in groups of six into an unfamiliar or isolated location, armed with map and compass, to find our way back to Camp at a precise time without civilian assistance of any kind, including hitchhiking.

Arms training exercises could be extremely hazardous, as they usually involved the use of live ammunition. Machine guns fired rounds narrowly over our heads while we scrambled around and underneath barbed wire obstacles, on our bellies.
Unfortunately, a fatal accident took place during one such exercise, a year before my arrival at Camp X. Chief Instructor, Captain Howard Benjamin Burgess, was shot through the head. Captain Burgess, a popular instructor, and by all accounts, a first-rate officer, was demonstrating to a group of recruits how to duck under enemy gunfire while scuttling beneath a barbed wire barrier…

Howard Benjamin Burgess, born August 15, 1915, in England, had worked briefly for the *London Daily News*. He enlisted in 1940 and was selected for admission to the Military Intelligence Training Centre at Matlock. While there, Burgess demonstrated his extraordinary talents and was 'spotted' by SOE for training at Beaulieu, the prestigious finishing school in England. Upon graduation, at the age of twenty-five, he was appointed directly to the college staff of Beaulieu, as Lieutenant Instructor, under Chief Instructor Major Richard 'Bill' Brooker. Major Brooker would subsequently be appointed second-in-command of the newly commissioned SOE STS-103, Camp X, in December 1941, under the first Commandant, Lieutenant-Colonel Terence Arthur Roper-Caldbeck. Major Brooker would later succeed Lieutenant-Colonel Roper-Caldbeck as Commandant. In 1942, Major Brooker inherited a problem. Major William Ewart Fairbairn, the SOE's 'star' Chief Instructor at Camp X had been seconded to the prototype American OSS training station, (RTU-11) in Maryland, at the express request of OSS chief, General 'Bill' Donovan. Major Brooker knew of only one man who could possibly replace the fifty-seven year old master William Fairbairn: Howard Burgess. Accordingly, Captain Burgess left Beaulieu to visit his parents briefly and embarked for his new assignment at STS-103, Canada in April 1942.

Intrepid frequently expedited such co-operative arrangements among OSS, SOE and BSC from his headquarters in Rockefeller Centre, New York City. Captain Burgess arrived in Halifax in late April 1942 where Captain Herbert Rowland, *Intrepid's* Canadian liaison representative, met him. They travelled by rail to Toronto's Union Station, a sixteen-hour journey. After an overnight rest at The Royal York Hotel, a Camp X staff car whisked them eastward along The King's Highway Number 2 to Thornton Road, then straight south to Camp X on Lake Ontario.

Howard Burgess took up his new duties as Chief Instructor with characteristic enthusiasm. He immediately undertook a personal review of the Camp's programs to ensure their compliance with the rigorous SOE Training Syllabus. His interpersonal abilities, initiative, intelligence, and leadership skills quickly won him the respect of his colleagues and students. Bill Brooker had done very well. Indeed, he had hired a Chief Instructor worthy of the mantle of the great man, Bill Fairbairn. However, it was to tragically end, too soon.

Captain Burgess' head wound was bleeding profusely. He was in severe shock and nearly unconscious. Camp security policy prohibited any emergency service vehicles inside the gates. Dr. Millman, the Camp's physician in Oshawa, was telephoned;

he ordered that Captain Burgess be rushed immediately by Camp staff car to the Oshawa General Hospital. The distraught Commandant, Lieutenant-Colonel Roper Caldbeck, accompanied him. Five days later, on June 3, 1942, Captain Burgess passed away of a cerebral haemorrhage, after a brave fight for his life. His stellar career at Camp X had been cut short.

Captain Burgess' remains were taken to the McIntosh Anderson Funeral Home on King Street in Oshawa. In 1999, Alan Longfield and Lynn-Philip Hodgson were permitted to examine the official 1942 funeral ledger. Captain Burgess' place of residence is given as The Sinclair Farm. The signatures of Dr. Millman, Roper-Caldbeck *et al* are still clearly legible. The fee for all service rendered, $110.00 is marked *paid in full.* All the vital details are complete and correct; however, the cause of death is blank. The attendant assured my friends that this is common, as it is officially recorded on the Ontario Death Certificate. The casket remained closed. With his fellow officers in attendance as pallbearers and mourners, Captain Burgess was laid to rest on a cold and rainy morning of June 5,1942 in the Oshawa Union Cemetery at Thornton Road and Highway 2. The burial permit and Death Certificate are reproduced on pages 56 and 58.

Captain Burgess' burial permit states that he died of a kidney disease, *acute glomerular nephritis*, not of a gunshot to the head. *Glomerular nephritis* is a severely debilitating illness which can reduce the sufferer to the state of an invalid. Why so outrageously misleading a falsehood? His place of residence is correctly given as "The Sinclair Farm." Why would the Camp's authorities misstate the cause of death of this brilliant young SOE officer? Here we are venturing into the ethical minefield of covert operations, where secrecy and deception are not only commonplace, they are essential. As Winston Churchill said, "In wartime, truth is so precious that she should always be attended by a bodyguard of lies". However, such duplicity seems inappropriate in the tragic circumstances of the twenty-seven year-old Captain's death. Perhaps, and I can only surmise, it was foreseen that a person or persons might be found to be answerable for this fatality in a civil lawsuit, unlikely as that would be in wartime, or, more probably, a board of inquiry. It is also theoretically possible that the authorities decided to suppress the details, anticipating that if they became public currency, it could rend open the carefully-woven fabric of secrecy surrounding the Camp and expose its covert nature. This would have jeopardised the Camp's very existence and created a catastrophic setback to SOE's operations planning and, as well, risked the exposure of agents who were active in the field. SOE's *modus operandi* of necessity was 'night and fog'. Perhaps SOE's standard operating procedure, 'need to know,

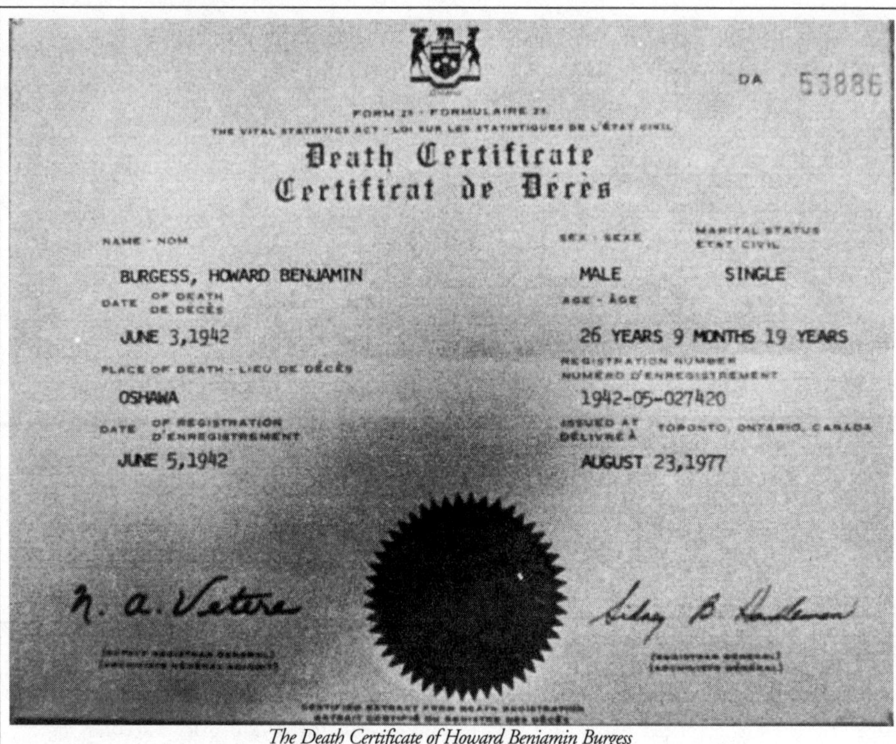

DA 53886

FORM 21 · FORMULAIRE 21

THE VITAL STATISTICS ACT · LOI SUR LES STATISTIQUES DE L'ÉTAT CIVIL

Death Certificate
Certificat de Décès

NAME · NOM: BURGESS, HOWARD BENJAMIN

SEX · SEXE: MALE

MARITAL STATUS · ÉTAT CIVIL: SINGLE

DATE OF DEATH · DATE DE DÉCÈS: JUNE 3,1942

AGE · ÂGE: 26 YEARS 9 MONTHS 19 YEARS

PLACE OF DEATH · LIEU DE DÉCÈS: OSHAWA

REGISTRATION NUMBER · NUMÉRO D'ENREGISTREMENT: 1942-05-027420

DATE OF REGISTRATION · DATE D'ENREGISTREMENT: JUNE 5,1942

ISSUED AT · DÉLIVRÉ À TORONTO, ONTARIO, CANADA: AUGUST 23,1977

(DEPUTY REGISTRAR GENERAL) (REGISTRAIRE GÉNÉRAL ADJOINT)

(REGISTRAR GENERAL) (REGISTRAIRE GÉNÉRAL)

CERTIFIED EXTRACT FROM DEATH REGISTRATION
EXTRAIT CERTIFIÉ DU REGISTRE DES DÉCÈS

The Death Certificate of Howard Benjamin Burgess

and no more', was so deeply ingrained and habitual that by reflex, truth was an orphan, even in the most innocent of circumstances. Unfortunately for historians, SOE staff burned eighty-seven percent of the Camp's records in bonfires, before turning over STS 103, in 1946, to the Canadian Department of National Defence. My search of the SOE Archives in England revealed no information on the subject of Captain Howard Benjamin Burgess. I was informed that the record "...is not available."

"Does this mean the same as 'destroyed?' " I asked.

"Not available, sir!" was the archivist's emphatic pronouncement on the subject.

It was never reported that any senior staff member referred to the case. I overheard a junior instructor say that Captain Burgess had suffered an acute cerebral haemorrhage, in his quarters, and had fallen stone dead, to the floor. *Glomerular nephritis*, indeed! It is my understanding that his family was informed that he gave his life 'in the line of duty'. Were they ever afforded the truth, that he was mortally wounded in a training mishap? Does it matter, even now? I think so. It was untimely, unfortunate, and preventable, but such accidents did occur. Captain Burgess' death was one of three casualties at the Camp, 1942-'43. Author Lynn-

Philip Hodgson has thoroughly researched and documented all three in *Inside-Camp X*. SOE's margin of acceptable loss by training misadventure was three per cent. If, by the most remote of possibilities, there had been reason to suspect foul play or third party negligence, one earnestly wishes to believe that a thorough and proper inquiry, *in camera*, would have been held and its findings put on the record. Nearly sixty years later, the SOE register is still "not available": Classified or…?

The gravestone at Union Cemetery in Oshawa

On August 15, 1943, the ten-week Camp X phase of our training was completed. My colleagues and I had written short exams throughout the training period, which were relatively easy, pertaining to a section of training that we just completed. Some of the questions were so basic that we would now call them 'no-brainers.' For example: "Can RDX be exploded by gunfire?" Never-the-less, some of our lads who had limited fluency with English needed to be coached by my friend, Alec Vass, or me, which rendered the results less than useless, as we often had to literally give them the answer. There was a final exam, which we all managed to pass, in the same fashion, with Honours, but I now question SOE's motives. Perhaps they cared less about the answers we gave than how we behaved as individuals to help our group members master the challenge.

We rarely met any of the trainees in the other sections, but stories did make the rounds that some had failed to make the cut. This was shocking to me; they were apparently shunted off to obscure desk jobs for the duration of the war.

BURIAL PERMIT

ONTARIO
Registrar-General

Registration Division of *Oshawa* County of *Ontario*

Whereas notice of the death of *Howard Benjamin Burgess*

which occurred at *Oshawa* County of *Ontario* Ontario

on the *2nd* day of *June* 19*42*, was duly filed in the prescribed form with me and registered in accordance with the provisions of The Vital Statistics Act, this permit for the burial or other disposition of the body as in The Vital Statistics Act provided is hereby issued.

The said notice stated that the cause of death was *Acute glomerular nephritis*

Given under my hand this *5th* day of *June* 19*42*

J. E. Hare
Registrar

This permit must be obtained before the burial or other disposition of any body may take place, and must be delivered before burial to the caretaker or owner of the cemetery in which such body is to be interred, or as otherwise provided by The Vital Statistics Act.

The Burial Permit for Howard Benjamin Burgess

My comrades and I were slated to continue on to Scotland and England, for advanced courses. In a gesture of generosity and goodwill, Commandant Lieutenant-Colonel Skilbeck hosted a grand farewell party in the mess hall. Abundant food, drink, and the most popular recorded music were supplied. All of the Camp's officers and staff, including many of the BSC female clerical workers from Hydra and the administrative office who were not on duty, attended. Despite the strict wartime rationing for Canadian civilians, we enjoyed excellent food and non-stop libations. It was an evening of fun and celebration, a time to reminisce with our instructors, to propose tipsy toasts and to enjoy the light-hearted revelry marking 'the end of our beginning'. We had cut our intelligence teeth at Camp X, were well trained in the basic arts of sabotage, subversion, and survival, were in superb physical condition, and were supremely confident that we would soon be joining that *élite* band of warriors: Special Operations Executive Secret Agents.

Camp X from the air 1968

CHAPTER 2
Bletchley and Beaulieu

At the end of August 1943, my mates from Camp X and I arrived by train in Halifax, as ordered. Our orders were to sail to Greenock, near Glasgow, Scotland on the converted Cunard luxury liner, *Queen Elizabeth*, which was loading troops in the magnificent Bedford Basin. We were all good friends; my closest chums were Alec Vass (code name Vincent) and Mike Turk (Thomas). Andrew Durovecz (Daniels) who passed away in 1998, wrote a fine memoir, *My Secret Mission*, (Lugus Publications, 1996) recounting his and our shared experiences at Camp X and in Hungary. The others who sailed with us were Adam Magyar (Murphy), Adam Herter (Herbert), and Gus Bodo (Bertrand). I would be given my *nom de guerre*, Joseph Gordon.[1] The similarity of the code name to our family name was purposefully done, to make it easier to remember.

Mike Turk (Thomas) 1944

None of us had been granted the promised rank of sergeant, bloody or otherwise. It was explained that we would be too conspicuous! No one raised an objection, as it would have seemed distinctly unpatriotic. We knew that we would be bounced around

England and Scotland, to acquire more specialised qualifications in our training, and finishing up, we hoped, at Beaulieu, from which all of our British STS instructors, including our Commandant, Lieutenant-Colonel Skilbeck, had graduated. Beaulieu, the SOE's fabled, prestigious finishing academy, was the final stage in the making of a secret agent. Beaulieu's graduates were deemed razor-sharp, ready for assignment to the target country of destination, and were favoured candidates for admission to the hallowed SOE Instructional Cadre.

The officer who had been charged with the responsibility for developing, vetting and nurturing SOE's unconventional warfare and intelligence training curriculum and director of operations was the brilliant, dapper, moustachioed Highland Scot, Colonel (later General, then Sir) Colin McVeagh Gubbins.

Special Operation Executive's brief, unusual and illustrious history, from 1940 to 1946 is a classic study of a loosely organised group working in a regimented environment. Its focus was on individual initiative and localised leadership, and it had to develop the knack of surviving political interference and the intrigues of traditionally-organised, (i.e. 'top down') government agencies and institutions. The military, Whitehall bureaucracy, and even Prime Minister Winston Churchill were not resistant to tinkering. Churchill also dictated policy and installed his personal choices in top posts within the Executive. Fortunately, history has proven that his hunches were unusually inspired and his appointments particularly adept. SOE was Sir Winston's express creation, when in the dark days of 1940, he charged its founder, Sir Charles Hambro, with the mission to "set Europe ablaze."[2] Under Sir Charles' successor, General Colin Gubbins, whose abilities as a soldier, authority on guerrilla warfare and repute as a gifted administrator won him the office, SOE rapidly gained the respect and admiration of General Gubbins' political masters, staff, and, as well, his colleagues in the military establishment.

As fairly naïve and idealistic young servicemen having the time of their lives, we knew nothing and would have cared little about the inner workings of our adopted service,

[1] *These aliases were not given until our arrival at Sandhurst, England. They were not treated frivolously in SOE circles. We knew that our survival in the very near future could depend on our capability to give only that code name, our rank and serial number, under questioning. We also knew that to divulge a comrade's true name could be lethal to him, to us or to an entire operation. In SOE's clandestine warfare organisation, a network of agents in an occupied country constituted a 'circuit'. Each circuit also had a specific code name. The Gestapo and SD cracked many SOE circuits by a prisoner's disclosure of just one name. The similarity to our real name was not accidental; it was hoped that we might have a better chance of retrieving it under psychological pressure or physical torture. German Intelligence services knew that some agents could be persuaded to talk, by appealing to their vanity and need for recognition, without excessive force. It was expected that the mandatory use of our code-names at all times might save a comrade, an operation, or a circuit, if one of us were to 'sing', regardless of the interrogation methods used.*

except we were intensely proud and very pleased to be Glasgow-bound, aboard the *Queen Elizabeth*, sergeants or not. It seemed to us, looking down to the wharf from the leviathan's mid deck, that the incoming stream of khaki-clad humanity was endless. What if a U-boat torpedoed us at sea? The loss of lives could be a calamity for the Allies. There were 19,000 service men and women on board. I tried to relate that number of humans to the throngs I had seen at 'Tent City' in the CNE grounds in Toronto and marvelled at the military's flair for cramming 'x' bodies into 'y' space, with 'z' left over, in case of emergencies. Finally, the great vessel's whistle shrieked our farewell to Halifax. As we heard the first clanking of the anchor chains being hoisted, a large convoy of American troop transports arrived on the quay, horns honking like the clappers of hell. Down went the gangways again and another khaki stream materialised from the trucks. As the soldiers boarded, I expected that the *Queen Elizabeth* would turn turtle with the additional mass of humanity, but she absorbed them all, without difficulty. Later that afternoon, I struck up a conversation with an Italian New Yorker, a GI named Luigi.

"Hey, my friends call me Louie. I'm from Brooklyn, New York. Where you from?"

I told him that I was Canadian, from Toronto. "What made you guys late"? I asked. "Doughboys, slow to rise again, eh?"

"Ah, the usual *snafu's*. Would you believe, Joe, the railroad lost a whole train for a day on a siding in Newark? Took the engine off and left the cars sitting there. Musta forgotten about it till someone started counting heads. 'Oh, oh, short about a grand! Gees, wonder where they could be?' The guys on board could have cared less. They had lots of food and just slept or played cards. Me? I was on a Liberty ship that'd had a run-in with a torpedo near-miss, off the coast of Newfoundland. Not enough to sink us, but the steering was screwed and we were towed back to Boston, half-sideways. Gees, how humiliatin'! Then a dive-bomber comes out of nowhere and clobbers the sub. Direct hit. It looked like a Texas gusher. No survivors; we counted 38 floaters, just like Saturday night in the East River. Man, I want to fly, and I'm gonna! Now, the real reason we're late? It takes a whole lot of time for 3,000 Yanks to kiss their broads goodbye

[2] *SOE was able to dodge and duck the bullets of petty officialdom and stay the course, despite obstructions and well-intentioned intrusions. Colonel Gubbins was a survivor of the political 'wars'. Between the first and second world wars, Colin Gubbins wrote two pamphlets for the War Office: The Partisan Leader's Handbook and The Art of Guerrilla Warfare, which are considered masterworks of unconventional warfare. Colonel Gubbins was appointed director of SOE training and operations in 1940. The Special Training Schools curriculum was his handiwork. Beaulieu, the jewel in the SOE crown, was Col. Gubbins' inspired conception. In 1942, he was promoted to Major General and Deputy head of SOE. General Gubbins was appointed Head of SOE in 1943. His code name was D.*

before you can get the show on the road," he laughed.

He reminded me of the bobby-soxers' idol, crooner Frank Sinatra, with his slim, swaggering, boyish good looks, slangy, tough guy talk, and glacial blue eyes. I took to him instantly. We became good friends on the five-day trip. Louie, a rabid Brooklyn Dodgers baseball fan, would entertain us by inventing play-by-play broadcasts of imaginary World Series games between the despised Broadway Yankees and his beloved Brooklyn 'Bums'. He could even make the sound of an ash bat smacking a ball. For intermission, he challenged us to name any player who had ever worn the Dodgers' colours and would reel off the man's season and lifetime statistics. Our new friendship almost came to an abrupt end when I called out "Joe DiMaggio."

A pained look came over his face. "Tell me that you're jokin' wit' me Joseph, okay"?

I thought I would get back into his good books and tried to recover with the only other ball player's name that I knew, besides Babe Ruth, the pride of the Yankees.

"Okay, then how about Yogi Berra?"

Louie's response was unprintable. But his good nature forgave my second gaffe and I was allowed to live to see another sunrise on the condition that, "You stick wit' ice hockey, or don't ever show your face down on Flatbush Ave! At least both your guys are Italian," he added, as if to compensate for my abysmal lack of knowledge about the great American pastime.

The vessel was now carrying 22,000 souls 'over there'. No sooner were we under steam, than the sedate *Queen Elizabeth* became transformed into one huge, floating casino. Hail Columbia! The Americans had every game of chance and gambling known to the world going, except horseracing, and who knew if that might be next. Gaming spread like the 'flu' and the epidemic was unstoppable. As quickly as the Military Police shut down one game, two more would start up. Unable to prohibit what was likely history's all-time biggest, floating crap game, the MP's consoled themselves by watching out for con artists, card sharps, pickpockets, and other grifters.

I had little experience with cards and none with craps, and watched the action with a lot of interest. Most of the bets were small, but there were some heavy weight players involved. I ventured a few dollars on side bets, which I lost immediately until Louie took me aside me. His system for betting on craps was based on the mathematical laws of probability and was infallible, "…plus or minus ten percent, trust me," he winked. Louie introduced me to his pal, a studious mathematical prodigy, 'The Wiz,'

("The Wizard of Odds, get it, Joe"?) The Wiz told me that he had taught sophomore and pre-college math at Brooklyn High, but had really learnt most of what he knew about 'probs and stats' from his students, who were street kids, rather than by studying Pascal's Triangle at NYU. I made some tidy profits, thanks to the Wiz and his Brooklyn brood.

We Canadian Hungarians bunked together; and ate two good meals a day at the same time, but not at the same table, as we had to line up to be served, then make a dive for any available seat. The sleeping accommodations were not *cabin: first class*; we were, after all, enlisted men. The officers, who had been assigned larger, fancier quarters, ended up with Louie, the Wiz and 2,998 GI's and Marines sardined in with them.

Concern for our safety in the Atlantic's 'submarine alley' was not a common topic of conversation, although we occasionally passed the time talking about our chances of surviving a hit. Louie said that he and several GI's and Marines were 'makin' book' on it.

"Even you guys who just got torpedoed? I asked.

"Oh yeah, us especially, Joe! We know the odds, right, Wizzo?"

The word that Louie got from the Chief Petty Officer was that the *Queen Elizabeth's* mighty turbines could generate more than enough steam to easily outrun the fastest German sub; she was only vulnerable to an ambush, by a head-on torpedo attack. We were assured that the ship sailed in complex zig-zag patterns, and stayed far away from known U-boat rendezvous zones. Proof came when we sighted a field of mountainous icebergs. *'Talk about going out of our way! Next stop, the North Pole?'* The thought of the doomed Titanic's hull lying a mile or more below us gave me a few seconds pause: iceberg…torpedo…whatever.

The *Queen Elizabeth* turned south on its approach toward Scotland. Finally, the enormous vessel eased gracefully into the slip at Greenock, near Glasgow. I was looking forward to being on land again, and was there much sooner than I expected as the crew and officers handled our disembarkation with outstanding efficiency.

It took me a while to overcome the sensation of being in constant motion on the *Queen*. A British officer directed us to a barracks for a short rest to recuperate after which we were rounded up and put aboard a train southward bound for Sandhurst, home of the famous Military Academy, near London. Sandhurst was a renowned, exclusive institution, intended for the *crème de la crème* of the British establishment. Among countless male scions of the nobility, the peerage, royalty, and the privileged class in general, Winston Churchill was among its notable graduates, as was the Scot David Niven, one of my favourite actors. It was here that our SOE code names were conferred. Afterwards, a cordial but restrained reception was held. An SOE officer led us into a dimly lit, dark-panelled room and put us at our ease with small talk, tea, and biscuits. He spoke quietly, giving a lengthy overview of our itinerary, and concluded his *tête a tête,* saying, "I am pleased to tell you, gentlemen, that you have been granted leave, to commence immediately, at the Mayers Hotel in Russell Square, London. I believe you will find everything there to your liking. Someone will be looking in on you, shortly. We have made arrangements for your luggage and transportation. Questions, gentlemen? Then do enjoy your stay. Good day."

We cabbed to the front entrance of the Mayers Hotel, a first-class hostelry, where a Concierge, whose magnificent uniform and stately manner bore a marked similarity to the Very Modern Major General in *H.M.S. Pinafore*, greeted us with a deference close to reverence.

After I unpacked, I lay down to test the luxurious bed. It was a far cry from my hammock on the *Queen*. I wondered if Louie, the Wiz and the boys were doing as well. Likely not. I hoped that Louie had been successful in applying for the United States Army Air Force. At six p.m. precisely, my bedside telephone chirped me awake. There was a gentleman waiting upon us in the drawing room beside the lobby, the clerk stated. This 'someone to look in on us' was an SOE major, with a very thick head cold, who had been dispatched to brief us on the 'approved list' of Hungarian ethnic clubs in London. With many apologies and much clearing of his throat, our SOE emissary listed the locations of choice: The Hungarian Club in Pembridge Square, The Democratic Club (President Count Mihaly Karolyi) and the Revai Club (for former Horthy diplomats who were pro-democracy). Mike Turk (Thomas) and I decided that we should personally research each of the recommended locations, as our patriotic duty.

On our first evening out, we became involved with two charming young women, who were Hungarian and Jewish with whom we spent several evenings, dining out and partying at the clubs, and then continuing at their rooms, after closing time. Mike and I had to vacate their apartment by 2:00 a.m.; it was the girls' inviolable house rule. We didn't have any cause to object and met them for dinner at the best restaurants as often as possible, which was nearly every night. There seemed to be no shortage of food, including a dazzling variety of seafood, which we all loved. Wartime steaks, though, were a different matter. Beef was rationed, and had been universally replaced by rabbit and horsemeat. Rabbit was not a problem for me, and I finally overcame my resistance to horseflesh in a

Soho nightclub when I courageously ordered a horsemeat steak, "Very well done, please. Burn it if you like." My London acquaintance with old Dobbin helped prepare me for steak *à la Russe* in Budapest.

We kept our friends supplied with silk stockings, chocolates, cigarettes, perfume and anything else we could get from the Canadian Army store or the American Forces' PX. Reality intruded when Mike and I had to say good-bye to our two lovely friends; our group was being shipped far north to Morar, close to Arisaig, the large Commando training centre near the Isle of Skye in the Scottish Highlands, for the next instalment.

Upon arrival at STS 25, Morar, we were lined up on the Parade Square in a downpour, and addressed by a Major who was wearing a kilt and sporran; he appeared to be in charge and was likely the Base Commandant. In the heavy rain, we couldn't understand a word that he was saying. We shuffled nervously, straining to look as though we knew what we were doing. This fierce - sounding man was a Commando; God knows what might happen if we appeared to be sloppy or inattentive. From behind me, a voice a whispered, 'Gaelic'. It might as well have been, 'Urdu'. Without a pause, the major broke into a delightfully rich, Highland Scots facsimile of the King's English as he outlined our activity roster at the camp. When he had finished, he invited, or rather commanded, us to attend a welcome party in the Officers' Mess, "Forthwith, gentlemen, forthwith!"

Left - Commando Monument near Arisaig

Sodden and hungry, we were relieved to accept his invitation 'forthwith'. Inside the warm mess hall, he and his staff entertained us in Highland Scots tradition. They were, to a man, grand fellows who proceeded to serve us wonderful, mysterious and appetising foods, washed down with large quantities of local ales, as a prelude to more serious drinking. As the reception progressed, the Major was moved to recite Robert Burns' stirring ballad, *Scots Wha Hae* and the *Ode to a Mouse*, in Gaelic and English alternately. A young officer turned to me to explain that the beloved Scottish bard's best body of work was in "the tongue." I have always been touched by poetry and found that I was deeply moved by the humanity of these stalwart warriors, who wore their nationalistic pride on their sleeves with such passion, without reservation or apology.

Our hosts imbibed single malt Scotch whiskey in quantities that might have staggered a plough horse. We Canadians managed not to 'let down our side', although at considerable personal cost the next morning.

The rigorous routine here was exactly what I had hoped for, except for the almost constant rain. I felt I was beginning to lose my physical edge because of the soft life in London. This would change. Early each morning before breakfast, we had a sixteen kilometre run: without fail, it rained bucketsful. It rained on each of the twenty-eight days we were at Morar. Paramilitary training included running across squelchy peat bogs while explosions were going off all around us, climbing rope ladders hand over hand, unarmed combat for hours, and always competing against the trainers at every chance.

Frequently, our travails were accompanied by the haunting skirl of the pipes, from somewhere in the distant reaches of the parade ground. Soon I was in the best physical condition of my young life. I thrived on the camp regimen, its physical and mental challenges, and respected the tough but fair and uncompromising, professional approach of the officers, particularly the Commandant. Before sitting down to breakfast - *Scots wha hae!* - we were served a generous tumbler of scotch, neat, fresh from the choicest vats of the local distillery. Kippered herrings, 'kippers', for which I developed an immediate dislike, were the preferred main course. I struck a bargain with the Major so that in return for my kippers and half of my amber eye-opener, I would inherit his bacon and eggs. He was obviously delighted and commended me for my "Calvinist charity," with a conspiratorial gleam in his eye.

Part of our training took us to Inverness, near the beautiful Loch Lomond. The scenery was spectacularly rugged and majestic, with a continuous overlay of drizzle: 'Scotch mist.' Like our Scots hosts, whose moods seemed to be immune to the constant mizzle –a delightful, local term which I believe aptly combined 'miserable' with 'drizzle', we Canadians surrendered and stopped thinking about the weather. Perhaps the Scots drank such quantities of whiskey to inoculate themselves against the constant damp of their dour climate. The Scottish pubs more than made up for the weather; they were warm, cosy, and hospitable, serving huge mugs of amber ale to wash down gargantuan plateloads of inexpensive and hearty, home-made fare. The Scottish lasses were gorgeous, with fair complexions like angels, and were very welcoming. I gained 12 kilos, going from 72 to 84 kg, without any fat. I felt and looked trim and fit.

We visited nearby Arisaig, the large Commando training centre. Our STS 25 camp was modelled after it, although on a smaller scale. An impressive bronze Commando statue was erected there after the war to commemorate the extraordinary deeds of daring, bravery and sacrifice by this band of heroes, many of whom were Canadian. It is a truly moving memorial to courage in the most perilous of circumstances. I recommend it as a 'must see' on your itinerary, should you ever visit the Highlands, to pause, reflect, and rededicate one's commitment to the perpetuation of Remembrance or Memorial Day, or by whatever name it is known in your country.

This phase of our SOE training was physically demanding, extremely strenuous, and thoroughly enjoyable. What more could a young fellow desire: first-class training in a splendid location blessed with wonderful people. But the terrible weather! I never saw sunshine while we were there. We all passed the requirements and returned south for a furlough in London after the rigors of Scottish training, Highland nectar, and constant damp. Our recovery included 'single malt scotch withdrawal therapy', courtesy of Drs. Guinness and Burton. Mike and I renewed our friendship with the two charming Hungarian women and together we haunted the same clubs and restaurants as we had on our first round. London is a truly exciting, cosmopolitan city. During wartime, it was the rest and recreation centre for hundreds of thousands of servicemen and women, offering diversions and 'entertainments' of all imaginable, and some unimaginable, descriptions. After leaving our friends' flat at 2:00 a.m., we would often walk over to Piccadilly Circus, to watch the non-stop street theatre. Mike and I enjoyed chatting up the pretty women, most of whom were seeking male companionship, and gave them cigarettes, chocolates, silk stockings, and any other favours which we had picked up at the base. The 'for hires' told us that they seldom charged a Canadian service man for services rendered, although we never tested this proposition. The Piccadilly pubs were teeming with our allied comrades in arms, of both genders. The saying *meet me in Piccadilly* was a truism then, as it is now.

Too soon, our leave was over. We took the train north to STS 33 Altricham, near Manchester, for the next great adventure, parachute training. I was looking forward to this course. The program was set up to start at a basic level of challenge and become progressively more daunting. We started from platforms 3 metres, 4 metres, and finally 5 metres off the ground, cushioned with piles of wood shavings. This was a 'piece of cake', as we had undergone similar training on the jump tower at Camp X. As I wanted to be the first one of my group to 'go for broke', I volunteered to jump from the 30 metre tower. I had no fear of heights and clambered quickly up the wooden rungs of the sloping tower, to its topmost part. On the platform, I slipped into a type of parachute harness, which, I was assured, was securely tethered to the top of the tower by means of a wire cable. My Jewish girlfriend in London had often used the Yiddish term, *Chutzpah*. '*So, this is what she meant,*' I reflected, proudly. At the dispatcher's command, "Go!" there wasn't time to reconsider my foolhardiness, so I launched myself down the incline, which ended abruptly, one metre above ground level. Our instructor had demonstrated how to roll upon landing to minimise the risk of injury, as you would in an actual jump from an aircraft. I executed the roll and stood up, shaking slightly, but feeling confident of my performance as I nonchalantly unfastened the harness. My pals were shouting and applauding; I glanced up at the dispatcher on the platform who gave me the 'thumbs up.' I was a convert! After a few more jumps from the static tower, which would barely pose a challenge to most of today's Intermediate-level bungee crowd, we were judged ready to add some motion. We jumped from the back of an army truck, moving at 32 kph. It was fun and wasn't fancy, but no one was hurt as we quickly perfected the roll landing and gained a sense of what was to come.

Before we were taken up to jump from a plane, we had to learn the art of packing our own parachute. Next, we were shown how to get out of the parachute harness quickly, to avoid being snarled in the guidelines. The double-edged Fairbairn-Sykes Commando knife was a godsend for freeing yourself, were you badly hung-up and unable to get clear. The famous blade was frequently the object of instruction, although it was not issued to me on either of my missions. Perhaps SOE knew that as a child in Hungary, I had once run with scissors.

After being certified *A-ready*, we eight climbed on board an aged Whitney aircraft from Ringway, which took off on a heading for Manchester's Tatton Park. On board were several other SOE novitiates, including three memorable French women, as well as an assortment of males: Norwegian, Dutch, and Polish. Our instructor lined us up at the more than generous opening in the Whitney's side, where its door had once been. We snapped our lifelines to the aircraft's static line. My heart was thumping against my ribcage; I was keyed up, but not afraid. The flashing red light over the opening turned green for 'safe' and with a 'Go' from the dispatcher, the first person jumped out, or was pushed. We followed, one by one, as the jumpmaster tapped us each on our left shoulder. It was impossible to refuse; the body behind was pushing and it was too late in the day to suggest a deferment: "Not at this time, thank you." Nor would it have been heard, above the competing blasts of the wind and engines. The person ahead of me hesitated momentarily. Push literally came to shove. With freshman's enthusiasm and impatience, I gave a hearty assist to launch the reluctant jumper. I believe that he or she landed safely; there were no reports of casualties, that day.

Among the greatest thrills of my wartime experiences were the parachute jumps. The first few seconds were an epiphany of extraordinary beauty. I hit the aircraft's slipstream, suspending my body in defiance of gravity as though I were nestled and protected in the hand of God, at a 30-degree angle. I was in space, but time was irrelevant. I could see ahead and beneath me as I was held momentarily weightless, in the slipstream, until Newton's Laws and the raging air currents regained control of my body and I began the free fall. The 'high' was positively addictive; I understand why skydivers whom I know suffer pangs of withdrawal until their next 'fix'. I thoroughly enjoyed almost every jump, whether in training or over enemy territory. At an altitude of 1,200 to 2,000 feet, one has to rapidly collect one's thoughts in order to concentrate, and anticipate landing using the proper procedure to avoid being banged up. In all of our training exercises, an instructor was situated on the ground to evaluate our jumps and landing techniques. Simply avoiding trees was an accomplishment in Tatton Park, but miraculously, only a few of us suffered bruises and there were no broken bones. Medics were always on duty, to attend to casualties.

The worst type of jump was from a balloon, from an altitude of 1,000 feet. The dispatcher, with a group of six trainees, sat in a swaying gondola, suspended beneath the gigantic gas-bag. There was a hole in the centre of the gondola's platform. Without a slipstream, your body plummeted straight down, as though a massive lead anchor was tied to your boots. No one I talked with liked jumping from a balloon basket, although we did it twice. Our instructor said that it was used to simulate jumping from various aircraft platforms. In my SOE career, I jumped from the side hatch of a DC3 Dakota, the belly of a Halifax bomber as well as the Whitney, yet for sheer terror, nothing rivalled the 'cannon-ball' balloon descent.

We all received 'pass' ratings in parachute training and enjoyed another short stay at Mayers Hotel before a week's leave at Northampton, near an ATS (Army Territorial Service) Camp, where we scouted out a friendly pub and passed some time with the Camp staff.

Our personal war was going extremely well for us. We had stayed together as a group, and had been wined and dined while experiencing the marvellous warmth and hospitality of Scotland and England, all the while being trained as SOE Secret Agents. Now, our hardy band was to be broken up. I was the only one of my group selected for specialised wireless telegraphy or W/T (Morse code and short-wave radio) training at Bletchley Park. I wished my friends good hunting and caught the train to Milton Keynes, Buckinghamshire.

Bletchley Park, a rambling Victorian manor estate, is located near Milton Keynes, within easy access of London, via the excellent British

Railway Service. The Foreign Office purchased the property after the death of its previous owner, Lady Frances Leon, in 1938. In 1939, the General Code and Cipher School, GC&CS (or, fondly, the 'Chalk and Cheese Society'), was established. Bletchley Park, along with its associated out-buildings was also known as Station X, and was crucial to the Allies' ultimate victory in many ways. The unique Intelligence establishment was far more than a top-secret radio interception base or a training and research laboratory. Its charming exterior with its myriad gabled roofs was home to a colourful group comprising the most gifted minds and unusually creative personalities to be found in British universities, or perhaps the universe. Professors in golf caps and plus fours mingled with colonels in battle dress, often lacking insignia. Here, in Hut 3, SIS secretly conducted Operation *Ultra*, which, by April 1940 had broken the supposedly impenetrable and indecipherable German Lorenz SZ 42 and the portable '*Enigma*' telegraphic cipher machines. This astounding feat eventually afforded the Allies unlimited and undetected access to top level German military and diplomatic traffic throughout the war. Knowledgeable historians credit Ultra with many of the most significant turnabouts of Allied fortunes, including the defeat of unrestricted German submarine attacks on our North Atlantic convoys and the success of D-Day. There is general agreement that *Ultra* shortened the war by between eighteen and twenty-four months. The story of *Ultra* is so incredible that any self-respecting editor would have rejected it as far-fetched science fiction, unworthy of even a third rate espionage potboiler. Yet, it is true. For example, an actual working German *Enigma* code machine, which had been stolen by a Polish national, was handed over to the British Secret Intelligence Service in 1938 after it was turned down by French Intelligence. Although hundreds of persons played significant roles in 'breaking the code', it was the astonishingly original minds of Alfred Knox, Cambridge-bred cryptanalyst and his assistant, a Cambridge and Princeton-educated mathematician, Alan Turing, together with their British, French and Polish 'brain trust', who invented the Turing *Bombe*, an electromechanical number sorter which 'crunched' and co-ordinated the data base of *Enigma's* 14,000,000 possible settings. The Bombes were precursors to the world's first true computer, *Colossus*, of which ten were built by the British Post Office and made operational at Bletchley, in 1943. Thus, the computer age was truly born, not in

[3] *The story of Enigma is a fascinating tale of human dedication, intuition, and inspired deduction, married with pure and applied mathematical logic, engineering virtuosity, incredible luck and serendipity. Dr. Leo Marks' memoir,* Between Silk and Cyanide, *Free Press, is an engaging, personal account of code making and politics by this brilliant, maverick head of SOE Cryptography. Bletchley Park Trust (http://www.bletchleypark.org.uk/) now operates as a public museum, with an active amateur radio club, some of whose members were among the original operators during WW II.*

America, but in England.

Dr. Leo Marks, SOE's brilliant chief cryptographer, and his associates, adapted and perfected the Soviet one-time code pad method (OTP) for SOE agents' field use. Theoretically, the OTP was unbreakable. Only the agent and his or her base had one of each page. However, it was severely compromised when a printer mistakenly ran off duplicates. Fortunately, the breach of security was detected, but not before damage had been inflicted on some field operations.[3]

We SOE W/T students had exclusive use of the wireless training facility, STS 52, on the main floor; our mess and sleeping quarters were all conveniently located close by. For obvious reasons of security, we were kept separate from the Cryptography Intelligence Section. I met and briefly chatted with a gracious older couple who I met unexpectedly on a staircase landing. To this day, I have no idea whether they were groundskeepers, SIS operatives, gardeners, or two of Dr. Turing's cryptanalysts. My classmates at Bletchley formed a microcosm of the Allied nations, including French-Canadians, Americans, Belgians, French, Dutch of both genders, Hungarians; Yugoslavs, Czechoslovakians, Poles and Dutch Indonesians, as well as an English professor of linguistics who was an acknowledged expert in several obscure Far Eastern languages. Our instructors, both women and men, were exceptionally talented professionals.

Rest and recreational pursuits were on tap at Thames Park near Oxford. In a local pub, I met some Poles from GC & CS who were dedicated sybarites. One, named Joe, and I became proficient at carrying out clandestine nightly raids on the Bletchley apple storage shed. I thought back fondly to Captain Pelham-Burn's chicken coop raids at Camp X with new appreciation for his wisdom; apples, or fresh eggs are extremely valuable when one is trying to survive in an unfamiliar setting, even one as benign as GC & CS. Joe's mission sent him into Poland. I do not know whether he survived the devastation of the Warsaw bombings by the Germans and Russians.

I also met Rolly, from Rhode Island, who was bilingual in English and French. His parents were originally from the Montreal area. Whenever we could wangle passes, Rolly and I went together to London. When it was available, we used one of the SOE safe houses in central London as our operations centre. We had both been taught how to burglarise as well as many other tools of the espionage trade and made good use of them, for the glory of King and Country.

We had been instructed not to use the flat without permission because there could be active agents temporarily in residence, whom we were forbidden to meet. Naturally, we couldn't pass up the chance to use some of our newly acquired skills and, against orders, made duplicate keys for the safe house. Fortunately, we didn't manage to breach anyone's 'cover'. Rolly and I had wonderful times in London, using our wits, while linking up with two charming English nurses whom we met regularly. They stayed with us in a hotel: even we wouldn't risk taking them to the house out of consideration for an agent's security. We four enjoyed many good times together, but eventually we were separated by the misfortunes of war.

My wireless training required that I be completely focussed and alert. Morse code needed to be perfected as if it were a second language, to be sent and received, without errors, at a minimum rate of twenty-five words per minute, in order to graduate. Each operator has his or her own unique 'sending signature' or 'fist' characteristics such as keying speed and touch, much like a typist's. These are as personal as a fingerprint, so that an impostor, such as an enemy counter-agent, could theoretically be detected immediately by the receiving operator. Of course, the receiving operator required practice in receiving messages in order to learn to recognise and memorise your signature. Wire recorders were in their infancy but German Intelligence had astutely learned to use them as a counter intelligence tool to duplicate the signature of a captured agent, as I was to discover.

We were issued special ciphers to be memorised and codes, thanks to Dr. Leo Marks' genius, which were printed on silk in case of capture. We were shown how 'one time' code pads worked and how to use them for secure communications. The OTP is virtually unbreakable, so long as it does not fall into hostile hands - or a careless printer. The agent and home station held the only two copies of random figures or letters, which are destroyed after one use. It was very difficult to destroy a piece of silk about 10 cm square, but they were of little use to enemy decipherers. RCAF and RAF pilots wore silk scarves imprinted with codes and escape route maps that were manufactured by the Timothy Eaton Company of Toronto. I already knew about the effect of the ionosphere on radio signals (skip) and learned how to best site or place my portable wireless by reading the signal strength meter, for sending and receiving signals. The concentrated course in W/T, particularly Morse code, was exacting and required painstaking study and continued practice for mastery. Consequently, we were permitted a lot of freedom to unwind after classes.

For relaxation, we were encouraged to go on safaris to stalk the estate's population of squirrels. This may have been intended as an exercise to hone our survival or handgun skills, but after shooting our first flea-ridden specimen, Rolly and I vowed to swear off. They were bold, tame, and entertaining to watch while I was studying in my dorm. They were also lowly rodents, which we thought to be *infra dig* as game for agents-in-training. We were trained to ride motor bikes, which I practised whenever the opportunity arose. As a bonus, I also learned how to stretch a piano wire tautly across a road to unseat a rider to disable or perhaps kill him by strangulation or decapitation. This technique is used to good effect by the late actor and motorcycle enthusiast, Steve McQueen, in the excellent 1963 film, *The Great Escape,* but I never had the opportunity to try it out.

I met some very interesting people at wireless school whom unfortunately I have never encountered again. Bill, a young Dutchman, and his girlfriend, both spoke English very well and were preparing to jump into Holland as soon as they completed the course. They planned to be married when the war was over. SOE policy normally prohibited such arrangements; the torture of one could be used to 'break' the other. Beau, a French-Canadian from Montreal, and I enjoyed good times together. John was a Belgian with whom I spent puttering around on a 'one banger', a single cylinder BSA 'Beezer' motor bike, terrorising the local countryside. Einar, a Norwegian, was a very special friend who told me to look him up in Norway after the war. He said that he was employed in a travel agency in Oslo. I went to Norway and visited every travel business in Oslo, but couldn't find him. All of these friends of course used their cover names. If they survived, I sincerely hope that this book will find them alive.[4]

I passed all of the courses and graduated from Bletchley's wireless STS 52. This had been the most challenging and enjoyable period in my preparation and I was looking forward eagerly to the next phase at Beaulieu Manor, in southern England. Winston Churchill had charged Sir Charles to "Set Europe Ablaze:" my SOE friends and I had done quite well at starting a few fires on our own. I stopped over in London for a few days' leave and my last visit with the English nurse. With fond farewells, I was *en route* to Beaulieu, the SOE finishing school.

Beaulieu Manor, set in the New Forest between Bournemouth and Southhampton, is a spectacular manor estate consisting of twelve elegant country homes, each of which was built by close friends of the Barons Montagu, the hereditary owners. Beaulieu (commonly pronounced *bew lee*) has been the Montagu ancestral home since the sixteenth century. The family's vast holdings include Beaulieu Abbey, on land given to the Cistercian Monks by King John, of Magna Carta notoriety,

[4] *Please contact me through Gath Ltd, in care of Blake Books Distribution, at the address shown inside the front cover of this book.*

in 1202. In 1940, Lord Montagu temporarily turned over the keys of his baronial estate to the British government for use by SOE. It became an operational Special Training School in 1941 and was returned to the Montagus in 1945. There was likely no other location, among the stately homes of England, to more perfectly match the esoteric needs of SOE.

Each 'house' has its own unique character, distinctive appearance, and name. The manor home is the magnificent Palace House. Others are The Rings, Inchmere, The Vineyards, The House in the Woods, Hartford House, Boarmans, The Drokes, and The House on the Shore. Each residence is set well apart from its neighbours, a great advantage, as each served as an independent, self-contained STS: The Rings was STS 31, Hartford STS 32 and my house, The Drokes, was STS 34. Trainees were grouped according to their prescribed courses and had little formal interaction with members of any of the other Schools. Over the door of each house was a sign to discourage unauthorised entry: "Trespassers will be shot." Depending on the particular course you were taking, your accommodation was conveniently close to your training school, but not necessarily with your chums. Beaulieu was not a social club, therefore arranging individual schedules to coincide was understandably not among the Commandant's priorities.

The staff members' range of expertise was staggering; they were as unusual a collection of eccentrics, wizards, and experts in secret warfare as one could find anywhere in Britain, with the possible exception of Bletchley Park. My pre-conceptions were shattered one by one as the Baron's groundskeeper (a convicted safe cracker), and a burglar on parole were introduced, among this gifted instructional cadre.

The curriculum was a review of all previous material in the STS instructional 'Bible'[5] except for parachute jumping, flavoured with 'enrichment opportunities' suited to our individual profiles and future assignment. In three weeks, I was instructed in arson, assassination, blackmail, break and enter, burglary, codes, code-breaking and ciphers, disguises, false pretences, forgery, invisible writing, key making, sabotage, and more silent killing, among others. Adolf Hitler, who was reputed to have harboured a personal hatred, bordering on paranoia, for SOE in general, referred to Beaulieu as "the gangster school." The Nazi state police organisation, most particularly the *SD* and *Gestapo*, had been issued standing orders to extract intelligence, by any means at their disposal, concerning Beaulieu's programs and personnel, from captured agents who were even

[5] *My sincere appreciation to Nathan Estey, who has kindly and generously given me permission to reproduce, in part, the SOE STS training manual in his possession. See Appendices.*

remotely suspected of having been trained there. Consequently, we were instructed on how to conduct ourselves under intense interrogation without divulging anything of a compromising nature. Failing that, we were expected to commit suicide by means of the cyanide 'L (lethal) pill', which was actually a small round capsule that was issued before a mission and conveniently sewn into your jacket's lining.

I loved the training. We were kept in peak physical condition with an eight km morning run in which I usually came in second or third. A Belgian was the consistent winner. The Americans on board the *Queen Elizabeth* had corrupted us; we developed a system of handicapping the top runners for betting on the outcome of the next day's run. The payoffs were usually accompanied by quantities of free beer at the mess each night. I enjoyed swimming as much as running and made a wager with the Belgian as to who could swim the most lengths of the large outdoor pool, in the morning. As the weather was quite nippy, the Belgian and I agreed that each contestant would be permitted to take a timed rest after so many lengths, wearing his army greatcoat. By this time, we had broken the rules about non-association with persons outside our house, and a crowd had gathered to watch. When I arrived at poolside, the water's surface was covered with a layer of ice. The Belgian's *clique* demanded that I pay up.

"Not in this lifetime, *mes amis*!" I proclaimed, to show my cosmopolitan nature. Addressing my handlers, I ordered, "Get some thick, heavy stakes and we'll show them what Canadians do every morning before breakfast!" The Belgians looked alarmed; by my bluster, perhaps they thought that Canadians thrashed Belgians regularly for morning exercise.

I wasn't sure that my scheme would actually work, as I showed my 'side' how to use the largest sticks as clubs to crack open a lane way in the ice. Then I plunged in, swam two lengths, and won the bet, to wild applause. I was very grateful for the greatcoat. That evening, I was carried into the mess on the shoulders of my supporters, like an Olympic medallist, to an enthusiastic reception hosted by my Belgian challenger and his pals.

My house of twenty students was composed of Poles, Americans, a Norwegian, an Alsatian and one Canadian, me. We were taught how to case and burglarise a house by a most unusual man, a convicted burglar, 'Blokey'. 'Blokey' was brought out of "the nick, choky, in durance vile" as he oftentimes described his sentence in prison, or most imposingly, "…in Indefinite Detention at His Majesty's Pleasure." I was immediately entranced; only a man who truly loved poetry as I did, especially the work of Robert Burns, could possibly have known, or tossed off, 'in durance vile', during the course of conversation. SOE had arranged for his release into their custody at Beaulieu to permit him to teach us his trade on the assumption that "It takes a thief… to teach thieving." He was a thorough gentleman, highly educated, superbly skilled at his profession and must have run into very bad luck to have been 'nicked'! He could pick any type of lock, manufacture a key, or pry any window. He taught us how to case, enter, and leave a house, without disturbing a fleck of dust. Blokey was kept under "crumpets and tea" - lock and key - when his talents were not needed. One night, we were enjoying ourselves at a mess party when a total stranger, edged his way over to me and whispered, "Mum's the word, mate!" he said, holding his finger to his lips. I looked at him, up and down. I had no idea who he was, although he bore a striking resemblance to my mental picture of Magwitch the convict, in *Great Expectations.* "Mum! Where?" I had met a somewhat mature Belgian *fille de joie* in Piccadilli who used 'Mum' for her own obscure reasons, as her preferred working name.

"Get me a glass of beer laddie, and I'll show you."

I came back with the beer but couldn't find either him or Mum, so I set down the mug on my table. A moment later, he re-appeared. "Thanks, Gordon, dear fellow. I'll remember this! It's me, Blokey!" he whispered in cultured Oxbridge, then winked as he shuffled off.

I was astonished at his clever deception. It was a masterpiece done with minimal makeover and theatrical touches. He confided later that it was 'dead easy' to escape from his room and did so often. "I slip out to take the fresh night air, or for a lark, visit the local pub for a beer or two and a little slap and tickle with the ladies. The disguise wasn't a major challenge, Gordon. I used to do a fair bit of acting at school, usually played an older person. You know, the bumbling headmaster or someone's idiot uncle from Brazil. So I make use of voice training and the basic tricks in the actor's stock in trade, to get the ageing effects, like hair colour, style, and skin tone. It's the eyes. Learn to exploit the eyes. You can always find a few cosmetic aids without much effort. This Czecho RDX works well in a pinch if you can't get hold of cotton batting, to change the facial structure. See? Just don't swallow it. Nasty, very nasty on the internal parts! Won't blow to bits, but you might wish it would."

He pulled out a clump of Semtech from his pocket. Ripping it into two halves, and kneading them, he inserted them carefully into his mouth. He turned away, momentarily. Within seconds, he turned around; the transformation was startling. This was an undocumented use of the material; of that I was quite sure. "The training manual's (SOE) damn useful too. I have my own copy, illegally of course, if you want to have a gander." He stayed at the mess party for the entire evening, with the knowledge of three or four other students whom he trusted, and then slipped away unnoticed to his room.

The next evening, my house met for a special assignment. An officer introduced it as a 'stealth game' and then had Blokey give us the details, in his best, old-school-tie manner. Nothing could have been simpler, he said. To win, a group had to gain entry to The House in the Woods and bring back some special documents, as proof. The rub, he said, was that you could not start before 9:00 p.m. nor use any of the materials he had covered during his lectures. The groups huddled together like conspirators, planning their strategies. As the 9:00 p.m. starting time grew near, we checked our watches anxiously. My group was primed. Then, at 8:55 p.m., Hugo, the little Frenchman from Alsace-Lorraine suddenly bounded into the lecture room brandishing some papers, which he handed to the instructor who glanced at them and gave them to Blokey, who calmly declared,

"Gentlemen, *les jeux sont fait!* The games are finished! Monsieur Hugo is the winner!"

Hugo had won? How? He confessed that he had started out at 8:30 p.m., half an hour before starting time! There was grumbling from the non-starters, with muttered comments that reflected on Hugo's parentage and his innate lack of a proper British sense of fair play. To further embarrass us, the instructor praised Hugo's initiative with the "All's fair in love and war" speech. Wisely, Blokey said nothing.

"When you are fighting for your life against an unscrupulous enemy, you cannot be governed by rules of what's fair; your objective must be to survive and win. The enemy not only does not play by the rules, he recognises no rules at all."

I was not about to give up. As the instructor waxed eloquent on his theme, I slipped from the room. Within 15 minutes, I returned with an ornate, gold-plated letter opener and quietly slipped it to Blokey. I had found a door that was unlocked at 10:00 p.m. and made my way up a back staircase to the study where I spotted the opener. To my surprise, the officer seemed rather pleased and I was awarded second place. Unknown to any of us, the instructors had posted guards at the house. Somehow, Hugo and I had managed to get in and out without alerting them. We celebrated Hugo's *élan* and my little victory that night.

As for the guards, Blokey said, "Simple enough, really. They were only told to be on the alert from starting time, 9:00 o'clock, and then "went for a Burton" when they were told about Hugo's caper. You both outfoxed the beggars! I live by my wits, lad, and always, always plan for the unexpected. You must too, if you're going to survive. Think first and always plan for the worst. Chances are it won't happen, but something just as bad likely will. At least you have a chance if you have your head about you. Plan your escape route. Never, ever panic! Might as well then put your revolver in your mouth and say your last 'Our Father...'"

Blokey added that he admired my spirit of adventure and abilities and that we might have a future together after his 'situation' was resolved.

My adventure in housebreaking gave me an idea. I enlisted a friendly Norwegian and together, at night, we broke into several of the Beaulieu houses to steal odd bits of equipment or rummaged through the personal effects of students to find a trophy. As we got braver, we would leave our secret 'calling card'. We always left the purloined items in a conspicuous place in the morning to be reclaimed by the owners. We were never caught. Despite the warning signs posted, security was poor, to non-existent. It was obvious, Blokey said, that SOE had given little thought to actually guarding the premises from students, believing that the honour system and the ominous warning signs were a sufficient deterrent. They underestimated our entrepreneurial nature; we were highly trained young buccaneers who were inclined to try out our illegitimate skills for fun. Eventually, security was tightened up, but by then, *Norway* and I had tired of the game.

I admired our small arms instructor tremendously. He was a crack shot with any pistol or revolver and taught us his technique for shooting from the hip that was easy and fast. He was light years ahead of his time. He had set up a pistol range with straw figures of enemy soldiers and civilians that actually moved just like the ducks in a carnival shooting gallery. At first, it was quite discouraging when he pointed out my misses and hits, particularly those shots that had taken down an innocent 'straw' civilian, but with practice under his expert eye, I improved. He challenged us to contests, but I never could out-shoot him. He used straw targets to demonstrate the effects of various pistols; his least favourite was the American service Colt 45, which, though delivering tremendous firepower, was too bulky and heavy to be concealed for our use in the field. I was impressed with the massive damage it inflicted on the targets, but agreed with him that the German Walther P38 was lighter and packed a punch which was more than adequate for fieldwork.

As at all other SOE schools, we continued a rigorous paramilitary training program with daily eight km runs and hours of unarmed combat. The lecture and demonstration sessions were intensely interesting, and densely packed with information. If Camp X was the Bachelor's degree, Beaulieu was the post-Doctoral level of espionage training. I was expected to keep my W/T speed at 25 words per minute, which was tested weekly through my operator at Bletchley. We delved further than I thought possible into codes, secret inks, and one time code systems, under our instructor, Paul Dehn[6], who knew the field thoroughly and went over coding procedures repeatedly. "It's your lifeline", was his mantra. It was pointed out how vulnerable we were in the field with the portable 'suitcase' W/T radio, which was heavy, difficult to conceal and easy to locate with electronic radio location equipment. The Germans had become expert in this technology, having had a head-start in the Reich, Austria and the occupied countries in the detection of clandestine civilian sets tuned in to BBC Radio International. We were cautioned to be on the lookout for any persons in the streets or cafes who seemed to be checking the time excessively. German counter-intelligence services had developed a sensitive, portable detection coil that was worn as a small vest under the clothing, with a radio signal strength meter cleverly disguised as a wristwatch.

"The only protection available is to use the W/T sparingly: set up, get in and out fast, then pray the SD berks were taking a pee break, while your carrier wave was switched on."

We had advanced instruction on housebreaking. Blokey's sessions were supplemented by Captain Green, nicknamed "Killer" and J. Ramensky, a Pole, who was an expert safecracker and delighted us with a demonstration of how to use Semtech, mixed in a paste with mud, to blow a small hole in a lock, and gain entry to a building. We learned about dead letter drops, couriers and how to choose them, as well as the dodgy economics of payment for services in the field.

"Count on the fact that they'd as soon rob and gut you, just for fun. Pay 'em too much and they'll assume you're as rich as Midas. They'll put that about when they're pissed and bingo; you're the target for every local villain to slip a blade between your ribs. Pay too little and they'll rat you out, just to be bloody-minded. Either way, my friends, you lose. Get it right the first time, or kill him, or her. Don't hesitate. You won't have a second go. He'll do it to you without blinking or a 'by your leave.'"

For diversion, the kindly Beaulieu groundskeeper taught us how to snare a rabbit, which seemed infinitely more sporting than hunting Bletchley Park's comic squirrels. He was a truly accomplished gamekeeper and master forester who could move about the woods as soundlessly as Robin Hood, without disturbing the smallest twig.

[6] *Mr. Dehn became a successful screen writer after the war, authoring several screenplays in the James Bond film series.*

His encyclopaedic knowledge of edible ferns, fronds, fungi, fruits, roots, and herbs was freely given. For heartier appetites, we ventured out of Beaulieu to learn the ancient arts of chicken thievery and cattle rustling without giving away the game and arousing the farm dog or its owner. Unlike Camp X, this SOE School apparently had no scruples about adversely affecting the local farmers' finances or depleting the town's rations. Perhaps they were repaid in some way. I hope so.

An American professor on loan from OSS delivered our political education lectures. He occasionally wore the uniform of a Major and it was rumoured that he was from Columbia University. He spoke knowledgeably about the political situation in many of the occupied countries, including Hungary, and provided valuable insights into the treatment that we could expect if captured, which later served me well. He recited some excerpts from the SOE 'Bible's' liturgy on disguise:

"Long hair is much easier to change than short hair; it can be cut, and dyed. Your clothes can be rearranged to alter your appearance. A limp (laughter), a limp can be produced with a small stone in the shoe. Never draw attention to yourself by glancing behind. It would make His Lordship the Archbishop of Canterbury look suspicious. Avoid talking with strangers while drinking, and don't ever, ever get drunk. Finally, if you're stupid enough to date a girl in an occupied country, you're damn well on your own."

My state of mind was analysed and re-analysed with batteries of tests administered by a platoon of psychologists and psychiatrists. At first, they were novel and stimulating, but I soon became annoyed by the repetitive questions about my mother, my history of bed-wetting, and my interpretation of inkblots that invariably looked like ghastly spiders, or simultaneously, witches and Edwardian *belles* in silhouette, wearing gigantic hats. I found that if I made up something slightly bizarre, it seemed to satisfy the examiners' needs more than a garden-variety response. Perhaps they were as bored as I was. I wondered if I had been subjected to so many sessions because my responses were sufficiently off-the-wall, without being psychotic, as to constitute a clinically useful case study. It would soon be appreciated as a useful rehearsal for the many lengthy future interrogations, hostile and 'friendly'. I hope that I contributed a helpful kernel or two towards some higher purpose [7]

I was once subjected to a late

[7] *In October, 1999, a hitherto classified SOE report,* Cyphers, Signals and Sex, *was released which reveals that intensive Freudian psychoanalysis was used to screen agents who may have harboured neurotic, self-destructive personality traits, that could lead to their capture and death. The anonymous researcher targeted unconscious exhibitionism, sado-masochistic tendencies, and awareness of the sexual symbolism of "droppings from the sky, holes in the earth, sudden explosions and many other activities in their daily life." Now I know.*

night interrogation. Two Gestapo officers stood over my bed, shouting commands in German. They half-dragged and frog-marched me, in my underwear, into a very cold, white room. I was brusquely ordered to sit down on a metal chair, beneath the stark glare of a blinding light. The room was sparsely equipped, with a wooden desk, three chairs and, on the wall behind the desk, a prominent Nazi swastika flag, and a colour portrait of Adolf Hitler, glaring balefully. I was disoriented but knew that I wasn't dreaming. The cold room and the unyielding metal chair were very real.

I tried to control my shivering by examining my interrogators' uniforms for insignia. At Camp X, there had been a room set up with a display of German uniforms, which we were expected to be able to recognise by branch of service and rank. I noted that the senior officer wore the insignia of an *Obersturmführer-SS* (1st Lieutenant). His junior was a *Scharführer-SS* (Sergeant). This had to be a prank, being played by my gang of jokers. Perhaps my midnight ramblings at the other houses had been traced. This was payback.

'Just like my good friends to steal them from a storage room here, for this little caper! I wish I had thought of it, first,' I reflected, struggling to put this nightmare into some sort of context. I thought of the writer, Franz Kafka. The absurdity of my predicament was the very stuff of his disturbing story about the victimisation of an innocent citizen, on obscure grounds, by an anonymous and capricious bureaucracy.

The *Obersturmführer* began the inquiry in accented English, in a manner that inspired a sense of helplessness, "You were trained at Camp X in Canada. We have incontrovertible proof of that. You really should not talk in your sleep, Agent Gordon" he remarked with a confidential air. He paused, while he examined his manicure. "We know all about your background. You are a spy, a subversive agent and can be executed at any time we decide you are of no further use to us. First, you will answer these simple questions. Tell us about your Communist countrymen."

"I have no idea what you mean. Come on, you jerks; fun is fun, but I've had enough already. I'm freezing my butt off!" My teeth were chattering. For a moment, I thought I would be slapped for my insolence, as the *Scharführer* rose from his chair and started toward me, his gloved right fist upraised. The Obersturmführer hissed a command and the sergeant retreated, visibly annoyed, to his chair.

The Lieutenant now looked at me with absolute disdain and smiled. "Heroes die just as miserably as cowards, here. You will gain nothing from cheap theatrics and dumb shows. Why would you, an anti-Bolshevik, want to protect these scum, the sworn enemies of your so-called democracy?"

He had spit out the last three words with venom. These guys were good. Very good. If this wasn't the real thing, it was a reasonable replica. *'Pay attention, Joe! Whatever's going on here, you'd better do your damnedest not to look like a fool! Concentrate*!" He repeated his question, and I responded,

The Sergeant snarled, "*Schweinhund*!" and saliva flew from the corners of his mouth.

My limbs were trembling and I was becoming angry. '*Careful, Joe. If you lose your temper...*'

The *Oberstürmführer* intervened, in a school masterly manner, as if correcting a faulty geometric proof. "Stupidity is a deadly sin here and will get you no further than a bullet in the back of your head. Consider your answer carefully, please, in that light." The next line he uttered was chillingly effective. "Agent Gordon, where did you last see your Bolshevik comrade, Andrew Durovecz aka Daniels?"

Perhaps it was the shock of hearing Andrew's name. Sweat was now trickling in cold streams from every pore of my body, onto the chair. I tried not to squirm, in discomfort. "Joseph Gordon, First Lieutenant..." I answered, like an automaton. The sparring, shouting and threats continued for another forty-five minutes.

Then, as though 'through a glass darkly,' I suddenly recognised my tormentors. The spell had been broken. The *Oberstürmführer* was a senior officer, the *Scharführer* a small arms instructor, neither of whom were associated with my house. Despite this 'shock of recognition', it was a surreal, utterly convincing, and chilling *tour de force*. As though they realised that I had caught on to the game, I was tossed a blanket and escorted wordlessly back to my cot. Although physical force had been only implied, the imminent threat of violence had been palpable. I was unable to sleep for the next three nights. Next morning, I saw the two investigators on my way to breakfast. The *Sharführer* briefly inclined his head in my direction, and continued walking, while his co-inquisitor ignored me. No mention of the incident was ever made. I knew better than to raise or discuss it with anyone; for SOE, it was a routine necessity, and as it turned out, quite civilised and tame in contrast with my treatment in Hungary.

Lectures by agent-officers recently returned from the field were always eagerly anticipated and informative. Their insights and recommendations, which were based upon the most current information, were always received with great interest. They invariably drilled into us that we were on a mission to defeat the enemy, regardless of the politics of the country we had infiltrated. Vigilance was to be our topmost concern; to detect and avoid informers, double agents, and criminals on the make, as well as the local militia and *polizei*. The 'pigeons' might be motivated by idealism, but it was more likely to be the assurance of reward money from the authorities, old–fashioned human greed. In all cases, they were to be assiduously avoided, or killed. Much of the guest lecturers' information echoed the NYU Professor's stock-in-trade, but was eminently worthy of repetition.

As I studied Blokey's copy of the SOE Training Syllabus, I knew nothing of Kim Philby, the British-born, Cambridge-educated, Soviet double agent. A brilliant, charming deceiver, Harold 'Kim' Philby, successfully outwitted and subverted Britain's Secret Intelligence Services: MI-5, MI-6 and MI-9, until he defected to Moscow, in 1956, without a scintilla of remorse. Philby boasted that he been promoted to the rank of KGB general, although the Soviet government vehemently denied that he had been accorded any official status. Nevertheless, Philby lived in relative comfort, thanks to a generous government pension, and boldly recounted his astonishing career in his memoirs, *My Silent War*.

Philby had managed to be recruited into the fledgling SOE in 1940 and served briefly an instructor at Beaulieu; he was a contributing author of the SOE training manual, or 'Bible.' Philby, who was certainly no slouch in the area of intelligence, highly regarded Major Bill Brooker, the first Chief Instructor at Beaulieu, and, subsequently at Camp X, where Major Brooker would become the second Commandant. In return, Major Brooker thought Kim Philby to be an exceptional mind. As a secret agent, Philby was, unfortunately, perhaps the master of all. He positioned himself inside SIS to vet pro-Communist recruits before selection for training by SOE. He cleverly 'stacked the deck', by inserting pro-Soviet agents wherever possible into Hungary, Yugoslavia, Czechoslovakia, Poland and elsewhere. As I have stated earlier, I was an exception. His schemes provided a solid launching pad for Joseph Stalin's eventual Soviet acquisition of those countries bordering Russia at the end of the Second World War. Russia swallowed up my native Hungary at the 1945 Yalta Conference in spite of Churchill's opposition to Joseph Stalin's megalomaniac plans, and a puppet Communist dictator was installed.

Philby and his Cambridge co-conspirators Guy Burgess, (Sir) Anthony Blount and Donald McLean, were collectively responsible for many of the most devastating breaches of security in the bleak history of the Cold War. As a direct result of their treachery, scores of British, American and other Allied and NATO agents were exposed in the Iron Curtain countries, tortured, and executed. The infamous 'Cambridge Circle' was able to operate above suspicion, even as evidence was mounting against Burgess and McLean in 1951. In the rarefied 'old boy' network, it was unthinkable that a member could betray England. SOE, MI-5, and MI-6 had a rule that members had to be born as subjects of the Crown. Many potentially useful recruits did not fit into this category, but accommodations were made when it was politically expedient.

As we approached the final phase of our training, we were instructed in the fine art of avoiding a 'tail'. For practice, we were dropped off either in Bournemouth or Northampton with instructions to 'spot and ditch' any would-be 'tails'. I was strolling in Northampton when I noticed that a man and woman were following me. To evade them, I slipped into a large clothing store and took cover behind a large stack of women's underwear. I could see them both perfectly from my vantage point. The man was covering the front entrance, absorbed in a newspaper, and the woman was watching the rear exit, while applying makeup, with the aid of a mirrored compact. They didn't seem anxious to leave, although I was sure they hadn't seen me. After an hour of 'frozen tag', I was desperately in need of the washroom, which was close to the rear of the store and beyond reach. Another half-hour passed. They were still there. I made a mental calculation of the cost if I were to lose control and 'water damage' the ladies' unmentionables. '*More than a month's salary*,' seemed a reasonable estimate. '*To hell with it! This is literally, 'do or die!*' I sneaked one last look at my silent tormentors. Miraculously, they had vanished! I just made it in time to the WC and was late for dinner. The instructor had warned us that these trials would be carried out at any time, without forewarning. I resolved in the future to pay close attention to my body's warnings.

I was delighted to re-discover my American friend Rolly, at Beaulieu. Since graduating from Bletchley, he had been appointed a full Lieutenant in the US Army, as were his chums. All had joined OSS before recruitment into SOE. The US Army had honoured its verbal commitment that the attainment of Lieutenant's rank was subject to their passing the prescribed OSS and SOE courses. The Americans were a multilingual group: Juri and Jan spoke fluent Czech, and Rolly and Ron were bilingual in English and French. They all knew how to separate work from relaxation.

Rolly and I soon resumed our old habits by going on the razzle in Bournemouth whenever we could get an evening or weekend pass. We worked out a system to 'cover' our tracks so that the ever-present tails would have no clues as to our whereabouts, and even enlisted our female companions as players in the game. They acted as decoys and did a bang up job of confusing the tails. We went into the Ladies' section of the same department store where I had had my first brush with SOE followers and switched coats with the girls.

I explained that we had a bet with two or three people that they couldn't catch Rolly or me on the weekend before we returned to Beaulieu. The girls thought it was great fun and played along enthusiastically.

On our most unforgettable weekend excursions in Bournemouth, we brought along Blokey, who, in his customary fashion simply 'doctored' his bed and slipped the lock of his bedroom door. Blokey's skills of deception, which he shared freely with me, would serve to be useful later in Hungary. He, Rolly, and I had a lovely old time. Blokey knew Bournemouth well and made sure that we didn't miss any of the highlights. He introduced some charming seaside girls, with whom we enjoyed the sights, sun, and sea. On another occasion, Blokey showed us some locations in 'the ways less travelled' where we spent a memorable evening with some of the loveliest ladies of Bournemouth. Whether or not we were tailed was academic by this time.

I had been at Beaulieu for three weeks when I received my final examination. My abilities as a spy were to be put to the test. This was a challenge that I relished! I signed out and tested my suitcase radio (Mark II), which weighed about fourteen and a half pounds , as well as the necessary secret codes on silk, one time only pads, and security identification numbers, then was off to Northampton, feeling like a dyed-in-the-wool secret agent.

Before leaving Beaulieu, my briefing officer had given me an address in Northhampton. I found it almost immediately; it was a house! First test passed! I rang the doorbell. A servant invited me inside. After a brief chat, another servant appeared and took my precious suitcase radio. I followed him upstairs as closely as possible and shut the bedroom door when he left. Suspiciously, I opened the lid of the leather case to inspect my radio set thoroughly for signs of sabotage. It appeared intact, but I would test it later. My host was a lawyer with whom I enjoyed a sumptuous breakfast. There was no shortage of excellent food or interesting conversation. I learned that he was a widower, but little else of a personal nature. He did not seem to be the least bit curious about me. After a leisurely breakfast, he departed for his office, leaving me free for the morning. A servant prepared lunch, which I ate by myself in the dining nook. Dinner was served promptly at 7:00 p.m., preceded by a drink with my host at 6:30. We then enjoyed a superb meal of soup, then a fish course, followed by the *entrée* course of roast beef accompanied by a superb French Burgundy. Dessert was served with tea and coffee, complete with sugar and thick, country cream. So much for the constraints of rationing! My host and I retired to his smoking room for an after dinner brandy and more polite conversation.

I was expected to set up my W/T radio and send messages daily to

Bletchley Headquarters with proper identification, to which they would reply with an acknowledgement and new orders. The radio was operating perfectly. I received instructions to wander around the town into areas that were out of bounds, 'looking for trouble'. I tried the next day but couldn't arouse anyone's suspicion.

After a few more days of fruitless escapades, I was directed to go to a town near Leicester to try again. Here, I was treated to lodgings in a first-class home belonging to a charming retired couple whose hospitality included morning tea and lovely meals. My operator at HQ encouraged me to tour around town, staying out of the local pubs and avoiding the girls, as we had been strongly advised at Beaulieu. Eventually, my efforts to be 'seen' paid off and I was brought in for questioning to the local police station. I tried valiantly but couldn't talk myself out of this fix; my papers, which I hadn't bothered to look at before setting out from Beaulieu, were obviously, undoubtedly, authentically German.

'*Thank you very much, Beaulieu*!'

I had visions of being thrown into solitary confinement to await trial in a Magistrate's Court, then sentenced to life imprisonment doing hard time in the dreaded Wormwood Scrubs. I tried to explain that it was all a misunderstanding, that I had picked up these papers accidentally. The coppers were having none of it. I couldn't reveal my mission or identity. The small interrogation room was becoming unbearably hot. I had one last chance. As I wasn't in manacles, I asked permission to make a telephone call. The sergeant and constables stared in silence. After a hushed discussion, the sergeant motioned me over to use his desk. I fumbled in my wallet as they all watched me closely, until I found the emergency number. Was this a serious enough problem to warrant its use? I thought so. The voice on the line asked for my identification number, which I supplied. After a few millennia of silence, she came back on, and asked to speak with the sergeant. Of course. It was a 'set up', staged by Beaulieu. The police must have had a good chuckle at my plight, but were considerate enough not to show it; although after the telephone call, had I detected an amused twinkle in their eyes? The policemen played their parts flawlessly and the performance concluded with a stern lecture by the Sergeant on wartime security measures and my civilian responsibilities. He omitted the nudge and wink. I thanked them all and retreated hastily.

I returned to Beaulieu and was sitting on the edge of my cot, reflecting on my ignominious brush with the law, when an orderly knocked and announced that I was summoned to a meeting. As I straightened my dishevelled uniform, I thought, '*This is the end. I will be discharged from*

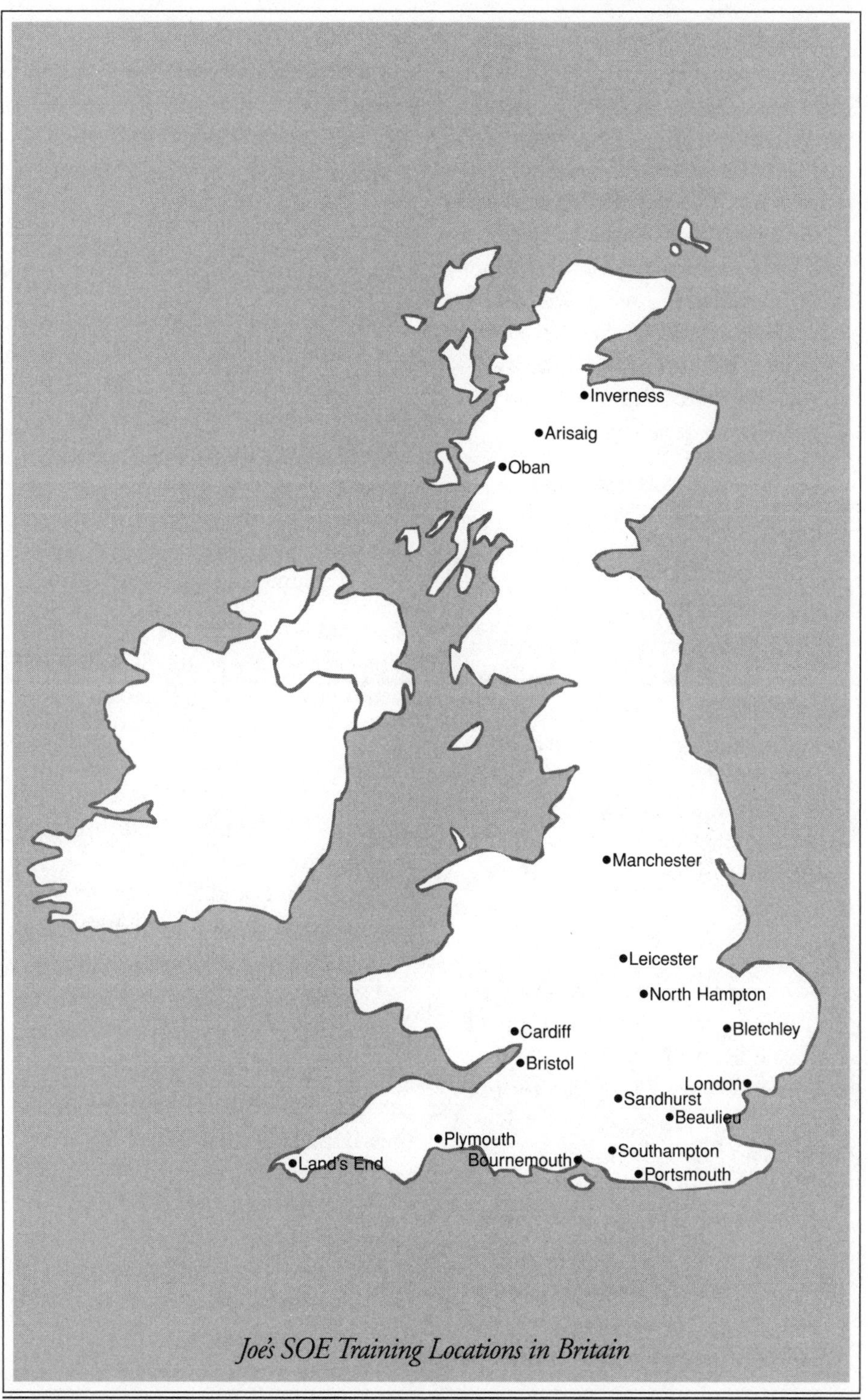

Joe's SOE Training Locations in Britain

SOE and serve as batman to a drink-sodden madman in Burma. Then, I will work my way back to Canada as second assistant to an assistant cook on the Queen Elizabeth. I will clean stalls at the bloody Horse Palace or hawk day-old flowers to the Bay Street elite. Dad and Helen will disown me. I will join the French Foreign Legion, and serve out my days in the sub-Sahara, battling sand flies and fierce Tuareg tribesmen (whoever they were!) until slipping into absinthe-induced dementia.'

The officer was reserved and humane, I thought, as he bid me sit down, shuffled his papers and then recounted, in excruciating detail, my activities in each town. I was astounded to find out that my SOE masters knew absolutely everything, all of the what, when, who and where, including every topic of conversation with my hosts. I listened to each word, full of dread, preparing for the inevitable, "Unfortunately, Gordon, SOE has no option but to arrange for your immediate transfer to the Army Service Corps…."

To my astonished ears, instead of a career stopper, I was hearing myself commended for maintaining my cover name, Joseph Gordon, for not committing any egregious breaches of security, and for adhering strictly to authorised radio procedures. The incident at the police station wasn't mentioned! Was that episode a hoax or a coincidence? Although I was originally a bit miffed about having to forego the usual pubbing and clubbing, I was now thankful that for once, I hadn't strayed. Loose lips can not only sink ships, but could have dashed my aspirations in disgrace: Beaulieu was a 'finishing' school in more than one way!

I completed the entire syllabus of required courses plus a few extras, and graduated from Beaulieu. It was very intensive but rewarding; everything I had expected, and more. At my last meeting with senior staff, they commended my dedication to SOE. I thanked them and I can recall responding, "I'm sure the courses I attended will help bring me back to see you again."

I did go back to Beaulieu, many years later. As I read the SOE commemorative plaque in Beaulieu Abbey Cloisters, dedicated in 1969, I reflected on my lost, missing and fallen friends, my many cherished comrades in arms. Then, I gave silent thanks to my Special Operations Commandants and STS instructors as well as the scores of marvellous people through whose friendship, support, and sacrifices I had been permitted to survive and return.

If I could not recall my fallen comrades to life, nor find them safe in their homelands, I vowed that I would commemorate and honour them, by daring to recreate some reflection, however inadequate, of our glorious days and dark nights, when we were princes, all.

Chapter 3
Across the Wide Drava...

Freshly ordained as a Second Lieutenant, and with a jeep and driver to confirm it, I was on my way to the south of England for a flight to Gibraltar. The Women's Army Corps driver, Master Sergeant Charlotte T., drove southward through Bristol and on to Cardiff, Wales, where we enjoyed tea on a terrace amidst the spectacular scenery. We then continued our leisurely journey along the meandering southern English coastline, through Plymouth, and towards Land's End where I was scheduled to catch the next flight out. I was billeted comfortably in the Officers' Quarters at the nearby army base. With the luxury of the driver and jeep at my disposal and freedom to tour wherever I pleased, I indulged in sightseeing, enjoying the museums, bistros, and picturesque charms of this historic town.

At 8:00 a.m. sharp on the appointed day, my driver, Charlotte, delivered me to the Land's End airfield. She went into the hangar to make inquiries and, when she returned, asserted, "That's the one, the Halifax, over there, Lieutenant." She pointed to a four-engine bomber, with an RAF Transport Command truck pulled up snug to its belly. "Doesn't look very cushy, does it, Sir?"

I wasn't particularly concerned about how I would get overseas, merely that I get there. I thanked her for her services and pleasant company and walked over to board the plane. A perspiring corporal and a private were wrestling bulky containers from the truck into the bomb bay. They stopped, saluted and each mopped his face with handkerchiefs that had apparently been used to wipe dry the aircraft's oil dipsticks. The corporal greeted me, "Morning, Lieutenant! Off to 'Gib' are you then? Might have about as much chance of makin' it non-stop as my Aunt Fanny gettin' to the Punjab on roller skates!"

"Excuse me, Corporal. Could you say that again please?"

He may have thought that my question was the mark of a freshly commissioned officer pulling rank, but I had simply not fathomed his accent.

"Well, Sir," he began, squinting into the sun. I had the feeling that I was about to hear the unofficial, plain truth, like it or not. His voice had lowered as though he was about to breach the Official Secrets Act "You see, Sir, my mate here, Private Willy Johnson, and I figure she's way over her load specs. If it were just bombs in this blighter's belly rather than all of this equipment and such, plus you lot, well.... Sorry, Sir! Trans Comm is stretched to the limit. We've lost three to Jerry this month alone. Mail must get through! Good flight, Sir."

Private Willy added, "Cheery bye then, Sir!"

'*Cheery indeed!*' Although I had to smile at their 'cheeky' familiarity, the Corporal's outlook did not inspire much confidence. I settled in as best I could while we readied for take-off from Land's End. My fellow travellers included a general, two captains, some others of indeterminate rank and a vast assortment of loose equipment, as well as six jumbo-sized cargo containers. A problem developed as we taxied slowly to await the signal flare; when it was fired, the engines were notched up to take-off speed. I braced myself. Then they packed it in...dead silence. We were obviously heavier than a sock full of lead shot. After a brief pause, the pilot restarted and gunned the motors. We began to rumble down the airstrip, under full throttle. Again, no go! The engines were cut back to idle, as though taking a final, deep breath. On the third try, we lumbered down the runway like a wounded duck, barely managing to get airborne.

The four Rolls Royce engines roared at maximum revs, slightly out of synchronisation, causing the aircraft to vibrate menacingly as if it were about to disintegrate. Screwing up my courage, I looked out the thick 'Perspex' window, which was buzzing and rattling in sympathy with the deafening cacophony. An alarming number of the flathead rivets on my starboard wing were actually pulsating like pistons under the stress. Not wanting to witness them popping out of the sheet metal and into the ocean only a few metres below, I sat back down on a packing crate as the Halifax continued to climb, groaning like a beast in pain. It seemed that an eternity passed before the pilot eased back on the throttle and levelled off the Halifax at cruising altitude. I swallowed to clear my ears; we were Gibraltar bound, *almost*, RAF Transport Command style!

Accommodation for passengers had not been considered, so we each claimed our personal living space, leaning against or bracing ourselves between those containers that seemed to be more or less securely anchored with ropes or straps. Some of the passengers were sprawled out, using machine parts and other military paraphernalia as makeshift pillows, dozing and perhaps dreaming of a safe touchdown. I would be happy with something resembling that, I thought, and I fervently hoped that our Halifax might avoid becoming 'lunch' for a grazing *Luftwaffe* hot shot.

The flight to Gibraltar couldn't have been longer, more boring (once we were airborne), or more uncomfortable, and I longed for the security of a parachute pack on my shoulders. I eventually drifted off but was awakened when the plane made an abrupt wing over to starboard and began to descend at a suprisingly rapid rate as though we were in a free fall. The cargo boxes groaned as they strained against their tethers. Looking through the Perspex side window, I could see individual white foam crests topping the waves on the surface of the blue Mediterranean, waiting to take us. I had been told at Land's End that the Gibraltar run-in could be a nail biter, but this was ridiculous. Our landing speed, I humbly suggested, was much too high and we were much too low. "Son of a bitch! We're going in the drink!"

"He's going to ditch in the bloody bay!"

"Holy Mother! Is he insane"?

We all huddled at the small window, staring in fascinated disbelief, as the bomber descended lower and lower, until it was barely skimming the surface of the water, seemingly a mere two metres above the waves. The Perspex porthole was dripping with saltspray. This was the end. There was no evidence of any effort to reduce our speed. We would either smash into the water or run into the monumental grey rock face looming ahead ever more closely. Suddenly, the plucky Halifax shuddered as the hydraulic undercarriage lowered; our wheels clawed at and then grasped the edge of the tarmac. The rock wall was fast approaching. I closed my eyes. The pilot applied the brakes; we swerved, skewing sideways, and came to a dead stop precisely in front of the small terminal building. He cut the engines. We each silently thanked the Supreme Being of Aviation as we stumbled down the steps, onto the solid tarmac. The pilot was already standing at the counter, chatting up an appealing WREN when I approached him.

"Hello, Flight Lieutenant. I'm Lieutenant Joseph Gordon. That was quite a take off and a bit of a hair-raising landing!" There was no sign of a navigator or any other crewmembers. Perhaps he flew solo – highly unlikely, but little wonder!

"Thanks awfully. Glad you enjoyed it, old chap. Nothing like a bit of excitement to get the blood pumping, what? Milk run…knew what the old kite was doing every sec. Should have been with me last time in! Bit of a squeaker, really. Cheerio!" He returned to his inter-service pursuits.

'*Milk run? Cheerio to you too*!'

We were taken to the Base as guests of the affable Commandant, and spent the next day exploring the Rock under the guidance of his personal driver. The fabled Rock Apes were swarming everywhere. They scampered over the jeep and attempted to remove its mirrors and control knobs at every spectacular, scenic stop. My precious new Lieutenant's hat was particularly attractive to the alpha male from whom I wrenched it as he was darting away to present it to a favoured concubine. Legend said that should the apes ever desert Gibraltar, Britain would lose possession. Judging by the present population, it seemed that the Rock would be firmly entrenched as a craggy outpost of the Empire for centuries to come!

Security was very tight as we toured the Rock and the Base; after a good dinner and the Commandant's informative travelogue, we went to bed. I dreamt of a Halifax, loaded with crates of wild apes, breaking out, seizing the controls….

The next morning, we took off from Gibraltar *en route* to North Africa: same Halifax, new pilot, complete with a copilot, but with neither cargo containers nor apes. Under the new command, the Halifax performed as though it had just received its certificate of airworthiness. Our approach to Tangiers swept us over the endless white sand beaches and oceanfront. As I stepped from the plane, the wave of heat rising from the asphalt strip was oppressive. '*Was it, 'dogs and mad Englishmen*', or, '*mad dogs and Englishmen*?' ' British Army Sergeant Teddy Williamson, who met us with the customary jeep, had apparently been appointed to explain Algerian traditions and behaviour to us, foreigners that we were, and his colourful prognosis for our survival was, apparently, not good. He delivered a rapid-fire crash course on Algerian culture and climate in rich Cockney as he drove us at breakneck speed around and mainly through a jumble of handcarts, bicycles, and pedestrians, to the hotel where we were to be billeted.

Sergeant Williamson stopped the covered jeep at an intersection and immediately a hand darted across my lap and grabbed a piece of luggage. With a vigorous Anglo-Saxon curse, the Sergeant jerked up the emergency brake lever, leapt out of the vehicle and apprehended a terrified native, a boy of no more than fourteen, whom he proceeded to pummel. This, he explained to us after, was a useless exercise. "The sod will do it over and over…'e's damn lucky, Sirs. I could 'ave turned 'im over to 'is coppers and the judge would 'ave 'is 'and off in a twinkle. It's the law 'ere for fievin', you should know, Sirs!"

Despite our hard-boiled training over the past months, we were shocked by this physical display of colonial superiority and bullying. As I thought afterward of the hapless, young Algerian '*almost* thief', I wondered what dire form of correction the Sergeant might have exacted on the Rock's mischievous primates.

This initial display of viciousness was never repeated in our presence. Teddy, in fact, proved to be a hospitable and informative guide and companion. His knowledge of the city's highlights and lowlife was encyclopaedic. We toured the fancy beach hotels and restaurants, as well as the casbah and seamiest parts of town, but with our two-fisted Sergeant Teddy as bodyguard, never worried for our personal security, even in the most disreputable of dives, which there were in abundance. He took us to his choice of the most exotic of erotically explicit nightclubs. In a society where women customarily wore the *hijab* veil in public and both sexes wore long robes in the eternal, infernal heat, the graphic displays of nudity seemed much more shocking here than in a Western setting. The women, he cautioned us, were best left alone, unless one brought him along as a guard to prevent theft or even worse. We took his advice seriously and restricted our activities to running, sunning, and swimming in the surprisingly cool Mediterranean Sea.

We had been issued notice to be ready for takeoff, "before nightfall." A general, two captains, three lieutenants, other army personnel, and I were on alert for a week, with bags packed and ready, until the Halifax finally took us aloft to Algiers.

Upon arrival, we were taken to Massingham, an SOE advanced training base, just outside the city. The courses were of the 'refresher' type, similar to Beaulieu's, but on a greatly reduced scale. The staff were excellent, and kept us occupied reviewing wireless procedures and practising Morse, memorising Leo Marks' clever code verses on the silk prints that we called 'silk handkerchiefs', reading maps and exercising, which I found extremely hard going under the sweltering African sun. SOE field veterans popped in and out regularly to give talks aimed at preparing us for the treatment we could expect as prisoners of the Third Reich or its minions. Perhaps Torquemada's Spanish Inquisition, but certainly not the Geneva Convention, would have endorsed the methods that they described in meticulously detailed lectures. And so we spent the week at Massingham, waiting for our flight to Naples.

It was March and instantly I fell deeply in love with *la bella Napoli,* like her countless other suitors over the ages. Unlike my alarming introduction to the Rock, which never detracted from its inherent majesty, the harbour of Naples was truly a magnificent panorama from the air. My friends Alec Vass (Vincent), Andrew Durovecz (Daniels), Adam Herter (Herbert), Adam Magyar (Murphy) and Gus Bodo (Bertrand) and I were put up at the Officers' Club at the Base, which boasted *prima cuisina*. As we had no particular duties, we hiked every day to the top of the volcanic mountain, to drink in and marvel at the breathtakingly splendid harbour below. In contrast with this peaceful scene, we could distinctly hear the rumble of artillery from the epic second battle for possession of the ancient monastery of Monte Cassino.

The Neapolitan women were beautiful and congenial. Although some sections of the town were depressingly squalid, it seemed that the natural optimism of the Neapolitan character made even the poorest citizens oblivious to their condition. Perhaps it was because of the music implanted deeply in the Neapolitan soul. The city seemed haunted by the ghost of its most famous son, the greatest *bel canto* tenor of the twentieth century, Enrico Caruso. His name and music permeated the atmosphere. Caruso was born here in poverty in 1873 and was so coolly received in his debut at the Teatro San Carlo in 1901 that he left town, to return home only once, to die of pleurisy in 1921.

Although never tiring of the idyllic splendour of the locale, we volunteered to lend a hand at the Base. The Commandant suggested that we might enjoy working with a small group of Italian Partisans, helping to train them to jump behind German lines in the northern part of the peninsula. "To help sharpen the saw," was his polite excuse for ending our slothfulness, giving us something to do other than wining, dining and romancing *le belle Donne*.

I felt like a newly knighted Beaulieu instructor. One morning, while on a cross-country run with our Partisans, we watched in disbelief as four parachutes drifted down, 1500 metres from where we had stopped to rest. I stood up to watch with my binoculars, mentally rating each on his landing. This was not a training drop and they were not in uniforms from 'our side'. This was much more exciting than the War Office Film Unit's training/propaganda tripe that we once had suffered through. These were the real enemy! A squad of Tommies appeared, running toward them, from a nearby wood. There were bursts of semi-automatic rifle fire. I signalled our group to get up and move quickly. We arrived in time to capture one of the jumpers who had bolted headfirst into a dry ditch.

Within seconds, all four were squatted on the ground, facing inward in a circle, hands locked behind their heads and covered by the rifles of six pleased British infantrymen. Our Partisans were chatting excitedly. Was this a dash of realism that we had arranged for their benefit? Three of the prisoners wore Italian uniforms, the fourth, a field grey German Army Major's. In my halting *Deutsch*, I told him he merited full marks, *zehn zum zehn*, (ten out of ten) on his landing technique. He looked at me, stone cold, expressionless. Either he did not understand my German, he had thoroughly mastered the art of masking his emotions, or he thought me utterly insane.

Then he smiled, slightly, and inclined his blonde head, "*Danke schön, Herr Leutnant.*"

For that moment, I felt a fleeting professional bond between us, "*Bitte, Herr Major.*" So, this was the face of the enemy! The troopers marched them away, at bayonet point.

Our next port of call was the lovely resort town of Bari, almost directly across the peninsula from Naples, on the Adriatic coast of Italy, and SOE's regional HQ and primary staging point for inserting agents into the Balkans and Hungary. We scouted out and commandeered an abandoned farmhouse on the outskirts of town, an estate of about ten acres, with abundant fruit orchards, chickens, and vegetable gardens. There was no pressing need here to steal apples or eggs! We had inherited a world class chef in our group who recruited some local Italians as assistant cooks. The meals they created were *magnifico*, as were the vintages that we liberated from the local winery.

At Bari, we were getting closer to the action that we all craved. Along with my continuing wireless duties, we were all kept busy with paramilitary training exercises for which we were split up into small working groups. We studied aerial photos of the area in Yugoslavia where we were expecting to land *en route* to Hungary. My Mission DEERHURST Commander, Lieutenant-Colonel Boughey, regularly conducted map and intelligence briefings with his second in command, Major Wright, and me. It was usual SOE practice that mission commanders were British Officers; we were all Lieutenants. Eventually, Lieutenant Vincent (Vass) replaced me, because of a misunderstanding with Colonel Boughey. Another group, Mission WINDPROOF, was made up of Major Sehmer, Lieutenant Daniels, and Lieutenant Zenopian. Their British radio operator was Corporal Davies.

Our off-duty activities usually involved consorting with the attractive and charmingly shy young Bari women whom, because of the wartime shortage of eligible homebred males, chose us as their main source of romantic diversion. We responded enthusiastically. We had the run of Bari and surrounding countryside most afternoons, including the oceanfront for swimming, sun bathing or kibitzing with the women, whose silvery laughter made us feel like schoolboys. Their cheerfulness and love of *la dolce vita* were a welcome antidote to the excitement as well as to the dark, secret thoughts that we all shared about the grim possibilities that lay ahead.

The mornings were spent in planning sessions with Colonel Boughey. He wanted to go behind enemy lines and had selected our group for this purpose. Although I was originally a member of DEERHURST, [1] after a minor misunderstanding, Colonel Boughey changed the group's membership. The Colonel planned to go in as a Sergeant in the Black Watch

Regiment for cover, in case of capture, which did in fact, happen. Nominally in charge was Major Wright of the British Army. Lieutenant Alec Vass (Vincent) was designated as Hungarian interpreter and liaison with the Partisans.

I was transferred to Mission DIBBLER. Captain John Coates was our Commander. I chose Lieutenant Mike Turk (Thomas) as our Hungarian liaison and interpreter. I, Lieutenant Gordon, W/T wireless operator, was put in charge of the radio equipment as well as our secret codes and money, some of which I had carefully sewn into the lining of my battledress jacket. Gus Bodo (Bertrand) was already in Hungary, as our advance liaison officer.

The explanation for my transfer from DEERHURST to DIBBLER is somewhat complicated, but may be of interest. Gus Bodo (Bertrand) had led off for DIBBLER by parachuting into Yugoslavia where Marshal Broz Tito's Communist Partisans infiltrated him into Hungary by boat across the River Drava. Inside Hungary, he was met by a Yugoslav Partisan courier sent directly by Marshal Tito after lengthy W/T negotiations between Bletchley and Tito's Yugoslav Partisan government.[2], with the assistance of SOE Captain Rolly Young's radio operator at Papuk, 6th Corps base. All arrangements were made through Tito, who exercised personal control over his Partisans. All foreign agents required Tito's explicit permission to enter his country or to liaise with his Partisans, both within and outside of Yugoslavia's borders. Tito, a staunch

Top row; L-R Magyar, Coates, Turk, Durovecz-Bottom row; L-R Herter, Sehmer, Vass, Gelleny on a Bari rooftop

Communist, and a fierce nationalist, played 'fast and loose with Stalin' and often broke ranks to disagree with him on issues affecting Yugoslav self-determination. In this instance, Tito may have been protecting his country from a possible build-up of Allied forces whose agents could possibly be the vanguard of a counter-offensive against Hitler, launched through Yugoslavia. This he did not want and sided with the Moscow party line of exercising total authority within his country and jealously guarding access to his military. Tito had also set up an extensive Partisan courier service and network of listening posts inside Hungary, to monitor developments in a country that he distrusted and whose people he personally disliked.

Gus (Bertrand) and his guide made their way towards the safe house in the industrial city of Pécs. It was a trap; the Hungarian Second Bureau had infiltrated Tito's courier service, without the knowledge of Gus' Partisan guide. Gus was captured, badly beaten and ultimately forced by his Hungarian captors to send a W/T message through SOE HQ in Bari, as SOE's W/T procedures expressly forbade direct agent-to-agent radio communications.

It was the curious circumstances surrounding Gus' message that led to the misunderstanding with Colonel Boughey, and my subsequent transfer out of his unit. The controversy centred on the interpretation of Gus' transmission. Gus and Mike (Thomas) had secretly worked out a highly-illegal arrangement in which Gus was to initiate his wires (messages) with one word in Hungarian, *egen*, (yes) to indicate "I'm OK". Gus' wire had omitted that, according to Mike. This non-approved practice, *added groups*, was prohibited in the W/T manual, but is a slick trick that is used in spy fiction and films.

I became embroiled when Mike asked me to inform Colonel Boughey that Gus' signal might indicate that he was in trouble. The Colonel, of course, wanted to know why we thought so. Mike could not say that he had made a special arrangement with Gus that was forbidden by iron-clad rules of procedure. Mike simply reported that Gus' wire did not give as much detail as he had promised. Colonel Boughey was not satisfied and was therefore reluctant to show us Bari's transcript of the wire. Eventually, however, he did. To me then, as now, it was unclear whether Gus had used the prohibited added groups. However, I 'blew it' when I came to Mike's defence. The Colonel

[1] *The British Foreign and Commonwealth Office in July 1999 made the sixth release comprising 1013 previously classified SOE records at http://www.feo.gov.uk/news/newstext.asp. The public can browse documents regarding specific SOE Missions: their personnel, objectives and outcomes. The missions are grouped by region(s) or country (ies) of insertion and activity.*

[2] *Tommy Drew-Brook, Intrepid's top Canadian BSC representative and talent recruiter extraordinaire, had been selected to parachute into Yugoslavia to serve as Tito's personal radio operator. He didn't get there. See Inside-Camp X, Lynn-Philip Hodgson, Blake Books, 1999.*

removed me immediately from his roster and substituted Lieutenant Alec Vass (Vincent) with Sergeant Manley, as his W/T operator. This decision added one extra man to the mission's complement. I had taken the blame for Mike, was likely insubordinate, and could have been court-martialled, but I joined a first-rate team, Mission DIBBLER. I should add that neither Gus nor Mike had been trained as W/T operators at Bletchley, although every SOE agent received basic instruction in W/T, Morse code, and ciphers. Unfortunately, Lieutenant Vincent was later killed during an Allied bombing raid, near Stuttgart; I was saddened when I heard of it, particularly in that Vincent had replaced me on that mission.

Colonel Boughey and I patched up our disagreement shortly after my transfer. He acknowledged that I was not a party to the Gus/Bertrand transmission problem and informed me that he had checked with HQ to confirm that my rank was now that of a full Lieutenant in the British Army, dated effective March 18, 1944.

Another of the SOE Hungarian Canadians to go into Hungary by way of Yugoslavia was Steve Markos who was recruited from the Canadian Army in England and trained in Britain. We received word that he had linked up with the Hungarian resistance; his whereabouts and whether or not he survived are not in any of the SOE records that I have examined.

Mission WINDPROOF was to go into Czechoslovakia with Major Sehmer as the British officer in command. Lieutenant Andy Durovecz (Daniels) was interpreter and liaison along with Lieutenant Zenopian and British Army Corporal Bill Davies as W/T operator. In September 1943, WINDPROOF left from Brindisi, Italy and was dropped into Slovakia near Banska Bistrica.[3] I saw them off, giving Andy a bottle of Scotch for good luck. Unfortunately, Major Sehmer was captured and shot by the Germans.

DIBBLER'S mission essentially was to contact and follow up on Gus' (Bertrand) liaison work with the resistance forces which, it was assumed, he had begun in Yugoslavia and was actively nurturing at present in Hungary. Specifically, our orders were to fly or parachute into the mountainous Papuk area of north-east Yugoslavia where there was an advance SOE base, 6th Corps, under the command of Captain R. 'Rolly' Young. As the SOE liaison officer on the ground, Captain Young co-ordinated all contacts between local Partisan guerrilla forces and SOE personnel, as well as American OSS agents in the Papuk area. Captain Young later remarked to me that he "…sometimes felt like a policeman directing traffic in Piccadilly Circus on Christmas Eve."

In a very limited sense this was true, but he was also much more. With Marshal Tito's permission,

Captain Young was charged with full responsibility for SOE operations at 6th Corps' Papuk base. Captain Young had a Bletchley-trained British wireless operator, Sergeant Scott, through whom he kept in contact with the hub in Bari, as well as with the American HQ. The volume of signals routed through Bari and Torre A Mare, Italy, by this excellent W/T operator was mind boggling. All of our DIBBLER traffic was, of course, routed through Captain Young.

Mike Turk (Thomas) and I received our official orders signed by Major Morton. The Directive, dated 15 August 1944, is headed **Top Secret, HQ Force 399, CMF**, and addressed to me, Lieutenant Gordon.

Directive to Lt. J. Gordon

1. Along with Lt. M. Thomas, you will form the advance party of mission DIBBLER. You will be in command of the party.

2. You will be dropped or landed as soon as possible to a reception committee in Yugoslavia, Papuk area, and will report at once to Capt. R. S. Young under whose orders you will be while in Yugoslav territory.

3. Object to contact Lt. Bertram and with him establish a reception ground in the area north of Pécs, into which Capt. Coates will drop as soon as he hears from you. You should confine yourselves solely to this object until Capt. Coates arrives.

4. Capt. Young to provide details as to your journey, contacts, any further necessary documents, etc.

5. Alternative if can't contact Lt. Bertram then endeavour nevertheless to carry out your object as in para. 3 (enter Hungary and set up reception for Capt. Coates).

6. Will take 200 gold napoleons and 25,000 *pengös* used for upkeep of mission, transport and the furtherance of our work by any means which appear promising. A rough account of expenditure expected at a later date.

7. W/T link will be with TORRE A MARE/ BARI. You will reduce your traffic to the barest minimum and limit yourself to your signals until dropping area established for Capt. Coates.

8. If you are in danger of capture and **if your escape would be facilitated by leaving Lt. Thomas behind to draw off the enemy you will give him orders to this effect**, as it is vital, in such circumstances, that you should be in a position to signal the home station. (Emphasis in bold as per original).

Each article in the orders was minutely examined by John, Mike, and me, as was the inventory of supplies that Mike and I would take into Yugoslavia and Hungary via the

[3] *Andrew Durovecz's personal account of* WINDPROOF *is told in* My Secret Mission, *Lugus Publications, 1996.*

Drava River. We were instructed to cross the Drava River by boat, or swim it, if necessary. "We'll walk across it if we have to," we boasted, not knowing how great the challenges lying ahead would prove.

All of these arrangements were relayed to Bari and confirmed by wireless through Captain Young's W/T operator, Scott. Mike and I were ready to go into Yugo at a moment's notice and eagerly awaited the call.

We received the orders informing us that *Lt. Thomas and Lt. Gordon would parachute into Papuk on August 10, 1944.* Mike and I forced ourselves to pay attention at the final briefing. We boarded an RAF Bristol Blenheim bomber at Brindisi Airport, Italy on an overcast evening. The plane was loaded to the hilt with the equipment which Mike and I would need, including my B MK III wireless set, as well as canisters of supplies for Captain Young. The Bristol's pilot handled his aircraft's takeoff without any theatrics or false starts, unlike a recent flight that I recalled. At cruising altitude, he flew with great precision, darting from cloud to cloud, to minimise our exposure in locations where German *Focke Wolff* night fighters were known to lurk. While in some particularly massive and forbidding clouds, the pilot turned to invite us each to take the controls and fly the damn plane, while he supervised! This was thrilling! He remarked in taking over the stick again, "Flying straight is quite easy, as you now know. It's the landings and takeoffs that can be a little dangerous, chaps." Amen! I thought better of mentioning my Gibraltar 'milk run', as pilots, particularly air force types, are a notoriously tightly knit group.

Mike and I shared an extra headset, courtesy of the pilot, so that we could listen in to the chatter among the crew, though there was very little due to the likelihood of enemy intercepts. Time passed quickly; I was surprised to hear the navigator break radio silence to notify our pilot that we were approaching our landing site. We broke out of the clouds and the pilot motioned for Mike and me to look downward. As we expected, we could clearly see the signal fires laid out in the form of a large candle. The pilot gave us an OK sign. We knew from our briefings that it was his duty to verify the signal pattern. If it were not laid out correctly, he would send a brief, coded signal to the ground for verification. In the event that he did not receive a precisely coded confirmation, he would, "Get the hell out of there and pray all the way."

SOE used the same visual system when DC3 Dakotas were landing supplies and personnel, though in much more level areas than our drop zone. The pilot brought the Bristol down to 1600 metres to compensate for the high winds blowing off the mountains; otherwise, we risked drifting off course with the likelihood of hurtling into the heavily forested mountain terrain which surrounded the drop zone.

Mike and I hooked up our static lines to the cord as we had done on every practice jump. At Altricham, we were told that it was SOE tradition that agent/parachutists carry a container of brandy, 'just in case.' I was prepared for a 'just in case', having purchased a sterling silver-plated flask during one of my trips to London. The dispatcher removed the bottom hatch cover. We looked with apprehension through the hole in the plane's belly to see hills and trees flashing by rapidly beneath us. The signal fires were less visible now, as the ground party had let them burn low in case of enemy spotting planes. The Bristol had completed its first circuit of the jump zone when I pulled the silver container from my breast pocket, and passed it ahead to Mike. He was unscrewing the cap when the red light turned to green and the dispatcher shouted, "Go!" For an instant, Mike was a deeply conflicted man. Training overcame trepidation as Mike, clutching the container in both hands, disappeared out the hatch. He and my sterling brandy flask from Harrods were airborne. I took a deep breath and slid out after him, bracing for the buffeting from the wind and backwash from the propellers. Mike's chute billowed like a giant white mushroom below me, and mine opened perfectly, placing me almost parallel with the plane's rudder, at a thirty degree angle. After the slipstream released me, I dropped in a vertical position, feet down, and chute above. I thought that this was the thrill above all others, including piloting the Bristol, but my euphoria ended rudely. I was losing control, dangerously close to being parallel with my chute. I suddenly felt pangs of fear as well as regret for having missed out on the brandy. The voice of our jump instructor at Altricham came to my rescue, "Gentlemen! If you're jumping near mountains, and chances are very good that you will at least once, the up and down thermals can play havoc. Your parachute can unexpectedly deflate and you'll find yourself descending on top of the canopy like a maraschino cherry on whipped cream. That, gentlemen, evacuates all remaining air from your chute, as you would expect. Hence, you will fall like a two-hundredweight stone."

I remembered how he had demonstrated three times the exact sequence that needed to be executed to adjust the cords. Grimly, I pulled the ropes in the order he had made us memorise. The silk canopy obeyed and swung above me swelling reassuringly, billowing with the air it had found. Thanks be to God! I descended quickly for a jump school-perfect landing. After removing my harness and gathering my chute, I looked about anxiously for Mike. A voice called me from somewhere overhead. Dangling upright in a huge oak tree, like a large and very distressed marionette, was Mike. I called up, "Hey hold on, I'll be right there! Where's my flask?"

"F… the flask and get me down!" he replied colourfully. I proceeded to shinny up the gnarled trunk and was helping to untangle his lines from the thick branches when I heard loud voices at very close range. We froze. With my right hand, I reached down slowly and undid the fastener on my P38's holster. I expected to see a squad of black-helmeted SS-men, with rifles and machine guns zeroed in on us. Out of the shadows, through the branches came a voice in English, "Joe! Joe! You OK?"

"Joe"? It was a goddamn German trick! I squinted down through the leafy clusters and saw at least a dozen figures, looking up at us, waving their arms in greeting, or anger? It was definitely a welcoming committee, whether Yugoslavian Partisans, arranged by Marshal Tito, or a *Waffen SS* Death's Head Truppe, arranged by Herr Schickelgruber; I had to make a decision.

"Help! My friend is caught!"

"Sure, stay there! We come, Joe!"

Within seconds, two men had scrambled up nimbly to cut Mike's cords and we slithered down to the ground without mishap. If they were German agents speaking idiomatic Slav, which my father spoke fluently, they were masters of Yugoslavian dialect.

I turned to the big, black-haired one whom seemed to be the leader, and asked in English, "You know my name?"

"Sure, SOE, Joe! We're all SOE Joe's here!" he replied, in English. 'Joe' was of course, Special Operations' generic name for an agent.

I mentally cringed at his egregious breaches of security.

"Friends…Tito, Churchill, Roosevelt, you, us. Okey dokey?" he asked.

"Okey dokey, friends" I replied. He embraced me in a bear hug. I was faintly amused at his use of 'Okey dokey' and wondered if slick little Brooklyn Louie would have approved.

Our new friends quickly recovered all of the supply canisters and chutes, which the Bristol had strewn, seemingly at random, around the site. One always had to keep in mind that a jump behind enemy lines was neither complete nor safe until the landing area was completely 'disinfected'. They hoisted everything onto trucks, horse-drawn wagons, or their own backs for transport to the base camp. Mike and I were helped into a horse cart and gratefully rode the three kilometres to the base. As we were climbing down, the leader looked at us closely, and whispered "Joe, are you guys Camp X?"

"What?"

"Camp X, Canada."

I wasn't prepared to divulge anything to this band that, as far as we knew so far, could be part of an elaborate trap.

"What's that?" I asked disingenuously.

"Genosha Hotel! Oshawa, King Street. Big, tough waiters...sometimes fights, and lot's of pretty girls from the General Motors factory."

"Don't know it, sorry "I replied, in absolute denial. In fact, my chums and I had spent more than a few enjoyable evenings relaxing in that venerable Oshawa landmark.[4]

He grinned, "Sure, okey dokey, Joe." He lowered his voice conspiratorially. "I saw you shooting seagulls at the lake. Hip shots: blam, you missed; blam, you got it; blam, blam, one more. Pretty damn good, Joe!"

'Do I have 'Camp X' branded on my forehead?' "Okey dokey." He came at me like white lightning; his bear hug threatened to collapse my ribcage. Mike received the same treatment. The topic of Camp X was never raised again, at least in Yugoslavia.

Upon arrival at the secluded Papuk 6th Corps base, via hairpin twisting mountain trails cut through the dense bush, a youngish and very hospitable Scot, Captain R. S. 'Rolly' Young, was waiting. He greeted us enthusiastically and introduced his W/T operator, Sergeant Scott, and then the entire Partisan welcoming party who had more than proven their mettle. This confirmed their *bona fides*; not surprisingly, "Okey dokey" proved to be the Partisan Lieutenant 2IC - Second in Command.

Formalities over, Captain Young declared that we should celebrate our safe arrival whereupon two brawny Yugoslavs opened a case of native plum brandy, Sljvovica. What a lovely party it was, fuelled with food, drink, and lusty folk singing in which Mike and I participated to the best of our linguistically-challenged abilities. Our Camp X comrade, Okey dokey, who possessed a fine tenor voice treated us to a melancholy serenade to a gypsy *femme fatale*, Veronica. By 3:00 a.m., we had wished Irene a sound goodnight in three or four distinguishable languages; I was exhausted, and acknowledged that Sljvovica's reputation as a potent brew was well deserved. Captain Young cheerfully informed us that we would be sleeping 'under the stars'. I laid out my groundsheet and sleeping bag at the base of a tree as best I could manage under the circumstances. At the bonfire, a good-natured OSS Captain Hamilton had advised Mike and me that it was the rule in Yugoslavian partisan company "to have your gun

[4] *For accounts of staff and recruits' adventures related to the Genosha Hotel, see Inside-Camp X, Blake Books, 1999; pp.8,127,135-36.*

within easy grasp, just in case." I had no reason not to believe him and tucked my revolver under the headpiece before saying goodnight to Captain Hamilton in the adjacent bedroll. As I was drifting off, I suddenly realised that Captain Hamilton was none other than the well-known Hollywood actor, Stirling Hayden.

We awoke to a beautiful sunny morning, made even better by the pungent aroma of strong coffee brewing in an open metal pot over a campfire. I ate a huge breakfast of sausages, eggs, and fried potatoes cooked to perfection by our partisan allies and gratefully declined the brandy 'eye-opener' they offered, remembering my morning reaction to Scotch whiskey and kippered herrings. At 10:00 sharp, Captain Young convened a detailed briefing with the Partisan leaders, Captain Hamilton, Mike, and me, which lasted until early afternoon.[5]

After a late lunch, Captain Rolly led us on the grand tour of his camp which I thought a practical blend of Robin Hood's retreat in Sherwood Forest and a rustic 'Bide a Wee'-type of family lodge as might be found in northern Ontario. The compound was placed in a clearing that had been carved out of a dense, old growth pine forest. Like Robin Hood's men, the sentries were invisible while on duty and, based on the previous night's evidence, could more than hold up their end in the merry-making department. Rolly assured us that they were scattered outside the perimeter and had a system to alert the camp immediately if there was any sign of Germans or anti-Tito Chetnick Partisans. The HQ and Ops building was about fifteen metres long and five metres wide, and stood two stories high. On the second level, Rolly had established his and the Partisans' W/T and command centres. The kitchen, mess, and other living essentials were on the ground level. The Partisans, as well as Rolly and his staff, were quartered in small cabins nearby. Rolly pointed out the forbidden places including the women's quarters, the ammunition magazine located a considerable distance away, and other 'sensitive' off-limits areas, designated as such by the Partisans.

Between August 10 and August 31 we waited for a wire giving Tito's permission for our mission into Hungary. I was given almost immediate clearance, but Mike's was over three weeks in coming through.

---

[5] *Every SOE member going behind enemy lines was educated in the subtle signs that the enemy would look for to prove that you were an agent. Every precaution had to be taken in the preparation for your mission, from the obvious such as clothing and labels which had to be European, and anything carried which had to be absolutely authentic: cigarettes, lighters, coins, keys, even condoms...In our case, all items were Hungarian. Both SOE and BSC had 'special' sections that employed scores of skilled artisans, tailors, counterfeiters and a host of other gifted specialists who could manufacture exact copies of anything that was needed, if the original item could not be unearthed, by whatever means. The Harrod's sterling silver brandy flask was best forgotten. I had been put in charge of most of the money. I kept an amount in my pocket, which would be unlikely to arouse suspicion, and had sewn a reserve into the lining of my Army jacket along with the special silk W/T codes and my secret verses.*

Stirling Hayden A.K.A. Captain Hamilton

card-carrying Marxist, was not. We had little to do but to exercise, target practice, read, and study maps; I faithfully practised my Morse code daily.

Stirling Hayden was using his new legal name, Hamilton. He was an imposing, handsome man: blonde, broad shouldered, almost six feet, six inches tall and extremely impressive in his American Rangers uniform, which he wore without insignia. He was taciturn, and spoke slowly, as though each word was precious and not to be wasted. Stirling invited Mike and me go for hikes through the woods when it was quiet at the base. He liked to kid me about having my revolver at the ready and would pretend to 'draw' on me,

Perhaps Tito didn't know about my Hungarian ancestry. That he was not fond of Hungarians was an understatement. Mike's background check would have revealed his ancestry. It was ironic that, I, a non-communist was quickly cleared whereas Mike, a like a matinee cowboy. I believe I impressed him with my 'shoot from the hip' style which I had worked so hard to perfect at Camp X and Beaulieu, when I shot a pinecone off the top of a lofty Papuk jack pine. "Not bad, kid! Next thing, you'll be roping wild horses and riding off into the sunset with the pretty lady!" I was surprised at this departure from his usually reserved nature. We spent many enjoyable hours hiking at a fast clip through the Papuk forests, and became friends.

Twice, Stirling asked me to accompany him on what he called 'excursions' to give whatever help I could in contacting and debriefing American and Allied fliers who had been given safe haven by courageous Yugoslavs. Stirling always brought along a Slav interpreter on these missions. The two safe 'houses' were many kilometres apart and completely innocuous in appearance.

On our first excursion, we walked due south for four hours from base camp to a small, isolated farmhouse. The interpreter went to the front door, knocked and spoke briefly to an inhabitant, then turned and gave us the 'all clear' signal. We followed him quickly inside. The owner and his wife, a peasant couple of indeterminate age, greeted Stirling and the interpreter with grand hugs and me with warm handshakes, then disappeared down the cellar stairs. A minute later, they returned, and proudly presented their secret lodger, 'New Jersey Johnny', Flight Lieutenant, United States Army Air Force (USAAF), the navigator and sole member of his crew to survive the crash of his B29. Johnny had managed to evade the Germans, by subsisting in the forest for two weeks, where Stirling 's Partisan agents found him, nearly dead from exposure and starvation. He looked unaffected by the experience; I was curious as to the reason why.

Johnny had been especially well attended to, the interpreter explained, as his hometown, Hoboken, was the birthplace of our hosts' favourite American singer, Mr. Frank Sinatra. Stirling examined Johnny's papers and spoke with him privately for about forty-five minutes, then with maps, instructed two Yugoslav couriers who had arrived to accompany Johnny to a pre-arranged DC-3 landing site the next night. Our hosts invited us to remain for the night but Stirling declined, thanked them graciously and we left.

Our second excursion, a week later, took us southwest on a rugged six hour hike from base. Stirling 's guide brought us to within a half kilometre of a modest country inn, which, he whispered, was a popular watering hole for German patrols. Stirling and I lay down in the tall grass to wait as the Yugoslav walked nonchalantly to the rear door of the lodge. He whistled to us and we ran up to the door, keeping low to the ground. Inside, the proprietor greeted us cheerfully. He then showed us into the kitchen, where he served strong Turkish chicory brew and sweetcakes and then left us to our business. Our guide positioned himself outside the kitchen door, his chair leaning against the wall, his rifle strap loosened across his chest. On the journey, I had asked Stirling how the safe house owners and couriers were compensated for the huge risks that they took on his behalf.

"The regular Partisans are looked after by Tito, but it's a challenge to get these other folks to accept anything. They're very committed to the cause and consider what they're doing to be their duty as good Yugoslavs to help defeat the Nazis. They're dedicated, completely trustworthy, and as idealistic as you and me. I have to find creative ways to repay them. Most would be deeply insulted if I offered money, directly. But we usually manage to balance the ledger." He smiled, but did not elaborate.

The publican returned with a slender, pale, unshaven male in a United States Air Force Flight Captain's brown leather flight jacket. Stirling invited him to sit down facing us at the kitchen table. I estimated him to be no older than twenty-five as Stirling introduced us and poured the nervous young man a mug of the powerful brew. Then he began the inquiry.

"How have you been Captain? Are they treating you well here? I understand that your papers were lost. Just tell Lieutenant Gordon and me everything, from the beginning; take as much time as you need."

"Thank you, Captain Hamilton. Yes, I'm doing very well, thanks to my hosts. A barrage of '88's (anti-aircraft artillery) hit the nose of my Mark II P51 (Mustang) out of nowhere. Must have been a mobile unit mounted on train tracks. That was about seventy-five miles southwest of Pécs, Hungary. The engine started to smoke and flames were coming now from the port exhausts. I hit the extinguisher switch, figuring I could just make it back to Italy, or at least ditch safely in the Adriatic if I nursed the throttle carefully. Then orange balls the size of Georgia peaches began to belch from the starboard headers and I knew it was in a heck of a lot of trouble. I checked my position, radioed Mayday and looked around for some place to bring it down. I could see the Drava glinting below and the mountains dead ahead. I figured my only chance was to try to slip down between the two."

Stirling nodded, "A party saw you way off to the east and said you looked as bright as the Star of Bethlehem!"

"Well, the cockpit was filling up with black smoke, Captain. By now, I couldn't see the instrument panel, I was sucking in hot castor oil through my mask and Christ knows what else, so I decided, what the hell am I waiting for? Uncle Sam can afford a new plane. My butt is a one-issue item. I'm buggin' out, I said to myself. So I took a guess at my altitude, popped the canopy and bailed."

"How was your jump?" I asked, always the parachute expert.

"Fast, very fast! The 'chute didn't open! I yanked, pulled, and jerked every one of the D (release) rings…nothing! A zombie must have packed it. Anyway, before I knew it, I had hit the ground feet first and…."

"So now, how do you credit you're still alive, Captain? Did you have a miraculous vision of angels on the way down?" asked Stirling, smiling sardonically.

"Better, sir. I landed in a peat bog and must have sunken in over my waist. By a real miracle, my legs weren't broken. I managed to claw out partway, then I think I passed out. Your guys said it took them two hours to reach me and that I was damn lucky I hadn't come in headfirst and suffocate. I didn't break anything! Want to see my bruises, Sir?" He stood and pulled up his trouser legs calf-high. They were black and blue.

"Sit down son. Save it for the girls at home. Guaranteed to get you a lot of dates, a hometown hero's write-up in *The Stars and Stripes* or, hopefully, both. '*Bogged down, but not out*'", Stirling joked, "there's your headline. Speaking of which, why Lieutenant Gordon and I are here: getting you home. We'll leave the girls up to you, son."

Stirling then proceeded to ask some very detailed questions about his squadron, his mission's primary target, secondary target, and related questions all while listening to his answers, very intently. I thought he was satisfied with the pilot's story until he turned slightly and nodded at me to join him in the tiny pantry.

"What do you think, Joe?" he whispered confidentially. "Is he a ringer or the real McCoy?"

I shrugged. "I couldn't overhear every word, but he sounds like he's on the level. Something doesn't check out for you, Stirling?"

"I always have doubts. It goes with the territory. The Germans have pulled off the shot-down-flier routine before and blew a courier network in Greece. Plus, he doesn't have any papers. He told the Partisans that they got lost while he was mucking around in the muskeg."

"How could he be lying? Didn't your men find him in the bog? I mean, no German would use the word 'zombies'", for God's sake!" My voice was no longer *sotto voce*.

"Ssshh! They found what was apparently a flier, two hours after the plane crashed and burned. There was nothing left of it but a charred shell. It is possible that German Intelligence could have found it first, sized things up, pulled out the pilot's remains and inserted their own guy in the swamp. Did it ever occur to you that some American-born German members of the *Bund* in the good old USA high-tailed it home to be of service before '41?" The *Bund*, I knew from the newsreels were American black-shirts: fascist, pseudo-Nazi rabble-rousers whose leader was addressed as *Der Führer*.

"This is a bit far fetched, Stirling. We're talking a B, or maybe a C movie script."

"Joe, listen to me. Berlin wants our networks shut down, at any price…now! The Allies are pounding the living daylights out of the Reich, with 1,000-bomber raids day and night over Hamburg, Cologne, Düsseldorf, Bremen, and Berlin, and the *Lutfwaffe's* chief, Hermann Goering's stock is sinking fast. You see, the fat bastard told the German people in '39 that if a single enemy bomber made it to the Fatherland, he'd change his name to Meyer. That's Jewish, in case you didn't know. Well, now he has the *Gestapo*, *SS*, *SD*, and Hitler's granny on the look-out to hunt down every single crash survivor. They've even got special action *SS Einsatzgrüppen* squads of bounty hunters on full time assignment. Too many of our boys are being cold–bloodedly executed where they're found. It's a favour I'll return with this one, if I'm not convinced otherwise in about one minute."

"Do you always have to be this suspicious?"

"No. Usually everything adds up and its just 'skeedaddle on out of here, kiddo, do exactly as you're told and you'll be drinking *vino* in the *piazza*, *domani*.'"

"Why did you give Jersey Johnny the okay so fast?"

"Because Rolly got me some very good background from HQ before we left Papuk. It only took me a few minutes to verify his story and codes."

"And this one?"

"Oh, just an old seadog's sixth sense, I guess. He may be kosher, or a ringer. He's got some explaining to do, or he's coming back with us, dead or alive."

I had a sudden inspiration. "Stirling, will you let me ask him one question?"

"If it's his mother's recipe for sauerkraut, by all means. I'm kidding. Be my guest."

We went back to the kitchen table where the young man was sitting. He looked up nervously at Stirling, and asked, "Excuse me, Captain, may I ask you a question?"

"Shoot!"

"Well Sir, I've been sitting here wondering what you were talking about out there, not that it's my business. And…."

"Go on, son."

"Sir, are you a sailor?

"Maybe. Why do you ask?"

"Well, at first I thought you were the movie actor, Stirling Hayden. But that's impossible. Jimmy Stewart's the only big star on active duty. He's a pilot, too. I'm from Boston, Captain, and it was a few years ago that I remember my Dad taking me to Gloucester to see the big ships and you sure look like that tall captain I saw on the deck of one brigantine."

Stirling 's mood mellowed. "Lieutenant Gordon," he smiled, "what's your question for this young man?"

"Okay. When did Babe Ruth play for the Brooklyn Dodgers?" I thought Louie would approve of this line of interrogation.

He looked deeply pained. "Lieutenant, no disrespect, but are you… *meshugganah*? George Herman Ruth never, ever played for Brooklyn. He was born in Baltimore on February 6, 1894 or 5, I forget, and joined Boston in 1914 as a southpaw pitcher. They won the Series in 1918. The Red Sox' owner needed money fast for some deal so Ruth was traded to New York in 1920 for 100,000 clams. He spent the rest of his illustrious career as 'The Sultan of Swat' in the Yankee outfield. Boston, to its eternal humiliation, hasn't won the Series since; it's 'the curse of the *Bambino*'".

Stirling reached out his right hand across the table. "Welcome aboard, son. *Meshugganah*, eh? Are you by any chance Jewish?"

"Close enough, Sir. My Dad was Jewish, born in Leipzig, Germany. Mom was Irish Catholic. I'm a hodgepodge myself, Samuel Liam Stern. I was born in Cleveland. We moved to Boston 'cause Pop had a hankering to be a deep sea fisherman."

"And was he?"

"Yes. Actually, Captain Hayden, he owned his own trawler, *Sam's Stern* and netted cod for twenty years off the Grand Banks!"

"That's correct, Sam!" Stirling grinned. "But my name's 'Hamilton' around here, thanks. Well, I'll be damned! I remember him, Slammin' Sammy Stern, the old cod walloper! I crewed out there for a few trips before joining up!"

"Sorry, Captain Hamilton, of course, Sir! That was Pops, all right, Samuel Benjamin Stern."

Stirling called out to the interpreter, "Drago, let's have some food. And bring us that jar of rotgut Sljvovica you're hoarding…with three glasses. Pronto!"

On our return journey, Stirling asked, "Joe, whatever made you ask a dumb question like that? It was brilliant!"

"Just a dyed in the wool ball fan, I guess."

"I guess" he replied. "Did you know the answer?"

"I take the Fifth! I was hoping you did."

"Thought so. Stick to hockey, pal, okay?"

"I don't know much about that, either. And you, Mr. Smart Guy, Grand Banks fisherman.... So you suspected he was at least part German from the start?"

"Accent on 'Herrrr mannn'. Then I figured if he was a Nazi, the Jewish bit would send him right around the bend and he'd give us the Aryan *übermensch* line." But the vernacular about 'The Babe' was Triple A American. Couldn't fake that and *Meshugganah* helped. The rest was damn interesting, too. It all fit together neatly. It's one for his grandkids," he chuckled.

At most times, Stirling 's character was that of a brooding, reflective poet. He enjoyed sitting in the forest's shade, his back propped against a tree. Our conversations were punctuated with long silences; he would wrinkle his brow and gaze into the distance as though he was composing his thoughts in complete sentences before uttering them. I remember one such occasion when I asked him about his film career and love affair with the sea.

"Making movies was a quick way to make a lot of money to indulge my real passion. I was still a kid of twenty-two when I skippered my first ship, if you can imagine, an eighty-nine foot brigantine from Gloucester, near Boston, to Tahiti. I figure I browned off too many people who thought I was too young, too chippy, too inexperienced...too everything. They were likely right. Anyway, it hit the East Coast papers; I got some publicity, even got marriage proposals, and all that baloney. I would have made the round trip completely, but a big tropical blow nearly scuttled us on the homeward leg. I was flat broke, owed a lot of money, and badly wanted another ship. Instead of getting on my case, the papers were very kind. Some reporter joker said that I had the looks of a movie star, so I figured, why not? I tested for Paramount in New York in '40 and, by May, was in Tinsel Town with a seven-year contract. Big mistake!"

"Why? I saw *Bahama Passage* in Toronto (actually Brampton, but I assumed that as a sailor, he would have heard of Toronto) and you were pretty good!"

"Exactly, Joe. Pretty good wasn't good enough for me. The New York critics were brutal. I wanted to do better work, but I had no training and I was too damn stubborn and impatient to take advice from anyone, much less some fancy-Dan acting teacher. Listen, Joe, I'm no student. I quit school at sixteen to go to sea! So, in '42, I did three smart things. I married Madeleine, skipped out on the Hollywood BS and joined the Marines. And she supported me all the way." Madeleine Carroll was his heavenly co-star in *Bahama Passage*. He enlisted in the USMC, passed basic training at Parris Island boot camp, came out as a Lieutenant, then requested, and received a transfer to OSS, where he rose rapidly to his Captaincy.

I never tired of hearing about his pitched battles for respect and better roles with certain egomaniacal studio czars. His stories were laced with ribald asides about Hollywood's most glamorous stars and satyrs, told with cynical wit, although he preferred discussing Canada's rich maritime history and surprised me with his knowledge of our naval traditions as far back as explorer Jacques Cartier. He was a well-read marine and naval historian, as well as a philosopher and searcher for the truth 'about myself'. He said that he was considering writing about about his "personal voyage, someday." And in 1963 he did, to critical acclaim and substantial sales and was featured as a selection by the Book of the Month Club.[6]

Our final adventure together was to accompany our Partisans to join a larger force bent on inflicting a major disaster on the Germans in Belgrade. The city had been bombed to a rubble by the *Luftwaffe* in 1941. With permission from Bari and Rolly, I accompanied Stirling to Belgrade to help supply the guerrillas' front lines with guns and ammunition, from Rolly's stores at Papuk. Although the Partisans fought courageously and held off the Germans for a considerable time, the enemy's superior numbers eventually forced the Partisans to retreat with a great loss of life. Tito sent in kids to fight in these vicious building-to-building street battles, with the excuse that it saved real soldiers' lives! Dejectedly, Stirling and I made the trek back to 6th Corps base.

After the war, I read that the American government had awarded Stirling the Silver Star for running arms and supplies to Tito's guerrilla forces. I know that he did that, but I also know from our two 'excursions' and conversations that his primary mission was to establish underground networks of safe houses and courier posts along escape routes to transfer downed American and Allied pilots out of Yugoslavia. I cannot understand why this courageous service to his country was omitted from his citation.

Despite Stirling's one unfortunate lapse of judgement in the Cold War McCarthy witch-hunt trials, which he deeply regretted,[7] my memories of 'Captain Hamilton' are of a deeply principled man of integrity, courage, humour and exceptional intellect for whom I have the deepest respect and affection. In the opinion of film critic Judith Crist, his portrayal of the mad, paranoid, cigar-chomping, ultra right-

[6] Wanderer, *Stirling Hayden, 1963, Alfred A. Knopf; reissued, 1977, W.W. Norton & Company.*

[7] Wanderer, *Stirling Hayden.*

wing General Jack D. Ripper, in his friend Stanley Kubrick's 1964 dark comedic masterpiece, *Dr. Strangelove*, is 'perfection.'

I sincerely hope that my friend, Stirling, the taciturn, solitary Viking from the forests of Papuk was at least gratified with the realisation that he had finally achieved film eminence by harpooning the two evils that he most despised: mindless militarism and fascism.

After three weeks, a wireless message was transmitted to Rolly from Marshal Tito's HQ, giving his authorisation to proceed with our mission. In retrospect, I don't believe that Captain Young had ever received or even requested permission from Tito, prior to our arrival, for our stay in the Partisan camp and the use of the facilities; or, most importantly, to engage a guide to take us across the Drava River into Hungary. It appeared that a political power game had also been in play. Neither the Russians, including Philby, nor Marshal Tito, wanted a single non-Communist Allied agent in Hungary, as Stalin had already selected Hungary for absorption as a Soviet satellite state at war's end, with Tito's consent. Our unauthorised presence coupled with our pre-emptive request for guides likely delayed the Yugoslavian *Supremo's* 'thumbs up' considerably. Perhaps, and I am only speculating, Tito's strategy had been to put off making a decision in the hopes that Mike and I would enter Hungary without a guide, be captured and thus be neutralised. On the other hand, we might simply tire of the waiting game and return to Italy.

We packed up my B Mark II wireless set and our clothes and equipment to make ready for our trip to the River Drava. Rolly and Stirling saw us off with "Good luck, we'll see you after the war!" We left 6th Corps camp early on a Saturday morning with our Partisan guide, whom Mike and I immediately nicknamed 'Papuski'. As we journeyed in a small buggy to the outskirts of Vocin, a village close to the camp, we were shocked to see rotting human corpses hanging from lampposts. Many seemed about to fall to pieces on the ground, in the final stages of decay. The odour of putrefying flesh was frightful. Papuski sought to educate us, explaining that these pitiful, scarecrow cadavers had been enemies of Tito, "Mihailovic's Chetnicks, Nazis, they're all the same!" he remarked scornfully.

"Why not just bury them and be done with it?" asked Mike.

He shrugged. "An example must be made, as a warning to other traitors. They'd do the same to us!"

I shuddered at the thought of our fate, if caught by the Chetnicks, in the company of our Titoist guide. The grisly scene was repeated at Slat and again at Drenovac. Mike and I were on the verge of retching.

No quarter was asked or given in the bloody feud for control of Yugoslavia. Draza Mihailovic had been the first resistance leader to seek and win British support. However, neither the British nor Americans trusted his motives and both judged him insufficiently anti-Nazi in his politics and war effort. Mihailovic's Royal Chetniks were, as the name suggests, supporters of the exiled King. Mihailovic and his Chetniks had helped 'run' scores of Allied flyers safely back to Italy. Nonetheless, Allied support swung behind Tito who fought the Germans with barbaric ferocity. With the support of Philby, McLean and Burgess, the Soviet's English agents, and upon Stalin's insistence, Tito was recognised as the Communist saviour of Yugoslavia. As the loser in this struggle for supremacy, Draza Mihailovic was court-martialled and executed for war crimes by Tito, in 1946.

As a result of Tito's good standing with Britain and The United States, Captain Young was permitted to run his clandestine mission in Papuk, which served the dual interests of Britain and Tito by infiltrating Communist SOE agents into Hungary and bolstering Tito's Communist forces with SOE-trained Yugoslavian guerrillas. Tito was very interested in having an underground courier service in Hungary in preparation for the upcoming Russian invasion. A further complication was Tito's intense hatred of Hungarians, which, as mentioned, was likely the reason for the delay that Mike had experienced. The Yugoslav and the Hungarian agents were all Communists, except for me, and all were recruited and initially trained in Canada, at Camp X. Despite the infernal politics and bloodletting, Mike and I enjoyed our time in Yugoslavia immensely and are forever grateful for the generous and warm hospitality we received everywhere we travelled.

As if to compensate for the dreadful reminders of the Partisan war we had encountered in the three villages, Papuski invited us to take a side trip to a Partisan wedding. We were hesitant, not wanting to be late for our rendezvous at the Drava. He assured me on his word of honour that we wouldn't miss it, and then asked me for some money. He and the cart disappeared down the forest trail and returned in a half-hour with a larger two-wheeled horse and cart, and our driver. With a smile, he proudly announced that we were now ready to proceed to a wedding, in true Serbian style!

The journey was a day's travel from camp, and the muted rhythm of the horse's hoofs on the soft, sandy soil and the warm sunshine prompted Mike and me to take turns dozing and staying on watch. We rested overnight close to the town of Mikleus, which I hoped we wouldn't have to enter and witness another 'chamber of horrors'. Next morning, we cautiously crossed the main road at Mikleus, and continued southeast towards Zdenci. After two hours, Papuski pointed out a dirt road to the driver, which soon brought us to an apparently abandoned and isolated farm. Isolated or not, we were certainly not alone. Crowds of people were milling about on the 'back forty' and a band was belting out folk tunes. Papuski assured us that Partisan guards were patrolling the boundaries to ensure there was no chance of a surprise raid by the Germans or Chetnicks.

It was as though we had magically transported into the wedding scene in a grand Balkan production of A *Midsummer Night's Dream*! All of the members of the wedding party were wearing Serbian national garments. The six bridesmaids wore identical flowered dresses with their hair adorned with halos of laurel leaves and white columbine. The statuesque, fair-haired young bride wed her handsome beau on a makeshift wooden platform under a bower of intertwined wild flowers. Close family members were seated on the dais while the guests literally overflowed onto the grass once the celebration was underway. Papuski was a cousin of the groom and Rolly had given him some liquor from his private stock. There was an abundant supply of Sljvovica plum brandy to which Mike and I had unknowingly contributed when Papuski went to hire the cart. Now I wished that I had given him more money, to buy the young couple a wedding present!

When the Partisan priest had given his final blessing, the pair kissed shyly at first and then with such passion that we all rose, cheering and applauding. They turned to us, blushing, and kissed again, then bowed deeply, like a rustic Romeo and Juliet taking a curtain call. The small band struck up a lively waltz and the couple led off while we clapped in time. An attractive young woman, whom I had noticed during the ceremony, swept me up onto the platform to join the bride and groom in the next waltz. Her movements were gracefully smooth and she was elegant. I was smitten! Her name was Elena. After the second dance, she excused herself and joined the women who were setting up the refreshment tables. I regret that I didn't dance with Elena again that afternoon.

The band played continuously, while individual musicians took short breaks without interrupting the flow of the music. The food was fresh, zestfully spicy, and abundant. It seemed that no plate or serving tray was ever allowed to be empty. Mike and I were like sailors after six months at sea. The women were beautiful and charming! We danced to the lively Czardas and Slav folk tunes, drinking in the women's grace, and their companionship, the heavenly scent of their bodies made even more alluring by their flowered wreaths. Yet, I longed to dance, just once more with Elena, the Serbian princess.

"Just like a Magyar wedding, but maybe a whole lot better, Joe!" Mike enthused.

I couldn't have agreed more. As evening fell, the festivities had gradually diminished with the departure of the very happy couple, in our horse cart now festooned with flowers. Papuski walked us to a safe house, where, he indicated, we would stay for the night, with his niece. We would meet our Drava River guide the next afternoon, as promised, he said. Sleep seemed the best option, as I was too 'high' on the day's excitement and Sljvovica to serve SOE with any semblance of distinction. However, it was not to be; Papuski had been busy arranging our actual accommodations with utmost discretion. He took Mike next door to the home of a charming and very attractive widow, who was a member of the wedding party's family. Papuski returned and bid me follow him outside. A few doors further down, he knocked softly. Framed in the open doorway, her golden hair let down to her waist, was my beautiful dancing partner, Elena. She gently took my arm to bring me inside, and shut the door. She led me into her sitting room, illuminated only by the light of two flickering tapers. Elena kissed me softly and poured two exquisite crystal spheres of homemade Sljvovica. We locked arms and drank from one another's glass. Slowly, she removed each of her shoes and then knelt in front of me, to take mine. We had not spoken, except briefly in greeting. In our bare feet, we kissed and with eyes closed, held one another tightly, as we slow danced to serenely romantic music on her gramophone, as the prologue to a magical night of passionate, unending, lovemaking.

Both women had lost their husbands in the war, Elena said. Although widowed, each would be a highly eligible wife after the war ended; it simply wouldn't do for the village to know that they had each entertained a strange man in her home. She told me that she had left me at the reception, to avoid gossip, so that we could spend this time together. I was very impressed by her foresight and discretion.

Mike and I reluctantly left our dear friends before dawn, after early breakfasts and sweet farewells. We promised to visit them on our way back and immediately felt like curs to have deceived them but couldn't bear to confess that the odds were strongly weighted against our return.

This sojourn did not in any way interfere with our mission. We were on schedule to rendezvous with our next escort that night. Captain Young's alliance with the Yugoslavs had provided us with the splendid Papuski, our loyal, resourceful partisan guide and interpreter who attended to our 'care and feeding' and more, with food, shelter, protection and the very special hospitality of his country's folk.

Exhausted, deliriously happy and a little hung-over, I took a ladle of water from Elena's well, after we had kissed goodbye indoors for the hundredth time. Instantly, I felt dizzy and nauseous. Papuski was with his lady friend who looked somewhat amused, as he took me by my arm and helped me into the back of the wagon. How could I have forgotten the wisdom of the Partisans of Papuk during Rolly's welcoming party? "You drink Sljvovica and you'll be drunk. You drink water next morning, you'll be drunk again!"

Fortunately, I had had no more than three small glasses of Sljvovica and my head soon cleared. Perhaps my vertigo was largely due to the after effects of Elena. Mike and I had vowed to be on the alert, for many reasons, before the reception had begun. We propped ourselves up in the cart, facing behind to look for any sign of trouble while our driver and guide, Papuski, covered the front. The Chetniks and Germans often used this road, he gravely warned us. That evening, we picked up our new Yugoslav guide, Steve, at a safe house, two-thirds of the way to the Drava River. Steve and Papuski had been told that the advance guard of a motorised German unit had been sighted within ten km of town. Without hesitation, Steve shoved us out the back door of the safe house to the barn; where there was a haystack about fifteen metres high. He instructed us to bury ourselves deeply in the straw. I looked at Papuski, who nodded and grinned encouragingly. He was obviously enjoying the irony of the contrast between our previous night's lodgings and this. Both men helped us burrow into the prickly, warm straw, much too enthusiastically, I thought. We had no difficulty falling asleep; our stalwart guides woke us at dawn with the news that the patrol had bypassed the village around midnight. Once the danger had passed, they said, they left us and went into the house to sleep.

"That's nice! Why the hell didn't you take us with you?" I inquired while we sneezed, brushing and shaking the straw and dust from one another's uniforms. Steve muttered that it was safer for us to say hidden. I decided not to argue with the fellow and we gratefully followed them into the house for a wash, shave, and breakfast. An ample, jolly Serbian woman cooked a hearty farm breakfast while humming what sounded suspiciously to me like Elena's phonograph ballads from the wedding night's tryst. As we ate I joked feebly about our romp in the hay and remarked that while it was far worse than the hospitality of the night before, it was far better than the fellowship of the *Gestapo*.

"Or Chetnicks, comrades," added Steve smilingly, with the internationally recognised gesture of a knife across the throat.

I was in radio contact daily with Captain Rolly's 6th Corps. At last, he signalled that Bari had ordered us to proceed with the crossing of the Drava River. This turned out not to be as straightforward as we had hoped. We made three attempts to get into Hungary with the Partisans' help, without achieving our objective. The first time we made it as far as Dakovacs where we were halted because Rolly's communications with Tito for Mike's permission to enter Hungary were ambiguous. When that was cleared up, we were at Polic, but were turned back when Steve's contact insisted that he needed at least four days to arrange some details for our reception in Hungary. On the third attempt, we were poised and ready, at Budakovacs, at the Drava. To our dismay, the crossing was halted this time because the full moon's reflection made the river's surface too bright, and worse, the boat had a bad leak. Three strikes! The Partisan boatman explained that it was too dangerous to take us by boat on a moonlit night, as the Hungarian border guards were very vigilant. We convinced him to try anyway, but less than half way across the broad Drava, we had taken on so much water that we were half-swamped and had to row back or we would likely have sunk. He puttered around on the beach but was unable to find another watertight boat. They had never warned us about leaky dinghies at any Secret Agent School! We were *almost* there, but not quite.

Mike and I were deeply disappointed and resolved to try again; we studied our map and pinpointed other locations around Cadavica, where we planned to lie low and make an attempt in a week's time. I sent Rolly a wire to let him know our new plan, which he forwarded to Bari HQ for approval. Rolly relayed back, "Bad luck, return to HQ 'soonest'". Mike and I were obliged to obey this order, but we agreed that 'soonest' could mean one day or possibly two. After all, we reasoned, we had boasted in Bari about walking across, if necessary. We would only give up after having 'a go' at swimming across, at the very least. Steve said it was best that we try during the daytime when many of the younger people went for a summer dip, so as not to arouse the suspicions of the Hungarian sentries who could be counted on to monitor the bathers with high powered German binoculars. The local jokesters often swam past the geographical centre of the Drava, taunting the Hungarian border police who occasionally shouted obscenities and waved at the young women. The Hungarians had put into effect a new system of guarding the river on September 1, which included spotting posts in tall trees, mobile one-man patrols, and sentry bunkers every kilometre, for this fifteen km stretch. A killing zone of 1,000 m had been cleared on the river embankment. The Drava is wide and flows at five to six km per hour at this spot but it was fun to swim and play in its warm currents. We made several attempts by day and night, without provoking even a curse from across the river. Steve, who had acted as look out, assured us that the sentries were watching us closely, nonetheless. We never tried to make it all the way across, without our equipment. My B Mark II portable radio was far too heavy and would have been completely destroyed by the water, had I been foolish enough to try. My codes on Leo' s silk squares and the paper money in my linings likely would have been impossible to restore. Like the Biblical Israelite Sampson, we would have been 'Eyeless in Gaza' without wireless, or codes, and flat broke, at the mercy of the Philistines.

We had been four weeks in Yugoslavia. Our guides, Papuski, and Steve had taught us so much and we had at least proven to ourselves that it was possible to slip into Hungary across the Drava, at night, if the gods were beaming down and the moon wasn't. Rolly warned us that Bari was insistent upon our immediate return and we had run out of stalling options. Mike and I realised that a cold drop would have been preferable and more efficient. Reluctantly, we turned our backs on the Drava and headed towards Papuk base. I couldn't help but wonder if DIBBLER had been sabotaged from the outset by the political intrigues of Tito and Stalin. Was it ordained to be the SOE Operation that was... *almost?*

CHAPTER 4
Blind Drop

Mike and I decided that the daylong trek back to Rolly's camp gave us a perfect excuse to detour to Zdenci, and visit our girlfriends. Papuski had no objection, adding gruffly that anything would be better than travelling back to base camp in such depressing company as we had been, thus far. We knew he also had met a woman companion at the wedding. I told him that I was simply thinking about the welfare of the horse, which surely would need to be fed and rested overnight.

"The horse is fine, Lieutenant Joe: healthy, strong, and well fed! Your grousing is driving me crazy. I may shoot you both before the Chetnicks do! But first I think that you two badly need some female company." Were we letting our frustration and aggravation show that much? Obviously!

We rested on the outskirts of town until it was dark. Papuski reached into his leather bag on the floor of the cart and held up three small bottles of the Yugoslavian standby, 'white lightning' Sljvovica. "Follow me and be back here, ready to leave, at five-thirty tomorrow morning. No excuses!" Within ten minutes, I was stealthily deposited at Elena's doorstep clutching my night's ration of plum brandy. Elena was very surprised and as happy to see me as I was to see her. We renewed our delightful relationship with passionate intensity. Difficult as it was to leave next morning, I crept out of Elena's house and ran to our rendezvous point, only fifteen minutes late, where a sleepy Mike and Papuski were more or less patiently waiting, with the driver. I made no mention of my stopover, nor did they, except that I yawned continually and dozed all the way back.

Rolly was in a state of high alert when we reached 6th Corps, Papuk Base. Mike and I had barely set down our kits when he called us in to a formal 'Sit Rep'; Mike and I gave a full situation report that was transcribed by Sergeant Scott, Rolly's W/T operator. Rolly reviewed the main points for the record and we then evaluated our situation. He had made tentative arrangements with Bari to send an aircraft to fly us out of Papuk to Brindisi, Italy, 'post haste'. I expressed my doubts that HQ would give us another chance at piercing Hungary.

"You're completely wrong on that, Joe. Bari wants to get your mission back on track, soonest! Blind drop this time, almost certain, but that's up to the top brass. Your turnaround time in Italy will be very brief. DIBBLER is on the front burner and your commander, John Coates, is packed, primed and waiting anxiously for your arrival at Brindisi. That's why we're working overtime to pull some strings and get a Dakota in ASAP. There's a very good chance that something can be lined up for a pickup tomorrow night. Wireless Willy will let us know the moment the met boys (meteorologists) in Italy give it their blessing."

'*Wireless Willy? Best not to question why*'. Rolly as usual, was being sound, sane, and very sensible. Bari was central HQ; no amount of wishing could get us into Hungary from Papuk without a Special Operations aircraft, full briefings with our DIBBLER Commander Captain John Coates, supplies, new codes, money and logistical support. The word around camp was that the Allies' post D-Day fortunes in Europe were steadily improving. Germany's armies were still potent and dangerous, despite Commander-in-Chief Adolf Hitler's demented 'no surrender, hold out to the last man' orders. Appalling losses among his battle-seasoned veterans, combined with his most brilliant commanders being dismissed on the *Führer's* whim, captured by the Red Army, or cut off without *materiel*, food or equipment, was forcing the once-invincible *Wehrmacht* to fall back towards the borders of the *Reich*. John, Mike, and I simply had to get into Hungary, to do our best to help defang the wounded beast.

Bari radioed that the weather probabilities for a DC3 landing near camp at 22:00 hours the next night were 'eighty percent promising'. Confirmation was expected in less than eight hours.

I had not seen Stirling since returning to Papuk. Rolly answered my question, "GWTW (gone with the wind), back to sweet *Italia*, almost a fortnight ago. Places to go, people to see, you know the drill. He did leave something for you. Come up and I'll fetch it." Rolly took a plain envelope from his desk drawer and handed it to me. It was addressed: 'Attn.: Lieutenant Gordon'. The hand-written note was an expression of his appreciation for my companionship and support on our three excursions, ending with best wishes to Mike and me for success in our mission. It was signed simply, 'Stirling'.[1]

The next morning, Sergeant Scott received a wire confirming a DC 3's arrival on schedule. Mike and I spent the day preparing our equipment and personal effects. I checked my radio and codes, and we then visited with Papuski for our private farewell. We recalled the wedding's delights and even laughed about our misfortunes, then hugged emotionally and departed. Papuski had refused our money; I had insisted, but to no avail. How right Stirling had been about the principles of these extraordinary people! While Mike and I were whiling away the time, a messenger arrived with a note from Rolly. Captain Young needed us up in HQ, immediately. We dashed upstairs into Rolly's operational command post; I was apprehensive that our flight was washed out. But it was an even more urgent situation. Rolly announced that the guards had sighted two German armoured troop carriers less than two kilometres from the perimeter of the camp. The Partisans, he said, estimated that there were twenty men in the detail. Rolly and Genosha had placed the base on high alert; the atmosphere was electric. Wireless Willy had shut down the radio. The Partisans on picket duty were keeping Rolly and Genosha in the picture by means of couriers. Rolly was scanning the perimeter of the camp with binoculars, while he talked.

"Here, have a look. You can see the blighters at 135°, due east" he indicated, handing me the instrument.

Through the trees, I could see two half-track vehicles stopped on the road, little more than a trail in the dense bush; four figures in *Wehrmacht* field grey stood in a tight cluster, beside the first carrier. "They're looking right in our direction…looks like they're having a parley. Ha, they didn't spot us! They're getting back in now. Rolly, the second one's backing up. It's turning around! Its back wheels are nearly over the edge of the cliff!"

Within fifteen minutes, the crisis had passed. Both armoured cars had turned tail and retreated down the hill. Rolly asked Genosha to send out the order for the Partisans to stand down. Our plans were still firmly on track.

"Do you think they're coming back with reinforcements?" asked Mike.

Genosha was shaking his head. "No, those guys were plenty nervous; I'll bet they're reporting to their CO right now that they searched every blade of grass but couldn't find a thing."

I could sympathise. Rolly and his Partisan allies owned every square centimetre of this neighbourhood. If the Germans had been foolish enough to penetrate any further, they faced certain extinction, at the hands of either Tito's forces or the Chetnicks. *Reichsführer-SS* Heinrich Himmler's racial policies, particularly as applied in predominantly Slavic Eastern European states, were fatally destined to turn potentially neutral peoples into bitter foes. Wherever the *SS* encountered officially designated 'racial undesirables' (i.e. almost all

[1] *I deeply regret that Stirling's farewell letter has 'gone missing' from my files. Were it available, it would be reproduced here.*

Joe Gelleny SOE

non-Aryans) in countries such as Russia, its *Gestapo*, *SD* and 'special action units' mercilessly enforced the most brutally repressive measures imaginable, thus arousing the formation and mobilisation of underground guerrilla forces which enacted bloody retribution, tying up thousands of German personnel who might otherwise have been deployed in conventional combat roles.

Final clearance for our inbound flight was received. While walking to the landing site in the evening, I gave Rolly some of our money that I had removed from my cache with a request to invent any pretence to pay our two intrepid guides for their services. At the very least, Rolly likely kept up 6th Corp's glorious tradition by hosting a rip-roaring party in honour of Papuski and Steve, the Drava dynamic duo.

The landing strip was a level hayfield located close to the camp. Needing some diversion to calm our nerves, Mike and I helped make the site ready and prepare the signal fires for lighting. I was fascinated to watch how carefully Rolly paced the landing area and dropped markers on the ground to indicate the precise location for each signal fire to be built. As I walked with him, Rolly explained, "The field's surface is ideally suited: flat, level, and resilient. In two days, all signs of the plane's wheels, the fires, drop canisters and our footprints will have vanished, old boy. The stubble will recover, without leaving so much as a dimple. Now, let's synchronise our watches. Get Sir Mike over here, if you would, please."

That 6th Corps at Papuk had survived undetected and unscathed by marauding Germans or Chetnicks was a tribute to Rolly's extraordinary leadership and trade craft, joined seamlessly with the Partisans' communications network, wariness and an indomitable will to outwit, outmanoeuvre and obliterate the Nazi interloper. Rolly and two Partisan leaders walked the field, stopping frequently to check the position of each signal, then joined Sergeant Scott and the rest of us lounging in the 'rough' at the side of the field, like spectators at a golf tournament. My pulse was racing as I lay back, staring up at the black, moonless sky, anticipating the arrival of the star player.

Presently, I sat up and glanced anxiously at the luminous dial on my wristwatch. It read 9:40. There was no sound of an approaching aircraft, only the crickets' mating calls. Sergeant Scott put on his headset, screwed the long antenna into its socket, and then positioned his portable unit. He looked over at me, pointing to the signal strength dial. I craned my neck to take a look; the needle was reading *maximum*. I gave the professional's nod of approval. At 9:45, I was pacing the edge of the field. At 9:50, Rolly and two Partisans lit torches with Genosha's trusty Zippo and walked the pattern, igniting the signal fires. It was amazing to me how quickly the fires caught and blazed.

"I always add a dash of Semtech and aviation petrol as a primer; it burns like Billy-ho, even in a downpour. The field isn't much scorched either. It means I don't have to sacrifice one ounce of our precious Sljvovica for the cause of freedom." Rolly could never be accused of taking himself seriously, only his mission.

"Rolly, I know agents have used Semtech to boil water in the field, but isn't this pushing your luck?" It was slow to ignite, but yielded an intense heat.

"I'm still here, with ten fingers and toes at last count which is more than I can say for some poor devils who handled dynamite with kid gloves in the mines up where I come from. No need to worry and, if you can be bothered to read the instructions on the box, perfectly safe, Joe. Right then, let's keep our eyes peeled."

Sergeant Scott called, "Captain Young!" He pointed toward the northwest. I checked my Bulova. It was exactly 9:59. Peering into the overcast sky, I could see nothing. Then, I heard the now very familiar drone of aircraft engines. Rolly pointed up. I could barely distinguish the grey, ghostly silhouette of a Dakota, emerging from the cloud cover. We stood up and waited while Scott engaged the pilot in the SOE air to ground verification protocol. Within seconds, Rolly called "He likes what he sees. All clear for landing! Dampen your fires, gentlemen. Quickly, quickly please. Bari says *Herr Focke-Wulf* is hungry tonight!"

Three Partisans scurried around hastily banking the signal pyres. The Dakota came down swiftly, its engines shutting down precisely when its brakes were fully locked. Makeshift chocks were jammed under the wheels. Six Partisans, who had been appointed with the task of unloading the DC3, opened the transport's hatch door, and with clockwork precision, in two teams, wrestled the heavy supply crates and canisters onto waiting horse carts. The pilot walked over to speak with Rolly who introduced him to me. He was the American flier who had dropped Stirling in here. As we were talking, a 'wagon train' of six horse-drawn conveyances bearing wounded Partisans materialised from the woods, at the edge of the field.

"Where in the hell did they come from?" I asked.

"The father of us all, Josef Tito", replied Rolly. "It's all part of the plan to get the Chief's 'thumbs up' for your flight. Heaven knows these poor devils need proper medical attention. There were several skirmishes in the last week while you and Mike were in God's country. Nothing close to us, fortunately."

"You'll be a bit cramped, Lieutenant" advised the pilot. "Sorry that the seats have been yanked out, fellas. I'll do my best to get you back safely and as quickly as I can manage. We're off in less than five minutes." He went over to supervise the loading of the remaining wounded.

Forty-eight of the fifty-two persons aboard were Tito Partisans, including their women and children. All of the men and some of the women were wounded; the most serious cases were loaded into the hold on makeshift stretchers. In a remarkably short time, the hatch was shut, the chocks pulled away and the aircraft was being turned around by a Partisan ground crew to face into the wind. Mike and I barely had time to thank Rolly for his leadership, good counsel and hospitality before bolting to board the plane, its twin engines were revving up for take off. As the pilot had said, all of the Dakota's passenger seats had been removed. We settled in as comfortably as we could manage on the floor of the fuselage among our less fortunate companions. To my surprise, two pilots, apparently British and unwounded, were sitting across from us. We shouted to them but the din of the engines, combined with the sounds and stench of the wounded, stifled any attempt at conversation.

Despite Bari's warning about ravenous Luftwaffe pilots, the flight was uneventful. Inside Brindisi airport, Captain John Coates introduced himself. "About time, you two! I was going to leave without you! I'm delighted you're here." I watched as three Warrant Officers escorted the two British fliers hurriedly past us into a back room.

"What's up with those two?" Mike asked. "D &D? Drunk and disorderly in Titoland? It's the rubber hose treatment for them, eh Sir?"

"Not at all Lieutenant. RAF escapers, without papers. Just a routine check. There are a few missing details to be followed up with Rolly in Yugo," John clarified.

I thought of Stirling's hard-nosed approach with Sam and hoped that if the two airmen were legitimate, everything would soon be 'okey dokey' for them. John, anxious to bring us up to speed, hurried us outside to his waiting car where we saw a stream of military ambulances loading the wounded Partisans.

At the barracks, Mike and I signed for our room key, stowed our luggage, then locked up and went to John's quarters across the hall. He produced three large gin and bitters and Mike and I began to talk, all at once. John listened politely as we babbled on about our Yugoslav woes. After two minutes, he interrupted.

"Joe. Mike. Time, gentlemen, please! I received a full report from Captain Young while you were *en route*. He omitted the naughty bits, you'll be pleased to know, so it's a short story."

I blushed.

"Our detailed business can wait

until our briefing at eight tomorrow morning. Now, tell me your impressions of Captain Young's operation at 6th Corps. The word is that the Partisans worship him." We chatted while finishing our drinks, then departed with a promise meet him in the mess at 7:00, sharp.

The two British airmen were loading up their trays. Their credentials had been vetted and verified and they were hoping to return to duty, they said, pending the arrival of replacement documents. We wished one another the best of luck.

Our DIBBLER status briefing with Captain Coates was lengthy, detailed, and extremely well presented. SOE had ordained an exact time frame; we would go within forty-eight hours, or not at all. John had planned the mission on the premise that we would be dropped into Hungary *cold*, that is, without a pre-arranged contact with Partisan liaisons on the ground. Our communications security procedures required close examination. Gus (Bertrand) was safe there, or so we hoped, and should have been in close contact with a Yugoslav Partisan network in Hungary, but John had worked out DIBBLER on the assumption that we would be fending for ourselves until we located Gus. The earlier DEERHURST communications *snafu* between Gus and Mike had raised serious doubts about Gus' status. He was still actively transmitting wires, but they were being treated as 'not above suspicion'. John and I decided to arrange our own set of passwords and security arrangements by W/T through the Partisans to cover us after we arrived. Thus, our drop would be *almost*, but not entirely cold, as there would not be a welcoming party physically on hand to meet us. When we had finished the four hour meeting it was clear that John's preparations were so thorough that there was little left for Mike and me to look after, except to help John check each item and stow our supplies and equipment in the three drop canisters.

I was appointed mission banker, along with my W/T duties. I decided to keep the gold coins, my B Mark I radio, and its crystals in my knapsack for security and immediate access. The coins, in a drawstring brown leather sack like a highwayman's booty bag, consisted of 200 gold Napoleons, valued at over $50 apiece. They would be safer to circulate than American eagles. I sewed several gold napoleons, two thousand dollars' worth of Hungarian paper *pengös*, and two hundred American dollars into the lining of my jacket. Combined with the remaining Drava stash, our net worth was well over $15,000. We studied maps and aerial photos of the area around Orfu, close to Pécs, where Gus was presumably located in a Partisan safe house. After much discussion and scrutiny of Divider air photos, we chose our drop point in a hilly sector of the fields near the small hamlet of Orfu. I had left

Hungary when I was eight, so it was almost a foreign country to me now, but Mike said it felt that he was returning home, even though he had been away for much longer, almost twenty years.

My duties as DIBBLER W/T operator meant that I had new codes to learn. I added a secret verse from a Hungarian *csardas* (*Az a sep akinek a semme kek, akinek a semme kek*) for my amusement. John had requisitioned a newer, larger and more powerful B Mark II wireless set, which I carefully packed on top of the supplies in the main canister to prevent it from being damaged. After I had sewn three silk-square codes and two one-time pads into another part of my jacket lining, I felt ready to push off at a moment's notice.

In our brief time together at Brindisi, I found out, although not from John, that he was a graduate of Cambridge University and a noted scholar of linguistics, fluent in both high and low German, with 'native-like' ability in Italian, French and Russian. Thus, it wasn't a great surprise when he addressed me in Hungarian as we were completing preparations, and we carried on a limited conversation. I liked him, admired his gentlemanly erudition, and respected him as a thoroughly professional officer. Mike and I agreed that John was not only a great companion, but would definitely be more than capable of leading Mission DIBBLER.

At last, our time had arrived. We took off from Brindisi in an RAF/ Special Operations Halifax bomber, on September 13, an overcast, moonless evening, the type so beloved of SOE, for obvious reasons. Our supplies had been stowed aboard in the three large canisters; each measured one cubic meter. The inventory was minimal, as agreed upon by John, Mike, and me, to provide us with enough equipment, munitions, weapons, and provisions to establish a base camp, to be supplemented with subsequent drops. The pilot, a friendly chap sporting a bushy RAF-style 'handlebar' moustache, invited us to visit him and the navigator in the cockpit. Mike and I let John do most of the talking about the details of our drop. This was merely a formality, I think, on the pilot's part, to satisfy our psychological need for assurance that all was going to go according to our plan. On the pilot's insistence, we each took turns briefly at the large bomber's control stick and pedals. Fortunately, we encountered no hostile Hun aircraft. As we approached the drop zone and began to lose altitude, John and the navigator had to interrupt their discussion of Italian grand opera to begin the approach for our drop. As this was a blind drop, by dead reckoning and without visual cues on the ground, the navigator's attention to his maps and instruments was critical to ensure that our position and altitude were, as he remarked, "...absolutely spot on."

Special Operations Halifax Bomber with RAF markings

After handshakes with our escorts, we three musketeers went aft to don our chutes; as I fastened my harness, I stared down through the open belly hatch. There were no flares or signal fires below to give us a sense of our altitude, only an utterly black space. My mouth felt hollow and parched; I had forgotten the brandy. The signal light flashed to steady green. John gave the thumbs up and jumped, followed by Mike, then me, as pre-planned. My free fall and controlled descent went beautifully, without swirling mountain gusts to upset my stability.

I landed on one side of a large hill, immediately removed my knapsack, then the chute, and bundled it up for a decent burial. There was no sign of my companions.

'*Simon says bury your chute. Okay, but where's the ruddy shovel?*' I hadn't packed a folding spade, because my heavily laden knapsack was brimming with other valuables. A small army spade was always attached to every canister; there were none in sight. The Halifax had dropped our supplies after we jumped, but I had no idea where to begin looking. The field was covered with recently mown hay stubble. On my hands and knees, I blindly groped around for a suitable burial place in the pitch dark, then decided that the treed area was a better starting point. Setting down my knapsack, with its precious contents, I walked down the hill. I quickly discovered a hole at the base of a large tree, stuffed the chute in, and covered the opening with leaves, branches, and other debris. To put off tracking dogs, I peed on the cache to erase my scent. I searched and listened for any signs of John and Mike. There were none. By now it was very late, and they had not responded to my SOS flashlight sig-

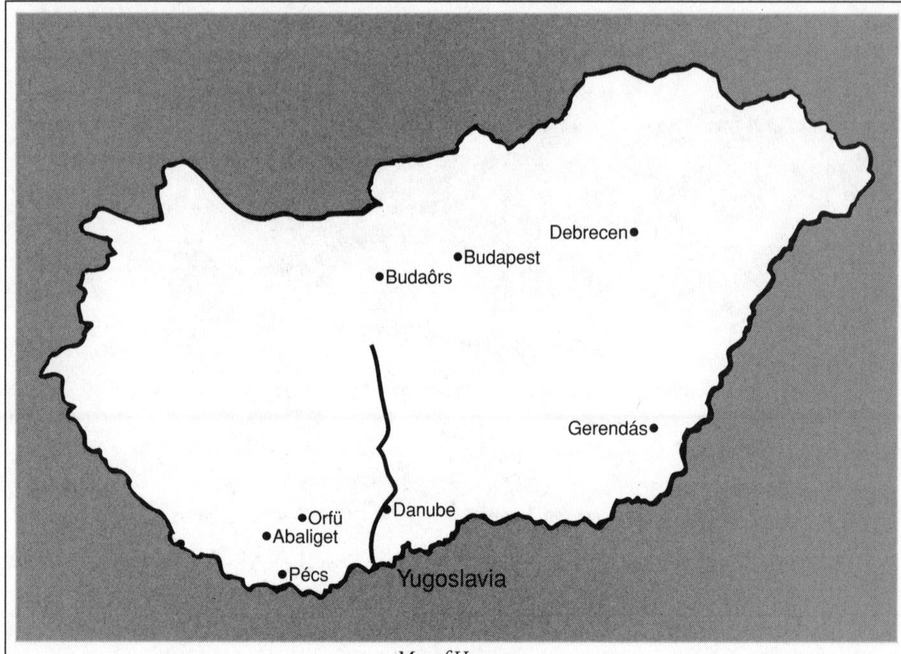

Map of Hungary

nals or shouts of 'DIBBLER!' Exhausted, disappointed, and very worried, I fell asleep under a tree.

The next day, September 14, dawned warm and sunny, a beautiful Hungarian late summer morning. I reckoned that it would be best to get organised and then spend the day searching for my partners. After a half-hour search, I found the main supply canister, removed the small shovel, and decided to bury my Mark 1 radio along with the crystals, and then the sack of gold napoleons separately. My plan was simple, based on the tales of buried treasure troves in *Pirates of the Spanish Main* that I had read as a little boy. I stripped to my waist, then using my 'base' tree as home, I carefully stepped off fifty paces in two directions, memorised the locations and placed markers on the ground just like Long John Silver, 'X marks the spot'. Then, at each marker, I dug a hole, and buried the articles. The radio was first. It was wrapped in cloth and protective oilskin, for just such an occasion. The gold coins were next. My next problem was to dispose of the mounds of soil that had accumulated. After more than two hours of sweaty labour, I had almost completed the job. Lying on my stomach to get the best perspective, with sweat stinging my eyes, I used my hands to sculpt and smooth the surface soil on each excavation to blend in with the surrounding earth, as best I could. For the closing ceremony, I peed on each burial place, to mask my spoor.

The canister was too large to

bury. I took out some packages of dry rations and then rolled it into a clump of bushes where I covered it well with foliage and branches to be retrieved in a day or two.

Dishevelled, unshaven, with my face and hair caked with dust, mud, and sweat, I lay down in the shade, tired and hungry, to rest for a moment. I thought of my old friend and master of disguise, Blokey, and hoped he was in a safer place than I.

Something awakened me with a start. Had I heard dogs yapping? A glance at my watch showed that I had slept for two hours. '*Yes, definitely they're dogs and dogs mean people. A search posse! Amscray, pronto! If John and Mike have been captured, the enemy must be sweeping the area looking for stragglers: me! I think we've jumped into a trap*'. Cautiously, I raised my head to look around for a better hiding place. It was foolhardy to expose myself to any passer-by, but to sit and wait to be caught was worse; it was suicidal. The barking and baying was fading into the distance. I waited for fifteen minutes, then decided to risk moving into the open. Belly close to the ground, I scuttled crabwise to a grove of birch and poplar trees, shinnied one, and when I had a secure foothold, scanned the surroundings. I was directly in line with, and could clearly see, the rustic little Abaliget train station. All was calm there; the stationmaster was sitting in the sun on the passenger bench, enjoying his newspaper and pipe. The immediate danger had passed as the 'dogs of war' were by now far in the distance and with them, I sincerely hoped, their two-legged companions.

I climbed down warily from my aerie and scampered over to the fast-flowing mountain creek, which rippled past my hiding place. The spring-fed water was clearer, colder, and more refreshing than any of the bottled brands that I have tasted ever since. I lay down on the bank and gratefully immersed my head. I took a long, luxuriant drink, then washed off the grime, and filled my plain metal flask.

Now, to find John and Mike. "DIBBLER! SOS! DIBBLER!" It was of no use and highly risky. I had to make a thorough ground search. For the next two hours, I scoured the area. I was completely baffled. If they had landed on the opposite side of the hill, surely we should have connected by now.

I made myself a roost in my perch, and nestled in, with my dry rations for comfort, for the second night. Awakening at dawn, it took a few seconds to orient myself to the reality that I was curled up snugly between the trunk and the limb of a tree, eight metres above the ground. It was misty, deathly quiet, and seemed a good time to descend and attend to my morning *toilette*. As I started to climb down, I stopped. I could distinctly hear the sounds of

Railroad station at Abaliget where my first interrogation took place

voices and yapping dogs, coming, very quickly, in my direction. Should I stay or make a run for it?

'*Get back up, silly bugger*' I heard Blokey saying. '*Stay stock-still and hope they pass you by. If they sight you, don't bolt. No heroic last stand. You won't have a snowball's chance if you run. 'Prisoner shot while attempting to escape'. Give yourself up calmly and count on using your wits.*' Swiftly, I went back up to the relative safety of my tree. My revolver holster was hanging on a branch; I reached for the strap and fastened it on. '*Die like an SOE agent, and take one or two of them with you.*'

The dogs, heading for the precise location of my tree were barking and howling, mad with the excitement of my scent. I estimated that there were at least eight hounds and forty armed men. The posse members were spread out, one metre apart, in a curved line, sweeping the field. The dogs had run ahead and were clustered at the base of my tree, jumping and snarling, in frantic attempts to scale the trunk. '*So this is what it meant to be treed by hounds.*' The search detail converged, shouting excitedly while a dozen stalwarts aimed their rifles up at me. They appeared to be a ragtag mix of *Honved*, the homeguard volunteer service, made up of WW1 veterans and men unable to qualify for army service. Some were wearing what appeared to be their uniforms from the 1914-1918 war, while others were in civilian garb. I was concerned that some of these old boys would be trigger-happy. Their leader, who appeared to be a young Gendarme, a civil police Lieutenant, called up to me, in English. "Throw down your weapons, then come down slowly and surrender. My men will not shoot if you do this!"

What choice did I have? Down went the gun holster, which the Lieutenant caught smartly. I had a knife, which I dropped as well. Perhaps fate had played a role in the fact that I didn't have a Fairbairn-Sykes dagger, which might have earned me a bullet at point blank range, in the nape of my neck. When I jumped the final metre to the ground, the officer gave a terse command to two guards who reined in the hounds, which up until then, had been voraciously sizing me up as kibble bits for breakfast. The lieutenant ordered me, in halting English, to put my hands on my head while two uniformed *Honved* regulars frisked me; a third and fourth trained their carbines squarely on my chest. My pockets were emptied. They didn't find the gold napoleons, paper money, or codes hidden in my jacket lining. One of the gun-toters, speaking in Hungarian, said quietly to his partner, "Shall I shoot him? My finger slipped, right? No questions?" I tried not to show a flicker of understanding.

"No, the Lieutenant wants to take him back for questioning, along with the Hungarian and English one. Maybe we'll shoot them after."

This was a break! John and Mike were alive, as was I, for the time being! My mind harkened back to my encounter with the captive parachutists in Italy. I hoped I could act as professionally as that German Captain had. They tied my hands tightly, but not brutally, with hemp rope, and escorted me the short distance over to the Abaliget train station, and into its gloomy, wood-panelled waiting room. It had the nostalgic aroma of my old Hungarian schoolhouse: fresh wax, old varnish, and carbolic acid. The stationmaster joined us, and, after a brief conversation with the Lieutenant, went over to his desk and picked up his telephone handset. The Lieutenant gestured that I sit down beside him on the hard, smooth wooden bench. He politely asked some routine questions in Hungarian. I looked at him blankly and shrugged. He repeated the queries in English. His troops were chatting quite excitedly about their 'catches,' discussing how to divvy up a triple-sized bounty payment for bringing in DIBBLER'S members, alive. He, in the striking navy blue Lieutenant's uniform of the Gendarmerie, pointed to the pips on my British Army jacket, "Lieutenant. English?"

I decided to come clean. "Yes, Lieutenant. British Army."

"You do not sound British."

"British Army, but Canadian."

He nodded. "Canada. Yes."

A grizzled *Honved* irregular, who had been shadowing me with his rifle, asked the Lieutenant for permission to speak with me, in English. "I lived in Canada, out west, in Saskatchewan. A hard life, wheat farming". I nodded that I understood him. "Many Hungarians lived there. No rain and dust storms meant no wheat, and no money. I came home in 1934. Very good people."

This unsolicited testimonial to our national character couldn't hurt my status as a Canadian PoW, if they bought it. I could sympathise with his leaving the hard scrabble prairies at the height or depth of the 'dirty thirties' dust bowl, as Dad might have done.

The Lieutenant was unfailingly polite throughout the interrogation, which seemed to have concluded more or less amicably, when we were interrupted by a loud commotion outside. The station's twin wooden doors swung open violently and a mass of perhaps thirty people pushed their way in, led by the stationmaster. This may have been the entire population of Abaliget. I was reminded of the scene where the enraged villagers confront Dr. Frankenstein's Monster. I, the foreign interloper in their homeland, was to be summarily weighed in the scales of mob justice by these incensed locals. Two brawny farm lads, standing at the high side window, were actually fashioning a running noose from hemp rope. The Lieutenant immediately ordered the *Honved* guards to shoo them out before, "He has no business being here! Hang the bastard!", and "String him up from the rafters!", translated into an impromptu, vigilante necktie party.

The *Honved* were experiencing considerable difficulty with crowd control and several shoving matches were underway. These villagers obviously scented blood: mine. Then the Lieutenant stepped onto the bench and fired his .38 service revolver into the ceiling. There was abrupt silence, except for the sudden mewling of an infant, perhaps startled by the gunshot.

"People! Settle down and listen to me. Now! I will arrest and fully prosecute anyone who attempts to interfere with my troopers or me in carrying out our duties. I am transporting this prisoner to Orfü for extensive questioning. He will be under close watch by security guards. It is my personal responsibility to ensure his arrival in Orfü, alive, which I fully intend to do. Kindly leave now, quietly! I thank you." He returned his revolver to its holster and remained standing, hands on hips, neither defiant nor arrogant, but in obvious control, while the rabble dispersed. He was an impressive piece of work; single-handedly, he had taken command and reversed a situation that was seriously career threatening to us both.

I thanked him. He bowed slight-

Orfű, where I was turned over to the Hungarian Second Buveau under Colonel Csongor

ly, like an actor receiving an impromptu accolade, and responded slowly, in English. "English I learned at the University in Budapest. It is still very difficult for me, so please excuse my errors. As you know, I am a Gendarme and must turn you over to our Intelligence Service, the Second Bureau. I am here unofficially. I am on a vacation leave in the area with my family when I was called up to command the militia. No one else of officer rank speaking English was available on…on short notice. I will report to the Bureau that you have been…co-operating. I will be with you for a short time in Orfű, and will do what I can for you there, but I want to go back and enjoy my new baby for a few more days. Good luck, Canada."

That resonated, but where had I heard it? The Horse Palace and the Bloody Sergeant! It seemed aeons ago.

As the last of the hangers-on were drifting out into the noontime sunlight, a dark blue sedan pulled up to the open entranceway. Two blue-uniformed members of the Hungarian Security Service, the Second Bureau, stepped inside. Thank God, they weren't *Gestapo*! After exchanging formalities with the Lieutenant, the guards led me out to the car with my wrists still bound, and pushed me to the middle of the rear seat. Each got in from opposite sides so that I was bracketed. The Lieutenant, as good as his word, joined us in the front passenger seat.

On September 15, 1944, we arrived at Orfü, where I was taken to Czvijak House, the Second Bureau's local HQ. As I entered the reception area, I was astonished to see John and Mike, in handcuffs, being escorted to the door of an interrogation room. John appeared to be in fairly good condition, but Mike seemed drawn and haggard. The jig was up. DIBBLER had obviously been fully compromised; how, by whom and to what extent I intended to find out.

A security police guard approached and ordered me, in English, to sit down on a bench. All of my training and common sense dictated that I must never let on to my captors that I understood and spoke Hungarian, under any circumstance. By this ploy, I planned to gain an 'edge' through hearing my interrogators' questions first in Magyar and then repeated in English by an interpreter. It might save my hide, if it worked as I hoped it would.

The valley of Orfü

The security guard stood in front of me and reached out his hands as if in mute supplication. I understood and raised my hands to him. He cut and removed the rope restraints with my confiscated knife! That was somehow symbolic, if only I could figure it out. Though loosely bound, the rough rope had severely chafed my wrists. I was silently celebrating my release from bondage but my freedom ended abruptly as he fastened police cuffs on my wrists and ratcheted them closed, tightly. I gasped at the shock of cold steel biting into my raw skin.

"Stand! Walk! Fast!" He took my arm and marched me down the hallway to an open door, across the hall from where John and Mike had gone. The room, barren except for a desk and five wooden chairs, was white, windowless, and illuminated by only one overhead bulb in a white enamel reflector. The door was slammed shut; a key turned in the lock. '*Shades of Interrogation Training Course 101, Beaulieu*!' Those SOE instructors had known what they were doing! At least in this mess, I was fully clothed, awake, focussed and the chair was wooden, not frigid metal. Unfortunately, this was not a rehearsal. As I waited for events to unfold, I tried to concentrate on my cover story.

After perhaps two hours had passed, the door was unlocked; the police Lieutenant from Abaliget and two officers of the security service entered and sat at the desk facing me, solemnly. The Lieutenant commenced the session in English. He led off as he had at Abaliget, with a reprise of my name, rank, and other particulars, in the classic opening of all military interrogations.

Replying politely, giving my ID as "Lieutenant Joseph Gordon, British Army; Canadian," I added, "As a regular army officer, I request that I be accorded treatment as a Prisoner of War, under the provisions of the Geneva Convention." The Lieutenant appeared unconcerned by my legalese as he translated for his colleagues.

The Bureau officers laughed heartily, as the Lieutenant responded, "You are not an officer, you're a damn British spy"! The Lieutenant repeated his opening questions, more forcefully, for effect.

I replied exactly as before. He seemed disappointed. A Bureau officer added in Hungarian, "We've heard this tripe from the others. He most assuredly is an Allied agent but will have to be made to admit it. We'll need Colonel Csongor's special expertise…and Imre his interpreter." He turned to the sergeant who was guarding the door "Go and ask for them both please."

"Kindly loosen those hand restraints on your way. We don't want Canada passing out" the Lieutenant interjected. The rest nodded, chuckling. I was relieved and grateful again to this man who so effortlessly integrated his chivalric code with the ethics of his profession.

While we waited for the 'expert' team to arrive, the panel quietly discussed the protocols under which my interrogation would proceed. I understood every word, thank God. It would turn nasty if I were evasive, hostile, or unforthcoming. The sergeant returned with the uniformed interpreter who seated himself beside the Lieutenant. A Security Service private and a corporal entered with two additional chairs, which they placed at either side of the desk. The corporal saluted and whispered to the Lieutenant, then he and the private exited, closing but not locking the door. Who was 'Csongor' and what was his special expertise? My Hungarian language heritage notwithstanding, I found the name 'Csongor' amusingly droll. I fantasised that he might suddenly materialise out of a cloud of smoke.

There was a lull, as we awaited Csongor's arrival. The Lieutenant took this time to review the background details of my case for the benefit of the earnest male interpreter. I surmised from his diminutive stature, banal appearance, and thick eyeglasses that he was a student conscript and then recalled that the loathsome Nazi Minister of Propaganda, Joseph Goebbels, held an accredited Ph.D. in Philosophy.

The Lieutenant briefed the interpreter telling him that Tito's courier organisation in the Pécs region had indeed been penetrated and thoroughly compromised. He described Bertrand's capture when he arrived at the 'safe' house, along with the Partisan courier, and confirmed that Gus was physically coerced into sending messages to Bari. Worse, Hungarian Counterintelligence had 'turned' Gus' radio and codes to intercept and decipher all of our W/T traffic with Bari, and had correctly deduced from our wires that we intended to drop into the Orfü area within a month of our Drava River fiasco. From time to time, they paused and looked at me directly as if sniffing for any scent of my understanding. It was extremely difficult not to betray my complete dismay as these shocking revelations were disclosed, all the while struggling to maintain my composure while feigning non-comprehension.

Neither German nor Hungarian Intelligence had been able to pinpoint our landing zone, a Bureau officer continued. Nonetheless, our Halifax was picked up on German radar screens well before we passed eastward over the Drava River and vectored us into Orfü airspace. German Intelligence immediately informed their Hungarian counterparts precisely where we had parachuted and 'the game was afoot'! We had indeed jumped blind, or, more exactly, blindly, into the waiting arms of that posse of superannuated scarecrows.

The door was flung open and the

room rose to attention. Hail the Mighty Csongor. The Lieutenant ordered that I also stand in the presence of Colonel Ference (Frank) Csongor, Hungarian Second Bureau. What a disappointment! Csongor the Great was an immaculately groomed, handsome, greying bureaucrat, in his mid-forties and of medium height and build, sporting conservative grey pinstripes and lustrous black patent shoes. His diamond-stud tiepin and massive cufflinks were the equivalent in value to the country's gross national product. His sidekick was a rather unlovely, pockmarked hulk, a Master Sergeant of the Bureau, carrying an ominous black leather case, similar to a medical doctor's satchel. I smelled trouble.

Csongor's opening questions, in English through the interpreter, ran according to interrogation routine, a recap of the Lieutenant's queries. He then tried again, without the interpreter, in Hungarian. I shook my head, feigning bewilderment. Not satisfied, he addressed me in Slav, of which I had a limited understanding, gained from my father. Again, I stared at him uncomprehendingly. For this, I received a boot in the shin of my right leg, from the 'sergeant doctor'. I shrugged as though it was beyond me to reply in a language of which I was ignorant. Another boot, this time for my insolence or ignorance, or both?

Now came German. "*Wo ist dein Funkgerät*?"

I thought it best to try to convince them that I had a minimal understanding, which was true, if it would prevent another application of the hobnailed boot. *Funkgerät* I knew was *radio*.

"*Ich habe kein Funkgerät.*"

This did not please Csongor, either grammatically or factually, who launched into a tirade that I could not follow, the gist seeming to be that they knew I had landed with one.

But I had two! If only they knew!

"Where have you hidden your codes?" he asked next, in German.

I responded with "*Keine codes*", which got me a laugh and another kick. He tried several more parries in German to which I answered *jawohl*, *nein*, or whatever came to mind, eliciting more laughter but no boots. I was obviously pathetically impoverished in *Deutsch*, and had overreached my limit.

The jousting was over. Colonel Ference Csongor picked up the black satchel and dumped its contents onto the desk, squarely in front of me. Like Galileo, brought before the Inquisition, I was being shown the instruments of torture, a strategy calculated to extract a confession by intimidation, then as now. Out tumbled a hand-cranked telephone magneto and a thick, rubber truncheon. The magneto had two long wires that ended in large alligator-jaw clips, attached to its terminals. As I looked on and speculated on my diminishing options, one of the soldiers unlaced my parachute boots and removed them, and my woollen socks. My chair was pulled away from the desk and a smaller chair, turned sideways, was placed about one-half metre in front. The interpreter ordered me to stretch out my legs with my calves on the seat of the far chair, so that my soles extended over its edge. My ankles were tightly lashed together with a long, rubber thong.

"Now, we'll start again. Why are you and your comrades here?" the interpreter repeated Csongor's words to me, in English. If ever I needed Blokey's wisdom, it was now!

I answered with name, rank and number. Csongor nodded to the 'doctor' who administered a stinging blow with the truncheon to the soles of my feet. I winced and bit my lower lip until it bled.

"Good, a very good warm-up," Csongor complemented the 'doctor' on his enthusiasm. "I want to get him to talk about radio procedures. First, ask him why he came here and keep at it, both of you, until I get the fully correct answer, which I already know."

I had little reason to doubt that he did. What a gift! I could 'listen in' before the bastard's questions were translated.

"Why did you come here, SOE Secret Agent Lieutenant Gordon: sabotage, assassination, or subversion? Answer!", the interpreter insisted.

I knew what to expect if I played dumb or stayed silent. To expedite my response, the doctor delivered a hard blow. I gasped and tried to draw up my knees, which earned me another great whack. If my feet had been thrust into boiling water the pain could not have been any more unpleasant; the after-effect was equally agonising, with lingering, throbbing waves and a burning sensation as if a thousand red hot needles were jabbed under the sensitive skin of each sole.

'*Time to talk, lad. Give him something to chew on, or it'll be a lot worse, but be economical with the truth.*' Blokey had come through, again.

"I was sent to meet with the Partisans in Hungary and help them resist the German occupation." Csongor grimaced, but didn't order a blow.

'*Good lad,*' whispered Blokey. '*There's a grain of truth in that and no harm done to John, Gus, or Mike. He resents the Germans for being here, pulling their* Übermensch *act on him night and day, and half wants to believe you. Keep it going, now.*'

The blessed St. Joan of Arc had been guided throughout her campaigns and trials by her 'voices', but ended up burned at the stake. Was she insane or divinely inspired? Was I insane or hallucinatory? Or both? Regardless, my dialogues with Blokey did give me confidence and a comforting forum for psychological second thought, debate, and counsel; so far, he hadn't misled me.

"What is your assignment?"

I had heard it coming, in Hungarian. "I am a British Army wireless radio operator."

"Why did they need you here? If the mission DIBBLER'S purpose was to liaise, we Hungarians have very competent radio operators. I believe you are a spy and will treat as such."

I protested that I was in a British uniform and ought to be treated as a PoW. He laughed and ignored my declaration.

"Where is your radio, then? Where are your crystals and codes? We're not stupid, Gordon. Did you bury them? If you did, the Lieutenant's men will find them all. A detail is out there at this moment, correct Lieutenant?" His next words were addressed to the Gendarme and not translated. "You should be with them to co-ordinate the search, Lieutenant, until my specialists have taken charge.

"Please accept my thanks for your fine work and give my very best to your lovely wife, your new baby and Chief Tamas! I will be telephoning him and sending a very favourable letter of commendation. You are dismissed, with my thanks and the gratitude of the Second Bureau, Lieutenant."

I thought I detected sympathy on the Lieutenant's aristocratic face as he squeezed past me.

"Where was your wireless training, Gordon?" continued Ference Csongor, without a pause.

"In England, sir."

"Where in England?"

'Don't mention Beaulieu, dear boy, the Führer's not a fan of 'gangster school' alumni. One way ticket to Prinz Albrecht Strasse to meet jolly what ho with Heinrich's [2] head office minions.'

"I'm a Canadian and really didn't get to know England very well in my short time there."

"Was it in the countryside or in a city?"

'Careful, Joe!'

"Kind of isolated, not close to much of anything, Colonel."

"Really! How quaint! Try again. Refresh his memory, Gregor, if you would, please." Gregor complied by applying his boot forcefully to my

[2] *Heinrich Himmler,* Reichsfuhrer-SS. *In 1936, Adolf Hitler appointed Himmler supreme head of all Nazi security and police services, including the KRIPO(criminal police), ORPO (civil police)* Gestapo *and* Sicherheitsdienst (SD) *security police. Secret Police HQ was located in Berlin, on Prinz Albrecht Strasse.*

right knee.

"Where did you and your chums go for fun?"

"Aberdeen, Colonel."

Gregor's knuckles rapped me soundly on the cheekbone.

"Scotland? I think not.

"I'm sorry, I just don't remember much about the location. It could have been somewhere in London," I replied, attempting to be vague and sound sincere, all at once.

"Ah, The Government Code and Cypher School, of course. Bletchley Park. I know Bletchley Park. Was that it?"

"Sounds familiar. It might have been sir. I'm just not sure."

"Bletchley Park, so that means that you must be a top dog wireless operator! I want you to show your expert skills by sending a signal to your HQ. We have one of your flimsy British Mark 1 radios next door, courtesy of your spy friend Zoltan. You don't know Zoltan, a.k.a. Bertrand? I'm sure that you must know Agent Bertrand."

How he loved to show off his knowledge: Mark 1, DIBBLER, Bletchley GC&CS, Zoltan/Bertrand. I was concerned that he might have already learned a great deal more from Gus.

"I'm sorry sir, I can't do that."

"Can't or won't?"

'Here it comes!' Doctor Gregor delivered three thumping blows to my throbbing feet. I could feel that the welts were wet. I tried to turn my soles inward to look for blood.

"Pay attention to me if you want to be able to walk upright to your own execution!" *'Not much motivation to sustain me.'*

"Can't...sir." The pain was so severe that I felt myself on the verge of nausea.

"Why not, Gordon? Have you forgotten how, since you landed? How inconvenient for you!" he laughed sardonically.

"I have no codes and the truth is, sir, there's no way to send to my HQ without them." That was weak. My jacket was lying in a heap on the floor. *'Please, don't let them search it!'*

"You are lying. All W/T operators have codes. Very well, you have forced me to be more persuasive." He turned to the 'doctor', "Gregor, I've had enough of this bastard's stalling. You two, unfasten his ankles. Remove his trousers and spread his legs; make sure you hold his knees apart."

'You knew this could happen, laddie. It was covered in your lectures by the Prof. and field vets. Doesn't make it feel any better, but others have survived it, and much worse. It's going to hurt like hell but

you'll live if you scream bloody blue blazes. Loudly! They don't want the truth. They already know the truth. He wants you to suffer. This villain's a sadist, a bully, maybe a psycho, and as vain as the Queen of Sheba into the bargain. Needs to be the master of any poor devil he can dominate. You're it. Loves to hurt, so give the audience what they paid to hear. You'll get through it and have many long years and babies, who, God willing, will look like their mother.'

"Gordon, you will be begging me to allow you to send a message before this day is out! Now, his feet!" His spoke matter-of-factly as if he had just audited my tax return and was describing the penalties to be assessed.

Gregor summoned the private to carry the magneto to the desk. As Gregor put on a pair of kid gloves from the satchel, the private carefully attached one of the two lead wires, with the giant-sized alligator clips to the side of each big toe. I thought I would literally 'go through the roof', as the metal fasteners bit into the skin. '*Dear Alexander Graham Bell, or was it that Hungarian tinkerer Nicola Tesla, why did you have to invent this infernal thing?*' I shut my eyes and tried to think of my lovely Helen's smile.

"Turn!" ordered Csongor. Gregor happily complied. I heard the mechanical whirring of internal gears and cogs as he rotated the hand crank. The charge of electricity that resulted seemed to ignite every neural pathway like a powder trail as it flashed up into my calves and crotch with white and blue flames. My legs thrashed in violent convulsions.

"Gregor doesn't like you, Gordon. Allied bombs annihilated his wife, two young children, and their grandparents in Budapest! I hand picked him for you. Again!"

This time, the gear's whining escalated rapidly in pitch as he cranked for vengeance. My legs were filled with flaming gasoline. I screamed.

"Stop! Give him water and pour the rest on his feet."

I heard the clink of glass against metal and the gushing of water being poured and I opened my right eye. The light was blinding. From a metal pitcher on the desk, the private was filling a drinking glass, the edge of which he thrust between my involuntarily clenched teeth and managed to half-empty the contents down my throat. With the dregs, he meticulously drenched each of my legs from toe to thigh.

"Feeling better? I hope you're refreshed because we're not through. When you're ready to stop playing hero and send the message, all of this will vanish, like waking from a bad dream, Gordon. Ready or not?"

"Not!" I barely managed to gasp it out, sputtering, recovering from the sudden, forced 'watering'.

"Oh, just so you know. You'll feel much more pain now. Water is such an excellent conductor."

'*Yes, Blokey, this is a first class, genuine bastard villain.*'

The interpreter's normal prison pallor was now suffused with a pale green patina, matching his bulging frog eyes.

"Again!" Now, thanks to the wonders of science, the pathway of agony was both inside my legs and like skittering lightning, dancing on my skin's surface. I screamed very loudly. Csongor held up his hand, like a traffic cop. He left the room. Within two minutes, he returned. Washroom break?

"You are a fool, a liar and a spy. Your partners in crime have just confessed to everything and we have located your radio and codes. Your civilian friend, Agent Thomas, is not doing well under our care. '*Mike had been caught in civilian clothes*!' He is also a Hungarian and is being treated as a traitor." He straightened his tie. "Will you send the message? Warm supper and sleep time. You must be exhausted, no?" he queried, buffing his immaculate cuticles on his suit jacket's sleeve.

I shook my head.

"Testacles!" he announced with finality.

'*Oh my God, is he going to castrate me?' Blokey, help me. Is this what you meant about babies? I didn't understand....*'

Mutt and Jeff guided Frog Eyes out of their field of operation. As Mutt removed each toe clip, he handed the copper wire to Jeff, whose gloved fingers delicately fastened the metal jaw clamp to the loose skin on the sides of my scrotum. I wondered if I would vomit and pass out simultaneously.

"Stand clear! Turn!"

Gregor was in his element, he was actually smiling as he leaned over the generator and powered the crank with joy and the volts jolted my manhood to eternal impotence, sterility, incontinence, and perhaps insanity. The agony, to use the term, was indescribably exquisite. I screamed as my body seized up, recoiled and I felt a hot wetness spurting over my loins. Perhaps I had exploded wide open.

"Clear of the puddle! Turn!"

He didn't mean me, only Mutt and Jeff. One of the goons had doused me with more water. My muscles spasmed, then locked in temporary rigor. I would have gladly denied the Lord thrice for a single moment's respite. I thought I would suffocate, or choke on the gorge rising in my gullet.

"Halt! Gregor, take a break while I try to reason with our Lieutenant." He was studiously polishing a green gemstone ring on his left pinkie, as he spoke, taking brief breaks to examine his handiwork.

"Listen to me. It is now evening and I am really quite tired of you. You have the night to consider whether your futile resistance is worth this discomfort or not. If you persist, so will the pain. The radio is ready at a moment's notice. Send the message and save yourself from days and weeks more of this. It will not stop until you co-operate, that I can promise you. Consider my words carefully, Gordon. You could be sleeping in a feather bed tonight in the most luxurious hotel suite in Pécs with the most voluptuous courtesan to service your every need. Or two, or three! Your choice: No radio? No nookie. Get him some food and lock him up, out of my sight!"

Was he serious? The concept of even one bedded courtesan, voluptuous or anaemic, was quite beyond me emotionally, intellectually, and most certainly, physically.

I cannot remember anything of that night or the next day, except that I was dragged to a basement cell, given my clothes, and collapsed onto the cot in my cell until a female guard awoke me the following afternoon. I ate the chunk of black bread with tasty and hearty cabbage soup and drank some green tea, then slipped out of consciousness for the duration of that day and night. Csongor did not call for me.

It was not until late in the afternoon of the following day that the numbness in my nether parts had begun to subside, to be replaced by a curious loss of feeling in my hands. I had tried to pick up the metal plate that the guard had placed on my cell floor only to have it tumble upside down in a soggy *lumpen* mass of soup and stale bread. I felt tears of frustration welling as I tried unsuccessfully to scoop up the remains, unable to cup my hands. I wept and cursed in rage at my own helplessness and slept fitfully that night on the cold, concrete floor.

In the morning, two guards awakened me, picked me up, and helped me stumble a short distance past two identical cells to an evil-smelling toilet and, when I had finished, stripped me of my clothes. One handed me a new bar of strong army soap and pointed to a shower stall. I was pleased to comply when he gestured that I enter. The water was lukewarm and wonderful: it was too difficult to hold onto the soap. The guards were quite amused at my clumsiness as I attempted to grasp the bar and repeatedly had to play 'chase the soap' as it slipped from my feeble hands onto the tile floor. Bending over was absolute misery, but I managed to inspect, lather and rinse all body parts gingerly and thoroughly. A fresh, rough army towel and clean, cotton prison coveralls completed the renewal process. I waddled back on the outsides of my soles, clutching my precious uniform, socks, and boots.

Back in my cell, the previous night's litter had been removed and replaced with a fresh bowl of warm soup and a large, ladle-like spoon. I ate greedily by holding the utensil with considerable difficulty in both hands and then lay down on the cot to consider my options, which evidently, were non-existent.

My reverie was rudely interrupted by Csongor's voice reverberating outside my cell door. He and Frog Eyes entered without the turnkey who was dismissed without ado, leaving the door open wide.

The Colonel's elegant, casual worsted wardrobe was undoubtedly contrived to remind me of a life that once I led and to which I must now earnestly aspire. However, the redolence of his expensive cologne, in combination with the carefully swept back, coifed hairdo (or was it a wig?) depicted the perfect pimp, hitman or habitué of that well-known upscale Budapest bordello. He began expansively, through Frog Eyes, "Well, Gordon. I see you've been sanitised and fed. Your hands, a little weak are they? Soon better, if you decide to be reasonable. I really don't expect that much. You won't be betraying you country. No, no! A little give by you here, a lot by me there. *Quid pro quo*. What do you say?"

I wanted to say that he was a smarmy bastard. "Sir, I'm a prisoner of war and I resent your mistreatment of my friends and myself!"

"Indeed, indeed. Come into my country by stealth, to overthrow the regime and expect to be treated like a tourist? You and your so-called friends are subversives, spies, British Secret Agents and that makes you immune from the Geneva rules, which we honour and follow to the letter with legitimate prisoners of war. I could shoot you right here as we talk and never lose a moment's sleep."

"Fine then. Shoot me. I am not a spy. You will be committing murder…."

"Shut up, you insolent bastard. I will see you upstairs."

He did and it was a replay of the electric circus, though briefer. I did receive one viciously large jolt when he informed me that I would actually be helping the Allies by sending a W/T message. My response was "Bullshit!" Frog Eye's skills were not required. Gregor cranked so vigorously that the wooden handle cracked and splintered and I feared that he might pick up the generator and use it to cave in my skull.

Ference was becoming bored with me or had a better place to be. The session was terminated, which visibly frustrated Gregor, who had added a replacement magneto as 'backup' to the tools in his kit bag.

Numb, I stumbled to my cell on infected, swollen feet, my eyes unable to focus except to register a jumble of intense white-hot halos radiating from the dim bulbs of the corridor's high overhead fixtures. With a migraine the size of Alberta, I attempted to sleep, squirming and turning in a thousand positions to ease the throbbing, aching waves, which overwhelmed me. Several times I awoke, my hands clenched so tightly over my eyes that my palms bled where my nails had made half-moon incisions. My dreams were a phantasmagoria of faces, falling through space. Csongor, the red-robed, hooded chief inquisitor, lit the faggots bundled at my bound feet with a phallic cigar, held in delicately outstretched fingers, as I was consumed in hell fire, while Steve and Papuksi danced the Csardas around the flames, with a naked Elena, in celebration.

It was the morning of 18 September, the aged female warder informed me in Hungarian. I gave my usual shrug of ignorance. She persisted; perhaps I spoke Magyar in my sleep. Finally, she relented, and spoke English.

"Gather your belongings and be ready for transfer to Second Bureau Headquarters in Pécs." Good information, if not good news.

A pale, slim Bureau Lieutenant with an elegant tortoise-shell cigarette holder helped me into the rear seat, then recklessly drove four *Honved* guards and me on a breathtakingly wild Grand Prix road circuit through the spectacular hilly countryside from Orfü to Pécs. Though my hands were tightly trussed, I was swaying on the hilly curves and just able to turn enough to see through the rear window the two similar vehicles in close pursuit. Were John and Mike coming along for the ride?

I was confident that I was young and healthy enough to withstand Csongor's torments and I resolved to be brave, to survive by whatever means I could muster from my training, short of co-operation with him, Heinrich Himmler or Jack the devil, for that matter. Feeling at peace with my decision, I smiled for the first time in four long days. The cavalcade stopped at a high, badly rusted metal gate to which was affixed a large red and white wooden sign announcing that we were about to enter the HQ, IV Hungarian Army Corps. The duty corporal saluted our dashing Lieutenant driver and raised the barricade. Standing there on the porch of a green wooden barracks, in all his glory, was Colonel Ference Csongor, Commander, Second Bureau District Pécs, in full dress uniform, waiting to receive us into his majestic presence. The fat lady had not sung, it was only the end of Act One.

CHAPTER 5
Colonel Csongor

Ference Csongor, resplendent in azure-blue Second Bureau Colonel's uniform, was prepared to receive us. The three immaculate limousines, in matching blue, were drawn up in military fashion, precisely ten metres apart. On his command, a formation of six Bureau warrant officers goose-stepped forward, then broke off into pairs to open the right rear doors of each vehicle with precision timing, and took us, the enemies of the state, into their custody. I was impressed. As I got out, I could see John and Mike emerging stiffly from the second and third cars. We all squinted at the glorious sun. I willed John to look at me and fancied that we exchanged furtive glances of mutual support. Mike was putting up a brave front, but his handsome face looked as though he had just gone ten rounds in the ring…and lost. His two escorts were half carrying, half dragging him.

'I have to find a way get him to hospital. I need to find just one guard here who I can bribe, even if it takes all of the money'.

With an imperial sweep of his hand, Colonel Csongor directed our warders to deliver us to a large army barracks building. A *Honved* guard later told me that the army had abandoned the base as obsolete, after World War I. It had been mothballed and lay dormant until the Bureau decided, in 1938, that it needed a branch office in the Pécs military district. The ramshackle structures were converted into an administration centre with separate confinement facilities for civilian and military detainees, serving as a penal halfway house for prisoners *en route* to Budapest.

John, Mike, and I were locked up in separate cells on the military side. I occupied myself that day in rookie prisoner fashion, by pacing my cell to measure my new living space, then dozing, and gazing absently out of my triple-barred rear window. It was uplifting to see the plot of green grass, which segregated our block from the civilian section behind. A mid-afternoon meal of salami with coarse but good-tasting peasant bread and lukewarm ersatz coffee was delivered at about 4:00. I counted my blessings, that my watch, money, and codes had not been confiscated.

The decent food and the wild ride from Orfu had made me quite drowsy and I drifted off. I awoke abruptly, in a cold sweat; it was pitch dark. Loud, piercing wails punctured the night, mixed with pitiful female screams, sobbing, and pleadings in Hungarian. Harsh male voices and the sound of blows responded. I knelt on my straw mattress to look out the window. The appalling noises were coming from the row of civilian cells behind. The shrieks and guttural, strident commands continued intermittently for hours; I tried to blot out the dreadful noises and the terrible visions that swirled inside my head. Sleep was futile; it was a night in hell. I lay awake, wide-eyed, twitching with every heart-wrenching cry.

The next day, September 19, was, by contrast, sunny, agreeably warm, quiet, and trauma-free. The horrors of the previous night had evaporated to be replaced by muffled shouts of command and crisp, unison responses in Magyar, drifting perhaps from a distant drill ground. There were no meetings, no beatings and the two meals provided were likely better fare than most Hungarian troops could scrounge in the field. I had overheard two *Honved* warders expressing their hope that Hungary's Regent, Admiral Horthy, would soon declare an armistice with the Allies. The majority of Hungarians were 'fed up to the teeth' with their country's involvement in a war that wasn't winnable, the men said.

Entering Pécs

"Hey, look over here! Hey, you there! Hey, you, look here! More to your right!"

I was staring abstractedly from my window at the sunlit tract of grass, while imagining a luxuriously leisurely 'bird and bottle' picnic with Elena. A deep, male voice was shouting at me, in Magyar. What in the name of heaven was going on? I looked behind, over to the far right, and tracked the voice to a cell window across the little grassy quadrangle. A black man was waving what appeared to be a red shirt through his cell window bars to get my attention. I acknowledged him with several waves, but didn't call out. He replied with a 'thumbs up' and then vanished. This was my first experience of a Hungarian-speaking African.

September 20 began routinely at 7:00, with a metal cup of something resembling coffee - dark, but not unpleasantly bitter – along with slices of spicy kolbasz sausage and a crusty bread roll. I was eating contentedly and wondering how long Blokey and the rest of the Beaulieu Houdini's would have needed to break out of here, when the sounds of voices, footsteps, and jangling keys approached. My cell door creaked open. Csongor, with six of his finest, in their Bureau best, had come to inspect me. Which of them, I wondered, were the perpetrators of last night's ordeal for those hapless 'subjects'? My surge of rage turned almost immediately to bewilderment; a spectre, an unearthly reincarnation of the assassinated Archduke Franz Ferdinand of the Hapsburg dynasty's Austro-Hungarian Empire, in full dress pre-1914 uniform, complete with a jewel-encrusted metre long sabre scabbard, white ostrich-feathered field marshal's tricorn hat, endless swirls of gold braid, and bright regalia, had materialised outside my cell. The short and stocky apparition halted and apprised itself of me, with its monocled right eye. Its white-gloved right hand rested on the sabre hilt, while the other carefully groomed its bushy moustache.

The sergeant of the inspection party addressed me, in English, "The prisoner stands at attention and salutes the Commandant!"

'*Commandant! My god, is this the prison Commandant?* Was he one of the rapists, too?' I stood up at attention, to be compliant.

"Prisoner, salute the Commandant!"

'*Do anything to avoid staring at His Goofiness!*'

The sergeant was losing face and patience in front of Colonel Csongor and the visiting potentate. He took a step closer, "Prisoner, saaaaalute!" he bellowed in my face. Startled, I took a backward step. His breath was heavily laden with the pungent aroma of garlic and a recently-interrupted encounter with cheap Tokai.

I gazed intently at a minor discoloration in the crumbling brick wall across the hallway, for which discourtesy he delivered a sharp clip to the side of my head.

I was going to lose my composure. The notion of a dead emperor, visiting from the happy hunting grounds in the skies was overwhelmingly silly. Not only was this preposterous popinjay's garb sadly outdated, he was abnormally short and slightly cross-eyed, like a hybrid of the silent screen's Charley Chase and the irreverent Groucho Marx, cast as the addled Emperor of Lower Ruratavia.

Once more, with feeling, "Prisoner, salutes!"

The 'little emperor's' grip on his sabre's ornate hilt tightened as if he were about to withdraw the blade to split my skull like a coconut. Instead, he shook his head in disbelief or disgust at my *lèse majesté*, coughed delicately into a gloved hand, and wafted on, the gold filigreed tip of his sheath, clinking against every cell bar, as he proceeded, like a one-note xylophone. The eerie spell broken, I sensed that I had not won a friend. Csongor and gang peremptorily slammed and locked my door, with unpleasant muttering, and hastened to follow in the wake of his serene highness. This place was cuckoo land, ruled by a nut case, with a sadistic megalomaniac as chief enforcer. I thought of the SOE 'head doctors' back at Beaulieu and the fertile subject matter that they were missing out on.

My insolence had acutely embarrassed Csongor. I was going to pay in 'spades', I was told, by the English-speaking *Honved* ex- Sakatchewan wheat farmer from Abaliget. That man, the toy Commandant, Sakatchewan explained, was directly responsible for each prisoner's rations and upkeep, so I had been doubly unwise to tweak the imperial nose. 'Sakatchewan' had applied to the Bureau for a transfer from Orfü to Pécs , he explained, as the prison kitchen here had a reputation of serving two solid 'squares' daily. 'Saskatchewan's,' name was Bela. He introduced his *Honved* comrade, Jozsi (Little Joe), who was also assigned to my section. Jozsi spoke a little English and less German. Nonetheless, we hit it off immediately; they deeply resented Colonel Csongor's arrogant contempt for the *Honved* volunteer militia and abhorred his callous brutality, which seemed even more vindictive and counter-productive in light of the growing unpopularity of Hungary's Axis alliance.

"Who was being abused my first night here? It sounded like women were being tortured out back."

"The Jewish and Gypsy women," Bela replied. "The Bureau keeps them here to clean their quarters. Csongor thinks it's good for the Bureau's morale to rape and abuse them, regardless of their physical condition or age. Two have died within three months. One was a grandma, older than me, and another, all of nineteen, was in her last month of pregnancy. It's disgusting. Csongor is

Remains of Pécs prison

worse than a common criminal: he's an educated monster. I am so ashamed to be here."

"I saw a black man across from here in the civilian wing, or was I dreaming?"

"No, not dreaming," said Bela. "That guy's name is Benjamin Lantos. He was picked up for selling American cigarettes to our soldiers. Can you imagine what a threat to our great leader Admiral Horthy's government that adds up to?"

"What will happen to him?"

Jozsi responded, "Not much. If he agrees to hand over most of his profits to Csongor, he will be beaten and then set free. If not, it might be not so good for him."

"Are there many Africans in Hungary?"

"Some, but not so many anymore."

"Please give Benjamin my best wishes." Sensing that I could trust these two worthies, I decided to make a small business proposition.

"Would you be willing to buy and smuggle…bring in fresh vegetables and any kind of fruit available, say, three times a week? Second, would you make sure that my comrades receive some, too? Of course I can pay you for your trouble and the risk."

"For sure!" volunteered Bela. "Jozsi and I are farm boys and know where to get the pick of the freshest produce, not that dried up *dreck* from the markets, and dirt cheap, too. We'll begin tomorrow morning, but we'll need a little start up cash before we go off shift at 6:00 tonight."

"One of you come by in a half-hour and I'll have it! But I need a large safety pin, please. See, I have this one to hold up my trousers but it's practically useless, it's almost bent out of shape."

Bela exploded in laughter. "Mr. Lady Killer! You wouldn't fit in too well in Regina, on a Saturday night, practically useless and bent out of shape!"

"It's the safety pin! My father was ready to head out on a train to Saskatchewan, but my uncle met him in Toronto and hijacked him to Welland, thank heavens!"

"If you have money, keep it well hidden, my friend. Csongor would be happy to find it, to prove that you are up to no good. But our lips our sealed, right Jozsi?"

"Right, brother Bela! Sealed so tight!"

I believed them, but I had no choice. Perhaps I had given away too much.

"Colonel Csongor, or as we sometimes call him, Vlad the Impaler,[1] would have you with a very long, dull stake, stuck up your rump, on the front grass, if he knew," added Bela.

"No thanks. But I thought Ference Csongor was a Hungarian name."

"There's no doubt of that. Old Vlad, the original devil, was either Hungarian or Rumanian, depending on which book you believe."

"Can you please tell me, how are my comrades? Have you been able to look in on them?"

"Captain John seems alright. Lieutenant Thomas, the Hungarian, is not doing so well. When he was caught, he was wearing street clothes for some strange reason. The third man, Bertrand, so we've heard, was also wearing civilian duds when he was picked up earlier in Pécs. He's also a Magyar, so the Bureau is trying to prove that they're both spies, and traitors. That means a trial and transport to Austria, maybe worse. In the meantime, Vlad's men are punishing

[1] *15th Century Prince Vlad Tepes of Wallachia, was also know as Dracula (literally, little devil). He gained legendary infamy for his exceptionally cruel, customary method of execution by impalement. Vlad's victims included thousands of his countrymen and women, and prisoners of war, especially Turks. His ancestry can be said to be Rumanian/Hungarian, because of the frequent disputes over the territories bordering both lands. His barbarous and depraved habits provided Bram Stoker the idea for his central character in the novel, Dracula. See websites, e.g. www.Dracula.com.*

them for their own amusement, beating the hell out of both of them nightly."

"And of course Csongor never dirties his own hands," Jozsi added as he set off. In less than five minutes, he was back with a large safety pin that he 'palmed' off through my cell bars into my waiting fingers.

I was truly blessed. I said a prayer for Gus[2] and Mike as I busied myself, picking at the threads in the lining of my prized, stained army jacket, with the tip of the pin. Soon I had removed a small sum in pengös, and had refastened the lining. My codes and one time pads were intact. I gathered the loose material around my ever-thinning waist and jabbed in the new pin. At Camp X, our Instructor had used a manikin to demonstrate and then coached us until we each had perfected the fine art of killing a man with a hatpin. Who knew when I might get my chance with Csongor? When Bela came by with my supper, I slipped him some bills. Without a word or glance, he departed. I wondered if I had naively put my trust in a clever con game, orchestrated by Ference. But I had to trust someone.

My cell door opened the next morning and Bela came to my cot. "Good morning, Joe. Sssh! Here's the first instalment. Eat it all up quickly and I'll come back before seven and take away the evidence."

From under his jacket, he produced two carrots, an apple, a cluster of green grapes, and a clutch of dark burgundy cherries.

"Fresh picked. Eat the carrot greens first! They're very good for you, you know. Everything's been washed."

I think I tried to kiss his gnarled hand. "*Kosz-o-nom*. Thank you, Bela. And thank Joszi. How are the other two, John and Mike?"

"*Kosz-o-nom*! That's pretty good, Joe! *Kosz-o-nom*."

"*Kosz-o-nom*," I repeated slowly.

"Jozsi is looking in on Captain Coates now and I'll see to Mike. Put the core, pits and stems in a little pile right there," he said pointing to the corner where my cell door abutted the wall. I'll be back. Enjoy, my friend!"

"*Koszonom*!"

He smiled and winked, "That's it!"

I wouldn't look this gift horse in the mouth, and enjoyed the image of those two mischievous brigands, lurking and leaping fences as the twin midnight scourges of local vegetable patches and orchards. I hoped that Bela and Jozsi were hoarding every pengö that I had given them. It was the best investment in people I had

[2] *I was never to see Gus again during the war. Mike had changed into civilian clothes after he landed near Orfü. John, however, wore his uniform, as I did.*

ever made, and was being returned one hundred-fold. Bela returned within the hour, with the regulation Pécs' prison breakfast.

"Eat up, Joe. Be hungry! They look for little signs like that, damn those devils! By the way, John and Mike were very happy and send you their best wishes." He reached down and scooped up the little mound of refuse from my high-vitamin binge, then as he straightened up confided, "Not to scare you witless, young fellow, but you're on Lord Csongor's list today. It's posted on the Orders of the Day Sheet, which I'm not allowed to see. Try not to piss him off again, old friend.

"Your breath is horrible. Here, chew this. It's an herb my mother used to give us to clean our teeth and sweeten our mouth. I'll look in on you later. God bless, Jozsi!"

With Bela's departure, fear returned like a rat, gnawing at my intestines. My resolve to survive by giving Csongor true but non-essential information buoyed me for the ordeal to come.

The interrogation room was bright, spacious, functional, and well equipped. I was reminded of the high-ceilinged physics laboratory in my Toronto high school, right down to the potted, wilting red geraniums on the windowsill. Four long counters, with immaculately white porcelain sinks and shining chromed fixtures lining either side, ran the length of the room. Glass-front storage cupboards on the walls were filled with neat rows of specimen jars. If they contained body parts, as I suspected, the sepia fluids inside mercifully obscured them. On one side wall, there was a larger than life-sized coloured chart graphically depicting a dissected human cadaver's nervous system. An imposingly large poster adorned the front wall, with Hungary's great patriotic leader, Admiral Horthy, in a winged helmet with sword aloft, heroically repelling the foe.

The instruments of torture were arrayed in groupings, by type, on the front counter. They resembled the sort of harmless apparatus our teacher would have laid out for investigations into simple machines: levers, forces, and, for enrichment, electrical energy. Dental and fingernail extractions were available options, for extra credit. There was even a tall green metal cylinder marked *Oxygen*, complete with a rubber facemask, close by, just in case. If this display were calculated to terrify and intimidate me, to force a voluntary confession, it would easily have done so to Joe Gelleny. As Joseph Gordon, SOE, I had been thoroughly indoctrinated by lectures, films, and mock interrogations to do everything possible to resist giving in to my natural impulses, which the instructors, from Camp X to North Africa, had assured us, would quickly lead to our demise.

I was held down while my hands

were tied behind the chair by guards on either flank. Grand Inquisitor Csongor, Assistant Gregor and Interpreter Lieutenant Imre, a.k.a. Frog Eyes, entered from an anteroom. All were robed in the long, pristine white and starched laboratory coats of surgeons, dentists, and manicurists. Gregor fastidiously snapped each finger of his latex gloves, for my edification, as he pulled them on each hand. '*This boy definitely has a serious character flaw. I wonder if he drowned kittens in the Danube as a kid?*'

"This inquiry, number 0-33-51 is the first of a series, with the subject, prisoner Joseph Gordon, Special Operations Executive, Canadian. Commencing at 09:30 hours, September 21, 1944, at Second Bureau Command Head Quarters, Pécs," intoned Frog Eyes, to a sour-faced male clerk, who dutifully transcribed shorthand scribbles on a yellow notepad for posterity. It did not take a Bay Street lawyer to grasp that Csongor was preparing his case file.

'*The first of a series? A fresh start, for the official record. Orfü never happened? I guess it was just for fun, yours maybe, but certainly not mine. Ference, does your mother know what you do for a living?*'

Déjà vu! He began reviewing, in exacting detail, all of the material that had been extracted in Orfu about the mission and my role as DIBBLER'S W/T specialist. It seemed that he knew very little beyond this, which was a very good sign, indicating to me that John, Mike and I were collectively holding to the 'party line,' in best SOE fashion. It also meant, I thought, that they hadn't found my caches in the straw field. I was wrong.

"Your pathetic attempt to bury your supplies failed miserably, as I told you it would. We have had the containers in our possession for several days. The contents are at odds with your fairy tales."

I felt a cold chill. '*But not the radios, please, God!*'

He gloated, "It is difficult for me to believe that you and the other two came here simply to link up with Hungarian patriots. I am convinced that you were sent to carry out sabotage and cause maximum disruption to our country's communications and rail systems. Your weapons and explosives are *prima facia* evidence of that. Agents Bertrand and Thomas, who by the way is a civilian, are both Hungarian nationals. Thomas has confessed it all, in a selfish, but wise attempt to gain clemency. He is not only a spy, he is also a traitor to Hungary and to you. Your commander John Coates has verified all of the information. All four of you are Allied secret agents, *de facto*. We'll return to this later."

My memory of one year's worth of high school Latin was spotty, but I recognised that Csongor was grandstanding, for future consideration.

"Now, I want an explanation for your performance!"

'What *performance*?' I was receiving this act double-barrelled, in Magyar and English, but still couldn't decipher his point. It was critical that I take my time, so as not to tip them off to my knowledge of Magyar. "By performance, what do you mean, Colonel"?

"Teach him some respect, Gregor!"

It was a struggle not to wince.

Gregor, evidently delighted to be unleashed on me again, swung his truncheon lustily twice against my soles, which had been improving incrementally in his absence. This would not help. '*So that was it! Respect! Respect for the comic book commandant!*'

"You showed flagrant disrespect for our commanding officer. That is insubordination, an offence in any army's code of conduct, is it not?"

'*How would you know anything about any army? And speaking of behaviour, yours comes straight from the cave!* '

"Colonel Csongor, I did show respect. I stood at attention for the entire time he was inspecting me."

"You were, not unreasonably I think, expected to salute the Colonel, to acknowledge his position and rank. But you refused! Are you his better, Mr. Canadian? Did he amuse you? What excuse can you possibly offer me?" He rose from his cushioned, wooden armchair.

"Sir, he did not appear to be an officer of any corps or regiment to which I owe any allegiance. That's all. It was not intended to be personal."

"Would you salute me? I am also a Colonel?"

"I would!" '*What* was *I saying*?' "But, I'd also salute Adolf Hitler while introducing him to the devil in Hell!" '*I had mangled that quotation. Was it by Winston Churchill?*'

My impertinence earned my tender soles four swift, heavy blows and Gregor's elbow jabbed up, under my chin, for good measure.

'*Enough, laddie. You've shown you have backbone. He has no sense of humour and more defiance will get you a wooden overcoat. Start thinking about John and Mike. They need you to calm down and think like a trained agent. They're trying their best, too. You're all doing well; he's getting nothing of any value at all. Now, I don't want to hear any more of this nonsense. D'you hear me? Use your common sense. One more crack like that and he'll dump you all in a concentration camp, if you're lucky. He caught proper hell from Budapest because of you and wants his pound of flesh. Straighten out the attitude and I mean, now, soldier!*'

"I apologise, Sir. I was wrong.

But I could think more clearly if your assistant would stop beating and abusing my friends and me. It does confuse my mind."

"Stop the session! Note: taking a recess. Record the time. Everyone out!" He stormed into his sanctum. The walls reverberated when he slammed his door.

'*Everyone out but me.*' My shoulders were aching from having been stretched unnaturally in this position for hours. I looked around the room for an avenue of escape. The window was not high, but was triple barred and locked. There was no sense in even considering a breakout until I could work out a plan with Mike and John. The three musketeers were in this together and, for now, would stay together. I had great faith that our chance would come, but not yet. A white-haired *Honved* guard had been posted to watch me, in case I made a bid for freedom, unlikely as that was. I was tied to the chair. Instead, I fell asleep.

When I awoke it was twilight. Csongor was bending over, hands on his hips, glaring at me. How very ordinary he looked…no fangs, no odour of sulphur, and no mark of Satan on his forehead; his was the feral joy of inflicting suffering, in the name of the state, without a shred of remorse. He was the perfect executioner.

"I want you to tell me all about your wireless training, Gordon. From the beginning, please." The sourpuss clerk stenographer arranged his pencils and whisked some eraser shreds from the page, waiting expectantly for me to spill my guts.

"Very well. As I…." and I told the same story, as at Orfü, without mentioning Bletchley. It was almost all a crock, but better than nothing or the insolent wisecracks which tended to get his back up.

"That is not good enough. Many details have been left out, purposely, and I was not fooled by your apology. This is not the type of cooperation I would expect from a man whose life is in the balance. Leniency is denied to those who refuse to see the error of their ways. Gregor will take over." Lieutenant Imre Frog Eyes blinked rapidly while conveying this notice. Was he excited or repelled by Csongor's sadism? Perhaps both, or…?

Gregor and his henchmen stripped me to my skivvies and hooked up a trusty new, fresh out of the box, hand magneto. The Hungarian Second Bureau seemed so enamoured of this infernal device that it might well have been incorporated into their coat of arms.

The old waves of indescribable agony pierced my manhood. I screamed as the lightning bolt struck, repeatedly. Gregor paid no attention and cranked harder and longer. I wet myself and tried vainly to rise from the chair, to tear my body away from the machine's torment. The liquid only served to quadruple the power of the electrical current searing my neurons. Would I be cooked from the inside out, smoke pouring from my eyes and ears, like a condemned murderer in the electric chair?

It stopped. But Gregor, the son of a bitch, gave the crank one mighty turn and a horrible jolt of pain shot through like a current of acid, into every joint and artery. "Where were you trained?" demanded Csongor's disembodied voice.

"In England, partly!"

"Were you trained at Bletchley Park?"

"At Squirrels!" I blurted out. '*Maybe he'll think I've finally snapped my twig*!'

"Squirrels? Where the hell is 'Squirrels'? Take this crazy bastard back to his cell. He's out of his mind."

The Bureau goons, Mutt and Jeff, dragged me to my cell and threw me like a sack of coal onto my cot. I buried my face in the pillow, unable to move or think. Fatigue and stress overwhelmed my pain and I blacked out. I woke up, believing I was drowning. In the pitch-blackness, Jozsi was wiping my face with a wet, cold cloth. When he had finished, he applied it gently to my soles. The effect was heavenly. When he stood up to go, I reached for his arm to get support, in an attempt to sit up. There was nothing there. The room was spinning wildly, and I fell back.

"Your fresh fruit is tucked under the cot. Eat it slowly. It will refresh and strengthen you. Bela will be by to clean up. Sleep now, Joe."

"Jozsi, is that you? You shouldn't be here, but thank God you are."

"Good night. Don't let the bedbugs bite!"

I blindly grasped on the floor underneath my bed. My hand found a package. It was a small paper bag, containing juicy pears and plums.

I sank into oblivion until Bela came on duty.

"Bela, was Jozsi here last night?"

"No, he left at 6: 00 p.m. to visit his daughter and son-in-law at Mohacs. They just had a baby boy. He's a proud grandfather, for the eighth time! He'll be back for duty tonight. Why do you ask?"

"Oh, just a strange feeling, that's all. Bela, did you by any chance leave me some fruit yesterday?"

"Under the bed. John and Mike got theirs too. Hope you enjoyed it. Where's the trash?"

Despite the post-operative ache of the voltage overload and nasty claws in my groin, my immediate worry was that the backs of my hands were going numb again, as though they had been anaesthetised. Basic physiology told me that it was caused by involuntary muscle spasms, when I clenched my fists. I would try to resist, although it was, by definition, impossible to prevent involuntary contractions with such powerful lightning bolts coursing through my nervous system. I intended to go back to Canada capable of productive work, not as an invalid.

Csongor was not convinced by my one-liner mad act. Late on the following afternoon, September 22, he resumed his quest to coerce me into sending a wireless signal to HQ.

"You admitted in Orfu that you had been trained at Bletchley, England. Look carefully at this photograph; is it familiar?"

My hands were trembling and so feeble, that the photo fluttered out of my fingers. Dependable Gregor retrieved and held it for show and tell.

"Yes, yes, it's familiar."

"And?"

"It looks like a place I was trained, Sir."

"Listen you oaf. Is it Bletchley Park?"

"Possibly, but it could be Buckingham Palace, too. Very possibly Bletchley." I was playing with fire, or electricity, but what the hell. He was such a creep and seemed to be under considerable pressure to have me perform. I was young, still fit and could resist a little longer, but had no illusions. I knew that he could break me eventually, but I would not go gracefully. The Bletchley W/T instructors had taught us how to fiddle a radio's settings so that it would not transmit properly, if it came to 'a gun at my head' showdown. I was not a hero, but I owed it to John, Mike, and Gus to stall, to buy as much time as I could. I was their DIBBLER conduit, the slender W/T link with the outside world. By my upbringing, I detested and was taught to stand up to all abusive, arrogant authoritarianism, whether a snarling streetcar conductor, a tyrannical cop, a schoolyard bully, or creatures that rape and murder women in the night. And I had no L-pill to bail me out.[3]

"This one. Is it familiar?"

"Yes, I'd say so." I was so tired and drained that I had no idea if it was an SOE base or the Leaning Tower of Pisa.

"Is it your parachute training base, Altricham, near Manchester?"

"Quite likely, yes."

"'Quite likely!'" he repeated, with disdain.

"Colonel, I am being truthful. It is difficult, because in many cases I spent little time outside of a barracks in these places, like any soldier."

"You want to play 'cat and mouse' games, still? You are such a

[3] *I had thrown mine away at Brindisi.*

fool. Your friends have taken the sensible route and have told us everything. They're resting comfortably right now. Probably showering and shaving. Look at you. You're a disgrace. And you are holding out, for what? Your pride? Your country? SOE and England don't give a damn about you. Do you really think your fat bosses in London give a damn whether you co-operate now or next week? They've already written you off. You're a zero to them, disposable…expendable, like their promises.

"Do you perform this way because you despise me, Lieutenant? It really means nothing, nothing at all." He lowered his voice to a near whisper, appealing to my reason.

"Be sensible and make the transmissions to Bari and to Papuk, Gordon. It's simple, painless and gets me out of your life. You'd like that now, wouldn't you? It's not worth anything, except more pain, if you are so stupid and pig-headed to continue resisting. No glory just to be aggravating. I'm ready to turn you over to the Germans and disown you all. But, I can also release you, just like that, with safe passage back into Yugoslavia. I do have that power…guaranteed no tricks. You'd be free as the birds to run riot in Bari, just like before.

'Before? A lucky guess, or…?'

"Colonel, are you willing to say that with Mike and John here? And Zoltan, what about him?"

He was silent, for a moment. "No, freedom only for you and your Captain Coates. But Agents Thomas and Zoltan/Bertrand will each receive a fair trial, in Budapest, not in Germany, although Zoltan is out of my jurisdiction. However, I would not recommend the death penalty for either one, in my report. This is my final offer. Take it and show your good faith by sending the transmissions tonight. I'll begin preparing your conveyance documents immediately."

'He's lying, laddie! Do not do it! Then, you will have no chips left. John has told him nothing. Use your wits and stall!'

He directed the Bureau goons, Mutt and Jeff, to help me stand up and walk a short distance down the hall to a small room that contained a long wooden table. In the centre there was a Mark I radio hooked up to wet cells. Perhaps it was Gus' set, but I was guessing. There were three chairs drawn up; soldiers with Signals service flashes on their epaulets occupied two of them, directly opposite one another. One wore the black shirt and uniform, with silver lapel insignia of the *SS*. His hat, which lay on the table, bore the death's head badge. The other man was Hungarian army. Both were wearing headsets as they turned to greet me with perfunctory smiles. They then re-directed their attention to a device the approximate size of my suitcase radio, with the top removed. It had two large metal wheels, which were slowly rotating. The manufacturer's name, *Telefunken*, was stamped on the faceplate. '*Quality German manufacturing, of course.*' Two wires were attached between the device and the Mark I. Was it a magneto, to shock me if I made an error? I was directed by Csongor to be seated on the chair in front of the radio. The conversation that was taking place in Hungarian behind me was enlightening and may have saved my life.

"When he transmits, we can make a wire recording of his key signature. When we have that, it's a straightforward matter to learn and perfect it, then we can duplicate his touch precisely. That's the beauty of this machine. Once it's recorded, he's no longer of any value. We'll have to sweat him another day or so to get his codes, first. Then we'll be chatting with his headquarters in Bari and they'll never know the difference. Imagine if they believe that he's operating. We'll be getting top level SOE traffic directly from the source! What a radio game that will be!"

Csongor addressed me. "Lieutenant Gordon. Please listen. The technicians assure me that this set will transmit. Just send a test signal to establish contact then I'll dictate the message." The two reels were turning slowly, as the slender, silver thread payed out, awaiting my signature.

"I don't think I can."

"Of course you can." He was being magnanimous, avuncular even, for his audience. "Send a transmission to Bari and tell them that you've been in hiding since you landed, and your radio was damaged when it was dropped. You're in a safe house and repairs have been made, from spare parts you found there. Do it, now. Your friends will thank you!"

"I do not have personal codes and Bari will not accept my transmission without them."

"Try. We'll see."

"No, it's useless to try. They're really far too clever to fall for that. It has been tried and has always failed."

"You're throwing away freedom for your friends, you short-sighted, selfish bastard!"

"Is that what you told the gypsy and Jewish women? 'Just be nice so me and the boys can have a party and then we'll let you all go free?'" Frog Eyes was obviously perturbed to have to relay this zinger. In his shoes, I would have tossed in, '*Please don't shoot the messenger, Colonel, but….*', for self-protection.

"Women, Gypsies and Jews? Those women are janitors. You dare to accuse me of consorting with charwomen? Get this piece of garbage out of my sight."

I had struck a nerve. I was dragged back to the 'lab' where Gregor retaliated, without waiting for direction, applying several savage blows to my battered soles. I surmised from his anger that he was upset at my implication that they had been slumming with the help. The rest of the afternoon was a savage vortex of beatings, shouting, and electroshock therapy, ending, mercifully, sometime around nightfall. They saved their nocturnal activities for the civilian population.

I can only vaguely recollect the next forty-eight hours. Csongor wouldn't let up; he was a man possessed. I would be made to send the wires. Somehow, Bela and Jozsi managed to carry me to a shower late one night where I sat on the floor, washed and then shaved without slicing my throat. I also brushed my teeth, with great difficulty. The metal mirror reflected a sunken-eyed stranger, a skin and bones, sad sack rag doll. My hands were palsied, my feet were on fire, and my testicles felt as though every lineman on the Toronto Argonauts had kneed me for practice. I was black, red, blue, and so hopelessly fragile that the splashing of water drops was torment. I could not stand; I could not walk. I was likely delirious, but apparently made no concessions to Csongor, except for admitting that I was trained at Bletchley, Bela assured me.

Then it stopped. September 25 was the first day in the last five without Csongor's electric circus. I was on edge all day, waiting for a call, but it never came, though the fruit and vegetables did. Jozsi, Bela and I had brief, whispered chats. Their status reports on my friends were somewhat reassuring, although Mike was going downhill. This hiatus ended on September 28. What could be worse than a fresh round of vigorous interrogation by Csongor, Gregor, et al? A fresh round of vigorous interrogation by the Reich Security Service, SD,

[4] *The* Sicherheitsdienst, SD, *state Security Service, was the intelligence arm of the* SS, *(elite defence echelon) within the massive central police and security apparatus, the* RSHA *(Reich Central Security Office). The* SD *comprised a combination of national and local police agencies. Staffed by enforcement professionals, and with responsibility for the security of Hitler, Party officials and the security of the Reich and its conquered territories,* Sturmmbannfuhrer *Reinhard Heydrich was its creator and Chief until his assassination in May, 1942. Heydrich wielded fearsome, arbitrary powers of life and death, with impunity. His ambition knew no bounds as he was determined to outdo his rivals in the Gestapo. In addition to traitors, subversives, and anyone else whom he deemed unworthy or a security risk; homosexuals, Jews, Christian Scientists, political dissidents, Communists, drunkards, war profiteers, petty thieves and prostitutes, the insane, even orphans, were his targets. Heydrich, 'The Hangman', never one to miss an opportunity for advancement, orchestrated his own appointment as Deputy Reich Protector of Bohemia-Moravia(Czechoslovakia). On May 29,1942, two SOE-trained Czech agents (code name Anthropoids) attacked his open Mercedes with a British-made bomb while he rode with a chauffeur in Prague. Heydrich died on June 4 of gangrene, from infected fragments of upholstery horsehair, embedded in his chest. It has been rumoured that the* SD *secretly, vainly and ludicrously attempted to entice England into trading penicillin for* PoW's. *In reprisal for the death of the* Fuhrer's *probable successor, the* SS *razed the Czech village of Lidice, near Prague. Its male residents were shot; a few of the children who were spared were taken to Germany for adoption. Surviving women were sent ot Ravensbruch death camp. The reprisals throughout Czechoslovakia were appalling. Ernst Kaltenbrunner, a seven-foot tall, brutal mediocrity eventually succeeded Heydrich as* SD *Chief. It has been theorized, but never substantiated, that Heydrich was haunted by the fear that Himmler's* SS *racial department may have concocted 'proof' that his ancestry included a Jewish forebearer. Heydrich's fiercely sadistic persecution of the Jews, by means of the Final Solution, may have been partially motivated by a perverse psychological need to overcompensate.*

Sicherheitsdienst! [4] Same room, same Csongor, Frog Eyes and Gregor, but the *Oberscharführer-SD* from *RSHA* HQ in Berlin, via Budapest, was an unknown factor. I expected the worst, if worse was possible.

Csongor and his Bureau cronies appeared to be on edge, although the *Oberscharführer* was not an SD potentate. His SD rank was equivalent to a master sergeant in the *Wehrmacht*. However, the mystique and fearsome reputation of the 'black order', as it was known, had its effect. Csongor cunningly played the role of a deferential host.

Oberscharführer Pheiler obviously packed a certain *cachet*, inversely proportional with his rank. Several times he was called to the telephone, which, as I overheard, was patched through to *Sicherheitsdienst* HQ Budapest, and linked to Berlin.

Pheiler, as I discovered, was a muscular, ex-middleweight boxer and cleric, determined and gruff, but surprisingly restrained with me. He was a mere one point five on my Sadism Scale, in comparison with Csongor's clear nine point five and Gregor's eleven. However, when we three musketeers finally met in Budapest, I found out that the Reverend Pheiler had confirmed Mike as a spy and had beaten him with his fists and elbows so viciously that Mike's ear was acutely inflamed, and he eventually became deaf. John's treatment was similar to mine.

Oberscharführer Pheiler's opening session with me was the 'same old, same old' which Csongor had already probed, ad nauseam. I was politely unforthcoming, in an effort not to antagonise him. Pheiler would wait impatiently while Frog Eyes translated his question from German into Hungarian, then into English, for me. My answers had to be translated into Hungarian, then German. Csongor also became ill at ease, but for a different reason. The SD had been invited to participate as observers by the Hungarian Second Bureau HQ in Budapest, as a courtesy but the divine Pheiler had taken the initiative upon his arrival. His mission was twofold: to unlock the mysteries of the British wireless training establishments, notably Bletchley, and to witness me bearing a false message to Bari. He was skilled in the rhetoric of debate, but I was able to keep myself out of deeper waters with him by answering in apparent good faith without divulging anything useful. It was soon too evident that *Oberscharführer* Pheiler's methodical plodding was not up to the Bureau's progressive standards. I was in trouble. Csongor insisted upon demonstrating his superior handiwork. It was actually Gregor's hand turning the magneto handle and wielding the truncheon. If the *Oberscharführer* was unsettled by my ordeals, he didn't register any objection during the sessions except to appear to be very annoyed by Csongor's interference.

Csongor's professional pride was piqued that I would not make the radio transmission for him in the presence of his guest. The abuse I received in retribution increased in duration and intensity. Gregor had perfected a diabolical system where he would stop the generator when he had delivered its maximum output and, while I was recovering, would suddenly give me a high voltage, wakeup jolt. He enjoyed experimenting with his craft, as an artist. Sometimes, the team would leave the room and I had to wait for hours, while a *Honved* guard sat behind, reading a newspaper. I frequently fell asleep.

The Bureau's methods were not proving effective; *Oberscharführer* Pheiler resumed his more rational inquiries concerning my training.

"Who were your instructors at Bletchley?" "How many students were there?" "What countries did they represent?" "What other bases did you train at?" "Did you get your parachute training at Altricham?"

My strategy of playing 'the naïve Canadian abroad' was effective: "I'm not exactly sure, *Oberscharführer*. Those English towns all seemed so alike." "Somewhere close to Manchester, if I recall." "That sounds like the place!" Or often, he would mention a place name, which was my cue to nod affirmatively, whether or not I had ever been there. The scribe was kept very busy, asking Frog Eyes for the English spellings.

After three days, it ended. The *Oberscharführer* had been recalled to Budapest. Now what?

On the morning of October 4, I was brought to Csongor's office. He was wearing civilian clothes and smoking a cigar. It was my performance review interview. Frog Eyes was there, also. Csongor read from a typed document, on official Bureau letterhead. I could read parts of the typed Magyar script, upside down, but thought better of that.

"We have found your radios and crystals. We have found all of the canisters, and your parachutes," he stated matter-of-factly.

'What about the gold coins?'

"There is much in these packages, as I have stated before, that causes us grave concern. Therefore, you will be taken directly from Pécs to headquarters in Budapest, where you will be treated as a Prisoner of War."

"Thank you. May I ask, Sir, about my friends?"

"Your commander Coates has been accorded PoW status, also. Agent Thomas is another matter. I can't discuss the details of his case with you.

"You must be ready to travel within an hour. Clean yourself up. There will be fresh clothes for you to wear. Be ready promptly. Questions?"

"If it's alright with you Sir, I'd like to keep my uniform. I am now officially a PoW and I believe it is my right to do so."

'I need my money, OTP's and codes!'

"Agreed. Dismissed!"

What luck! At least John and I might have some chance to lobby on Mike's behalf, as PoW's. I disposed gratefully of my ragged British Army underwear and threadbare socks in exchange for the fresh Hungarian issue. Jozsi came to say goodbye. I thanked him and inquired about Bela. In the few minutes remaining, I opened my jacket lining, removed some money, and handed it to him. He refused it adamantly.

"Take it, please. I have more and you'll need it for food and diapers for that new grandchild. There's more than enough here for Bela, as well. Please! You have both been so good to me and John and Mike. Put it in your church collection box if you won't keep it. I have to go. Please, take it, Jozsi! It's not payment. It's insurance."

"God bless you and good luck to you all. I wish you could be here under different circumstances to be Godfather for the little one's christening. May we use Joseph as his middle name?"

"I would be thrilled and honoured. Yes, by all means. Goodbye, my Saskatchewan friend." We shook hands warmly and hugged as only Hungarian men can do.

"Good bye Joe. Don't let the bedbugs bite!"

A Bureau escort came for me. Two staff cars were waiting near the gate. John and Mike were put together in the back seat of one. I was shown into the back of the other where Csongor was waiting, impatiently. The sentry raised the barricade and we sped off, bound for the Pécs railway station.

Our train to Budapest had been delayed on Csongor's orders. The railway police who hastened to put us aboard treated him with great deference. Ference was to be my travelling companion. I hoped that he didn't indulge in cheap cigars on long train journeys. The train whistle shrieked briefly twice, with the characteristic unearthly European squeal and we began to pull away from the platform. We had survived, but more importantly, we had not betrayed our country, SOE, or ourselves. No matter what Budapest might hold in store, our personal bonds of loyalty and honour had proven to be stronger than Csongor's dire threats and crude bullying. And he knew it.

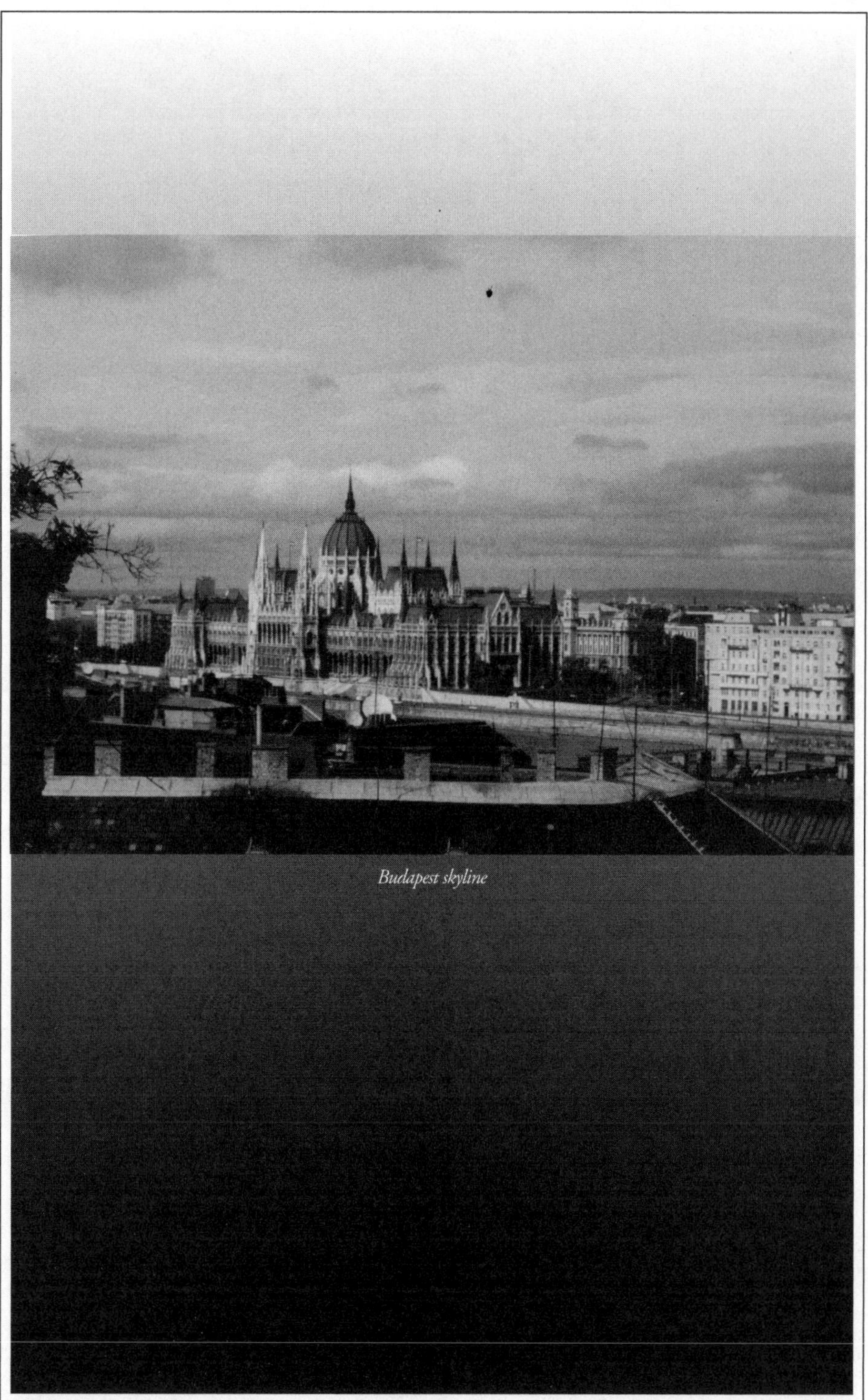

Budapest skyline

CHAPTER 6
Radio Games and the Admiral

Our journey to Budapest was not what I had expected. Instead of being tossed, hog-tied and gagged, onto the floor of a grimy baggage car, the guards escorted us into a regular day coach, which had been reserved for the Bureau's exclusive use. The interior was a reminder of the old Empire days, like a faded *grande dame* from another era. It was panelled in fine-grained, polished walnut with burnished brass hardware, including ornate reading lamps. The bench seats, which at one time might have qualified as decadently overstuffed, were like the carpeting: shabby, faded, and compacted by the passage of too many years. The coach windows were large, double paned, and barred, which was very disappointing. At either end of the car, there was a small washroom cubicle.

John was seated mid-coach and Mike was at the opposite end; both were facing away from me, so that we could not establish eye contact. I recognised four plainclothes Bureau security guards; there were two others, whom I supposed to be *Honved* volunteers. Csongor demonstrated his superiority by taking authoritative strolls the length of the coach, pausing to converse briefly with his Bureau confederates. He never acknowledged the militia's presence.

October's early glory was playing in living Technicolor; the tidy, bustling village markets and the ripened fields were bursting with the fruits of an abundant harvest. Where were the signs of wartime shortages? If this was war-torn Hungary, what might peacetime look like? And how long would it take for the Germans to 'liberate' this bountiful harvest bonanza, down to the last kernel of wheat?

When he wasn't pompously patrolling the aisle, the Colonel sat on the seat across from mine, his right leg outstretched, with an immaculate black patent Oxford resting on the cushion beside me. While he read, he made notations with a gold fountain pen on a ream of papers in neatly labelled yellow and blue manila file folders, of which there was apparently an infinite number. A black, kid leather briefcase, not unlike Gregor's dreaded black bag, lay open on the floor but proved to hold nothing more ominous than more files, a fresh orange which was as rare as Arabian coffee beans in wartime Hungary, and a small Swiss Army pocket-knife. After about an hour, he retrieved, methodically peeled, and then sectioned the orange with surgical precision. A large, red breast pocket handkerchief was spread out daintily on his lap as a napkin. Affably, he offered one-half to me. I took it without hesitation. If he was carrying a gun, it was well concealed.

It was distressing that this outwardly civilised, suave, charming and avuncular intelligence officer, who so disgraced the Hungarian Intelligence Service by his depraved disregard and callous indifference to the fundamental humanity of defenceless prisoners, particularly females, could pass invisibly and with impunity throughout society. His neighbours and acquaintances likely perceived a dedicated civil servant, a top mandarin, whose classified duties were obviously essential to the war effort, requiring his absence for weeks on end. For all I knew, he was a dutiful husband and devoted father, perhaps a doting grandfather. His venality was well cloaked in a mantle of bourgeois respectability.

Farmers were bringing the rich yield of their fields and orchards into the picture postcard villages. Entire families wearing floppy-brimmed straw hats were waiting for us at every whistle stop, their wagons and horse carts brimming with produce. This was so reminiscent of fall in my adopted home, Ontario, that my eyes began to water with memories of my first train ride to Niagara Falls as a ten-year old child. I had not thought often about Welland or Toronto and my Dad, but rather had worked hard to lock up that part of my life and throw away the key, for fear of awakening some dormant demon of weakness. Perhaps it was an acquired SOE reflex. Something about the wheat and honey hue of a beautiful girl's upswept hair as we rumbled past one of the many station platforms, or perhaps a shaft of mellow sun on a rippling pond's surface touched a vulnerable place in my heart, and I was instantly, desperately homesick. I knew that my Dad would be upset and worried by my long silence. I had not written to him since my final day in Brindisi.

A reminder that this peaceful, pastoral land was at war intruded abruptly in my reveries as a convoy of silver American Air Force B-29's with twelve fighter escorts thundered directly overhead, at medium altitude. The train windows shook as the airborne flotilla banked toward Budapest in the northeast, etching cotton candy heat trails in the autumn sky.

"God damn Amerika!" This was the Bureau's regulation response to anything American, particularly their aircraft, as I had learned at Pécs, when we had been taken outside by the guards to lie in trenches, while flights of USAF bombers rumbled overhead.

"Don't worry, Colonel" I remarked blithely. "Yanks don't bomb civilian trains. Only Germans do that." *'What did you think of that,*

Stirling?'

He ignored my propaganda while he settled down to read a slim, blue and white spiral bound report, the title of which, in Magyar, I could read clearly:

Top Secret

Second Bureau

Final report

The Enemy in Our Land: The Interrogation of SOE Agent Joseph Gordon

by Colonel F. Csongor, Pécs District Station

Second Bureau, Kir Haditechnikai Intezet, Budapest

If this was meant as a trap, it wasn't subtle. *'No comment! Don't register any interest by gawking. The slightest glance will give away the game!'* I stared resolutely out the window, trying to visualise the reunification of the three musketeers, free of Csongor, in Budapest.

Collectively, we had given him little to merit a leg-up the Bureau ladder. Ironically, the missing element, the one thing he needed to crown his efforts, was a false, coded W/T message to Bari. This was my trump card. Without me, it was not going to happen. In his report, he had unquestionably managed to paint himself in the best possible light as the true patriot, heroic defender of the faith, and the last bulwark against the 'knavish tricks' of Britain.

The coach door at our end, which did not have a window, was apparently locked. On an inaudible signal, one of the guards walked over and opened it to admit a red-nosed, rheumy-eyed railway agent who tottered over to inspect our passes, which were on display, in veteran tourist style, forming a perfectly symmetrical 'V for victory', in the metal frame of the window shade's catch.

'Dit dit dit Daa! Ference Csongor, the fascist, a secret admirer of the great democrat, Winston Churchill? Im-bloody-possible!'

The agent squinted at the small pasteboards, then saluted Csongor, and with a rolling gait, proceeded down the car. A waiter followed on his heels to set up a serving tray with sandwiches, cakes, coffee and tea, and two generous snifters of brandy. The thought of assassination, of 'doing Csongor in', using a dinner knife, his fountain pen or Swiss army knife, Fairbairn style, was tempting, but I rejected it. I had the strength. It would be justified before man and God, and extremely satisfying, but in that I lacked a plan or even the remotest possibility of escape, it would guarantee some very nasty business for John, Mike, and me. A noose or garrotte or Bureau bullet would be far too swift and merciful. Truncheons, elbows and electrodes would seem only minor inconveniences to convey the Bureau's deep regret at the untimely loss of their esteemed Colonel. Still, the thought of escape kept my mind occupied. A visiting instructor at Beaulieu had described, in entertaining fashion, how he and a female accomplice had tricked their guards and managed to break out, 'scarper,' from a passenger train on the way to a *Gestapo* prison, in Germany. However, without John and Mike as co-conspirators, it would be senseless.

I could get quite used to this lifestyle, under different circumstances; now it was time to freshen up. Csongor nodded his assent, without looking up from his report, when I pointed toward the washroom. It was a stainless steel cocoon, without a lock on the door, supplied with all of the toilette necessaries for the refined voyageur, except a window. I indulged in the creamy shaving lather, a soft, badger hair shaving brush and Gillette razor, the pleasures of scented soap, and finally a liberal dowsing of *Kölnisch Wasser*: the pathetic scarecrow of Pécs, in the metal mirror, had been recalled to life.

"Better, Gordon?"

"Yes, better, Colonel."

"Lieutenant, I won't be smoking cigars if you go back inside and wash off that sickening perfume."

I judged 'Lieutenant' a positive sign, although I assumed that he had not taken the leap in logic to connect my appearance with the recent unpleasantness at Pécs.

Dinner was a culinary *tour de force*, which included fresh vegetable soup, tender, boiled potatoes, and beef or chicken *paprikás*, complete with Leibfraumilch and Hungarian red Bika Ver. Csongor pointed to his meat, "Beefsteak, Gordon. Argentina. Peron." I knew horsemeat when I saw it and was glad I had ordered the chicken.

We took all our meals and slept uncomfortably upright in the compartment, arriving at Budapest's rococo Empire-style station at 4:00 p.m., October 5. Bureau Staff cars whisked us into the city.

Kir Haditechnikai Intezet, Hadik Prison, a low, ugly structure, was located in the Second Bureau Headquarters, which squatted on the intersection of Horthy Miklós ut (road) and Zenta utca (street).

After he signed us in, Csongor vanished down a corridor, leaving an acrid trail of cigar smoke. When we were brought to the lockup, John, Mike, and I took advantage of the Hadik guards' apparent lack of information, to be housed together in one cell.

We had not had any communication since September 13, on board the Halifax, the night of our jump into Orfü. I tried not to stare at them but the ordeals of the past month had taken a heavy toll. Mike had suffered the most. He had aged ten years. His infected ear was causing him extreme pain, exuding thick yellow pus, and he had a fever. John and I promised to find some way to get him to a hospital, quickly, and discussed plans for our escape, once Mike had been looked after.

We whispered for hours, about the landing snafu near Orfü, then recounted our personal odysseys from there to here.

"Who beat you, Mike?" I asked.

"All of them. Csongor and his creeps were no Boy Scouts. Man, that gorilla Gregor loved his truncheon! The *SD* bruiser Pheiler did this to my ear. I think he broke my eardrum with one cuff, the son of a bitch!" Mike shook his head. "Damn, even that hurts!"

"Take it easy, lad. John asked, "Joe, where in the dickens did you land? Mike and I searched for hours and couldn't find a trace!"

"Me too! I think from what you've said that we were on opposite sides of the same hill." I drew an outline of the hill on the floor, with my finger. "That's me, here. Here's the station…" I thought of mentioning that they were arrested before I was, but declined, as it seemed ungallant and pointless now.

"Exactly!" exclaimed John. "We were, …here, opposite you, right Mike? We all were going 'round and 'round the mulberry bush."

John wanted all of the details about the whereabouts of the two radios and the secret codes, which, of course, I told him.

"Look lads, we've finally managed to get together but I'm certain that the Bureau and SD have more up their sleeves for us. It's the radio. Csongor is going spare; he really needs to show the Counter Intelligence boss here, and the Jerries, that he can play the *funkspiel*[1] with the best of the SD's W/T counter-intelligence *wunderkind.*

"Going what, John?" Mike asked.

"Spare." You North Americans say, 'nuts.' What is happening with Gus and where is he?"

"Last I heard, he was using the cover name Zoltan H., and in custody. It's not looking…" I paused.

"I know. He and I are being held for trial," Mike responded bleakly.

"Joe and I will do everything we can to keep that from happening, Mike. I've heard that Bureau Chief Garzuly is a decent chap. At least he's not in the same league as Csongor." John, ever the leader, was doing his best to buoy us up.

"You have both done splendidly. But we must keep the flag flying. Don't admit to anything that hasn't been covered up to now. Agreed? Can you hold the fort on the radio and codes, Joe?"

"Yes, sir! I've managed to, so far. I'll just stick with my story. No crystal, no codes, the usual 'no can do' BS."

"Good man. It's the single most important factor in keeping us alive. Without your really superb resistance, Joe, we should all be pushing up daffodils in Pécs, by now."

We discussed everything, from Abaliget to Bertrand/Zoltan (Gus), whom no one had seen, and the canisters, too.

Next morning, Lieutenant Colonel Garzuly, the Second Bureau head of Counter Espionage, had realised his blunder, and we were separated. John's new cell was quite close to mine, though Mike's was a little more distant. Hadik was old, cold, and infested with fleas, lice, and bedbugs; the nocturnal rats and mice were more often heard, than seen. The Bureau controlled twenty double cells on the first floor. The luxuries of the train coach were gone, but not forgotten, although the Hadik regimen did provide us lukewarm showers, twice weekly. My wounds and aches were healing nicely.

Our Hadik prison guards were as good-natured a collection of professional gold-brickers as you could find in any army, a contingent of friendly, cheerfully profane slackers, numbering two sergeants (*Ormester*), one corporal (*Tizedes*), and two privates. Their duty roster, if it existed, was a mystery, although the faces generally mutated around 2:00 p.m. They became even more sociable when I put it about, by sign language, that I would pay them to smuggle in fresh food, with bonuses for freshness and selection, and hush money for insurance. One guard in particular, named Istvan Demian,[2] went out of his way to be helpful, cheery and kind.

In no time, Istvan and his chums were showering me daily with fresh pears, apples, paprika's, sweet red peppers and whatever else was at hand, which they passed along to John and Mike. The standard prison rations were, at best, meagre to very poor. The day began with a mug of chicory ersatz coffee, and one kaiser-sized bread roll. Lunch was better: thick vegetable soup *(gemüsa)*, with floating bits of real vegetables. Supper was the same: soup, but without the vegetables, i.e. almost water. The fruit and peppers likely prevented scurvy, as Hungarian sweet peppers are rich with vitamin C. John later told me that he had never eaten one before in his life.

For amusement, I recited my favourite poems, which I had memorised in my senior year high school English class: *In Flanders' Fields, Indian Summer* and *'What is this life if full of care…'*

I never witnessed any abuse or humiliation of a prisoner by the Hungarian Hadik guards, nor were

---

[1] *Deceptive radio practices, literally "radio games".*

they the least inclined to interfere with our chats between cells. My scribbled notes to John and Mike were written with contraband pencils and paper, provided by Istvan as part of room service, he said jokingly. The DIBBLER money was holding out well and gave me a huge advantage over the other inmates, so I made certain that the smallest favours and acts of kindness were rewarded.

One morning, I was astonished to hear English-speaking voices; Canadian, American and English accents were coming from somewhere down the concrete corridor. I motioned to one of the guards, called Pista, who spoke some English, and asked him what was going on.

"Fliers, Joe! Allied fliers, shot down." He made the 'chukkka, chukka' sound of a machine gun while imitating a falling aircraft with his hand.

"Why are they here?"

"Bosses have to talk to them before they go."

"Go where?"

"Prisoner of war camp. Maybe here, maybe Germany, I don't know."

"Can you get a message to tell them I'm a Canadian and would like to talk with them?"

"I'll try, Joe. They come and go. Stay only one or two days. Air bosses keep them busy with questions."

I scrawled this information on my little notepad.

"Pista, take this note to John, okay? I'll pay you."

"It's okay, Joe. No pay. John likes peppers. He wants more peppers, maybe?"

"Ask him yourself, Pista!"

We never did connect with the airmen, but found out that most were automatically and properly classified as PoW's by the Bureau's Air Section, and not as 'politicals,' to keep them out of the clutches of the SD's hard boys. It appeared that a turnabout in Regent Horthy's Axis alliance, a *rapprochement*, was around the corner.

Another sign was a meeting with Counter Intelligence Chief Lieutenant Colonel Garzuly, on October 8. He came to my cell with an interpreter.

"I hope you are well, Lieutenant." The Lieutenant Colonel's manner was brisk and professional, but not unfriendly. "I want to introduce my English interpreter, Zoltan Perisich."

Perisich offered me his hand. I stood up. "I'm alright, thanks, Colonel. The food is terrible, though I would rather be here than upstairs".

"Agreed. The *SD* does have its

[2] *Istvan Demian was cited by the British Government in 1945 for his 'friendly attitude and the many small services...rendered...to bring cheer and comfort" (to) "Allied soldiers who had the misfortune to find themselves behind barded wire...in the Hadik prison..." For his services, he received a payment of 25,000 pengös.*

own interesting methods of gathering intelligence. Quite rigorous, even harsh; they do sometimes get valuable information, but it goes against my grain to torture a man or woman to the point where he or she might blurt out anything at all, just to please their interrogator or to end the ordeal."

'But your man Csongor and friends don't seem to agree, Colonel. They outshone the Master Race, in my recent experience.' Nonetheless, Colonel Garzuly's admission was a sign of something. Just what was his game?

The cell door was wide open and they were standing inside, without side arms. I couldn't quite believe what he was saying, but I remained silent. My brief experience as a secret agent had taught me to never take anything said by the enemy, or just about anyone, at face value. *'Look for the hook, and keep quiet!'* But I owed it to Mike to try something on his behalf.

"Colonel Garzuly, Lieutenant Thomas is in very serious condition and needs to be examined by a doctor, Sir. His ear is badly infected. Captain Coates thinks that he will lose his hearing if it's not treated immediately in a hospital. Can you help us?"

"I can see about making some arrangements, but it may take a day or two. Things are, as you say, in an uproar. My telephone doesn't stop ringing. We will talk again tomorrow, perhaps. Incidentally, Lieutenant, you are an SOE-trained W/T operator, no?"

"Correction, Sir! I am a British Army W/T operator." That was not an outright lie. My quick notes to Mike and John were cheerful, to give Mike a boost, but I felt that the hook was being set: *'No radio message, no help for Mike.'*

When I lay down on the bed to think about this new information, my eyes wandered to the wall, just above my eye level. Faintly scratched into the dull grey paint, I could just make out,

Sgt. John Connor. Black Watch. I was here.

Captain Boughey, the leader of DEERHURST, had been an inmate in this very cell! I took a closer look and just above his was the inscription:

Lt. Bertrand.

Gus, too! The Bureau had bagged a lot of game, indeed!

On October 9, my suspicions were proven correct. Early that morning, I was handcuffed lightly by a *Honved* guardian and taken from my cell to a small interrogation room, where I was turned over to Lt. Colonel Garzuly, Zoltan Perisich and two or three Bureau officials. All wore civilian suits. Unlike Pécs, this interrogation room was rather small and contained no instruments of terror or persuasion, either medieval or contemporary. Almost graciously, Colonel Garzuly bade me be seated. I obliged him. He spoke rapidly to Perisich whose English translation betrayed very little Magyar influence.

"Lieutenant Gordon, I'll come right to the point. Your stubborn refusal to comply with past requests for your co-operation has gotten you and your chums no further than if you had agreed to work with Colonel Csongor in the first instance. In reality, you and you alone have dragged yourself, Coates and Thomas, further and deeper into difficulties." He paused to let his words sink in.

"But, you have the opportunity to help them now, especially Thomas, who, as you have said, is unwell. I urge you to consider your limited options. You are not in a position to bargain with me. No chips, Mr. Gordon! Send the message to Bari on your very own radio set and we'll get on with the arrangements. It's already here."

'You son of a bitch! Of course, you would use Mike.' He was a Nazi, just like his sick underling, Ference. *'So much for yesterday's anti-SD speech. Wait for the translation. Take your time!'* "My radio, Colonel?"

"Yours. You knew in Pécs that all of your buried treasures were recovered. Colonel Csongor told you. It's in his report, right here. Please don't waste my time with your denials of fact. Bring in the radio, please, Corporal."

There it was, my Old Faithful, Mark 1. *'Now what? Careful, don't make him angry. Mike has to get to a hospital. Thank heavens I had fiddled with the settings in Brindisi.'*

"It is yours Lieutenant. Now, let's get on with business. Please put on the earphones and switch it on, Lieutenant."

"The crystals are missing and there's no generator for power." *'Why did I mention that? Second Bureau had no lack of those devices!'*

"Lieutenant, where were you trained? Bletchley, no? I'm sure that you were told about dry cell batteries at some point. Let's move on, please."

"Yes sir. I've forgotten so much." Garzuly was sharp. *'I'm going to have to do something to try to look as though I'm being co-operative.'*

"It's on, but there's no signal strength showing on the meter, if you'd like to look, Sir. You can't send or receive without the correct frequency crystals."

Colonel Garzuly peered over my shoulder at the dial. The needle was hugging zero. The crystals and codes, which made the difference between collaboration and resistance, were safely tucked away in my jacket lining.

"I understand. But we have several available, that will fit in that socket. One of them must be the exact frequency."

"Sir, there are literally thousands of frequencies. I'll try them, but it's a waste of time, in my opinion."

Garzuly looked at his wristwatch. "I'll give you all the time you require. Here are the crystals. Try each one. Gentlemen, let's leave the Lieutenant to his work." This last statement was not translated. As they left the room, a *Honved* watchman came in and sat on a chair nearby. He nodded his head in acknowledgement, then removed, cleaned and adjusted his glasses and proceeded to read a pocket novel. This scarecrow was a decoy. Garzuly was going to be monitoring every move. *'It's for sure that he has a technician listening in. Get to work, Joe! John and Mike are hostages. Don't put them in danger.'*

The time passed quickly. There were fifteen crystals in the box. Dutifully, I inserted, pretended to test, and then removed each one, all of which was made awkward by the short link between my hand restraints. Seeing my problem the guard unlocked and removed the cuffs. Even if one of the crystals hit the jackpot, the radio was jimmied so cleverly, thanks to my training at Bletchley, that only a highly skilled W/T operator would likely catch on. When all had been tested, I switched off the power and asked permission to go to the washroom. The guard replaced the handcuffs and accompanied me. The temptation to overpower him and run was offset by reality. It was not the time. It would come.

When we returned, the room was empty. I sat down, lay my head on my arms on the desktop, and was soon asleep.

Perisich was tapping my shoulder. "Wake, wake, Gordon! Colonel Garzuly is on his way here." I was hungry and wanted to go back to sleep. They would be counting on my weakened resistance.

"So Gordon, any luck?" inquired the Colonel. He appeared well fed and freshly rested.

"No Sir, nothing worked."

"How unfortunate. Tomorrow, we'll use another one. You are dismissed. Take him back. No cuffs, but watch him!"

'Another what... box of quartz crystals? A new radio? Heaven forbid!'

On my walk down the corridor, I passed John's cell; he looked at me quizzically, as though expecting a sign. I curled by thumb and index finger to give him the "OK." He smiled and signed back.

Back in the custody of the Hadik guards, I was looking forward to being able to relax and enjoy the fresh victuals that they had been leaving. But the day was not over. A distinguished gentleman caller came by my cell. In perfect, public school English he began, "Excuse me. I'm sorry to bother you, but I thought you might care for some hot tea. It's fresh and I assure you, it's the real thing." He looked tall and distinguished, wearing the uniform of a Hungarian Air Force officer, although the insignia had been removed. Before I could reply, he was inserting a mug between the bars of my door.

"Just take it and try it. You have had a full day. By the way, my name is Colonel Matyas Pirithy; Matyas, will do."

"Joseph Gordon, Matyas. Thank you. I haven't had a real cup of tea for over a month." It was hot and tasty. "Are you on staff here, Matyas?"

"No, no, I'm more of a Lucifer, a fallen angel. I'm a prisoner of conscience. Spoke out too often to the wrong people. So, I'm being put up here, to keep me out of mischief. No need to fear that I'm an *agent provocateur*, or a stool pigeon, as they say in American movies."

"A conscientious objector, then?"

"Exactly, old boy. I consider myself a Hungarian patriot first and foremost. Colonel Garzuly's quite a decent fellow, and so long as I don't cause him any problems, I can pretty much do as I damn well please. Except leave. Which is fine with me. I'd really rather not be flaming any more Allied pilots. We got in on the wrong side. I'm damn lucky not to have been shot. Regent Horthy knew dear old Dad. Uncle's a top general and a staunch supporter of the current regime. Rescued me from a firing squad through the old boy network at the court martial. The Advocate General got a personal call, from the Boss in Budapest,[3] the night before I was to be sentenced. Lucky me."

"You speak English magnificently. Better than most Canadians that I know."

"That's the English upbringing. We lived in London from my birth until I was fourteen. Father and mother were both in the Hungarian diplomatic service. I was at boarding school for nine months out of the year and an embassy brat when I was home. A bad combination and it still shows. Well, Joseph, time and tide! The mug please. I'll come by tomorrow with a fresh cuppa. I enjoyed our chinwag although I did most of it: my deepest apologies. 'Till tomorrow. Carry on."

'Carry on, where?' My mind was overtaxed with the events of the day. If Matyas was a stoolie, I consoled myself with the knowledge that I hadn't been given the chance to say anything worth reporting. Perhaps he could get help for poor, sick Mike.

Early the next morning, October 10, I was taken, without handcuffs,

[3] *The Regent of Hungary, Admiral Miklós Horthy.*

back into the interrogation room. Colonel Garzuly and Zoltan Perisich were talking as I was being seated. The Colonel waved the *Honved* escort out of the room. Perisich had some opening remarks.

"Lieutenant, or so you call yourself, we are not clear yet about some points in Colonel Csongor's report. I, for one, am convinced that there were a total of four, and not three men sent here. Your comments?"

He was smooth. "No, just the three of us."

"Colonel Garzuly and I are convinced that you and your crew, likely four men, are British secret agents, spies. It is well known that Britain sends hundreds like you to carry out sabotage and assassinations. Our cells are full of them, as you have seen. Many simply disappear. Do you know what happens to spies here?"

"No, I don't."

"We take them down to the Danube and shoot them, is what we do!"

Poor Gus, if they linked him with us. Perisich was flying solo. His threat reminded me of the Bloody Sergeant's appraisal of that river's probable colour, back at the Horse Palace, one hundred years ago. I had no reason to doubt Zoltan Perisichs' sincerity or intent. Upon firing that warning shot across my bow, he sat down to await his superior's pleasure.

I was astonished to hear the Colonel instruct him to "back off" and to get on with the review of Csongor's report. It was a tedious, tiresome process, which consumed two hours, by my wristwatch. But it was better than faking a radio breakdown. For obvious reasons, my training sites, especially Bletchley Park, were of major interest. I gave no more information than I had at Pécs. Garzuly/Perisich were not content with my answers about our number: three vs. four. They returned to the point half a dozen times. I believe they really wanted to nail us and drag Gus along to the execution. I reiterated my hard-won status as a PoW, ducking and dodging Garzuly's/Perisich's rather clever, sinuous questioning was very tiring. At noon, they left me to consider my ways, in the company of a *Honved* guard who kindly shared his ham sandwich. After a brief washroom break, I leaned back in my chair and dozed, to wait for act two.

I should have seen it coming! Garzuly and Perisich returned from lunch with an *SD Hauptsturmführer*.[4] He was not an ethnic, but a fully-fledged *Übermensch*, a German, named Wilhelm von Richter: early thirties, dark, chunky and soft-spoken. His right eyelid drooped, lending him a sinister air. He was wearing black kid gloves with thick ridges. I braced myself for chal-

[4] *Captain.*

lenging times ahead. The *Hauptsturmführer* was all business. He reminded me of a busy physician, about to examine his twentieth patient of the day during an outbreak of the 'flu'. He spoke no English, which gave me a lot of lead-time to shape my answers, as with his reverend colleague in Pécs. He had obviously discussed Csongor's report with Colonel Garzuly and began the questioning with queries about details of my training at Bletchley. He not only wished to know more about the GC&CS, but who my classmates were and the names of my instructors. I was not very forthcoming which earned me a hard slap on my ear with the back of his gloved hand. My ear throbbed for an hour. Several more questions on the theme, with variations, followed, which I did my best to answer non-committally.[5]

"*Hauptsturmführer* von Richter, I think he slept through his classes there. He's barely able to recognise pictures of the damn place," interjected Garzuly, through Perisich.

'Hello? What's this? Colonel Garzuly for the defence, now? What is going on?' The SD officer was displeased with the Hungarian's intervention and suddenly veered, through Peresich, to probe my connections with SOE. It was either a fishing expedition or else he knew something about the training at Beaulieu, which was more alarming than Perisich's threats. The next statement was a heart-stopper.

"You had two friends there, who were Dutch, a man and a woman. What were their names and their destination?"

"Sir, I'm sorry; I have no idea. I know absolutely nothing about that place. I'm a British Army PoW, plain and simple."

I was rewarded for my insolence with a stinging blow to my face from a glove in a clenched fist. The sickeningly sweet, warm taste of blood made me want to throw up urgently on his immaculate black boots.

"Your French-speaking American friend, Rolly, and you had some exciting times with the pretty ladies in Bournemouth, no? Tell me, where did his mission take him in France?"

I was dumfounded. If this continued, I was canned meat and so were John and Mike.

I looked at him blankly and prepared for the *coup de grâce.*

Once again, good old Garzuly rode to the rescue. Although he outranked the German, it was not everyone who would have the courage to take on a member of the sacred order.

"*Hauptsturmführer*, he is hopeless. I've gone over and over this line of questioning and am convinced he

[5] *The ongoing fascination with Bletchley Park was, I'm sure, only coincidental with the Ultra secret. There is no evidence to date, of which I am aware, that suggests any knowledge of Ultra by German Intelligence.*

has nothing to tell. I don't think he's being obstinate; he's really just too stupid to have been recruited by SOE. One look at him and that tells you everything you need to know. It's an utter waste of your time. I can't imagine him charming any *Fraülein*, even English. I have several more leads to investigate in other areas and can't say when I'll be finished. I'll likely be sending the three to a military tribunal. But, perhaps you wish to take him upstairs with you now to explore this SOE topic further?"

There was dead silence. As I waited to hear my fate, words from a poem, *The passing of Arthur*, which I had memorised in high school, ran through my head,

'And slowly answer'd Arthur from the barge:

The old order changeth, yielding place to new;

And God fulfils himself in many ways…'

"Colonel Garzuly, I'm due to depart for Berlin within the hour. You can keep him occupied until I'm back tomorrow, I'm sure. I'll let you know my decision then. In the meantime, I know you will do your duty. *Heil Hitler!*"

"*Heil Hitler!*"

'Please God, let him be shot down!'

The *Honved* warder was instructed to take me to my cell, where Matyas greeted me with a hot cuppa.

"Bit of a dustup with the Blackshirt, I hear. How's the ear, old man?"

"You are uncanny. How did you know that, Matyas?"

"The ears have walls."

"Pardon?"

"Money loosens lips. Not to worry about *Gestapo* Wilhelm, they have bigger fish to fry right now. No disrespect, Joseph, but something quite a lot more earth shaking is about to appear."

"What?"

"Call me a fool, but I think Admiral Horthy is going to sue for peace. He's been reading the tea leaves and doesn't want Hungary to be euchred for the second time this century. Naturally, Adolf's knickers are in a knot. So the top chaps are huddling in the Berlin bunker to plan their next move. German Intelligence is very, very good. Listen old chap, why not come down to my digs, the door's always open, the bikkies are edible, and Garzuly's not going to object. I have someone else you should meet, as well as newspapers and books that you might want to look over." He spoke quietly to the *Honved* guard, who shrugged, and left us.

His cell door was ajar. I could see that it was equipped with an alcohol heater for boiling water, a tall narrow wardrobe with a mirror on the door, and a washbasin, and was littered with a scattering of newspapers, magazines, and books. Sitting on a straight-backed chair at the end of the cot was a Hungarian Army captain, reading a newspaper, which I think was German. Matyas introduced Captain Andras Hegedus, who, Matyas assured me, was fully trustworthy. Hegedus was wearing his regular army dress uniform, which was a brilliant red.

"Palinka, gentlemen, or Scotch?"

Andras and I eagerly accepted the pear brandy. I still hadn't forgotten my first unhappy breakfast experience in Scotland. Matyas produced a full bottle from the cupboard and filled three brandy glasses.

"Hungary, gentlemen." Andras responded with the same words, in Magyar.

We soon were engrossed in a discussion of Hungary's options, which if Matyas' source was correct, included the distinct threat of Russian troops replacing the hated Nazis, when Istvan, the guard, burst into the cell.

"Joe, Boss wants you. Now! His office! Wash your face and follow me! I'll wait. Any cookies today, Matyas? Can I have a taste of the booze? You can smell it down the hallway. Two minutes, Joe!"

Boss did indeed want me, that October 12, 1944. An orderly ushered me in to his inner sanctum; a distinguished Second Bureau general sat at the Colonel's large mahogany desk. This was the big time. A black telephone, a single red rose in a slim crystal vase, an ornate silver cigarette lighter, and a silver letter opener lay beside it on the otherwise bare desktop. Garzuly, Perisich and Andras were seated at the general's right side, on three of four plush armchairs. The orderly indicated that the fourth was mine, and without asking, brought me a cup of tea, in a china cup and saucer, and sesame sweetcakes.

'Now what? Matyas has set me up! And Andras is a stooge.'

Colonel Garzuly spoke in Magyar to the General. "Lieutenant Joseph Gordon is the Canadian W/T officer about whom I've been speaking, General. He's stubborn, tough as hell, seems impervious to intimidation and is likely an SOE secret agent from what I know of them. He's Bletchley trained, so he's very good around wireless. Perisich suspects that he knows much, much more than he has admitted. He's also a clever enough liar to have survived Orfü, Pécs and that fanatic von Richter today. The *SD* in Pécs and our ambitious Colonel Ference together couldn't break him. He's been through a lot and likely wouldn't trust his own mother by now, but we may be able get to him if he is convinced we're one hundred percent sincere. Oh, by the way, if he is SOE, he's a British Commando-style killer, so be careful. My revolver's in the centre drawer. It has a full clip and the safety's off. I'm sure he's been tempted before. So let's be very careful not to rub him the wrong way."

'Sure. You betcha; I'm a real William Fairbairn!'

"We're going to have to be very gentle but persuasive, to win his trust. He can handle a lot of physical and mental abuse; he just plays dumb and clams up. However, we must keep him and his colleagues away from the *SD*. Von Richter was very close to taking him away for more treatment. I tried a bluff and won, this time. If the *SD* get their hooks in him, we won't get him back."

'Wow! Thanks for the glowing compliments! This is better than my performance review at Beaulieu! So Garzuly was in fact, protecting me. But for what reason?'

Zoltan Perisich began interpreting Garzuly's opening remarks.

"Lieutenant, the General would prefer that his name not be known. He wishes to interview you concerning your expertise as a wireless operator. Please do your best to answer his questions as completely as possible and take your time. I assure you that your personal well being and that of your friends' will not be compromised by anything that you say here. Nothing will be repeated outside of this room. I give you my solemn oath as an officer. So please, relax and enjoy the refreshments. Please proceed, General."

'Well la de dah. Aren't you just the greatest bunch of guys! What do you think, Blokey old pal?'

'Better listen. You've got nothing to lose. Remember your friends John and Mike are counting on you to play the radio game as your ace in the hole. It's going to be dealt very soon.'

The General's remarks were very lengthy; he asked some rather innocuous questions about Bletchley, which I answered, but I quickly became bored with his rambling digressions. It was twice as dreary to be forced to listen to everything twice. He seemed hesitant to get to the point. The old boy said nothing that might have motivated me to attack him with the letter opener, but I was strongly tempted to get up and leave.

Perisich, sensing my edginess, intervened, "Excuse me General, may I try?"

"Please do." He lit a cigarette and inhaled with the deep satisfaction of a confirmed addict.

"Lieutenant. What the General is saying essentially is this: we have a rather serious problem. Our country is almost certainly pulling out of the war within the week and an urgent message must be sent to Bari, in order to alert the Allies. Now, I understand that you smell a rat. But let me assure you, this is not a trick, or a game that we've concocted to make you betray your friends. There's no one here who wants you to believe us more than me. I swear on my oath as an officer that this is the truth."

"Tell me again. What do you want me to do?"

Garzuly answered. "We need you to send a message to your HQ in Bari."

"Even if I did believe you, how could I?"

"We have your radio. I know you've done things with the settings. I know you can reset them and fix the crystal problem, as well. I know nothing about short wave radio, but I do know you're a top W/T man, Joseph. You were very highly trained in England. We need those skills. Hungary needs you."

Andras joined in. "Joseph, if the Allies aren't warned, Hitler and Stalin are going to be picking at a dead corpse: Hungary. It will be Armageddon. As Hungarian patriots, we beg you to reconsider. Please?"

"Look gentlemen, I'm worn out: damn mad, tired, and hungry. You haven't been playing by the rules of the Geneva Convention and your Colonel Csongor is worse than the SD. Why in the name of heaven should I help you out of your jam? Mike is sick and John's slipping daily. I need a better deal, some guarantees. Hungary's future is not my immediate concern, although it would be better for the Allies, I suppose, if she got out now and stayed neutral until the war's over. I need to speak privately with Colonel Garzuly and Zoltan."

"Very well" interjected the General. "Colonel Garzuly, let's take a dinner break now and convene in an hour."

The General left to go to another room in the executive suite. Garzuly reached under his desk. The gun! Within a minute, two white-jacketed trusties wheeled in a cart and had set up a complete dinner service, including a linen tablecloth on the desk. He waited for them to retire, then continued, "We know that the Regent is deadly serious in his commitment. But the British and the Americans don't want to, or won't, believe him. HQ here has made several overtures, by radio and backalley diplomacy. 'No dice', as the Americans like to say. I suppose we've done little as a nation to earn your trust over the last four or five years. What's that saying, 'With a Hungarian for a friend, who needs an enemy?'

"The General is Admiral Horthy's special envoy and has the confidence of the anti-Nazi officer cadre. Word about you got back quickly to the highest levels of the Intelligence Service soon after Lieutenant Pataki picked you up at Abaliget. There is a small but extremely influential group of senior officers who immediately realised your value as a wireless operator with access to Bari. If they hadn't gotten up

Colonel Csongor's nose, he would have finished you off. He hates your guts with a deep and abiding passion. He'll never make the General List because of you, you obstinate so and so! Good for you! Now, if you can't, or won't, get the message through, we are all quite likely screwed, royally."

'This is a major dilemma: If I do it and it's a game, John, Mike and I are done for; if I don't do it, Hungary, my birthplace, which I love, but not as dearly as Canada, could be a rubble heap; or, things will continue as they are now, down to the inevitable defeat. 'To be, or not....'"

"I want all three of us taken care of if all hell breaks loose. I want Mike taken to hospital. I want no further contact with the *SD*, *SS*, *Gestapo* or any other Nazi vermin, for that matter. I also want my radio back. I want to see the message, written out in clear, and I demand total privacy when I prepare to transmit and when I'm DX'ing.[6] No technicians listening in. No recording machine. Nothing! And, the wire must be brief. The longer I'm sending on air, the better the chance of a German intercept picking me up."

"Accepted. Thank God! Bless you, Joseph. I know you're ready to drop with exhaustion, but it's imperative that it be sent tonight. Can you manage?"

[6] *Jargon for long distance radio transmission/reception.*

"Yes."

He looked at Perisich. "Zoltan, inform the General and Andras that we will start in exactly thirty-five minutes, at eight o'clock. Joseph, some wine?"

"No, thanks very much. More coffee, please. It's real, not ersatz, no? However, there is one more item, Colonel. I never want to see or hear of Csongor, again. I want you to tell the General about his abuse of female prisoners, who are mainly Jewish or Romany Gypsies. He's a disgrace to your Service!"

"I will inform him personally while you are present."

"That's good, but not good enough. He should, at the very least, be removed from contact with any prisoners. He is a virulent anti-Semite, a sadist and a criminal sexual pervert."

"I will make the point very, very strongly, Lieutenant. I promise."

'I am so naïve!' But he did. The General's response was shocked indignation as I recounted the outrages at Pécs. His hands were trembling as he picked up Garzuly's Bureau phone and ordered the operator to call HQ. I could hear the conversation at both ends and understood every word. Csongor was being transferred immediately to the Quartermaster General's Corps, in Budapest. Starting tomorrow.

Perisich remarked, "He'll be under the General's thumb, the highest-ranking drudge ever, counting tin potties and sorting army blankets for the duration, Lieutenant."

'Ah, sweet justice. A court martial with firing squad would have been preferable, but this was acceptable.' I was now fully convinced of their sincerity and was eager to do my part for the Allies and Hungary. I excused myself to wash up in the ensuite bathroom. My crystal and codes were safe. When I returned, there was my radio, complete with new earphones and a fresh battery pack, set up on the desk. Lying beside it was a Bureau memo pad, fresh pencils, and to the side, a tray with a carafe of water and drinking glasses.

"We are leaving you to your business, Lieutenant," said Andras. "You'll see the message is printed clearly on the pad. Zoltan has produced an accurate English translation of the message approved by the General's associates. I checked it, of course." Zoltan Perisich nodded and smiled, wanly.

"If you require anything at all, press this button under the desk. Feel free to move around. Good luck! Oh, yes, I almost forgot. Please let us know when we can come in. Just buzz!"

"There is one little complication, gentlemen. I'm sorry, I can't read it.

"What?" There was stunned silence. I felt like crawling under the desk.

Finally, Perisich ventured, "Damn it Joe! I thought we were all through with deceptions and games! What are you...?"

"It's not a game, Zoltan. I guess I lost my glasses in the confusion when we were leaving Pécs."

"Just what the doctor ordered," responded Garzuly, pulling open his drawer. "*Voilà*, a magnifier!" He handed the large reading glass to me.

"Thanks, Colonel. Sorry to alarm you all, but I had forgotten completely how blind I am. Not a lot of reading to do here in Hadik. Just a minute, this is much too long. The *Sicherheitsdienst* will be sending in the troops before I'm halfway finished."

"What do you want us to do?"

"I'd suggest that you cut the flowery introduction and background paragraph. Everything else is okay. Can you get it down to one hundred words?"

They worked at it and Zoltan handed it back. "One hundred and five!"

"Thanks, it looks great; now let me get started or the operators in Bari are going to be asleep at the switch. I'll let you know when I want you back."

"Good. Turn the lock on the door after we leave, please!"

I did that and also closed the drapes to cover the two large windows, for insurance. *'This is it! My God, I have the chance of a lifetime. Maybe this will change the course of history. Don't screw up, Joe. One step at a time, right Blokey? Okay, first, get the crystal and codes out of my lining.'*

The radio's Polish-made vacuum tubes glowed reassuringly when I fastened the two battery leads to the contact posts. I switched it off, to install the all-important quartz crystal in its socket. '*Damn! I dropped it! It's on the carpet.*' My hands were trembling with excitement compounded by the fact that they still hadn't regained full flexibility. *'Down on your hands and knees under the table to retrieve the pesky little silver cylinder. Where is it?'* Without my glasses, I couldn't see anything but the intricate pattern of the rug, which was a sea of white and silver swirls. *'Feel around for it! It has to be here! Not there, try under the chairs…victory! Here's the little darling'!* By this point, I was drenched.

The quartz crystal was the heart of the radio's capabilities to transmit and receive messages. Because of its peculiar physical property, its atoms vibrated, exactly in synch with the frequency of the station in Bari. I carefully wiped off any moisture with my sleeve and then gingerly inserted the crystal by its metal base, using the fingertips of both hands, into the small receptacle. After an eternity there was a satisfying 'snap' as it slid into the small socket. *'Push down, gently, to make sure it's seated. Ah, good. Next! Power on. Earphones. Antenna attached. Adjust the settings.'* It took a few minutes to recall and recalibrate the changes that I had made at Brindisi. *'Check the signal strength meter. About half; not enough! It has to get there loud and clear on first crack and hope to God the Germans aren't listening. Count on the fact that they are!'*

Stretching the antenna wire towards the nearest window and wrapping it around the end of the curtain rod worked perfectly: maximum output…five by nine!

'Now for my one-time code pad.'
There it was, nestled inside the lining.

I tore off the top page. It took ten minutes to read, break into groups, and encode the message.

> Admiral Miklós Horthy is to make a speech 15 October 1944, asking for an armistice with the Allies. He wishes acknowledgement by the British and Americans so that he can secretly arrange, if agreed by the Allies, to send a small force by parachute to a designated safe area in Hungary. This would hasten the pullout by German troops and facilitate the safe passage of Russian soldiers through, without any actual fighting in Hungary. Russia is not to occupy Hungary. An Allied force is to be in control of Hungary. This will save thousands of lives: Hungarian, Russian, and Jewish.
>
> Signed: Committee for a Neutral Hungary, including Horthy.

I hadn't touched a Morse key in many months, but after a few preliminaries, I found my 'fist'[7] and sent the message without hesitation to Bari, Papuk and Istanbul. Almost immediately after it was sent, I received a confirmation from Bari, "Message received and understood." Using the fancy silver desk lighter, I burnt the one time pad page in the wastebasket. For good measure, I added the Bureau note pad to the conflagration. After five minutes, I poured a half-cup of water on the smouldering ashes, dumped the contents into and flushed the toilet, then unlocked the door and called down the corridor,

"Colonel, General, Andras, Zoltan, break out the champagne!"

[7] A W/T operator's unique keying speed and characteristic sending style. It is interesting that repetitive strain injury (RSI) of the wrist and forearm was not uncommon until advances were made in key design. W/T jargon for RSI was descriptive: glass arm.

Chapter 7

The Play's the Thing

The following day, October 13, I sent the conspirators' message again to Papuk, for emphasis, knowing that I could rely on Captain Rolly Young's exceptional W/T operator, Sergeant Scott, to relay it to Bari. It was a backup procedure that I felt would guarantee clarity at HQ, had there been any problem with the meaning of the original signal. Then, for insurance, I transmitted it to Allied Command, Istanbul, and again to Bari directly. No confirmations were received this time. However, I was confident that I had fulfilled my duty by covering all of the bases twice.

In the next days leading up to Regent Horthy's broadcast, I was kept on alert in the event that some indication of Allied intentions was received from Italy or Turkey HQ's. On my advice, Colonel Garzuly had installed Hungarian W/T operators at Hadik to monitor traffic around the clock, with instructions to notify me first if a signal was received. Admiral Horthy's people had followed our lead and instituted a similar watch. We were all on edge. I had chats with the Hadik guards and with Matyas, who visited my cell regularly with news, rumours, and treats.

Matyas confirmed that Colonel Garzuly was extremely busy but had been successful in keeping *SD Hauptsturmführer* von Richter at bay by insisting that we three were still undergoing intensive questioning. My cell was locked for the sake of appearances only. Apparently, Colonel Garzuly had told the German that he was about to prepare our papers for a military tribunal or order us transported directly to a PoW camp in Austria, which, Andras assured me, the Colonel had absolutely no intention of doing. How he got away with these fabrications, no one knew; however, the man was living up to his promise.

I hadn't told John or Mike about my W/T exploits, on the assumption that Colonel Garzuly had done so. Apparently, this was not the case, as I would later find out.

During the afternoon of October 15, Andras Hegedus and Zoltan Perisich rushed to my cell. They were extremely agitated. In a state of high excitement they announced, almost in unison, "Joe, come now. Hurry! The Regent's address is being broadcast in the next half-hour."

"Where are we going?"

"The Colonel's office: let's go!" smiled Zoltan. Captain John was already there when we arrived.

The Regent's address was emotional, brief, and politically astute. He declared Hungary's unconditional surrender to the Allies with a direct appeal for their intervention in keeping Hungary free of further bloodshed, exactly as detailed in the signals that I had sent. Immediately afterward, the room broke into cheers, with hugs and handshaking. Colonel Garzuly had arranged for champagne and refreshments that were wheeled in. When a glass has been poured for everyone, Matyas, who had been appointed as spokesman, proposed toasts to Hungary and to the Allies, in Magyar and in English, for the benefit of John and me.

The plan, which the Horthy camp embraced, was doomed from the outset. Joseph Stalin and his British Secret Intelligence Service mole, Kim Philby, would never have agreed to Hungary's withdrawal from the war on these terms, allowing it to slip from Russian hands by permitting an occupation by Allied armies. Russia's plans for Eastern Europe dictated that she exercise absolute control over all territories destined to come under the Soviet hammer and sickle. We knew nothing that day of the magnitude of the impending disaster for post-war Europe: The Cold War.

"The Germans have surrounded Budapest with tanks!"

"Admiral Horthy has been captured!"

"Prince Regent Horthy has been shot!" Jubilation quickly turned to dismay and paranoia as rumours swirled in the vortex of the prison, fed by the panic in the streets. It was evident, Matyas said, that Germany would act swiftly to install a strong pro-Nazi government figurehead and impose martial law. Hungary would be sacrificed as Germany's stalking horse, to absorb and blunt the Russian thrust westward into the Reich. Hungary's defences would serve to bleed the Red Army white.

"Colonel, what becomes of us, now?" I asked.

Garzuly expressed his concerns for all of the prisoners, as he himself expected to be arrested and replaced at any time, by an *SD* officer, perhaps von Richter. We had to get to a safe house, he insisted. Matyas Pirithy worked feverishly through his uncle, a general, to arrange to have us whisked out through the prison's air raid shelter that evening. At the same time, Matyas and Zoltan were attempting, without much success, to get reliable intelligence about troop movements, German, Russian or British.

While we waited impatiently for confirmation of an escape plan, John stated emphatically that as DIBBLER'S commanding officer, it was clearly his duty to contact our HQ to inform Bari of recent developments. The Hungarians had not wanted John to know about my previous signals, for reasons that Colonel Garzuly did not explain to me. I hadn't told him either, by default, but not out of a wish to be secretive. Naturally, I agreed to send the message as he wished, but my radio was becoming undependable, showing the effects of moisture, neglect and a lack of maintenance. With some tinkering, the Hungarian Hadik W/T operator and I were able to get it fixed up and working. John wrote out the message in plain, then left it to me to transcribe and transmit the signal using my codes. Bari immediately acknowledged receipt.

Hadik was bedlam. The inmates and the guards led by Istvan had united and taken over the prison. The Hadik guards, happy-go-lucky loafers at the best of times, were hosting a grand jubilee. Wine and beer flowed and black-market delicacies, which had materialised from nowhere, were suddenly in abundance. An impromptu indoor soccer match had been organised by Matyas. As the guards and the prisoners were well lubricated, the game threatened to erupt into a riot as the prisoners consistently outscored their erstwhile warders. Elsewhere, prisoners and guards sprawled helter-skelter in the corridors, smoking cigars, playing cards and shooting craps, as well as a few games that I didn't recognise, despite my crash course on the *Queen Elizabeth*.

John, Mike, and I wandered out into the exercise yard behind and one floor below the cells, to get some much-needed fresh air. Scanning the open windows three metres above, I was certain that I could see my Camp X mate, Andy Durovecz (Daniels) of Mission WINDPROOF. It was Andy; he and I established eye contact. We were relieved to know that he was apparently well and in the same building. The soccer game was now a *melée*, split into two parallel contests, which ebbed and flowed throughout the prison's confines, spilling outdoors.

My own cell was occupied. Pista and a young clerk from the Colonel's office named Rachel were locked in the throes of passion, on my cot. I excused myself for my intrusion and left the fortunate couple. Eventually, despite the noise and confusion, I found peace on the floor of Matyas' quarters, and after rifling through his private stock, consumed two warm Czech beers and half a sausage, then fell asleep.

The news on October 16 was very bad, but not unexpected; overnight, Matyas reported, Hitler had installed a puppet dictator, his Nazi toady, Ferenc Szállási. The new government had adopted the name of Szállási's fascist party, The Arrow Cross. Szállási had the well-earned reputation of a zealous disciple of the Nazi policy of genocide, *Die Endlösung*, Final Solution. Everything that we had predicted for Hungary was coming to pass. The Allies' lack of decisive action had allowed Hitler to have his way. Soon, the Red Army would be swarming over the borders, thus guaranteeing the nation's devastation.

Matyas and I sprinted to tell Colonel Garzuly's office. The duty officer told us that the Colonel could not be disturbed, under any circumstances. Undaunted, Matyas brushed past him and entered the inner office. I followed with only slightly less temerity. Garzuly, Andras and Zoltan were in their shirtsleeves, stoking a raging blaze in the fireplace. They looked up in surprise, sweaty and red-faced, as Matyas addressed them, in Magyar.

"A bit early for the old 'chestnuts roasting on an open fire' routine, isn't it?"

"What?" Colonel Garzuly queried, looking extremely puzzled.

"Burning the evidence, no?" Matyas persisted.

"We're disposing of a few hundred sensitive documents. Care to join in the fun?" the Colonel asked us, in Hungarian.

"A pleasure!" responded Matyas. He turned and addressed me in English, "Joe, shall we?"

And pitch in we did, literally. Every fifteen minutes or so, two guards came in to shovel the smoking ashes into large metal containers which were dutifully carted away.

Matyas joked about damnation and hellfire without stop, in Magyar and English, until we were nearly breathless with laughter at his banter. "Open the window! We're going to asphyxiate ourselves!"

"Don't burn the damn carpet you idiot!" shouted one of the two ash-men, to his *Honved* partner, as a container came perilously close to spilling its smoking contents. "Sorry, Sir! But he's from Gerendas, you know." '*How dare they insult my little town*!'

I watched with mixed feelings as Csongor's report of my interrogation was consigned to the flames." '*If only I could...*'

The immolation of the Second Bureau's records consumed two hours. When the merriment died down with the embers, I thanked the Colonel, through Zoltan Perisich, saying that it was an act requiring courage and resolve, for which Mike, John and I and the many other prisoners, particularly those who were Jewish, would forever be grateful.

"You've earned it by your service to Hungary. Andras and Zoltan have found all three of you civilian clothes and a safe...."

"Colonel. Please come quickly!" the desk duty officer broke in.

The Colonel hastily straightened his tie, and donned his hat and uniform jacket. As he was rushing out, he ordered, "Wait here. No one leaves; let no person in but me! Here's my gun. Use it if you have to!"

"Colonel, stop!" shouted Matyas, in Magyar. "Your face is covered in soot. Rinse it off before you go out there!"

He came back in less than five minutes, looking fresh and dapper. "How do I look now, girls?"

When he returned he was serious and sombre. "Andras, shut the door and lock it, please. Zoltan, translate this exactly for Joe." He sat down at his desk and looked straight ahead. "Gentlemen, we are occupied. Hadik has been taken over completely by German Security and Arrow Cross *Nyilasok.*[1] All of my guards have been replaced or are relegated to kitchen or cleanup duties. It is my feeling that we all stand to be imprisoned and transferred to the Reich. *SD Gruppenführer*[2] Hauser, who is now in charge here, is not convinced of my loyalty to the new regime and has demanded that I account for all Second Bureau prisoners with their dossiers complete with full particulars, clearly stated, within one week.

"If I don't meet this demand, he will begin shooting prisoners at random, two per day. 'I will begin with your precious Jews', was exactly what he said. I believe him. He was wounded at the Russian Front, is a Nazi zealot, and as tough as a soldier's shoe leather."

"But we have no Jews here, right Colonel? Now that the records are destroyed, who knows?" asked Matyas.

"He suspects that I destroyed the most vital records and says if I try to play any 'race games' as he called it, I'll be shot, first. By him, personally. He's threatening to call in *Gestapo* racial experts, or some such Aryan nonsense. From now on, we are going to have to be extremely cautious. These meetings are no longer possible. Andras, you will be our go-between. I'll be doing everything I can to make arrangements for the safety of the Jewish inmates and to get you three to the safe house. I'm going to need your co-operation and assistance. I have a plan, but it requires more thought. That's all for now. Good luck!"

"One question, if I may Colonel?"

"Yes, Lieutenant Gordon…Joe?"

"I've heard nothing, but have you had any response from Bari or Istanbul?"

"No, zero. My W/T man can't ask to go to the washroom now without the SD or *Abwehr* intercepting him. My radio is monitored and is likely to go *kaput* anytime. I don't understand what it all means, but that's what the technician reported.

"But, there is one piece of intelligence that's eighty-percent reliable.

[1] *Nyilasok were the Arrow Cross Secret Police.*

[2] *Lieutenant-general SS.*

German security is holding the Regent, Admiral Horthy, under house arrest. One of my sources got that tidbit from a ten-year-old urchin who claims that when he delivered a German newspaper to a building yesterday, a sentry bragged that he would be personally taking it to 'the old man himself.' It's simply too bizarre to be fiction. Now go. Get out of here! And be very careful around the guards! They're nasty, brutal, and short-tempered. They're very edgy and their guns are never on safety."

The Colonel's plan, which Andras whispered through my cell-door that night, was brilliant: simple, elegant, and dangerous. John and I would interview ourselves!

"Sure, but how, Andras?"

"You'll basically make it up!"

"You mean…a play?"

"Yes! But you'll improvise it; you know, just like when actors write the script as they go along."

"What about a rehearsal? John and I can't just blab about anything. I need to know what questions are going to be asked so we'll have a vague idea what we're going to say!"

"Sure enough. The Colonel and Zoltan are arranging that. In the meantime, be thinking of what you want on the record for Berlin to read, and what you don't! I must go. A guard is due here in …forty-five seconds, exactly."

"Andras, please let Mike know what we're doing and why, and that he'll be alright. He'll understand you better if you tell him in Magyar."

"I will."

John and I would meet with Colonel Garzuly and Zoltan Perisich, Andras confimed, to sketch out our script, before curtain time.

Three days later, Colonel Garzuly and Zoltan came to round us up. Two surly, well-armed, menacing SS *Totenkopf*[3] non-coms accompanied them.

Stopping at the outer doorway, Colonel Garzuly turned to the SS corporal and snarled a stream of commands, in German. The man seemed to be about to argue. I understood from Garzuly's brusque response:'…*sehr geheim!*…*Verboten*! *Verstanden*?' that he was telling them to butt out and mind their own business. '*Very courageous and extremely risky of him*!'

'*Jawohl, Colonel! Heil Hitler!*' He had won, this time.

'*Heil Hitler!*' Garzuly led us into his office and shut the door. Act One had begun.

Zoltan tersely explained the pur-

[3] Totenkopfverbande, *the* Waffen SS *Death's Head Division had earned a fearsome reputation in Russia for genocidal brutality paralleling that of* SS *Divisions:* Das Reich, Wiking *and* Leibstandarte-SS *Adolph Hitler. Special* Totenkopf *units also provided the majority of* SS *concentration camp guards.*

pose of the meeting. John, Garzuly and I would construct and conduct phoney interviews to mislead our new masters, well enough, he hoped, to save us from a boxcar to Buchenwald.

"The Colonel is under great pressure, as you know. So, let's get to work on the questions, then you can work out your answers, on your own. We'll have to be ready by tomorrow afternoon, at the latest."

Perisich sat down at an old German *Adler* and typed in Magyar, while John and I dictated the questions, in English. When each one was completed, he read it to the Colonel, for approval.

Garzuly was obliging and made very few changes. In less than two hours, we had created a list of twenty-five questions, which we then broke down into two parts; the 'A' list covered the most essential elements, the 'B' list items were 'for the reader's interest', as Perisich explained.

Now John and I rewrote our stories, to fit the questions, while Zoltan listened, pacing, and making suggestions. We giggled and guffawed like college kids planning a prank in the dormitory as we painted a picture of three boy scouts, ordinary British soldiers, sent into Hungary to gather intelligence and report on the state of the Hungarian armed forces. Our most egregious deviations from fact were critiqued by Zoltan: "Come, come now, do you think all Germans are stupid? These guys weren't promoted because they're good listeners." "Even your mothers wouldn't believe you did that!" "No, absolutely not! You can't get away with saying that! We're trying to keep you three heroes alive!" "Could you try a little harder to sound believable, or do you really want to be shot at dawn?" As he was about to summon the guards to take back us to our cells, he whispered, "Look worried, depressed, in pain… something. This is not going to work at all if you just *futz* around. I'm counting on you to be professional tomorrow. You are SOE Secret Agents!" '*As if we need to be reminded*'. John and I in reality were serious, deadly serious, although we gave Zoltan the impression that we were treating it as a joke. Our enthusiasm was due to our mutual sense of enjoyment and excitement to be working together, at last. We confided to Zoltan that nothing in our training had prepared either of us for this assignment.

The English transcripts had been given to us for study and memorisation. John worked tirelessly to ensure that both statements were convincing and consistent with the yarns that we had spun earlier for *Hauptsturmführer* von Richter. John's scholarly training as a linguist was invaluable in assuring their ring of authenticity. When John was finished, Zoltan re-read the reports and made the necessary corrections to the Magyar versions. These he sent on to the Colonel who returned them within a day. Perisich showed us Garzuly's hand-written notes, which indicated that he was quite satisfied; he had made very few corrections or recommendations.

We were then 'interviewed' separately over two days. Colonel Garzuly and Zoltan were magnificent. It was a smashing success!

As John and I didn't want to be separated from Mike, a suitably large safe house couldn't be found. Andras told us to be ready for transfer to Zugliget, a Hungarian prisoner of war camp, if *Gruppenführer* Hauser accepted the validity of the mock interrogations. We were not yet home free. Upon reading the transcripts, *Gruppenführer* Hauser informed Colonel Garzuly that he had limited confidence in the integrity of the Second Bureau's methods of investigation. The SD would conduct its own independent interrogations forthwith. Had our plot been exposed? John and I feared that Mike would be targeted for harsh treatment again.

Andras was assigned by John to brief Mike. On November 4, 1944, Mike was taken upstairs for questioning. Later that night, at great personal risk, Andras stopped by his cell to make certain that he was coping and at ease with the prepared 'script'. It worked. After two days, the SD finished the questioning and Mike was sent back without having experienced any major difficulties, Andras informed us.

Now, it was my turn. Thanks to John's meticulous preparation, the opening session was almost 'a piece of cake'. Despite our tomfoolery, we had accurately predicted most of the questions. I used Blokey's sage stage advice, listening intently (German/Hungarian/English), pausing reflectively before responding with politeness, and asking for clarification once or twice to show my earnest sincerity. In general, I had the feeling that I had not set a foot wrong. There were no blows, cuffs, or kicks, but only an occasional '*Ach so!*' with nods of assent.

Next came the predictable questions about my W/T training. The interrogator was intensely focussed and showed considerable insight into specific aspects of the British Army's signals training curriculum. At noon, I was allowed to relax and ate a box lunch, supervised by a *Nyilas* guard.

The afternoon session was entirely different; they had decided to take a direct 'hands on' approach. I was taken to a radio room on the top floor of Hadik, outfitted with a powerful German short wave radio, complete with an operator. The agenda was clearly set: to have me send a transmission to Bari. The stakes were suddenly raised. I gave the only excuse that made sense: my codebook had been lost. It was made clear that further resistance would not be tolerated; the transmission could and would be made, without the codes. '*Just how thorough was their knowledge of radio procedure?*' The SD radioman, Paul, a youngish, blue eyed Aryan-type, looked up from his dials, removed his earphones, and shook his head in disagreement, causing the long ash from his cigarette to scatter like dandruff onto his tunic. I understood him to be saying that it wouldn't work. Undeterred, his superior ordered that Paul place my right hand on the Morse key, and hold my wrist. With the petulant sigh of superior knowledge surrendering to the sovereign power of total ignorance, he reluctantly complied. '*The International Alliance of Wireless Wonks?*'

"What is the message, please?" I asked.

"*Hier!*"

"But it's in German! I can't read it!"

"*Du bist ein dummkopf, Schmidt!*"

I understood that. The luckless, invisible Schmidt had not translated the signal for the *Englander*. The interpreter quickly rectified this oversight and the scribbled message was set before me.

The gist of the message was an inquiry about plans for an Allied landing in Yugoslavia. *'Fat chance!'* Without my one-time pad or any other coding, it was a useless exercise. '*Well, give them what they think they paid for.*'

'*Mary had a little lamb/ Its fleece was white as snow,*' I keyed. I waited: ten seconds, fifteen seconds, twenty seconds...no response. Paul was listening intently.

'*Take me out to the ballgame/Take me out with the crowd.*'

'*Funny, it's not working!*' "They don't seem to be responding. Let me try the top priority emergency group. Quiet, please, I need to concentrate closely. *Danke schön.*"

"*Mairzy doats and doazy doats/and little lamsy divey.*'

"It's no use. That last group is reserved, so it almost always gets an immediate confirmation!"

And that was the end of my little *funkspiel*. If Rolly's Sergeant Scott caught that last burst, and had recognised my fist, he would have concluded that I had 'gone spare.'

Day Two was devoted to my wireless training, again. If only they realised how little I truly knew about Bletchley, they would have thrown in the towel! But I was in for an unexpectedly pleasant surprise. There was a new interpreter, an *SD Obersturmführer*[4] whose education in the United States had imparted flawless, fluent English. He was unforgettable! He not only translated the German slowly and precisely, he fre-

[4] *Lieutenant*

quently coached me to reconsider and revise my responses to cast them in the most favourable context, for his superior officer, *Grüppenführer* Hauser. In several instances, he edited my statements on the fly when he felt I was venturing into treacherous ground. During a recess, I asked him about his background. He said that he had spent many enjoyable years studying and travelling in the USA, so that he felt as much American as German. Summoning up my courage, I asked why he was helping me.

"I'm no hero. I am German, but that doesn't mean that my notion of fair play is completely dead, Lieutenant. At this moment, we hold all the cards. The deck is stacked against you and your comrades. If I had thought for one minute that you were a gang of bloody-minded SOE hoodlums, I would not hesitate to help railroad you. However, you're clearly not. We're soldiers, trying to do our duty as we see fit, for our countries. There's still a place for honour, I hope, even in these times."

We were interrupted before I could learn this compassionate and courageous man's name. I am forever grateful to him for his extraordinary generosity and humanity.

The interrogations had been a farce that ended in a draw. The SD had learned nothing of value and no message had been sent, but I had not gained any insight into their plans for the three musketeers, although Zugliget sounded vaguely ominous.

John's two days of questioning were intensive and exhausting, but bearable, he said. The planning and rehearsals with Zoltan and Garzuly had prepared him so thoroughly that the outcome was 'almost a sure bet', he said. Before this, we only had hope; now, we were almost invincible.

November arrived and with it, Hadik prison became even more frigid, gloomy, and dank. The food was vile and the loss of Istvan and our friendly guards had meant the end of my supply of fresh vegetables. All night, the corridors echoed with the racking coughs of prisoners, many of whom, it was rumoured, had pneumonia or tuberculosis. Twice in one week, a blue-coated SS medical doctor attempted to conduct a sick parade, without success. No one in his or her right mind dared show up, no matter how terribly ill they felt, in fear of the probable consequences of 'Doctor Death's' diagnosis. After the second 'no show clinic', a guard announced that we would be taken and examined forcefully if we continued to resist the good doctor's services. Luckily, he didn't return to make good on this threat. My gums had become extremely sensitive and my joints were painful; I was worried that I was contracting scurvy or something worse. It was far more serious for Mike, I feared, as his condition was considerably more fragile. We had to get out of this hellhole.

Early on the morning of November 9, Zoltan Perisich[5] came down to my cell with a canvas bag containing civilian clothes and excellent news.

"You're moving out!"

"Whoa, wonderful! To where? Who else is coming?"

Mike, John, Andrew, and I were being moved to Zugliget. Furthermore, he had been able to locate two safe houses! Zoltan slipped a small piece of paper into a trouser

Remains of Zugliget, 1997

pocket then squeezed the garment bag through the bars.

"You'll be needing that. Keep it well hidden. You can thank the Colonel. He and I have made the arrangements for your transfer. Everything is set. Hauser is happy to get you out of his hair. I should add that Colonel Garzuly is very

[5] *Zoltan Perisich's courage and resourcefulness were recognised by the British Government in 1945. His citation states, in part, "…as an English interpreter (at Hadik) you helped skilfully to sabotage effective interrogations of a party of three British Army officers, under the leadership of Captain J.G. Coates. In co-operation with Lt. Col. Garzuly, you…arranged…to transport them to Zugliget." He is also correctly credited with supplying us clothes and several vital subsequent services. Zoltan's acts of bravery were rewarded with a payment of 125,000 pengös. (Approximately $100 at the time of payment)*

impressed with all of you.

"Please let him know that the feeling is mutual."

Zoltan left before I could thank him or find out more details. I knew nothing more about Zugliget, than it was a wooded campground in northwest Budapest. Any place was better than Hadik! A few minutes later, Andras Hegedus came to tell me that Zugliget was a PoW transfer-camp, with *Honved* guards and a physical layout that made it "secure as Swiss cheese". We were moving out within the hour. I wanted very much to thank Matyas before we left, but Andras could not find him.

Zoltan had arranged to have the Colonel's driver take us in Garzuly's Second Bureau limousine. The trip was almost leisurely in contrast with the Grand Prix of Pécs.

Zugliget was exactly as Andras had painted it: woodsy, with several worn-down chalets which a travel brochure in better times might have described as 'rustically charming', and a two-storey main stone building that served as the canteen and central lock-up, to use the term rather loosely. John and I were housed in one of several small apartments, with a common inner balcony, much like a contemporary motel. It was a very low rent Beaulieu. Situated in lovely park land known as Janoshegy (John's Hills), it had seen better days as a once popular and inexpensive summer retreat for a century to Budapest families, but now served as an internment compound for prisoners of war awaiting transfer to German or Austrian *stalags* - PoW camps. During our stay, we met fourteen prisoner officers including Polish, British, Americans, Romanians, and Russians.

Zugliget was a home-away-from-home for a large Polish refugee population who had fled the Nazis after the Blitzkreig had smashed Poland's heroic armed forces in 1939. Horthy's Hungary had welcomed and provided them sanctuary at Zugliget. The guards were a good-natured collection of seasoned *Honved* militia; the Camp Commandant, a captain, turned out to be a valuable ally.

Colonel Garzuly and Zoltan were truly miracle-workers. Not only were John, Mike and I together, but we were also re-united with Andrew Durovecz. It was a joyous Camp X Alumni homecoming. We had a lot of catching up to do.

Andy told us that he had been badly beaten several times and, like Mike, was losing his hearing in one ear. Mike and I talked privately about Gus' mysterious radio message, which had landed me in hot water with Colonel Boughey. It was apparent that Gus had been subjected to a lot of abuse at the time, but was trying to warn us of the danger at Orfu. Unfortunately, none of us knew where he was being held.

The Poles were very social, helpful and evidently wielded more influence around Zugliget than the *Honved*. They not only had the run of the place, but also carried papers granting them permission to travel around Budapest, with no curfew and few restrictions. We quickly grasped the opportunities for escape and went out of our way to befriend them. Security inside the compound, to be charitable, ranged from transparent to haphazard. During the first day or two, a *Honved* guard accompanied us to the canteen or the exercise yard, but soon grew tired of this rigorous duty and we were left to wander the grounds quite freely. The Poles cautioned us not to try venturing outside the perimeter fence, since *Nyilasok* sharpshooters had replaced *Honved* sentries in the aftermath of a recent escape. Naturally, we wanted to know all about it.

"One of your British officers, a Captain Reynolds, walked out of the camp, one morning. He would have hoofed it all the way to Yugoslavia, but someone reported him to a *Nyilas* security cop in town." The speaker was a forty-something Pole. John and I were impressed with his fluency in English.

"Where did you learn to speak English so well?" asked John.

"Wuj."

"Where?" I asked.

"Wuj! Wuj!"

"I've never heard of the place. Is it in Poland?"

He repeated it, "Yes, Wuj!"

"Please spell it, in English."

John was mildly amused.

"Sure: L-O-D-Z."

"Oh, Lodz, that I do know."

"Wuj!"

"Wuj it is." And thus was his nickname born. 'Wuj' had learned English in an American Jesuit seminary, where he had been studying to enter the Society of Jesus, until a German tank ripped the building apart. He was the sole survivor.

Finally, I got back to the point. "But I spoke with Captain Reynolds, the day before yesterday, just after we arrived. He didn't say anything about planning an escape! He had some vague ideas, but nothing definite."

"I spoke with him, too," John added quietly. "Interesting chap. He was very 'close to the vest' at first. Perhaps he suspected that I was a police informer, for all I know. But he did open up and told me that he was actually a Flight Lieutenant with the RAF, had been shot down in North Africa, and taken captive by Erwin Rommel's *Afrika Korps*, who treated him well. How he ended up here is a long and hair-raising story, but he falsified his ID, as Hungarians are not inclined to think highly of Allied fliers."

'How well I remember: A Boy's Guide to the Magneto for Fun and Vengeance!'

"He was being taken to Budapest to be questioned about a Hungarian General Ujhaszy. He was certain that there is a Dutch-run PoW escape circuit operating in Budapest. He showed me a note that I checked out when I went for a stroll last night. There was supposed to be a representative at the gate at eleven, but I didn't find anyone. The organisation's chief is a chap named Van Huttingen. I do speak enough Dutch and looked forward to the contact. Oh, yes, he had sketched a map of this place, which he gave to me, saying it was mine to keep, as he had no further use of it. Joe, I want you to file it away it inside your jacket, if you would please?"

"I wish I could let my folks know that I'm alive." Mike spoke for us all.

The following morning, John went to see the Commandant. He returned with the good news that the Captain would send Red Cross letter cards on behalf of us all!

I had studied Captain Reynold's map that night to look for any features of Zugliget and the surrounding neighbourhood, which might be exploited. "Do you mind if I go over to see him this afternoon, John?" I asked.

"Please yourself."

The Commandant was a friendly and courteous gentleman whose politics were closer to Horthy's than to Szállási's rabid Arrow Cross pro-Nazi fascism. He introduced his two Lieutenants. Through an interpreter, they enthusiastically described the history and development of the Zugliget area. I asked when and to where we were likely to be transferred. When I left the Captain's office, I felt pleased that I had obtained a better understanding of these three key people and, the inner workings of camp administration. As a parting gift, the Commandant gave me a stack of PoW letter cards for us to fill out, which, he promised, would then be forwarded. What I had actually wanted was to steal a street map.

John and I realised that our window of opportunity was closing very quickly. When the door was slammed, there would be no second chance, no turning back, once we were consigned for transport to Austria.

John and I held a council of war.

"Mike has to go to hospital, John! He's suffering with raging headaches, and he's almost deaf in his infected ear," I stated.

"I know. Where are the addresses of those safe houses?"

"Here, in my jacket. But we need a map to find them, or someone who knows the city and can give good directions."

"What about the *Honved* guards? Do you think there's one who would

Tel. No.: Abbey 6131

The War Office,
Whitehall,
London, S.W.1.

Any further communication on this subject should be addressed to:—

Capt. J.V. Houseman

21st April 1944.

JVH/GEN/3239

John J. Gelleny Esq.,
97 Wilton Avenue,
Welland, Ontario,
Canada.

Dear Mr. Gelleny,

I am taking the liberty of writing you a short personal note in order that you will not be worried at the irregularity of your son, Joseph Gelleny's mail.

He is very busy indeed on special duties and will not find time to write as often as he has done in the past.

You may rest assured that he is in excellent health and everything possible is being done for his well being.

Yours sincerely,

J. V. Houseman.

(J.V. HOUSEMAN)

Capt.

Letter from the War Office to John Gelleny, my father, noting that " he is very busy indeed on special duty... and will not find time to write as often as he has done in the past" give us a hand and not turn us in for thirty pieces of silver? Do we have enough money in case?"

"I have enough left. It may be tight, now that Andy is depending on us, but I'll manage. I need to get enough change for fares on the Budapest buses and trams. The canteen should be good for that. I'll approach one or two of the friendliest old boys tomorrow and hope they're not greedy."

"Good, and I'll see what specifics our Poles have to offer. We'll meet again at suppertime, tomorrow."

John was charged up. "I was with the Polish ranking officer for an hour. His name is Lieutenant-Colonel Jan Wolszlieger and he's rather well connected. Step outside for a bit of fresh air."

As we walked the grounds, we could still see the see the impressions of the countless tent pegs that had been hammered into the ground, silent mementoes of happier times for Hungarians.

"How did make out with your reconnoitring?"

"Bull's eye and aces all the way for me, John. Tell me your news first, though! And I dare you to say his name again, graduate linguist or not!"

"Wolszlieger, my boy. Wolszlieger. Lieutenant-Colonel Jan Wolszlieger is the ringmaster of a circuit operating out of here. He's cosy with Van Huttingen's Dutch group that Reynolds talked about."

"I know. There's also another, a Polish Communist circuit operating on the outside. They'll all work together for us."

"Heaven knows how many PoW's they have slipped through the Germans' tentacles. I would venture to guess fifty, perhaps more. I do have maps of Budapest and public transportation schedules" John stated.

"Good! I have money for tramcars, maps, schedules, and I now have a royal stomach ache. I drank at least five litres of coffee to have an excuse for hanging around the canteen bar all afternoon. What a great listening post! Lots of local intelligence about police patrols, roadblocks, and houses of ill repute to avoid because the rooms are sound recorded by the *SD*, ...the whole gamut of gossip. Most of it I picked up in Hungarian, with a smattering of German and a little Polish. Tonight, you and I are being taken by our new friends, the Polish Cultural Society, for a late night guided tour of the grounds, to check on possible escape routes."

"Fine work, Joe. Let's go inside and scan our maps, then after supper we can get a few winks."

The Polish Cultural Society met in a secluded corner of the canteen at 9:00 p.m. sharp. The Chairman, Lieutenant-Colonel Jan Wolszlieger, dressed in the clothes of a labourer, our interpreter Wuj from Lodz, and two silent, pipe-smoking seniors, comprised a quorum. Jan seemed oblivious to the presence of the canteen's late night regulars, as he quietly gave us a complete spy's guide to survival in Budapest. The city had arguably the best electric tram systems in Eastern Europe, he said, but fares could not be purchased from the drivers. That little fact I had forgotten, if ever I had known it!

"Only bought from news stands, always using small bills or change and never, never board without your ticket. That could get you labelled as suspiciously foreign and hauled away by the transit gendarmes. Now, show us your map; I don't want to know the addresses of your safe houses, just the main intersections, for your security. Then we'll be able to find the best route, and an alternate, just in case you feel that you're ever being followed."

The two seniors bent over the street maps, the smoke from their knobbly pipes circling their snowy-white heads like two Father Christmases. Jan had many other tips and hints to share as the two pointed to the grids with their pipe stems and leaned back, puffing knowingly. Sometime after 10:00, we got up and moved toward the door. "Fresh air, father! Too much damn smoke in here. Good night," Jan commented as we edged past the drowsy *Honved* watchman.

The tour of inspection was enlightening. This was the *forte* of the two older gallants. They moved as nimbly as kittens, crouching low and counting aloud, then scrambling from tree to tree, to dodge the synchronised searchlights, pausing occasionally to point out weak points in the fencing where there was adequate ground cover to conceal oneself. John and I were straining just to keep up with them, as we cruised the entire perimeter. I had brought along a sketch map, on which we made 'X's and marked the recommended escape exits. We regrouped behind one of the furthermost chalets. The Poles were not even breathing heavily. John and I were puffing; I was badly out of shape. '*Your Belgian Beaulieu pal would not be impressed.*' Putting the map into my jacket lining, we thanked them and wished them goodnight.

"Tomorrow, November 11, is a special treat: roast pig, Polski style! Come, celebrate Armistice Day with us! You've never tasted anything like it!"

How right Jan was. John and I supposed that such a speciality might be too fatty, too rich and too undercooked for our sensitive stomachs to handle after more than a month of spare prison fare. So, we decided not to be spongers, and paid in advance. This way, we reasoned, would it not be all right to insist upon extra-well done servings?

An hour into the banquet, John and I exchanged pained glances. I told him that he looked like hell. Then, I was gripped by stomach cramps and nausea. We excused ourselves and ran desperately for our room. I had never felt so wretched. For the next two miserable days, we were the 24-hour latrine twins. I will spare the details; whether it was simple food poisoning or pork-induced flux, tapeworms, or dysentery, the Jews and Moslems have it right!

Monday November 13, 1944, is a date that is seared into my memory. Jan had visited us early in the morning to express his personal regrets at our plight. John and I were still weak, but had found enough strength to shower and shave and were recuperating from the effort, lying in our underwear on our cots, quietly chatting about our imminent breakout. There was a knock at the door.

"Come in!" I shouted, expecting another well wisher.

The Commandant entered, with a Lieutenant. They were obviously ill at ease. When I heard his words in Magyar, I was in shock. The interpreter translated, "There are two German and two Arrow Cross security police officers in my office to interview you, Captain Coates and Lieutenant Gordon. I am very sorry. I will be waiting downstairs." He saluted and walked out.

The mystery guest was none other than *Hauptsturmführer* Von Richter, from Hadik, accompanied by an *Oberscharführer*[6] Messinger and two professionally nondescript *Nyilasok* plain-clothes officers in fedoras. The interview may have lasted five minutes. Von Richter gave us a cursory glance, standing while he closed the snaps on his briefcase, and announced that he would be returning tomorrow to question John. They strode out and sped off in an immense black Mercedes Benz with *SS* flags flying atop the front fenders.

Word had travelled quickly through the camp. Jan made his second visit of the day to bolster our spirits. It was a kind gesture, but we were too depressed to be grateful. Early Tuesday morning, November 14, John was summoned to appear at the Commandant's office. He put on his uniform. Messinger and another *Oberscharführer* were waiting for him, without the Hungarian coppers or von Richter. For two straight days, John was interrogated closely by Messinger while the *Oberscharführer* translated and typed.

Afterwards, John said that the questioning, though thorough, had covered the same ground as all of the pre-

[6] *Master sergeant*

[7] *Field police*

vious inquiries. He weaved and bobbed, following our Hadik mental script without any deviation.

On the evening of November 15, the Polish Cultural Society held an emergency meeting in Jan's quarters. We insisted that we had to break out within the next twenty-four hours. John and I felt that, failing a clandestine escape, we might just as well take our chances and walk away as Reynolds had done. Jan was horrified and tried to appeal to logic. We argued with him, eventually conceding that it would be a foolhardy act of bravado; we would be signing our death warrants. It would also be grossly unfair to leave Andrew and Mike to shoulder the grim consequences, whether we were dead or alive. Reluctantly, we agreed to be patient and wait a bit longer.

We were home free, *almost*. On Thursday November 16, at 9:30 a.m., a *Honved* man was dispatched to bring us to the Commandant's office, where *Oberscharführer* Messinger was pacing, impatiently tapping his boot tops with his riding crop. Outside, his driver was languorously polishing the windshield of the idling Mercedes, while two SS *Feldpolizei*[7], wearing the copper breast plates with chains which distinguished their service, smoked and glanced at their watches, their weapons leaning upright against the running board. We were obviously going somewhere: to German HQ? John understood Messinger to have told the Commandant that our few personal belongings could be safely left in our rooms, as he would bring us back in the morning.

A third guard, with a machine pistol as motivation, escorted two unhappy Hungarians, Andrew and Mike, as well as John, into the room. He saluted Messinger and goose-stepped to the door, narrowly missing the Commandant's beloved Pekinese. It didn't require much imagination to smell a rat. Messinger snarled a command to the would be dog kicker, who bellowed out the door. The two field policemen butted their cigarettes and clattered up the steps. Each took John and I by an arm and bundled us into the car. The driver closed the doors firmly and got in. We were like slabs of meat, sandwiched together in the rear seat, between the two SS men. I can clearly remember the feelings of bewilderment, helplessness, and rage. The windows were tightly sealed; the high-powered stream of hot air, tinged with gasoline fumes from the heater made my head reel. My still-sensitive stomach recoiled at the rankness of sweat and stale cigarettes imprinted on their uniforms, mixed with the acrid odours of machine oil and cordite on their automatic sidearms. I felt on the verge of throwing up on my captors' shiny breastplates. Desperate, I tried to slide my right hand toward the window crank handle. The *Feldpolizei's* meaty paw intercepted me; he laughed as he smashed the tip of the gun barrel on my knuckles. I gagged with the pain. At full throttle, the driver engaged first gear and let out the clutch as the engine howled in protest, spinning our rear tires on the wet grass, soaked by an overnight downpour. We lurched wildly and then hurtled forward, passing under the just-raised arm of the barricade. The tires screamed in protest as we leaped the curb and skidded onto the slick concrete roadway, fishtailing wildly from side to side, while accelerating like a demon.

We had been kidnapped.

Chapter 8

Escape From Zugliget

If it weren't so dismally depressing, it would have been almost laughable that the *Sicherheitsdienst* were apparently unable to part with us. The auto pulled into a concrete bunker garage at *SD* headquarters, at Tarogato utca #6. It had the appeal of a bombed-out tractor factory. We were hustled up a rusty steel staircase, then Mike and I were separated. I was escorted into what is euphemistically called an Interview Room, furnished in basic *SD* Interrogation Chamber. Here, a four-man *SS* board of inquiry waited impatiently for me, as warmly welcoming as delegates at an undertakers' convention. Blonde, blue-eyed, and athletically fit in the ideal Aryan sense of spit *und* polish, with *strength through joy* fervour glinting in his eyes, an *Obersturmbannführer-SS*[1] began the overture and first movement. He perched in splendid isolation from the inferior ranks and me, on the corner of an impossibly smooth, rich-grained mahogany desk, as broad as a grand piano, while he gave my Hadik 'phony' interview file a cursory scrutiny. Without comment, he slid it delicately into the wastebasket with the tip of the obligatory *SS* riding crop. He stood up, way up. Hands on black serge uniformed hips, he presented six menacing feet of contemptuous *über*-being. He addressed the assembled onlookers like a chief surgeon explaining a gall bladder transection to a class of awestruck first-year residents. With the smattering of German that I had managed to absorb, it was obvious that *Obersturmbannführer* Wolff was conducting a demonstration class in Interrogation Methods 101.

"No questions at this time, please, gentlemen. I have only three points to make:

"We are fed up with the prisoner's deceitfulness!

"We know all of his stupid, futile tricks and games.

"This time, he will give us the whole truth!"

In case I had missed the point of this psychodrama, the interpreter stated his version of the *Obersturmbannführer's* agenda in English: "a) your previous testimony was all lies; b) we will discover the true and complete facts this time, and c) you will send a message to Bari."

[1] *Lieutenant-colonel*

It was essential now not to abandon hope nor to waver from the script and be cowed by the bully's threats and intimidation. He began, in a serious mode, with detailed questions about the mission's objectives, our abortive landings and onward to Pécs. My answers were almost carbon copies of the Perisich/Garzuly interviews. I realised that by carrying on in this fashion, I was risking the most severe physical retaliation if I overstepped the bounds of his lordship's credulity, and would be hauled away for a sound flogging while hanged by the heels, or some appendage even more uncomfortable.

Herr Messinger entered the room, on cue, and chimed in, "We know that you have lied, continuously. We have used your own wireless set to contact Bari HQ. We were able to determine from our highly skilled deception techniques that most of the statements you have been mouthing are nothing but fairy tales...complete fabrications. What do you have to say to that, Mr. British Secret Agent?"

It was as though Gregor had given me a jolt. '*What if it were true...? No, not possible. You detuned the radio after sending the Horthy message to Istanbul, didn't you? And Andras had said that Garzuly ordered the Second Bureau to hide the damn thing, before the Arrow Cross could get their hands on it. These were lies; what he was saying was absolutely, definitely impossible!*'

"Not so, sir. I am a radio operator with the British Army, and remind you that my companions and I are prisoners of war."

An extremely ugly, pockmarked *SD* corporal who had been viewing me with contempt jumped up from his chair and brayed, spraying spittle in my face, "You lying bastard! You'll send a message to Bari yourself today or you'll be singing a different tune when I'm finished with you!" That said, he sat down, and continued to glare stilettos.

The corporal's outburst apparently was not taken from the same page of *Obersturmbannführer* Wolff's script. With a trace of annoyance, Wolff cleared his throat, and continued his pursuit of truth and beauty. His wristwatch showed 5:00 p.m. I had been in the chair for over three hours and asked for a washroom break, which was granted.

Now Messinger took charge. He used threats and harangues but stopped short of assault to induce me to send a signal, which I refused to do, citing the usual excuses: non-existent codes and crystals. Abruptly at 7:00 p.m., he proclaimed with finality that I would be packed off to an Austrian prison where the *SD* had 'special means' to effectively deal with the most 'difficult criminal subjects'. The bully corporal grabbed my right arm, marched me from the room, down a gloomy, grey concrete corridor, and flung me into a tiny cubicle.

It reeked of urine-fouled straw, sweat, and human misery. I was kept there in chilly semi-darkness for perhaps forty-eight hours, picking lice from my jacket, drinking cold cabbage flavoured water twice a day, with only an overflowing slop bucket for my personal needs.

Then, we were on the move again. Handcuffed, linked together by a chain, and herded into a police van, Mike, John, and I huddled closely, whispering, sharing our war stories. Messinger had beaten Mike, whereas John and I had only undergone some rigorous interrogation, with a side order of threats. Our captors had their wires crossed; they had mistakenly believed that John was also a trained W/T operator, but he disabused them of that notion. Now reclassified as criminals, we had been sentenced to extended incarceration in Vienna, the adoptive home of Wolfgang Mozart, Ludwig van Beethoven, and raging Nazism.

First, we had to survive Pestvideki Prison, on Fo utca,[2] in hilly Pest. This was not only depressingly regressive, but I was losing complete track of jails, jailers, and my accumulated time behind bars. This was not why I had joined SOE! I thought of my gentle chum Blokey, condemned for twenty to life: a dreadful, living death sentence for a man of his *joie de vivre*, talents, and fine sensibilities. Our section of Pestvideki was a holding tank for prisoners of all types and stripes, loosely classified as 'politicals': Hungarians, Yugoslav and Slovak Communists, a Russian Marxist *agent provocateur*, and some Hungarian Jews who were separated from us, ghettoised. Limited freedom to circulate was granted to some inmate 'trustees', ostensibly for the purpose of cleaning the dungeons. A few Jewish prisoners who had this 'privilege' were the most dependable couriers, running messages promptly from section to section, but their movements were restricted each to his own floor.

My cell was on the fifth floor, which was ruled by a gang of boorish, young *SD* louts, barely out of their Hitler Youth *lederhosen*. Many were ethnic *SD* and *Gestapo*, composed of Hungarian-German recruits from Swabia and Saxony, an unpleasant lot who claimed total sovereignty over the four upper levels.

Over the past month, I had tried to occupy my mind with my poetry and songs, or in trying to understand how Nazism's death grip had taken hold of so progressive and civilised a nation as Germany. The sign at Camp X had commanded recruits to KNOW YOUR ENEMY.

As a European, it was impossible not to have been saturated with Germany's distinguished contributions to music, film, architecture, literature, theology, and philosophy, not to mention the sciences, engineering

[2] *utca means street.*

and medicine. How did the land that nurtured Goethe, the pillar of German letters, and Felix Mendelssohn, the brilliant Jewish composer, get from there, to here: evil totalitarianism, institutionalised anti-Semitism, all driven by the unshakeable belief in an inalienable destiny to dominate the world? Was it in revenge for The Treaty of Versailles under the feeble post-war Weimar Republic? A national identity crisis? An infantile need for respect, or recognition? Was it Tribalism carried to the extreme? Tribalism serves to preserve cultural traditions, prescribes behaviour for the band and individuals, establishes a common identity, and fulfils the basic human need for affiliation - a sense of belonging to a group. Could its dark side be the basis of our wretched human record of intolerance, hatred, and savagery, a fatal flaw in our makeup?

The Nazi magus, the transplanted Austrian Corporal, Adolf Hitler, had conjured up a mystic vision of *Das Volk*, as an almost supernatural element of nature. He cleverly stirred up his adopted tribe's grievances (Versailles) into a frenzy of xenophobia, anti-Semitism, and the promise of restitution and glorification as the Aryan master tribe. The swastika emblazoned on a blood-red field – the blood flag, *Blut Fahne*, was a potent runic symbol woven into the rites and rituals of superbly-orchestrated 'sound and light' tribal gatherings to celebrate the triumph of the collective tribal will over those who sought to dilute the purity of the tribal (racial) blood stock. Who could resist the seductive power of the hocus-pocus, the brilliant oratory of the charismatic psychopath, *Der Führer*, the shaman and chieftain who would lead an invincible Teutonic *volk* to supremacy in a new world order, the One Thousand-Year Reich. Those who resisted or doubted the vision were branded as enemies of the state, i.e. tribe, 're-educated' to death in concentration camps, or otherwise eliminated mercilessly.

In order to survive in Austria, I needed to understand my enemy. To do that, I would become a student of German *kultur*. But to succeed, I would have to learn the language.

A quick study of the guards led me to pick out a young German *SD* Corporal, Karl Heinz Schrader, who spoke English, and, by appearances, was more civilised than his semi-alcoholic comrades-in-arms. My estimate was correct; he welcomed my request for some pre-primer readers, a German picture dictionary, and a simple grammar book so that I could begin learning to read, write, and speak *Deutsch*. He said his hometown was the port city of Hamburg, where he had aspirations of becoming either a university professor of Modern Languages or a stowaway. He not only supplied books which I had requested, but he became my tutor of sorts, stopping by to coach my pronunciation or to explain the intricacies of German gender, case and verb forms. Karl was using his off-duty hours to study Magyar. So that we could learn together, he bought a Hungarian dictionary and some elementary books. I made a concerted effort to study the German texts, to keep up appearances, but revelled in secretly reading Hungarian.

When Karl was not on duty, his messmates did the bare minimum as jail keeps, which suited me perfectly. My housebreaking experiences at Beaulieu encouraged me to pick the lock of the cell door, which was ridiculously easy, so that I could wander the fifth floor, almost at will. I realised how much Matyas must have valued his freedom, at Hadik. The problem was that I had nowhere to go at Pestvideki. There was absolutely no way out. There was a balcony, overlooking the main floor entrance five floors below, but unfortunately, heavy wire mesh netting separated each level. If I were to jump for a lark, I would have landed in the 'cage.' That surely would have reversed the steady headway I was making with Karl Heinz. A few of the guards became interested in my educational progress, and smiled if I thanked them or tried to chat, haltingly, in German, when they delivered my meal trays. Had my food improved incrementally in quantity and quality, or was it my imagination?

As at Pécs, the nights at Pestvideki were not calm and bright. It was a good time to get out of the confines of the cell for thirty-minute intervals to stretch my legs; I could see the lights inside the women's prison building. Unfortunately, those women were treated very badly; their nocturnal sobs and screams were bone-chilling reminders of the appalling record of mankind's heartless inhumanity to our fellow humans. When I asked Karl what was going on, he stated that he did not know; he had never ventured over there, as it "...was not my business".

Three weeks had passed since our abduction on November 17. When was the train leaving to take us to Vienna? At 11:00 a.m., December 6, Karl rushed to my cell. This was the third anniversary of the opening of Camp X.

"Joe, get your belongings and be ready to come with me, *in fünf minuten*!"

"*Wo*? Where are we going, Karl? *Wien*?" My voice was shaking.

"*Nein*!"

'*Oh my God! What next? Another abduction? If not Vienna, then where?*' At Hadik, I had heard whispered rumours of the horrors of Mauthausen, the main Austrian death camp.

"*Fünf minuten, schnell, bitte!* Five minutes. Quickly!"

Karl took me down two flights of stairs, to the guardhouse on the third floor. John, Mike, and Andy were standing sullenly against the wall, their bits of gear heaped on the crazed green linoleum floor. Messinger came out from his office squiring a Norse Brunnhilde, a full-figured, bleached-blond female SS interpreter. She was bathed in a perfume whose aroma made my head spin, but her heavily-inflected English was understandable. Thanks to Karl, I understood the gist of what was about to happen, before the fraulein finished her translation. It took a moment for the full meaning to sink in. 'We are going back to Zugliget.' It took all of my self-control to avoid blurting, '*Did you say, Zugliget,* mein Herr*? Surely you jest*!'

I didn't and he wasn't. We were quickly shuttled down to the garage, and shoved unceremoniously into a waiting limousine, to merry old Camp Zugliget. We drove slowly as the major roads were clogged with German military vehicles: troop carriers, tanks, mobile artillery, motorcycles, and armour of all descriptions streaming from the east. The traffic converging at major intersections was under the control of white-gloved *Feldpolizei*. Most of them looked prepared to shoot any driver, regardless of rank, who dared to deviate from or disobey, their directions. We turned off the main thoroughfare and arrived in less than an hour.

"Is this good news or bad, John?" We had been deposited at the Commander's HQ and shown back to our quarters by a cheerfully profane *Honved* guard.

"I'd have to say that they can't decide what to do with us and want us out of the way, for now. They've shown that they can get at us anytime, which they'll do again, when Messinger's finally ready to ship us to Austria. What do you make of it?"

"I'm not sure. Maybe Garzuly was working his magic."

"I don't think so, Joe. I can't imagine the Germans caring at all for his opinion. After all, the testimony we gave at Hadik was completely discredited by Messinger and his cronies. How could he possibly have any influence with them?"

"I don't know. But doesn't it seem hard to explain why the *SD* wouldn't have simply shipped us third class directly to *Österreich*? John, I truly, honestly believe we were almost on our way there, and someone, or fate intervened. Since I don't believe in miracles, or the kindness of strangers, I have to think it was partly because of Zoltan and the Colonel."

"Don't forget, Joe, the Nazis are facing the advancing Red Army, and Comrade Ivan is not taking prisoners. The Russians are swarming like bees to the hive. We're an added pain in their fascist rear ends."

"But we're officially criminals, John, so why not just shoot us and be done with us?"

"You have a point!"

I was determined to find out more, from Jan's Cultural Society.

"Welcome back, Lazarus! Back for another pork dinner?" boomed Jan. All of the inhabitants of the canteen turned to stare. Several old-timers waved and greeted me, including the rheumy-eyed *Honved* door guard. Jan lowered his voice. "See, Joe, I have English, but not much!"

Wuj, the '*almost* Jesuit', interpreter continued, "Get a coffee and meet us outside, behind the chalet with the blue roof. You remember, where we met after the grand tour."

We sat down on the wooden steps. Jan began. "So! Tell us all about Pest!"

I did.

"You're one lucky fellow, actually, all of you. My colleagues found out you were due back today. You're not going anywhere but to Austria, my lad, unless you get the hell out of here. I really never expected to clap eyes on you again when they tore out of here."

"How in the world...?"

He laughed. "A *pfennig* here, a smile there. The incorruptible *SS übermensch* can be bought, just like any one else, maybe more easily. Those boys are a long way from hearth and home. It works especially well when my 'girls of the night' treat them to a wink, a schnapps, and a massage."

"They deserve a medal for that," I remarked, thinking of Messinger and the toad-like sergeant from Pestvideki.

"They are thorough professionals, in the best sense, and know exactly what they can and can't get away with. Most soldiers, German, Poles, or English, just crave female companionship, someone to talk to and share a drink with. When it starts getting more complicated, we always have backup waiting in the wings to bail them out."

"Sounds well thought out. What are our chances, Jan?"

"The indications are that you're going to be force-marched to Austria, with several thousand Jews, from Sopron or Pilisvorosvar. Szállási's a vile, murdering bastard and is out-Caesaring Caesar, co-operating one hundred ten percent with the Nazis. Horthy was able to keep most Hungarian Jews out of the *SS*' clutches. He had a better record than Poland, so far as that goes. It's unlikely that most poor souls, yourselves included, could make it all the way to Austria. Disease, starvation, cold, exhaustion and beatings, and if you do get there, you'll be dumped like rubbish into a slave labour camp. Average life span there: three months, tops. I'd strongly advise that you avoid this trip.

"Give me until tomorrow and I'll have more details. I'm looking over my shoulder these days too, Joe.

Three of my best people have been taken away since you left."

"Not the two old boys?"

"Yes. They were not what they appeared; perhaps you get my meaning. The *Nyilashok* took Little Peter, too, whom you didn't meet. I'm afraid they're undergoing intensive interrogation in your Pest *SD* prison. No one can withstand torture indefinitely. We'll keep the circuit limping along, for now. Things will take a little longer, that's for sure. But that's always the way with old men, or so my dear wife would say. We'll get you out. Meet us back here tomorrow night, at eight."

'Could they be SOE? Of course! They spoke very little, had beards, wore caps to cover their hair, and they moved like young alley cats on a prowl. Now that the SD *had them, God help them! This wonderful man, Captain Jan Wolszleiger, is now in grave danger himself; he is either extremely courageous or mad!'*

John was enthused when I reported Jan's news. I asked him to join us. He was my mission commander. The night sky glittered with ice crystals like diamonds in the searchlights' beams. Jan was well prepared and covered the details with a finely honed precision. It was a masterpiece of intelligence briefing. He condensed the information that we needed to know, in meaningful chunks, and no more. Then he reviewed the vital details.

"Any questions?"

"Yes, one thing, if I may, Jan."

"Okay, John, but hush! Arrow Cross patrols have been doubled at night."

"What will we do about Mike?"

"Hah, I almost forgot! I am so glad that you asked! Tomorrow morning, he will be taken to one of the best hospitals in Budapest."

"That's for certain?" I didn't doubt Jan's word, but needed re-assurance that Mike would not be dumped and forgotten.

"Yes, for certain, Joe. We have arranged to send him to *Uj Szent Janos Korhaz* (St. John's Hospital). He will receive the very best of care. I promise, on my honour as a Polish Officer… "

"You're fantastic! Thank you, Jan! It's damn cold out here!"

"Now I have a pressing matter to discuss with Daniels. But I must change the location. We can't be too careful. Can you please find him? Ask him to our come to our friend's room, in ten minutes."

"Sure, but where?" I queried.

Wuj interjected, "My place."

"Now, you two must leave. We'll meet tomorrow, same place, and same time. Wear a coat! Good night!"

Right; Andy Durovecz (Daniels) at Bari, Italy

The next day, December 8, 1944, was eventful. Mike was transported to St. John's Hospital and Andy Daniels walked out of Zugliget, boldly passing himself off as a Pole. The *Honved*, and *Nyilasok* sentries didn't blink when a Polish internee carrying valid identity papers presented a day pass, signed by the Commandant, at the guard house. Andy strolled through the gate, hopped on public transit, and arrived at a designated Budapest safe house, where he turned over the Polish ID papers to a waiting Group 3 agent.[3]

The operation was brilliantly conceived and flawlessly executed. By its transparent simplicity, John and I concluded that it was a set piece of professional fieldcraft. Only Captain Jan Wolszlieger and his Group 3 associates had the resources, finesse, and external links with the Dutch circuit in Budapest, to pull off such an audacious feat. On a personal level, John and I were very happy for Daniels that the ruse had been a roaring success. But, had he been recognised, Szállási's *SD* and *Gestapo*-trained *Nyilasok* minions would have subjected Andy to endlessly brutal physical and mental torture to extract his accomplices' names and the complete details of the operation.

At Camp X and Beaulieu, agents were instructed in the techniques of interrogation. It was an expectation that each recruit recognise and accept his inherent limitations, a kind of personal pain profile. Borrowing from their Russian counterparts' explorations of drug-induced confessions for Stalin's 'show trial' purges of the Communist party and armed forces in the 1930s, SS doctors and medical researchers had developed diabolically effective chemical means of obtaining 'confessions'. Fortunately, I was never subjected to injections of the 'truth serum', scopolamine. Twisted medicine was now combined with the *SD's* 'advanced' methods of physical abuse, which together, were nearly infallible. Hence, the SOE's legendary 'suicide pill', 'L-Pill', or cyanide capsule was routinely issued to agents before embarking on missions. I had disposed of mine in Brindisi while packing my radios and gear.

Our confidence in Jan's abilities was beyond question, but as the SOE ranking officer in Zugliget, John was, by default, Andy's commander and wanted answers.

"Why have we had been kept in the dark?"

Jan responded that Andy had insisted, for his own reasons that he never made clear. Jan explained that the original plan hinged upon getting Mike to St. John's Hospital. Then, the trio of John, Andy and I would follow. After interviews with Andy, Group 3 decided not to attempt a triple defection. It was judged far too

[3] *Andrew Durovecz,* My Secret Mission, *Lugus Publications, 1996.*

risky and unworkable. Andy was told that he had to go solo. He would be disguised as a Pole, carrying valid Polish identity papers. The technical aspects presented several challenges, not the least of which involved coaching Andy in Polish and split second co-ordination with the guards' duty schedule, but it worked spectacularly.

While in hiding in Budapest with Mrs. Tihany Belane and her husband, at Realtanoda utca 19, Andy provided invaluable assistance to other Allies behind enemy lines, until the Russian occupation.[4]

The Daniels/Durovecz incident triggered an immediate reprimand from Szállási's HQ along with a fresh infusion of Arrow Cross security troopers. Patrols and roll calls increased dramatically overnight. Jan's sources knew that the resident *Nyilasok* informers had been ordered to perform as expected or face military courts martial before being shot. Although Group 3 had pegged ninety-nine per cent of the stoolies, we would have been arrogant, foolhardy, or dim-witted not to be on the alert at all times.

John and I met with Jan and Wuj in Jan's quarters on December 12 to finalise our scheme. Jan's message on behalf of Group 3 was unambiguous: it had to be now or never. There could be no doubt that 'never' meant a forced march to certain death in Austria.

Jan reiterated that the plan called for the evacuation of all prisoners in three stages. Andy's getaway, along with Mike's transfer, accomplished the completion of Phase One, the advance group. John and I were slated to go in Phase Two. Poles and the remaining PoW's would filter out, in Phase Three. Captain Jan Wolszlieger, "the bravest of the brave," planned to remain until the last man was gone.

Jan locked his door and directed me to spread out the street grids, tram schedules, safe house addresses, and sketches of Zugliget which were concealed inside my jacket lining. He and Wuj carefully scrutinised each one in turn.

"These are current. Memorise them."

I assured him that John and I had already done so, as I re-folded and stuffed the papers away.

He smiled, "Of course, you were trained to do that. Very good! You are going out tomorrow night, December 13. Now listen carefully. Questions, when I've finished. A sentry will be here in, I make it, eighteen minutes."

At last! Tomorrow, December 13, 1944, is our Freedom Day!

'Three months a prisoner, battered but unbowed, shuttled back and

[4] *Andrew Durovecz.*

forth, from one hell-hole to another.' I lay in bed, too excited to close my eyes, visualising the sweet possibilities. 'Home for Christmas? No, not possible, but at least I might find a way to write. How much I miss Dad and Helen. They must be worried sick. Maybe they think that I'm dead. What if Helen's married! I'll be like Tom Sawyer and go home to my own funeral. What a surprise!'

We spent the morning puttering around, putting in time. Jan and Wuj came by for a visit after lunch, ostensibly to see if we needed anything. I was too tightly wound up to make small talk, and happily let John carry on chatting.

Wuj suddenly broke off mid-sentence. "Oh, oh," he whistled softly, "we have problems, gentlemen, many problems. Come and see."

We did indeed have a very serious problem. Down below, two sizeable truckloads of Red Army prisoners were being unloaded, by a mass of *Nyilasok* security guards.

Wuj and Jan became engaged in a rapid-fire, heated discussion, which John understood. Our plans for tonight would be in jeopardy if the *Nyilasok* convoy was posted here to guard this lot. We counted as the ragged internees were taken off the trucks. "Ten, fifteen, twenty, twenty-five. God, there's thirty!" The prisoners were a pathetic reminder of this dirty war as they shuffled on makeshift crutches, wearing filthy, blood-caked bandages, many without hats or greatcoats and some, minus boots, with only ersatz sandals made of straw or tire carcasses tied with binder twine, to cover their feet. Even from a distance, the white patches of advanced frostbite on their Slavic features, fingers, and their blistered feet were evident.

We held our breath, as we watched to see what happened next. To our immense relief, the Lieutenant signed over the custody of the Russians to our Zugliget Commandant. With a snap salute, he vaulted with athletic *élan* onto the flatbed of the transport truck, and fastened the tailgate. The transmission clashed and whined like a banshee as it laboured to apply traction to the drive wheels in the slippery, half-frozen muck. I had an instant flashback to the Gibraltar flight: the Halifax' roaring engines, as it lumbered like a wounded duck to get airborne. The Daimler engine snarled, straining to extricate the large truck from the icy ruts. The result was that it slid sideways and stalled, at a precarious angle, which threatened to tip it over. The eight toy soldiers scrambled over the side like shipwrecked sailors. The driver tried to restart, cranking the motor for an eternity, until it turned over. Then it sputtered. I held my breath, willing it to life. It coughed again, belching blue-grey smoke, and died. The silence was deafening. The first truck had disappeared. For one harrowing instant, I had a vision of this truck, abandoned and derelict with its pistons seized, or cylinder head blown; Zugliget would be the overnight host to nine additional Arrow Cross men and their unhappy Lieutenant. The Morar Commandant's recitation of Robbie Burns' reflection on mice and men came to mind, neatly summing up our predicament.

Angrily, the Lieutenant trudged to the cab. After a short, sharp exchange, the driver sheepishly surrendered the controls to his superior. Upon taking the wheel, the lieutenant shouted an order to his men, who quickly took up positions with their shoulders against the tilting truck frame. The engine coughed twice, turned over reluctantly, then started.

'*The boy knows how to restart a 'flooder', just like my chum Beanie had shown me in Welland. "Jive for five, Joe, then pedal to the floor and vroom!*" '

With a Herculean effort, the knights of the Arrow Cross, including the erstwhile driver, heaved the Daimler sideways, then rushed to push from the rear and jumped on as if they were kids cavorting on a sleigh ride. It lumbered forward, rear wheels spinning and spitting twin rooster tails of mud and slush, until it was out of our sight.

"A close call. Your luck held, boys." Wuj crossed himself. "I almost thought yours had run out this time!" Wuj commented on Jan's behalf. "Get the straw whenever the way is clear. Be ready to move out at ten."

The arrival of the thirty new Russian prisoners to process and house had stirred the *Honved* into unusually frenetic activity. While they were busily escorting their charges to quarters, John and I slipped out unnoticed and retrieved a half bale of straw from the back yard which Group 3 had set aside the day before. Our task was to make up our beds, shaping the straw to give the appearance of sleeping bodies. We worked well together, sculpting the forms as realistically as we could manage. In the dim light, I could easily have been fooled by their appearance. This was the second time in my SOE experience that humble straw had served me well. After one last glance of approval, we jammed the door shut and walked down nonchalantly for supper. We ate slowly and lingered afterward in the canteen, but did not socialise with Jan and Wuj.

Upon returning to our quarters, we heard the disturbing sounds of a man, weeping, coming from the room next door. We froze. John motioned to me to try the door latch. '*What next?*' I turned the knob very slowly. A startlingly youthful soldier in a tattered Red Army uniform sat on the bed, rocking and sobbing. He threw up his hands over his eyes, palms outward, as though to protect his face. I smiled to assure him that I meant no harm to the poor fellow, while motioning to John to join me. John walked over and knelt, priestlike, as if administering the last rites. He spoke softly in Russian.

"Are you Russian, lad?"

"*Nyet,* Lithuanian."

John continued quietly in Russian. The bedraggled fellow nodded, apparently taking it in. As John spoke, the kid gazed at him, smiling sweetly, like an adoring child. His ragged uniform was soaking wet, as were the shabby straw 'clogs' on his feet. He began to shiver, uncontrollably. I whisked out to our room and removed the blanket from my bed, then carefully rearranged the props to maintain my deception. When I returned, John calmly instructed "Jonas" to take off his drenched uniform, then wrapped him inside the blanket, all the while continuing to speak reassuringly. John told me that Jonas was a farm boy of sixteen from a village near Kaunas, on the Baltic, when the Russians began mass deportations in June 1941. With his male schoolmates, he was force-marched into Russia. There, he had the choice of a labour camp in Siberia or conscription into the Army. He loathed both the Germans and the Soviets who had alternately invaded, occupied, and plundered his country, but his dislike for Russia was greater. At first, he said, he had been thankful to have been captured by the Germans, but was now fearful of his fate in a Nazi PoW camp, with the eastern war going badly for Germany.

We had stashed a few slices of bread and pieces of sausage from the canteen in our room, which I fetched for him. I took some Hungarian money from my jacket and pressed it into his cold, trembling fingers. John explained how and where to get food and drink from the canteen, and bid him a goodnight.

We were no more than ten minutes in our room, when there was a knock on the door. John opened it a crack. It was Jonas, our Kaunas Kid, beaming happily, holding three steaming mugs of coffee. He had located the canteen and had come by to show his appreciation. John thanked him and chatted as we hastily downed the hot drinks. John sensed what I was thinking and yawned, explaining that we were both extremely tired and would be going to bed straightaway. He hugged us both as he was leaving. Jonas was a nice kid, a frightened, lonely boy, and a prisoner in a strange land, but we had to be certain that he would soon be asleep, which was problematic, unless he was immune to the canteen's super-caffeinated ersatz brew.

At nine-thirty, John tiptoed over to check on Jonas. The kid had passed out; sheer exhaustion had overcome the canteen caffeine. At nine fifty, something glanced off our window. I turned out the light. Jan was looking up; he waved once and then vanished into the shadows of the moonless night. John opened our door slightly. Grandpa Charley, an affable *Honved* guard, was ambling along the corridor toward our room, wheezing while whistling a lively gypsy tune. Charley was the most conscientious of the veteran *Honved* guards: only a jug of vodka could detain him in performing his appointed rounds. Jan had also prepared for this eventuality, if necessary. We were quite sure that we had at least twenty minutes of grace.

We threw kisses to our sleeping dummies, with a "Good night, girls!" for luck as we waited for Charley to pass by. We crept out; I jammed the lock shut. Our primary objective was to make our way stealthily, and, we prayed, invisibly, along the thirty-metre balcony, by going literally from pillar to post. Sturdy, thick, wooden pillars supporting the overhanging roof were spaced at five metre intervals, along the balcony's outer edge. An iron safety railing one metre high linked the columns. The Polish Cultural Society had debated and rejected any attempt on our part to climb the railing and jump down. For two experienced paratroopers, it should not have presented a challenge. It was a five-metre drop from the balcony onto a narrow shelf on the ground below, which was not a concern, if we could manage to land squarely. "If..." The Society's concern was compounded by the inescapable fact that the earth sloped steeply downward from the ledge for nearly four mud-slicked metres, posing the threat of a free fall down the slippery slope. The risk of fractures putting an end to our dreams of freedom quickly scuttled that possibility. We would put all our faith in the pillars.

We opened Jonas' door to let ourselves inside. He was at peace, snoring at Force Five, when unexpectedly, he shouted one word, very loudly. The hairs on my neck prickled. John whispered, "Mother!" I suspended my breathing while I inched over to his cot for a closer inspection. The kid's eyelids were fluttering. John and I stood together watching him, with our heads bowed, as though paying our final respects to the dear departed.

The door handle turned, slightly. Charley had come back to check on the rumpus. I stepped back to avoid the incoming sliver of light. At that moment, I was prepared to overpower and subdue the stocky old man. If he struggled or resisted, I wouldn't hesitate to kill him. '*What to do with the body*? John looked at me for one instant and nodded, in tacit agreement. I flashed back to the gruelling, grisly Commando exercises on the training grounds of Camp X, Morar and everywhere else. '*Can you do it*?' I knew that John certainly would, if I hesitated. Charlie's left arm was extended inside the room as his hand groped spider-like for the light switch. I held up the fingers on my right hand and started the count down, silently. On one, we would haul him inside. Four, three...at two, Jonas kick-started his guttural breathing.

Charlie's hand stopped. John began another silent countdown. At three, Charley closed the door quietly, as though he was satisfied that everything was as it should be. We could hear him resume whistling and assumed he had continued his beat. John cracked open the door, and peeked out, cautiously. With his right hand, he gave the "Follow me" signal. We tiptoed out, single file, like cartoon villains, and sprinted across the hallway to the two nearest uprights.

We hugged our pillars, watched, and waited. I could just make out Grandpa's broad shoulders receding down the corridor, as the butt of his rifle bumped rhythmically against his ample backside. I took a deep breath. For the first time, I realised that my heart was pounding against my ribcage. We had *almost* fouled up, most royally.

Now we began the cat and mouse game, in earnest. As Charley walked, we advanced, cat-like, creeping from pillar to pillar, with John in the lead. Tonight, Charley was taking his responsibilities very seriously, stopping to check apartment doors, and moving on to the next. It was obvious that Andy's caper had caused considerable consternation among the 'brass' with a subsequent 'tightening up' of security precautions.

John signalled, "Go!" At that moment, Charley turned around and came directly towards us. I could smell pinesap in my nostrils as I flattened myself, face-first, against the wooden upright. '*What is the damn fool doing?*' He was less than five metres away. '*Thank God and Jan there's no moon tonight and the perimeter lights are shining outward, not in. If he spots me, we're done for.* I saw the glint of the silver emergency whistle that was hanging by a braided white lanyard, around his neck. '*Choke him with the cord before he gets a chance to blow it! Ready…*'

Charley halted. Slowly, he removed his fur cap and stroked his scalp; his chubby, red face a portrait of bemusement, as if he was struggling to remember exactly why he was out alone, so to speak, on a dark, frigid night, patrolling a prison balcony. He took one step hesitantly towards us; then spun decisively on his heel, and went back down the corridor. '*That's two. Seven lives to go, Mr. Charley Catman!*'

We moved warily ahead to the next set of columns. Bingo! Charley was doing famously, walking at a moderate pace, stopping to try each door handle, jauntily following his route. John motioned to me to stir myself and move along. We were now at our third set of stations. We barely paused and darted forward again. There were ten pillars lining the section of balcony that we had to traverse. We were almost halfway along.

Charley had been well ahead of John, but was dawdling again. At my eighth station stop, I strained to make out John's shadowy figure in the gloom. It was absolutely, eerily silent.

'Come on, John. Let's put a nickel in the damn machine and get going!'

Without warning, a petite dark-haired female flung open the apartment door, across from my pillar. I instinctively crouched and scuttled away to the opposite side of the post. She was balancing a large white porcelain dishpan, the contents of which, I feared, she intended to slosh over the railing. She was winding up, preparing to launch the slop, when she shouted over her shoulder, in Polish.

Instantly, I envisioned John, Jan and I, three bloodied pulps in a Pestvediki interrogation chamber, being injected with mind-altering chemicals, and forced to look on helplessly as *Wollf's SD* and *Gestapo* specialists brutally tortured our weakest comrade, Mike, to forcibly extract our final testaments.

Her eyes locked with mine, for an eternity. *'She's seen me! Yes, now she's panicking, and she'll call for help.'* A male voice responded churlishly from inside the apartment. Abruptly, she hesitated, mid-windup, causing the liquid to splash over the sides of the container and soak her apron. I understood the Polish words she called out in righteous indignation to her unseen partner, "Don't bother to help, you! I've done it!"

A sheet of kitchen wastewater smelling of stale pork fat and cabbage flew past my face...and then again, as she emptied the dregs. She turned and stomped inside, slamming the door.

'Could have been worse, Joe! It might have been a chamber pot.'

She had almost scored a direct hit. Shaken, I frantically scraped the slimy scraps of mystery material and viscous liquid from my face, with my frayed battle dress jacket's cuff. The liquid trickled in greasy rivulets down from my hair and forehead, and invaded my eyes and mouth. My stomach roiled violently at this memento of last month's miserable misadventure with roast pork. I gasped, fighting down waves of nausea, and forced myself to concentrate on keeping up with John's freshened pace. Once again, we had narrowly escaped disaster.

'Perhaps she didn't see me. But, maybe she did and was a member of Jan's underground. Or, maybe she did and simply reacted as a decent human being.' I prefer to believe the latter, that I owed my life to a brave, quick-witted Polish woman.

When we reached the end of the balcony corridor, I traced John's steps down the slope, then made for cover behind a large pine tree. I checked my wristwatch. It was fifteen minutes to midnight. Without a moment to

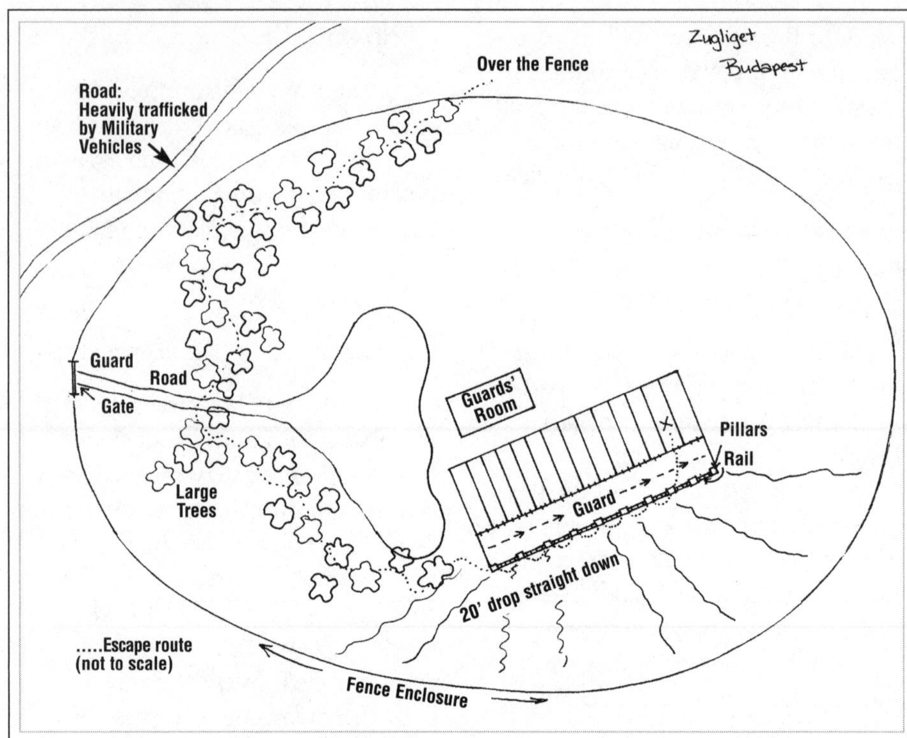

Zugliget showing our escape route

waste, we set out, sneaking from tree to tree, as our instructor had demonstrated on those exhilarating survival excursions one hundred years ago, back at Camp X and Rice Lake.

By midnight, we were within five metres of the gate. It was necessary that we separate in order to reconnoitre. I could see the guards clearly and hear their conversations. Their helmets were German. They wore metal breastplates with chain mail necklaces. Orders were being given in German! These were Germans, or more precisely, *Waffen SS* and *Feldpolizei!* I lay down flat and listened intently, but could understand only a few fragments. John rejoined me.

"Just bloody wonderful!" he whispered, shaking his head. He looked at me "My God, man, what happened to you back there? You're a ruddy awful mess!"

"You don't know, John?"

"Know what, for heaven's sake? Did somebody dip you head-first in cabbage soup?"

I described my involuntary baptism. John thought it hugely entertaining and was racked with spasms of silent laughter. "You didn't flinch or yell bloody murder? That's the old Special Op's spirit! Here's my handkerchief."

"Thanks a lot. Sit rep: situation

report, please Captain! What in the hell are *SS* troops doing here? Jan didn't warn us of this wrinkle!"

"He couldn't, Joe, because the blighter didn't know. They're newcomers. The *Hauptsturmführer*[5] told his *Nyilas* counterpart that they arrived fifty minutes ago."

"I'd estimate there are thirty in total. What do think, John?"

"Not sure. I'd guess thirty, too.

"What do you suggest we do, Captain?"

"What do you suggest, Lieutenant?"

"Go doggo! If we can't walk out heads up, *à la Daniels*, we can bloody well crawl out. Not as dignified, but…."

"Show me the perimeter map, Joe."

We retraced our path through the thick grove of trees, to the far side of the grounds, behind the main structure. '*Over the river and through the woods*, I hummed, to relieve the pent-up tension. I looked up to see Grandpa Charley heading into the backstretch of the balcony.

"Sorry old fellow, but you're in for it this morning!" John commented, *sotto voce*. "Glad we didn't have to wring the old darlings' neck!"

"Check. The *Nyilasok* gangsters will do it for us, undoubtedly. I hope not, though."

"There's the broken fence. Tut, tut! And it still hasn't been mended! After you, my dear Alphonse." John stood on the twisted barbed wire to let me pass over, without emasculation, then I returned the courtesy, from the other side.

"Still singin' tenor, and you? Stay low, move slow," John intoned, as though coaching a class of recruits.

"Words to live by, John, from the book of helpful fieldcraft hints."

"Time, Joe?"

"Twelve-thirty a.m."

"Can't be, man!"

"Yes, 'tis. Big Ben time! Where's your watch?"

"Don't question your commanding officer, son. The map, please" he said, dryly.

"I know the way", I assured him patting my jacket. "It's all part of a radioman's advanced training. Follow me, *mon capitaine*."

We dodged and ducked behind the large, sheltering tree trunks, clearing the camp boundary in less than ten minutes, and set out briskly, towards the safe house, as though it was a perfectly normal thing to be taking the night air at 1:00 a.m.

[5] SS *captain*

The first safe house

We encountered no one else. Far off dogs barked intermittently. Our Polish military all-weather coats, which Jan had scrounged to cover our uniforms, gave us a sense of security. We found the address easily, slipped down the side passageway, and gently opened the backyard gate. Once inside, I tried to latch it shut. It was rusted and bent. The gate swung open, creaking loudly enough to alert the guardhouse back at Zugliget. I tried again, failed, and gave up. We were in someone's backyard. Suddenly, all hell broke loose as an ominously large, dark shape lunged at me. I positioned myself in the Fairbairn-approved self-defence mode. I felt my assailant's hot, rancid breath on my cheek.

It licked my face.

"Down!" To my relief, the gangly Alsatian pup sat perched in front of me, tail wagging, expectantly.

John was doubled up with silent laughter.

"Just knock it off! It,…it scared the hell out of me! "

"Sorry, old man. Your blood and

guts reaction got me going. I would have done the same thing. Can you convince it to go away?"

With coaxing, it went, reluctantly, to its shelter.

We crouched on the damp ground behind a large clump of shrubbery to wait for some sign of life inside.

At 4:30, a light flickered on in the kitchen. The back porch door opened. We kissed the dewy ground. A short, chubby man, dark hair awry, wearing German army trousers with suspenders over a khaki undershirt all accessorised with a flowered apron, stepped out to take stock of the day.

He upended a pack of cigarettes, tapped it, and extracted a smoke, struck a match on the metal railing, inhaled deeply, and yawned as he appraised the cool morning. Then, he carefully balanced his cigarette on the railing, unbuttoned his trousers, and proceeded to relieve himself over the edge of the porch. The sky was lightening faintly in the east.

"If he spots us, you must take him," John whispered. "Get over to his left side, as close in as you can. I'll go to the right, as backup. Come in like bloody blue blazes and drop him while he's still peeing. Not a sound, no second chance. Set?"

"Set."

Safe house, Krusper Utca, 3 Budapest, Karola's apartment building

"Good luck."

I scuttled crablike to get into position, hunched against the low brick wall of the porch. The sharp aroma of the cigarette was going to make me sneeze. The birds were already chirping, insanely loudly. We had less than thirty minutes, I estimated, before sunup. My hands were stiff from the cold. I rubbed them together in readiness for the attack.

The cook, fastening his fly, was coming directly towards me. I made a quick reckoning of the distance that I needed to cover in one leap.

"*Schmidt, wo ist du?*" "Where are you?"

"*Hier, mein Kapitan!*"

"Where is my breakfast, I must be gone by six! *Macht schnell, bitte*!"

"*Jawohl, Herr Oberst!* Right away!"

The hastily discarded, smouldering cigarette landed on my head, as he muttered a fighting man's invocation of a biological impossibility and went in to do his master's bidding. My German tuition at Pestvideki was not all high-culture nor the glory of Nazism in Karl's *Der Völkischer Beobachter.*[6]

'*Blimey, Blokey, isn't this enough damn excitement for one night?*'

We flew through the gate and were out on the street in less that a minute. Across the road, an electric tram was loading a long queue of passengers. We parleyed and agreed that it might be faster and safer to ride than to walk to the alternate safe house on Krusper utca 3, at the end of the tramline. By now, the bed checks would have revealed our absence, triggering alarms at Zugliget, with rampaging squads of *Nyilasok* rummaging through every building, ripping up floorboards, searching attics, mouse holes, and sewer pipes. All prisoners would have been 'locked down' in their rooms, while the suspected collaborators would have been thrown into solitary cells to begin the questioning. A bulletin would have been flashed by teletype to every police precinct in Budapest simultaneously. We thought that we might be less conspicuous by hiding in plain sight, buried anonymously amidst the crowds of morning commuters.

The Poles had strongly advised us to purchase the tram tickets at a kiosk. There was no kiosk here. I had no choice. I told John what I was going to do. He was uncomfortable with it, but we boarded the tram and as I approached the female conductor, I quickly made a major decision. On only one occasion had I spoken Hungarian since landing at Abaliget. This would be my second. I reasoned

[6] *The Racial Observer, the official newspaper of the Nazi Party, was noted for its reportorial inaccuracies, outrageously anti-Semitic editorial bias, and unconditionally fawning praise for the ruling hierarchy. Adolf Hitler used it near the war's end as a means to issue an editorial challenge to all Germans to resist the invaders, even if to do so meant the utter destruction of the Fatherland.*

that it might be less memorable to the agent than a ham-fisted attempt to 'sign' my way through the transaction. I pushed the exact change towards her and uttered the fateful word, *Ketö* (two). Without glancing up, she scanned a dog-eared rate schedule through her thick eyeglasses. Two tickets were produced as she muttered, "Move along." Trying to appear casual, I glanced along the sea of faces and spotted John near the rear of the tram. As I worked my way through the crush, something poked me in the back. Annoyed and startled, I turned around to size up this unexpected threat. A middle-aged man pointed at the conductor's booth. The ticket agent was beckoning me. '*Fight or flight?*'

'*Use your wits, laddie. Be calm, but be ready!*'

"Ma'am?"

"Your tickets are good to the last stop."

I thanked her and walked to join John. We rode to the end of the line without incident, relaxing and enjoying the heady tonic of freedom.

At our stop, we found the apartment building and were admitted, somewhat hesitantly, by our contact. I introduced John and myself to our hostess, Karola Koschwitz, who seemed rather cool and unwelcoming. We stood in her hall entranceway, while John spoke with her in German, re assuring her of our *bona fides*. I heard her say Perisich in Magyar. John responded, "Zoltan." She took John's hand in hers', and then hugged us each warmly.

We were invited into her living room, where she served us tea with cream and sugar – all real – not ersazt. Our dark leather greatcoats, she explained, made us suspiciously similar in appearance to the *Nyilasok* secret police, who at that moment, were conducting a massive dragnet for Jews and escaped prisoners. Karola had every reason to be wary; as we would discover, she was risking her life by hiding a fugitive in the apartment.

This courageous and remarkable woman, Karola Koschwitz, would be my salvation, for the next two months.

CHAPTER 9
Safe House at Krusper utca 3 and Mr. Raoul

From a prisoner of Zugliget, to this suddenly almost normal existence was a change for which I was almost unprepared, although I couldn't count how many times I had dreamt of it, both awake and asleep. It was splendid to be free of the grey, mind-numbing drudgery of confinement (even at lax Zugliget), the boredom of predictable routines, and, most especially, the supreme arrogance of supermen in shiny boots. It felt luxuriously decadent to laze around for hours in a warm bed, instead of a prickly straw tic, without being jarred into semi-consciousness by strident commands at morning roll call. Perhaps the most pleasant aspect of all was to be able to relish the civilising companionship of a woman.

In total defiance of logic and common sense, I actually considered escorting Karola out for a night 'on the town', to the best restaurant, with all of the trimmings. Blokey's instructions of the arts of disguise encouraged me to think that I could walk around Budapest incognito. Fortunately, I came to my senses before even mentioning the idea to Karola or John. The harsh reality was that he and I were escaped PoW's, with a price on our heads. As far as Karola's personal safety was concerned, we were Class A liabilities. Yet she went about her business as though she were hosting a meeting of the Budapest Floral Society. She never mentioned the potential risk that we represented and was always positive, generous and completely fearless. It was only after an incident into which I stumbled accidentally during our first day with her, that I truly came to appreciate these qualities.

I entered the bathroom and received a pleasant shock. In the bathtub, immersed in a sea of bubbles, was a water sprite: a very attractive young female. Where had she been hiding? In my confusion and embarrassment I heard myself mumble in textbook German, " Oh, excuse me! I'm Joe, by the way. Who are you?"

"How do you do, Joe? I'm Mitzi!" Her voice was seductively low-pitched and musical.

"H-h-h-hello, Mitzi. I h-h-h-hope you're having a wonderful bub-bub-b-bath. Goodbye!" The peals of her laughter resounded in my ears as I beat a hasty retreat; I hoped I hadn't seemed a total fool as I recalled the incident that had caused me one week of woe at my new school in Welland.

Karola thought my timing was absolutely hilarious; after she had regained her composure sufficiently to relate the details of my gaffe to John, she conducted us to the second bathroom, off the master bedroom. Previously, Mitzi had been snugly tucked away in the front living room, where she slept and took her meals.

The unfamiliarity of my new surroundings made me become fixated upon the possibility that we would be discovered. For the first two or three days, every creak of the floorboards or cough in the hallway was sufficient to push me into a state of high alert. A sudden laugh, a toilet flushing too often, a suspiciously large accumulation of trash, or one fleeting, unguarded glance at a window, risked an informer's call to the *Nyilasok*. A lethal chain of events would then ensue: painstakingly thorough closet to cupboard searches, certain discovery, arrest and death, whether immediate – which was doubtful – or lingering, in a torture chamber and/or concentration camp. Despite these real possibilities, Karola never complained nor stinted in her efforts to amuse, accommodate, and feed us magnificently. She carried on cheerily, unconcernedly, frequently expressing her contempt for the madness outside with racy quips and risqué jokes in German and English, with some spicy Magyar, for added colour, which I pretended not to understand.

"Did I tell you about the German sergeant from Bavaria and the Russian prostitute?"

John expressed our gratitude with customary eloquence when he offered grace on our second evening together with Karola and Mitzi. "We are here by the grace of God, who, in his mercy, has brought us to his courageous Karola Koschwitz, through Jan Wolzlieger, Andras Hegedus, Zoltan Perisich, Matyas Pirithy and Colonel Garzuly. May He bless and protect us all. Thank you Lord, Amen."

It was difficult not to notice our hostess' 'comings and goings' at unusual hours, the stream of mysterious visitors after dark, the availability and abundance of good food and household luxuries: toilet paper, English soap, and scented bath powders, (for the exclusive use of Mitzi and Karola, of course).

My fluency in Magyar was still my carefully guarded secret. Unbeknownst to others, I couldn't avoid overhearing remarks, which made it obvious that Karola was more than a 'bit player' in the pro-neutral Hungary underground movement. Despite this, I was determined that John and I would contribute to our 'care and feeding'. With his fluent German to assist me, I approached Karola with a proposal for payment.

"No, I won't hear of it. It is being looked after."

"Nevertheless, Karola, John and I

insist!"

"If I didn't want you here, that would be entirely different. If and when it becomes a problem, we can discuss other options. I'm managing very well for the time being and enjoying your company, boys. Put the money away. You're going to need it eventually."

John and I continued to press our case, but she was adamant. I thought of a compromise. "Then would you consider this a donation to help Mitzi and her friends to get out of Budapest? I'm sure there's a pressing need for money to take care of the arrangements."

She gave me a peculiar look as though she sensed that I understood her involvement in an 'underground railway.' "Yes, but it can wait until the right time. *Shalom*." She kissed us each warmly on both cheeks. I took this as acceptance. Afterward, I returned the money to my secret cache behind the dresser in the master bedroom, where I had also squirreled away my codes. Karola had insisted upon cleaning and mending my jacket.

Karola's energetic *joie de vivre* and positive outlook were exactly the tonic that John and I craved. Besides, she was an excellent cook who could turn the plainest of ingredients into a gourmet feast.

"Perhaps you are *cordon bleu* certified?" I asked haltingly, in German/English, as I helped myself to some delicious leftovers.

"No, Joe, just a peasant Hungarian cook…but certifiable, me? Yes, for sure!"

I estimated that Karola was in her early thirties, an intriguing age. Her confident yet compassionate manner, combined with her physical attributes, created an alluring mystique. Karola's piercing, crystal blue eyes, set in her oval, pale face, were framed with heaps of dark brown ringlets which reflected the soul of a girl/ woman who thrived on excitement and challenges, with an appetite for *l'amour*, but on her terms, under conditions of her choosing.

Late in the evening of our second full day at Krusper utca 3, she knocked softly at my door. "Joe, can you come out? Someone is here to see you." The last part was spoken almost musically, as though she was sending a warning.

'*Not Messinger and his gang again! I'll take my chances by jumping out the damn window rather than go to Austria*.' Hastily, I threw on my freshly laundered and pressed battle-dress jacket and trousers and strode out to meet the devil.

"Joseph Gordon, I presume."

"Andras? Andras Hegedus?"

"The very same. How are you, my friend?"

As we shook hands warmly, I managed to blurt out, "My goodness, man, it is great to see you again. What are you doing here?"

"Your landlady and I are well-acquainted. Actually, I am making my pre-Christmas rounds. Now where is that Captain John hiding?"

John came out to be greeted with a similar show of warmth. We wanted to hear about our friends: Colonel Garzuly, Zoltan Perisich and Matyas Pirithy.

"All are safe and well and they send their very best wishes." This news was the best Christmas present that I could have asked for.

Andras was interested in finding out the details of our escape from Zugliget. He was impressed by our exploits. "That's truly amazing. I'm delighted that you made it, of course. After Daniels, you would expect that they would have learned their lesson."

"There must be hell to pay. Our friendly Commandant is likely in Pestvidki, poor sod," John added. "Joe and I feel sorry for Grandpa Charley, the *Honved* guard who was patrolling that night."

"Yes we do. He was a harmless old soul, eh John?"

"I hear what you're both saying, but you're soldiers, as he is, or was, and you did what the military code expects of PoW's."

"Have you had any communication with Captain Jan Wolzlieger? Before our breakout, the *Nyilasok* snatched two of his men, who we suspect may have been Allied agents. I hope to God they're all holding up."

"No, I've heard nothing at all from or about Group 3....."

"How far away from here do you live, Andras?" I queried, not expecting a definitive answer.

"Only a few blocks. My wife Ilona and I would love to have you visit. Now, I will be off. That nosy witch next door is likely listening to every sound with the water glass she puts her teeth into at night pressed against the wall. Watch this." He hit the plaster at shoulder level with his elbow. There was an audible thump from the other side of the wall. "That'll teach you, Margarethe, you old fascist crow!" he whispered.

"John, Joe, for the time being, you must stay indoors, out of sight. When it's safe for you to venture out, I'll let Karola know. We'll see you before Christmas though. Merry Christmas...I almost forgot to mention; when the heat is off, both of you fellows might want to join me for a bit of a nighttime frolic. What do you think, Karola?"

"If it's a bar crawling, boys' night out, I think, not yet. Otherwise..." she shrugged and turned expectantly to John and I.

"Why not!"

"I'm game!"

"Excellent. Good night, all!"

By the afternoon of our third day, John and I realised that we were creating supply and security problems for our hostess, although she had never let on. We whispered as we discussed our options.

"One of has to go, Joe. It's better sooner, rather than later. Karola can't be expected to put us both up indefinitely…."

"I agree, John. She has enough on her hands with Mitzi. What if we were traced here? She and Mitzi will be the victims of our carelessness. Any suggestions?"

"Let Karola choose" he offered.

"How about a duel, just like the good old days?"

"You'd cheat. Next thought?"

"John, frankly, your first idea is the best way. Let's spell out our concerns openly and let her decide."

"Agreed. I'll bring it up tonight."

During the course of the evening, John found the appropriate moment to mention the topic diplomatically. I was surprised when he volunteered to move to another location, which, Karola assured us, would be safe and more secure. She said it was the home of an old friend, Count Markovics, situated at Marvany utca 13. John agreed immediately after which Karola left to make a brief, private telephone call. When she returned to the room, she confirmed that arrangements were being made for his transfer within the week. There was no further discussion of the topic. Seven days before Christmas, on the evening of December 18, 1944, a courier arrived at our apartment. Karola introduced us to the very attractive woman, Elek Klari, a Jewish member of Karola's group, who told us that she preferred to be called Mari Nenni (Aunt Mary). She didn't look like any aunt that I had ever known.

John and I exchanged farewells, as if we were boarding school dormitory mates, leaving for the Christmas vacation. It was all pretence; we each knew that our paths were unlikely to cross in the near future, if ever again. As Louie might have said, "It's a crap shoot, guys, six ways from Sunday. You can take that to the five and dime!"[1]

That night, after John and Mari Nenni left, Andras called in to relay an urgent message. He seemed agitated, with very good reason. The news was grim: our building was now under twenty-four-hour-a-day surveillance, by the *Sicherheitsdienst*.

[1] John and Mary Nenni arrived safely at Count Markovic's home. The Count decided to send them out of the city, to live with his daughter and son-in-law in Kamaraerdo, at a considerable distance from Budapest. Using his linguistic gifts, John successfully posed as a Swabian, of German and Hungarian origin. He remained in Kamaraerdo until his liberation by the Russians. John was unable to locate Aunt Mary after the war.

"Plan on having some unwelcome Christmas guests on your doorstep; I don't expect they'll be the Three Wise Men. Thus far, I have no idea why you're in the cross hairs, but I intend to find out. In the meantime, best you bone up on your German: *Willkommen und Frohe Weihnachten!* I'll return tomorrow."

Karola called Mitzi and I to join her at the kitchen table. Speaking German, English and some Yiddish, slowly, for my benefit, she reaffirmed her intention to continue sheltering us. This was more than anyone might expect. I had to speak up. I announced that I would not continue to live rent-free, insisting that I could afford to contribute my share, and Mitzi's. I finished by affirming my pledge of support to the underground, for its work with Budapest's Jews. Karola accepted on this basis.

The next topic was our accommodation. "Not to take anything away from Andras," she began, "but I have been thinking about the possibility that we could be searched. So, there will be some changes made to our living arrangements.

"I'll sleep anywhere, even in the closet, if it will help," I offered gallantly.

"I think I can do better that that, Joe", she said, smiling. "You will bunk in with Mitzi, in the spare bedroom."

'*I think I could manage that.*' I gulped, struggling to appear blasé.

"Are you alright, Joe?"

"Sure, sure! What about Mitzi, though?"

"Oh, she's already agreed, haven't you dear?"

"Could you please say that again, Karola, slowly?"

Mitzi reached over and patted my hand. "It's fine, Joe. I know you're a gentleman."

"Good, then that's done. All this time, I thought that you were a confirmed old bachelor, Joe: pipe and slippers, no place in your life for a woman to upset your routine, no? Well, I am relieved. Now let's make the place fit the plan."

'*Is Karola playing the yenta here...the village matchmaker?*' I didn't have to wait long for an answer. Mitzi excused herself after dinner, to collect her belongings from the living room. Karola motioned to me to join her, at the sink. She threw me a dishtowel.

"She's extremely fragile, Joe. She puts up a brave front, but she has been terribly...ill-used, by German...soldiers, to use the term loosely."

I had to interrupt her to ask that she try to explain in English.

"Alright. Mitzi has been violated...not only once, but..."

The ornate china platter slipped from my hand and shattered on the linoleum. I was kneeling to gather the shards.

"Leave it. No matter. I'll get a whisk and dustpan," she said gently. "I've been looking for an excuse to get rid of that damned ugly relic. Anyway, Mitzi needs a friend, a brother, someone to trust. She's not looking for a lover. Can you be that person?"

"Yes, of course."

"And just in case that halo starts to slip, Joseph, she can likely thrash you with her right arm tied behind her back. She's sweet and petite but don't let that fool you. She's a real survivor, since her youngest days…very deceptive.

"But to be very serious and frank, Mitzi may, and I repeat may, have been infected with what you soldiers call VD."

I went and sat alone, in the dark living room. Through a crack in the shutters, I could see snow crystals glistening in the streetlight's arc. I awoke as the mantel clock chimed midnight. '*You can't sit here and freeze. Why are you avoiding her*?' I tiptoed to the master bedroom door, tapped uneasily, and listened for a sound.

"Yes?"

"Mitzi, it's Joe."

"Joe, come in."

"Sorry if I wakened you. I came to get my night clothes; I'll be gone in a few seconds." The bedside lamp cast my distorted shadow on the wall as if I was a night prowler in a low budget thriller.

"You can change in here, Joe. My eyes are closed, tightly. I promise." Her fluency in English, supplemented by some familiar phrases in German and Yiddish, was remarkable.

"Thanks."

There was a long silence. As I was turning to leave the room, Mitzi spoke gently. "You can sleep here, Joe."

"It is cold out there on the couch, but I don't want to..."

"Come. Don't be silly."

I slipped into the bed, well over on the side.

"Good night, Mitzi."

"'Night, Joe. Sleep well."

Within a few minutes, her breathing had deepened. I lay motionless, staring into the dark at the invisible ceiling. The clock on the mantelpiece chimed twelve-fifteen, then twelve-thirty.

"Joe, are you asleep?"

"No. You?"

"No, I'm restless. I can sense that you're uneasy. What's the matter?"

"Too much coffee, I guess."

She was silent for a few moments until suddenly, the wind battered the shutters. Startled, she whispered anxiously, "What was that?"

"Just the wind picking up. It's a wild night outside!"

She rolled onto her side, facing me. Her foot touched my calf. Carefully and deliberately, I slid my leg away. The mantel clock announced twelve forty-five.

"Do you want to talk about it, or just lie here awake all night?"

Her directness was unnerving. I didn't respond for a moment. "Mitzi, I've never known a woman as complex as you."

"Karola told you, didn't she?'

"About what?"

"Me."

"Yes…she did."

"So you're shocked, disgusted and upset to be lying in bed with a cheap tramp, yes?"

"No, Mitzi. Shocked maybe, but certainly not the rest. No, of course not!"

"I think you do protest too much. May I show you something?"

"Anything."

She sat up and switched on the table lamp. Then she stood up facing me, as she discretely drew her nightgown above her knees. Her thighs were criss-crossed with a horrifyingly cross-hatching of angry welts. She switched off the light, and lay down.

"There are more. I don't want to turn your stomach. Do you want to know how?"

"Yes. I do want to know."

She sat up, leaning her pillow against the headboard and spoke quietly and deliberately. "It was the middle of September, last year. It was already starting to get dark. I was hurrying through a small park, with a sack of groceries after work, when I caught a glimpse of a very tall German lieutenant and three other soldiers watching me. I tried not to pay attention. One of them whistled and called something like, 'Hey Jewish bitch! Come here.' I walked faster, averting my eyes, but they had me surrounded in no time. One of them, a cross-eyed, pimply kid, grabbed my bag and threw it on the grass. I asked if he would mind picking it up. That was a big joke. The lieutenant lit a cigarette and used the match to start the matchbox. When it was burning, he tossed it into the paper bag. It started to smoke.

"He laughed. 'See boys, the Jews are so rich, they burn food, while the rest of the country goes hungry. You pick it up, rich bitch!' His hand was on his holster, so I thought I'd better make the effort. Before I could reach down, he had grabbed my arm, spun me around and was pawing me and trying to kiss me. I couldn't stand it anymore, so I fought back.

"He was very strong, very angry and tried to force me to the ground. He was shouting with drool coming from his mouth as he literally screamed that Jewish women are forbidden to defy the master race. I fell down, sprawled on my back. The rest was predictable, except for the dagger cuts that I've just shown to you. He said they were his signature, or calling card…or something like that. I was too terrified to remember exactly."

"Then he left you alone?"

"Oh, no, unfortunately. Perhaps the thrill of bloodying his knife made him all the more violent; I expected that he was going to slit my throat. I bit and scratched at his face and tried to gouge out his eyes. He hit me so hard on the side of my head, that I was almost knocked unconscious. Then, he raped me again. My stomach turned with the stench of beer and tobacco. For that, he dislocated my jaw. I wasn't a pretty sight. Can you imagine that the three others joined in, after? They did their carvings, too. I won't show you…" Her shoulders trembled as she struggled to restrain silent sobs.

"How did you get help?"

"Apparently, they left me lying face down in the park, naked. A male nurse, to whom I am forever grateful, found me around one in the morning, covered me with his overcoat, and carried me to the hospital. I was treated very well there. That's the story."

"What about the police? Were they notified?"

"Oh, yes. The hospital filed a complaint and a very kind and sympathetic Police Inspector, who took a lengthy statement, visited me. That was it. I'm sure the authorities hushed it up."

"I wish I could pay them back."

"Just be my friend." She reached out timidly and took my hand. We slept.

The old alarm clock showed 7:00 a.m., when Karola knocked lightly. I went out into the hallway.

"Good morning. Get Mitzi up and the two of you get dressed. I have a feeling that it's inspection day. The room can't show any signs of you, or her. I'll help if you need me. Coffee and breakfast in ten minutes. Andras is due now. Hurry!"

Mitzi, having overheard Karola, had sprung into action. We dressed and scrambled to follow Karola's instructions. When we arrived in the kitchen, Andras was seated, eating breakfast. We joined him for a feast of sausages, fried eggs, and freshly baked rolls, with coffee brewed from beans.

"This is incredible, Karola!" I enthused. "How do you manage to do it?"

"Should I tell him?" Andras looked at Karola. "Mitzi probably knows. Joe, our innocent Karola is the Queen of the Budapest black market, aren't you my dear?"

"If you say so, Captain."

"Oh, indeed. Even the Germans know that fact. Now, here's the real news. My reliable source says that your building will be ransacked today. They're not likely to be looking for coffee, or eggs, or for that matter, butter, unfortunately, but hunting down Jews.

"There are several mixed Gentile and Jewish married couples living here. The race lunatics in Berlin have taken control, despite that fact that the Russians are breathing down their necks. Himmler has threatened Szállási that if he can't guarantee that Hungary will be one-hundred percent *Juden frei* by the spring, he will personally cut off his…my apologies, ladies. I'm sorry to alarm you, Mitzi, but we'll need to take every precaution. As for you, Joe, you're a prize trophy, a real bonus for these gangsters to haul in."

Mitzi's face showed no discomfort with his observations. Andras stood up, brushing a few minuscule crumbs from his immaculate jacket. "I'll be here and will try to fend them off. Thank you, as always, for the excellent breakfast Karola," he said, kissing her hand gallantly. "Dear Mitzi," he kissed her forehead. "*Geht mit Gött's hilf.* (Go with God). Obey Karola, unquestioningly, both of you! Good luck, Joe. We'll get through this together, somehow."

Mitzi looked up, smiled, and clasped his hand. "*Danke schön, Herr Kapitan.*"

Karola walked with him to the front door. When she returned, we cleaned up the kitchen and then scoured the apartment, looking for any forgotten clues which might tip off a search party.

"Karola, shall we find Mitzi and me a hideout?"

"The bedroom."

We stood at the bedroom doorway, casing the room. I opened the closet. It was much deeper than I had noticed. "This looks big enough. We can bury ourselves behind the clothing racks. What do you two think?"

Mitzi was inspecting a large feather comforter, or *duna*, which was lying on the floor, on the far side of the bed. "This is mine!" she exclaimed, as she was lifting it up.

"Sure, bring it with you, in the closet," Karola remarked.

"No, what I mean is, this is my hiding place. Underneath it."

"Nonsense! You can't mean that you intend to lie under that, and nothing else. Where are you going to hide? We're not dealing with the Boy

Scouts, for heaven's sake!"

"Karola, I've made up my mind."

"Stop, please. Mitzi, why won't you consider the closet?"

"Because I can't, Joe! I have a problem. Karola please explain this to him." She proceeded to speak rapidly in Magyar as she told Karola of her dread of enclosed spaces. I understood her explanation, acute claustrophobia, but I didn't let on. When Karola had translated for me, I still felt compelled to try to override Mitzi's reservations.

"I'll be with you every second. The *duna's* not good enough. Let's try the closet now, just for one minute, with the door left open. You might find that it's not so bad."

She thanked me and refused the offer. That was the end of the discussion. Her fear of being shut away was totally irrational and dysfunctional and as menacing to her as my loathing of spiders, whiskey and kippers. We could only make every effort to support her, and pray.

While she and Karola arranged the *duna*, I took the opportunity to burrow into the thick layers of garments so that I was nested at the rear of the closet, tucked behind two racks of clothing. Then I came out and went to the kitchen to fetch a carving knife, which I carefully placed on the floor of my cubicle. It crossed my mind that Mitzi was likely more than capable of 'slicing and dicing' with the best of them. However, both she and Karola rejected the idea of arming her.

To keep us occupied, Karola had planned the afternoon. Mitzi and I were shown two large cardboard boxes that held the Christmas decorations. When we had finished our tasks, after two hours of kibitzing, Karola inspected our handiwork. The wreaths, paper holly, and red and green garlands were approved, but the mistletoe had to be moved from the light fixture high in the entranceway to the centre of the living room ceiling, as Karola explained, "… to prevent unfortunate misunderstandings with our expected visitors." Mitzi and I rushed to comply.

When that was finished, Mitzi decided to create a small 'entertainment' for our amusement. We scrounged a scratched makeup mirror, white tissue paper, toothpicks, and pipe cleaners and cleared the centre of the sideboard. Mitzi, who was a talented artist, made excellent use of the scraps to produce a winter village skating rink tableau, complete with stick-figure people, dogs and trees and even a sleigh. We giggled as we pretended to frolic in our miniature scene. The gaiety ended abruptly with a heavy knock on the door and a coarse male voice demanding entry, in Magyar. Karola, dressed in a svelte red dress, didn't have to shoo us to our room.

Mitzi lay down on her stomach

beside the bed while I covered her with the duna. I tried as best I could to flatten it on her small form. She pulled it over her head. Others had joined the voice in the hall. I noticed a strand of golden hair, which had trickled out. As I tucked it carefully inside the cover, she looked up and winked.

"Are you sure?" I asked.

Her head nodded under the coverlet.

I wanted to pick her up and take her with me inside the closet, as I slipped into the relative safety of my refuge. Moments later, I heard the door latched shut… '*Karola*!'

It was difficult to hear what was happening through the layers of clothes and the closed door. Apart from my own rapid breathing, I could just make out Karola's and Andras' voices, and those of two or possibly three intruders. The sounds that had at first been muffled now seemed to be coming from the bedroom. Doors were slammed, heavily. The distant din of clashing metal created a mental picture of rifle muzzles with fixed bayonets poking and rummaging through Karola's kitchen and immaculate cupboards. Heavy footsteps reverberated in the hallway. A fourth voice, speaking strident German with piercing nasality, demanded a bayonet. I heard the unmistakable clink of it being detached from a rifle barrel. The odour of moth crystals inside the closet was nauseating. The German, now directly outside my door, ordered Captain Hegedus to open the closet.

"Is the Captain looking for a Christmas gown for his lady?" Andras' voice was positively dripping with irony. "There's nothing in here but women's frillies. Don't waste your time, now. Why not come back with your lovely young lady friend tomorrow and Karola will treat her to a fancy little something, right off the rack from Paris, eh Miss Koschwitz?"

"Exactly, Captain. Anything she wishes."

I was in a crouch position, prepared to disarm the German, and thrust the bayonet into his neck, below his ear, as we had been taught to do and had practised so often at Camp X.

"*Was ist los*?"

I heard the thud of something splitting wood. '*He's stabbing the floor with the bayonet! My god, Mitzi*!' A blood-chilling scream pierced the air. '*I'm coming out*!' I pushed my way through the wall of clothes and grabbed for the door handle. There wasn't one. '*Closets don't have inside handles; at least, not this one.*' Karola had made very sure that it was tightly shut. The screams rose in pitch and frequency and were joined by an angry chorus of male voices, cursing loudly in German and Magyar. With all my strength, I jammed my shoulder against the wooden door. It would not budge. I tried again, the sweat running into my eyes. It was useless; I was powerless to help. If I yelled, it would distract them while they routed me out, but it wouldn't save Mitzi. The chaotic screaming, profanity, and loud thumping of bodies colliding abruptly peaked but was immediately replaced by angry shouting between Andras and the German. The German seemed to be hell bent on taking Mitzi down to the Danube and shooting her.

Andras was arguing vociferously.

The German shouted, "Fine then. You'll be responsible. I will be writing this up, Captain. Expect to hear from my C.O. Sergeant Nagy, cuff this bitch and get her into the van, now! Watch her closely. What? So, put some ice on them, you fool. From the icebox, you dolt! One false move, you can shoot her."

The clatter of boots faded from the bedroom and proceeded down the hallway. The front door slammed. In the ensuing silence, seconds seemed an eternity.

"Joe, it's Karola. Are you alright?" As she pulled open the closet door, fresh air rushed in, reviving me like a splash of cold water in the face.

"Where have they taken Mitzi? Where is Andras? Tell me everything."

Over coffee, Karola told the entire story. Andras' excellent old-boy connections in the military and his well-heeled family's pull gave him a certain *cachet*, an ability to insinuate himself into situations which far exceeded the privileges of his rank.

"He saved Mitzi from being run through with a bayonet. The *Hauptsturmführer* noticed a bulge in the duna and jammed the bayonet right through it, into the floor. Thank God, he missed her, but she let out such a scream. That was it. Lord, did she fight them! Tooth and nail, literally. I think that the younger *Nyilas* man will be, how does one say, permanently disabled? She was incredible: a real tigress. Andras and I tried to prevent the Nazi from running her through and Andras was thrown headfirst against the wall. What an actor that Hegedus is! Could you hear his performance?"

"He sure as hell saved my skin! If he hadn't been here, they probably would have strangled her. Where is Mitzi now?"

"I don't know, Joe, but we'll find out tonight."

One question, Karola. It's a capital crime to hide Jews now, no? So, why aren't you outside in the van with her? I mean, it was obvious…"

"Any of those greedy fools can be bought. It's remarkably easy, really. A nudge here, a wink there, flash a few bills… I wish I could have had time to negotiate Mitzi's freedom before the fracas. They have to fill their quotas or end up as cannon fodder themselves. I know a few effective ways to corrupt the average person, which is what most of them are, but after the battle they were too angry and humiliated and not open to any negotiations."

Our concern was for Mitzi's whereabouts. Andras, as usual, had the information we desperately wanted to hear when he returned later in the evening. Mitzi had been spared immediate execution. Andras credited Karola for that, and she, him. Mitzi was in custody, but he didn't know where.[2] Andras' forehead had been patched, but he looked older and exhausted.

The *SS* and *Nyilasok* had raided several other suites in our building, and a Jewish couple had been taken out, driven down to the Danube, where, along with several score more, they were stripped, shot, and their bodies were thrown naked into the river. Mixed couples had been left alone, for now. That historic, romantic waterway was now a killing field of unimaginable horror, an endless blood bath of monstrous proportions. My 'bloody' Sergeant at the Toronto Horse Palace had been visionary.

The apartment had been professionally tossed. The kitchen, as well as the bedroom floor and walls, suffered some minor damage but Karola was unconcerned, except that her eggbeater was missing, which she attributed to the German. Her annual Christmas party was set for the following evening, December 22 and she was determined to carry on, eggbeater or no. I was assigned the task of coming up with an alternative, which she resolved with a large fork and my determined efforts to whip a dozen of these 'scarce-as-the-proverbial-hen's-teeth' cackle berries to her exacting standards of billowy fluff.

We had scrubbed the walls but couldn't completely erase the dark bloodstains imprinted by Andras' head wound. They and the jagged holes in the hardwood floor haunted me. I was not in a party mood.

'If only you had pushed on the door a bit harder.'

'Come, come, laddie, do you really think that you could have rescued her? They would have shot Mitzi, Karola, you, and Andras too, on the spot. She's alive.'

'Ya, cold comfort, Blokie!'

Karola's magic had produced a respectable wardrobe, including a jacket and grey trousers, which fit perfectly, *almost*. She had laundered my threadbare army shirt but shoes were more problematic as her dress code forbade a khaki shirt together with parachute jump boots. Andras solved this dilemma with a spare pair of military dress Oxfords that were only a half size too small.

[2] *Years later, I searched unsuccessfully in Budapest for people who might have had information about Mitzi. With her fighting spirit and strong principles, I would like to believe that she survived.*

Karola, as I expected, was a superb hostess and the extent of her connections with the black market was astonishing. Everything, from the impossible-to-buy delicacies, the traditional Hungarian Christmas fare, the punch, wines, and even the décor, was simply first class. I was reminded of that glorious fall day at the partisan wedding in Yugoslavia and my beautiful Serbian lover.

Instead of a peasant band to provide the music, I kept the Victrola wound up and fitted with cactus gramophone needles. I played an eclectic selection of Hungarian Csardas, seasonal songs, and carols, all spiced with hot Cuban tangos.

Most of the guests were our neighbours and several couples were of mixed Jewish-Gentile marriages. They were a spirited group who enjoyed themselves immensely. Karola had "just happened to find", as she explained, a small stock of kosher meats, breads, and sweets, complete with two bottles of sacramental wine. She had warned me against mingling too much with the guests, except for the three shadowy representatives from the Resistance, whom she pointed out. They were well dressed, ate little, and drank less, while observing the proceedings inconspicuously from the sidelines. Andras and his charming wife, Ilona, schmoozed with everyone else. I didn't know at the time that he and she were quietly warning the mixed couples to get far away, very quickly, as the local SD, *Gestapo* and *Nyilasok* had broadened their dragnet, in a concerted bid to outscore each other in the drive to eradicate Budapest's Jewish population.

Nevertheless, the dancing, uproarious singsongs, covert and indiscreet flirting, whispered kitchen accusations, teary resolutions and dalliances under the mistletoe and elsewhere, and general merry-making continued until past 2:30 a.m. To ensure that we had no complaints from sleep-deprived neighbours, Karola had invited most of the tenants, with the exception of the sullen, Szállási sympathiser next door. Some came by for a sweet treat and cup of wassail, they professed, but stayed for the fun, food and companionship. Although it was frustrating not to be able to socialise in Magyar, which I thought a wise precaution, I did carry on in hybrid Germano-English and sign language, with the designated 'safe' guests, particularly a gorgeous, black-haired woman who might have been a Parisian fashion model. They were all unfailingly polite, non-intrusive, and obviously saw through my *nom de guerre* and cover story that I was simply an escaped Canadian officer in the British Army.

It was well after 3:00 when Karola and I, still coasting along in a gala party mood, began to clear a pathway from the living room to the kitchen. She sang softly and tunelessly to herself as we tackled the mountain of soiled dishes and leftovers. We then retrieved the post-party debris, which included nothing more scandalously intriguing than one maroon silk handkerchief, a tube of ruby lipstick and one ornate fourteen karat gold earring which had likely flown off and skittered under the sofa during a Csardas or tango frenzy.

We chatted and laughed about the party's highlights and the salacious carryings-on of some of the more lubricated *tangoistas*, as Karola tied a flowered apron around my waist. "Very cute!" Her lips brushed gently against mind for a moment, then she turned and resumed scraping and submerging the dishes and silverware in the soapy sink water.

"Joe, you were a sweetie this evening and were very well behaved. Thank you for helping to make the evening a success." Then she added, "Andras thinks that yesterday's raid was not the last. I don't know if you overheard him and Ilona warning the mixed couples to make tracks, *schnell*. I think I have found you a better hiding place! Those need to soak for a few minutes. Come with me."

The master bedroom had what is now fashionably called an *ensuite* bathroom. "Your new residence," she exclaimed proudly, pointing to the small bathroom window. "Try it out!"

I looked at her blankly, without a glimmer of understanding. '*Does she expect me to hang out the window like Harold Lloyd*?'

"You'll have to climb on the toilet seat to get to the window. Here, take my hand."

I squeezed my shoulders through the narrow window, which opened into a concrete ventilation shaft/skylight. It had two small apertures at the top, on opposite sides, to provide circulation and admit light. The interior was approximately one metre square, consisting of nothing but cement walls; it was cold, dank, and surprisingly dark, like a vertical attic. The concrete floor was bare except for shrivelled leaves, bird droppings and assorted litter, which in large part consisted of partially smoked, lipstick-stained, cork tipped cigarette butts. I surmised that they were the incriminating evidence tossed away by a secret smoker, after a few furtive puffs. When I had crawled back into the bathroom, Karola assured me that it was possible, though very unlikely, that an upstairs tenant would stick her or his head through their window and see me. '*But what about that mysterious smoker*?' I could hear the scream for the police.

Sometime after 4:00 a.m., she insisted that I go to bed. Gratefully, I agreed. At 9:00, Andras arrived on our doorstep, looking exceedingly well rested and sober as though he'd 'had one or two at the club, then home and asleep by ten.'

"Sorry to disturb you, but as you can see, Ilona sent me out to reconnoitre at this ungodly hour. Please take this before I drop it." He handed Karola a magnificent, scarlet-red poinsettia.

"It's gorgeous. You can report to Ilona on my behalf that you accomplished your mission."

"I was passing by that little book and florist's shop on Uj ut, remember, the one that was run by the old Jewish couple? New owners. This was the last one, maybe in all of Budapest. Thank you again for a grand time."

"Can you stay for some coffee?"

"Thank you, no, I must be off." *Sotto voce*, he added, "We're being monitored." He mimed someone using binoculars and earphones. Barely speaking above a whisper he confided, "You'll be hit today. Mid to late afternoon. Joe, stay low." He continued, "Thanks again, Karola, we had a wonderful time. *Auf Wiedersehn!*"

With Teutonic precision, as the mantle clock chimed 3:00 p.m., the search party arrived. I headed to the bathroom, clambered across the obstacle course, through the window and dropped lightly onto to cement floor. I checked my watch: twenty seconds! I had left the bathroom door slightly ajar. I tried to reach up to shut the window tightly, but without success. It was jammed. Indistinctly, I could hear Karola welcoming them, in German, while apologising for the disarray, which was likely visible only to her. Now, she was offering them coffee and leftover cookies, the perfect *Hausfrau*. There were three male voices, two German, one Magyar. The familiar German voice asked her a question, in a high-pitched drone.

"Any more surprises *Fraülein*? May we check the closet this time?" inquired the *Hauptsturmführer*.

"No surprises, *Herr Oberst*. Please feel free to look anywhere you wish and take your time, please."

She was magnificent. The banter continued as Karola escorted the men down the hallway, towards the master bedroom. As they entered, the *Hauptsturmführer* proudly drew his comrades' attention to the recent signs of battle. Indicating the bayonet hole in the floorboards, he regaled them with an heroic account of his struggle to subdue Mitzi, 'the notorious female Jew black-market bandit.'

"Private, go inspect the bathroom and keep your light fingers off this lady's belongings."

An *SS* patch-emblazoned black helmet appeared in the doorway. I shrank against the wall, and held my breath. I watched as the helmet walked over to the bathtub and jerked back the shower curtain, picked up Mitzi's bar of lavender-scented soap, sniffed it warily, and then sniffed it again. My legs were trembling so much that I thought I might collapse. The helmet replaced the soap bar in the seashell dish and wiped its hands

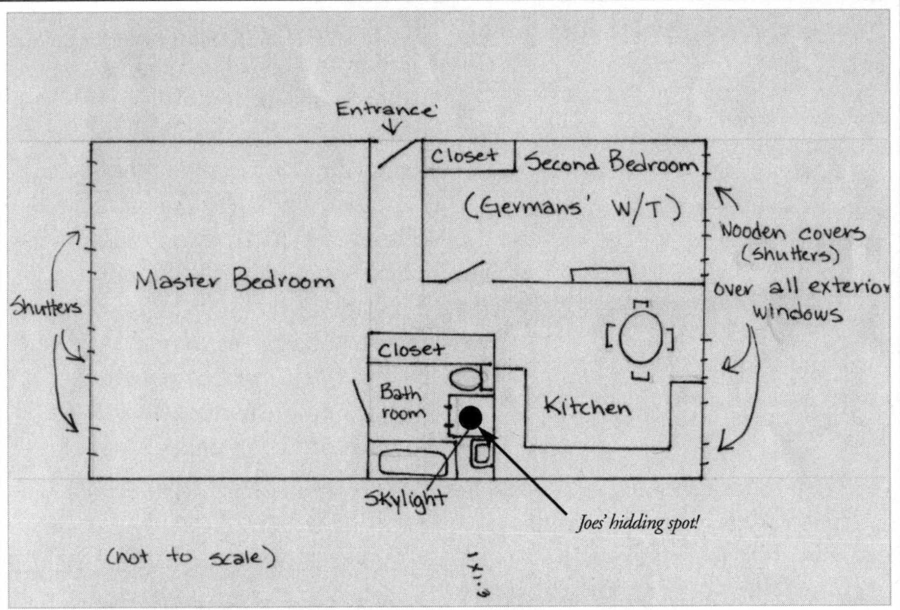

Interior of Karola's apartment, Krusper Utca 3, showing ventilation shaft where Joe hid

on its trouser leg. Then, it leaned over, out of my sight. It straightened up. As it examined itself in the mirror, I saw, reflected, the face of a schoolteacher, or carpenter or accountant. He patted his jacket pocket and then adjusted his helmet.

"Private, what in hell are you doing in there? I told you to search, not fall asleep on the can!"

"No, Sir! I'm coming, right away, Sir!"

To my dismay, the helmet became an SS *mann*, approaching the window. I crept to the far corner and crouched, imagining myself the size of a football, mentally struggling to control my breathing, which, to me, sounded as deafening as a tornado. He pushed up the window until it jammed three-quarters open. Putting his head partway through, his rifle barrel hit the wooden sash, causing him to curse soundly. He withdrew and then reappeared, *sans* gun. This time, the top of his helmet grazed the top sash. He looked down, then to his left and his right, slowly scanning the near-total darkness. He stopped, staring in my direction. I could see the mole on his left cheek. *'Think. I'm invisible. Say it! I'm invisible! That's it, he's seen me! I can break his neck, by lunging across and pushing upward with all my strength on the point of his chin. If I'm lucky, I can grab his shoulders before he drops and haul the body through.'* He spat heartily and withdrew. *'Thank God he didn't have a flashlight!'* After an eternity, I heard the toilet flush. I slowly raised my head and peered inside. The bathroom door was wide open.

"Now, *Fraülein* Koschwitz, open the closet door."

"As you wish. Did the *Hauptsturmführer* wish to make a selection, now?"

"Kindly move aside, *Fraülein*. I have no time for your games." The swishing of metal clothes hangers on metal rods obscured the rest of their exchange.

Hobnailed footsteps and harsh voices once again faded down the hallway. The apartment door slammed shut. I heard something fall.

A moment later, Karola came to the window to fetch me.

"What was that noise?"

"My Chinese figurine. It fell off the shelf."

"Sorry. Was it valuable?"

"Mm, yes, a reminder of someone. You might be able to mend it for me, someday?"

"Sure. I guess he didn't find what he was looking for."

"Apparently not. Come, let's take a peek out the front shutters, Joe. There's something going on outside." Through a crack, we could see two civilian police vans, idling curbside. I counted three *SD* men and two plainclothes *Nyilasok* in various military 'hurry up and wait' poses: standing, smoking and waiting; talking, smoking and waiting; or sitting, smoking, talking and waiting. Across the street, a *Nyilas* in a brown leather trench coat, was leaning against the lamppost, smoking, while glancing occasionally at our window. His service revolver's holster was unsnapped. This still-life tableau lasted for fifteen minutes. Suddenly, as one, they were energised as cigarettes were hastily flicked into the gutter and arms were shouldered. For a moment, the cause of this reaction was not apparent, but it was soon all too evident.

"My God, Karola, they're taking away all of our Jewish neighbours!"

It was a heart-wrenching scene. As I watched in disbelief, Karola softly intoned fourteen names, as each person appeared, single file. Every Jewish partner of a mixed marriage was being marched, pushed or jostled outside, directly into the rear of the waiting paddy wagons. Regardless of age, gender or physical condition, the distraught Gentile spouses who tried to reach out and touch or hold onto their loved ones were pushed aside. Two elderly men were clubbed for their trouble with *SD* rifle butts and lay bleeding from their head wounds, on the sidewalk. Suddenly, a gunshot rang out. The *Nyilas* cop across the street, his service revolver drawn, had killed one of the Jews, a young woman, who had tried to make a break for it. She lay sprawled, motionless, in the awkwardness of sudden death, face down, in the gutter. Her blonde hair was caked with fresh blood, the colour of her dress. I thought of Mitzi.

Seconds later, a small, dark green car, in the shape of a beetle, drove up noisily and stopped beside the *Nyilas* shooter, who was calmly replacing his revolver back in his holster. The driver emerged; he was tall, well-dressed, and darkly handsome, with the general appearance of a professional: a doctor or a lawyer. The stranger reached through the open passenger window of the strange little auto and produced an attaché case, which he opened and then set on the sidewalk. He spoke to the *Nyilas*, who appeared extremely annoyed with the intruder.

"Who's that, Karola, a lawyer? Does he want to get shot?"

"The angel of Budapest. Watch!"

Three of the previous night's merry company now lay inert, limbs askew, like broken puppets, their heads and faces oozing thick red liquid, which was congealing into obscene dark puddles, on the cement sidewalk.

The stranger had taken some documents from his briefcase, which he was showing to, or rather, almost shoving into the face of, the *Nyilas*. The policeman turned his back and walked away. The stranger followed doggedly, waving the sheaf of papers. The besieged *Nyilas* shouted at him, "Go to hell!" The soldiers on our side of the street had stopped to watch, but did not intervene.

The last person in line, frail, white-haired Byelorussian grandma Baba Yaga, was sitting on the steps watching, or simply was unable to move any further. The *SS* soap thief picked her up and threw her bodily, with brute force, into the back of the second van.

The argument across the street was now becoming more heated. The *Nyilas* was pointing his gun at 'the angel', who appeared unperturbed. I expected to see the stranger crumple to the sidewalk, a bullet in his brain for his daring. The remaining soldiers jumped into the second van before its back doors were shut and latched by the driver. Both vehicles were pulling away when the *Nyilas* shouted. Running, while still arguing at the top of his voice with the stranger, he got into the first truck, which then roared off. Abruptly, it braked and reversed, narrowly avoiding a collision with the vehicle following it. A soldier clambered out and picked up the lifeless body of the young woman, which he unceremoniously tossed into the rear. He then shut the back door, re-entering the passenger side and the van accelerated. As if watching an instant replay of the last scene, the second van stopped suddenly and with loud clashing and whining of its transmission, reversed at high speed, careening to a stop at the curb, directly outside our window. The front passenger door opened. The *Hauptsturmführer* alighted to delicately place Karola's china teacup and saucer, which he had obviously taken with him upon his earlier departure, on the top step of the entranceway. Karola pushed me well back from the window, so that I was just able to see him look up and salute with exaggerated civility, then re-enter the vehicle.

"Murderous bastard!" Tears of rage and frustration glistened in her eyes.

I knew I had truly seen the face of evil. The stranger, his valise and beetle car had vanished as mysteriously as they had appeared.

"They were all my friends, Joe, and they're gone...Helene, Jakob, Karin, Isaac, Herschel, Abel, Hanna...pouf! Even harmless, dotty dear Baba Yaga...why? What harm did she ever do, or any of them?" She was sobbing. I was in shock but tried my best to comfort her, holding her trembling body in my arms.

"Karola, you've got to tell me. Who was that remarkable man?"

"You'll find out, soon. I promise."

"Who was the young woman?"

"I don't know. She dropped in briefly last night. She must have been visiting someone. Oh, God, what a terrible time to be alive."

"Look, I'll do anything to help. Tell Andras that I need to do something. I have a fair bit of money and I can forge documents fairly well. I can work with someone to help make passports, if you or Andras know someone who can use me."

"Good, but now, I'm going to see what help I can give to those two old dears. Karl's nearly blind with cataracts and Ivan's almost eighty. They both have heart conditions. We must bring them indoors, before they catch their....get pneumonia."

Joe, please go to the medicine cabinet and find the iodine. Put on the kettle; we'll need lots of clean cloth for bandages. Go into the linen closet and take a fresh sheet. Tear it into wide strips; do you know how to make bandages?"

"Yes, of course. I can lend a hand outside, Karola! I'm qualified in first aid."

"Thanks Joe, but you must stay here. You've had far too much exposure already at the party. It was my mistake. Just do as I ask, please, and stay out of sight, as Andras said."

I couldn't argue with her logic. The searches of the apartment were certainly not accidental. Someone may have tipped off the authorities. I would be endangering Karola if I were seen again. The two injured seniors, Karl, and Ivan, Baba's Gentile Russian husband, were looked after by Karola and the others. She later told me that the men were semi-conscious, but were too dazed and bewildered to understand the atrocity which had occurred at Krusper utca 3.

The next day was Christmas Eve, 1944. It would prove to be the most significant December 24 of my life. Andras, Karola said gravely, had arranged a clandestine meeting with a very important member of the underground. Hegedus would meet me at 10:00 p.m. at an undisclosed location. She was not at liberty to tell me any more details, she said, until I was leaving. Was this the opportunity that I had been waiting for? It was personal now. The spectacle of the previous afternoon, and Mitzi's arrest, had turned me from a concerned observer into a champion of Hungary's oppressed Jewish people. I was deeply shocked and outraged, as a Christian and as a Canadian male, at these demonstrations of barbaric disregard for basic human rights. My motivation was less than noble; I longed for revenge.

It was difficult to just wait, so I napped after supper until 9:30 p.m. I retrieved and then counted the remainder of my money. Karola gave me a pair of overshoes and the last piece of my instructions as I was buttoning up the borrowed overcoat.

The park was less than a ten-minute walk away, but, as I assumed that I would be tailed, I took a creative route, arriving at the gate at 10:00 p.m. It was bitterly cold, moonless and eerily silent. It was an ideal night for thieves, lovers, and conspirators. The snowfall made visibility almost nil. There was no sign of Andras. I picked up some snow and hurled a missile at the unprotected overhead street lamp. It fused brightly and briefly before it faded out. In the total darkness, I made a three-hundred and sixty degree scan. I was alone but my instincts told me that there were eyes in the darkness, waiting, watching, and evaluating. By 10:15, I was certain that I had missed the appointment or it had been cancelled. I was about to return to Karola's for a cup of cheer, when a couple, walking a small terrier, appeared at the park entrance. '*Damn it, where is he?*' I checked my wristwatch for the last time: 10:20. I began to trudge towards the gate. The dog and woman had vanished. In their place stood Andras, facing me, less than a metre away.

"Good evening, sorry to keep you. Stay half a block behind me on the opposite side."

I followed him as he had directed, matching his brisk pace. The snow was blowing directly into my face making Andras barely visible up ahead. After six blocks, an auto drew up beside him and stopped. '*Gestapo!*' The rear door opened, he got inside, and the car pulled away. I walked on, hoping that was the right thing to do. After another block, I stopped to check the reflections in a shop window. A pair of partially blacked-out headlights was approaching. I heard the scrunch of tires on dry snow. I resumed walking, at a normal pace. The Buick pulled ahead of me and stopped, idling silently.

The left rear window rolled down. "Get in, quickly."

We drove for a half-hour, in complete silence. Andras was reading and marking up a document by the dim pillar light beside his head. The female driver, who wore a tam *à la mode français*, seemed vaguely familiar. As she drove around a corner, I could see her profile. '*How can I forget a face like that? This is the smashingly beautiful guest at Karola's party with whom I made small talk in fractured German*'. I had been hypnotised by her immense coal black eyes, Carrera marble skin and raven, shoulder-length hair.

My reverie was interrupted by Andras, "Did they teach you that in Canada?"

"I'm sorry. What, Andras?"

"Snowballs, as lethal weapons?"

"You were watching, all the time?"

"For a while. I had to make sure that you hadn't been followed."

It seemed to me that the goddess was driving in circles. Eventually, she wheeled through the non-existent front gate of a nondescript warehouse near the synagogue. Ahead, a massive, rusted steel door loomed like the cliffs of Gibraltar. I closed my eyes in anticipation that the goddess would smash into it at full throttle. She honked and it started to roll up. A split second later, she rolled at breakneck speed into the loading dock area, which appeared to be a repository for the world's stock of large oil drums. We halted only centimetres from a stocky man with a Sten gun. He waved and signalled to the goddess to kill the headlights.

'*Should I speak to her? And say what, 'Good driving, goddess?*"

Before I could, Andras spoke. "Joe, this way, please. Go up those metal stairs, watch your step, and around the corner on your right. I'll be with you in a moment."

"Right-oh!" I followed his directions but was blocked from going further by another, even stockier man, also toting a Sten and wearing a broad-brimmed grey fedora, just like the newspaper photos of the mobster Alphonse Capone. Andras caught up and we followed Big Al to a wooden door with bumpy, translucent glass in the window that I remembered touching as a kid, when going into the dentist's office. I anticipated that we were about to be ushered into the presence of a ferocious warlord, or, perhaps, the lair of Budapest's arch-criminal mastermind. Big Al opened the door and my hopes were dashed. My first impression was that of a Hollywood set designer's recreation of a big city newspaper office. A dozen or so men and women were standing around, or sitting on desktops, speaking rapidly, while two or three others sat quietly on wooden chairs at small desks, bent over archaic typewriters.

Everyone seemed to be smoking either a pipe, a cigar or a cigarette.

'*What are they doing here? It's Christmas Eve!*'

The voices were speaking Hungarian, flavoured with an unfamiliar dialect. I turned to Andras, who had read my mind: "Yiddish."

"I knew that." I recalled his final conversation with Mitzi, in Karola's kitchen. We threaded our way around the room. Several people greeted Andras as if he were visiting royalty.

A tiny and very tired evergreen tree, leaning forlornly in a water pitcher on an empty desk, flopped onto the floor as I accidentially brushed against it.

"Seven years of bad luck, Joe!"

Big Al led us to a small corner office where he delivered us into the care and custody of a striking woman with a killer smile and honey blonde hair heaped like freshly-cut hay. She was sheathed in a severely expensive black suit. In delightfully accented English, she welcomed Captain Hegedus, who introduced me to "Sonja."

'*Hungarian she is not: Scandinavian, maybe.*'

"Mr. Raoul will be with you in a moment. Please do make yourselves comfortable. May I bring you some Christmas cookies and tea?"

'*Yes, yes! Who is Mr. Raoul and where did he find this knockout?*'

"Sugar, Lieutenant?" She used the American pronunciation: loo-tenant. At that moment, a tall, darkly handsome man materialised.

'*My God, it's the 'stranger.'*'

Andras and I rose. "Raoul, may I present Lieutenant Joseph Gordon. Joe, this is Raoul."

I was flabbergasted. "Sir, I'm overwhelmed. I saw you on Krusper utca. You were, well, quite frankly, Sir, a sight to behold. How did you know that the Nyilas wouldn't shoot you?"

"I didn't actually," he laughed gently, "but thank you. That was not one of my shining moments. Please don't be too impressed, Lieutenant. As Captain Hegedus will tell you, I'm simply trying to provide a basic service despite some rather challenging circumstances." Raoul had the bearing and graceful poise of an Olympic decathlete, international polo champion or fighter pilot: tall, impossibly, youthfully handsome, athletically slim, and intensely charming and charismatic. He was dressed impeccably in a navy blue three-piece suit, which emphasised his piercing gaze. He took us into his office and thanked us for meeting with him on Christmas Eve. "Yes? Very well,

[3] *Please see Chapter 10 for more about Mr. Raoul.*

Sonja. Excuse me gentlemen, there's a call I must take on the scrambled line. I will be right back."

Andras filled me in briefly on Raoul's recent efforts to rescue Budapest's Jews.[3]

Raoul returned. "You must be wondering about all the activity here tonight, Lieutenant. Most of the staff, with the exception of Sonja and me, are Jewish. The offices back at the Legation were a little too frantic with merry-making this afternoon." He paused. "Just one moment, please. You must go, now, Sonja! No, no more…thank you. Go home and give Lars a big Christmas kiss. *God jul!*"

'*Lucky Lars!*'

"Excuse me, but she'd stay through New Year's Day if I let her. She's quite unusual for a Minnesota-born Swedish-Lutheran girl. Christmas is a big family affair where she comes from. However, things are quite busy here these days. Has Andras told you about my business? Good. Now, Lieutenant, tell me what you wish to do." He spoke English exceptionally well, with a Swedish accent, tinged with a trace of New England salt cod. This was a very interesting man. He had not mentioned a family of his own.

I explained the reasons for my need to contribute to his work, beginning with Mitzi's abduction. "Frankly, sir, I'm appalled at the wretched treatment of these people by Germans and Hungarians. I just can't stand by any longer. I'm more than a little bit lucky to be alive, myself."

"Lieutenant, please call me Raoul. I'm not a diplomat, so we can dispense with formalities. You are Joseph, if that's all right? Now, I have something that may interest you both. Have a look." He picked up a buff-coloured file, which he handed to Andras who opened and held it so I could view the contents. Inside were what appeared to be citizenship papers, mint, embossed with the triple gold crowns of Sweden.

Andras let out a low whistle. "Their work gets better and better, Raoul. How much?"

"This one's real, Andras. Joseph, if you want to have it copied, I'll give it to you, providing I can have it back."

"Yes, I want to do that."

"I don't know how much you can afford."

"How many do you need, Raoul?"

"We could make good use of any number, five…fifty would be ideal. We are usually able to reuse them, so fifty might gain the release of two or three hundred people, perhaps more. Are you still interested?"

"Fifty it is. How do I…?" I knew that John and Mike would have approved this use of our remaining

DIBBLER funds.

"Andras will place the order. Andras, these two names here are my most reliable specialists. I'm fortunate to have a pool of very skilled and discrete, shall I say, 'artisans', in the city, Joseph. Their work is flawless. Now gentlemen, thank you for your good will and your time. Speaking of which, good heavens, Merry Christmas!" The wall clock read 12:45. "I can ask Madeleine to drive you back, if you wish."

"No, but thanks, Raoul. We can walk back in half an hour, okay Joe?"

'So, the goddess is Madeleine. Speak for yourself, Captain Hegedus!'

As we stood to leave, Raoul took my hand and looked directly into my eyes. "I can't thank you enough. You've made this Christmas particularly meaningful, Joseph. Interesting isn't it, that we were discussing these things when we might have been at home with our closest friends, celebrating our Lord's birth, himself a Jew who was persecuted. God bless you both. *God jul!*"

I crept into the apartment at 1:30 to find Karola waiting up for me in the kitchen. The large breastbone of a goose was jutting above the water line in the sink, like the conning tower of a submarine. "So, tell me all about Mr. Raoul." We sat at the table drinking hot chocolate while I recounted my meeting with 'the stranger,' casually mentioning the two goddesses. I was in an euphoric state and rattled on until 2:00.

"Andras probably neglected to tell you that Raoul is a well-to-do Swedish business man, a Gentile, and came here to help, voluntarily. Merry Christmas, Joszi!"

"Merry Christmas, Karola!" We kissed platonically, and went to our separate beds.

Christmas Day was cold, bright, and best of all, raid free. The *Nyilasok* and *SD* had apparently taken the day off from their vile business. "A day of rest for the wicked" I quipped. Karola and I worked off and on in the kitchen together, until she insisted that she would be better off finishing the preparations herself. I went into the living room and cranked up the Victrola.

"What do you want to hear?"

"Liszt and Strauss. When you're done with them, play some happy gypsy tunes."

Andras came in for a brief visit to let me know that the orders for fifty sets had been placed. The total cost was fifty napoleons, which I gave him. We had brandies to toast Raoul and our success.

Christmas dinner was a miracle. Karola had pulled out all the stops. By 4:00, the apartment was filled with the aroma of roast goose. Although we ate by ourselves, as Andras and

Ilona had been invited elsewhere, we enjoyed a sumptuous banquet of stuffed roast goose, potatoes and 'the trimmings', complete with wine, culminating with mince tarts covered with her special hard sauce. Wearing tissue paper queen and king crowns, we got very silly and tipsy. I presented Karola with a home made card containing some pengös; she replied with a new pair of fleecy slippers. We toasted all of our friends and sang carols until the wine bottle was drained.

The next day was business as usual. A Nazi/*Nyilasok* coalition arrived at 10:00. Slightly hungover, I was shooed out of my warm bed, across the toilet barrier with barely time to use it, without flushing, and into my deep freeze hideaway, wearing pyjamas, my new slippers and the borrowed overcoat; it was ice-cold in 'the box.' I don't now if I was quivering with the DT's, fear, or shivering with the blast of Siberian air swooping down from the vents when a gigantic, grizzled guardian of the Third Reich poked his huge head partway into my inner sanctum and looked around, for an eternity. Something metallic clattered onto the concrete floor and rolled toward me, then stopped. Muttering, he tried to reach in to pick it up. Unsuccessful, he tried again, using his bayonet as a probe. I heard the point scraping the floor, less than a metre away. If it were attached to his rifle, he could have gutted me. He swore in frustration; then the bayonet and he withdrew. I didn't dare move in case he was intending to come in. I mentally prepared myself for a short, sharp round of unarmed combat, which was one of my strongest suits during my STS stints. Disappointedly, I heard the toilet flush and his hobnailed boots clunking out. '*Don't these guys ever wash their hands?' Thank the frugal German Quartermaster General that this goon wasn't issued a flashlight!*' As I was about to climb back into the bathroom, I kicked the object of Fritz' desire with my slipper. I bent down and picked it up. It was round, a silver capsule, with ornately-carved script in an unknown language. When I showed it to Karola, she instantly recognised it.

"That's a *mezuzah*. Most Jews, and nearly all Orthodox ones, have them fastened at the entrance to their home. Open it, carefully."

I did so. Inside, in unimaginably small script, were several tiny pages tightly rolled together. "It looks like the writing on the synagogue we drove past last night. So I assume that it's Hebrew."

"It is that. Those are the first five books of the Old Testament, the Pentateuch."

"He obviously stole it, probably hoping to sell it. It's made of sterling silver, I'd bet."

We decided that it was time to sit down and evaluate our situation. This search party, she said, had consisted of three soldiers. Two were Germans: *SD* and regular *Wehrmacht*, with a Signals shoulder flash. The third man was *Nyilas*. It was clearly not coincidence that our flat was being targeted. The critical question was, why?" I suggested that we 'think like the enemy' and come up with some possible explanations. Our final list consisted of five theories:

1. Suspicion of Karola, the acknowledged Queen of the black-market and probable Resistance sympathiser;

2. Mitzi had been caught here, therefore there might be more Jews in hiding;

3. The three Zugliget PoW escapees, Andrew, John and I, were still on the loose, likely holed up in one or more safe houses in Budapest;

4. All of the above;

5. None of the above.

Events soon proved that one of our theories was one hundred percent correct, as we were about to discover.

CHAPTER 10
Red Storm

Accounts of the wholesale slaughter of Jews on the banks of the Danube would have been too incredible to be believed had they not been described in horrifying detail by Andras Hegedus, an unimpeachable eye-witness. Karola and I had heard shots from the vicinity of the river, which was not far from her apartment. For proof, Andras had taken me on a quick tour, late one night. As we crept down toward the river's edge, I could clearly see gangs of workers in prison garb collecting the bodies which lay scattered like broken dolls on the Danube's banks, slopes, and even the pavement above. Working in pairs, the convicts were pushing, rolling, or throwing the corpses into the dark waters, under the attentive eyes of their German and Arrow Cross guards. Many of the cadavers that were clothed wore a yellow Star of David armband. I was overwhelmed with anger, sorrow, and nausea. 'By reason of insanity' was the only possible explanation for this deliberate, public massacre by the Hungarian and German authorities; my country of birth had been disgraced, turned into a charnel house, a living hell.

Andras was working frantically with Raoul's organisation to intercede with the SS and Arrow Cross High Command in Budapest. He told me a great number of remarkable stories concerning Raoul, which Karola verified. As an American-educated businessman who had visited Hungary often before the war, Raoul Wallenberg, a Gentile, gave up the comfort and safety of his life in Stockholm, Sweden in July 1944, to go to Budapest. There, with the cooperation of the Swedish Legation, he became a modern-day 'Scarlet Pimpernel' in an heroic effort to rescue Hungary's remaining 200,000 Jews. Using brilliant tactics, Raoul's network established the '*Schutzpass*' (protective pass) which placed the bearer under the protection of the Swedish legation. The person was then taken by courier to one of a number of safe houses flying the Swedish flag, in and near the ghetto area of Budapest. Raoul had effectively foiled the Germans and the Hungarian fascist secret police, the *Nyilasok*, by having these houses declared Swedish territory, thus shielding the person under the protection of the Swedish king. He was exceptionally skilled at inventing complex bureaucratic boondoggles to delay and derail Himmler's 'Jewish expert',

Obersturmbannführer-SS Adolf Eichmann's[1] deportation of Jews to the death camps in Austria and the Reich. Raoul, Andras said, often expressed his frustration that his personal efforts never seemed adequate. The genocidal fury being perpetrated by Eichmann's *SD Amt 11* (*Department 11-Jewish Section*) and the Szállási forces in Budapest and throughout Hungary actually escalated as the Red Army surged nearer to Budapest, spilling into the outskirts.[2] Andras assured me that the forgers had performed miracles, fulfilling my order with flawless precision in an extraordinarily short time. The artisans had actually returned some of the gold coins, to help underwrite Raoul's enterprises.

Raoul Wallenberg knew that the *SS* was thoroughly corrupt and of course, amoral. With the possible exception of their peculiarly puritanical, mass-murdering chief, *Reichsführer-SS* Heinrich Himmler, the senior officer cadre and bureaucracy, medical doctors, and ranks were shamelessly venal and could be bought off, often surprisingly cheaply. I do not know how many Jewish lives Raoul had saved by a combination of bribery, using my surplus DIBBLER napoleons, and the shrewd deployment of the fifty sets of Swedish identity papers. Andras told us of one dramatic rescue, among many, in which Raoul literally browbeat the German and Hungarian officers who were supervising the loading of Jews onto cattle cars at the Budapest train station. Using his diplomatic status, and by dint of his incredible courage, he waved a sheaf of bogus Swedish citizenship papers under the noses of the officials. He calmly asserted that the persons named were Swedish nationals, and demanded their release. He persisted. Annoyed and baffled, the officers complied. Wallenberg's single most daring act was to intimidate the *SS* general who was to about to order the destruction of the Budapest ghetto. Raoul calmly informed the commander, General Schmidthuber, that he would inevitably be executed after the war, if the liquidation proceeded, saying, "If you do not stop this now, I can guarantee you will be hanged as a war criminal." Schmidthuber, taken aback by this display of sheer bravado, reconsidered his options, and withdrew his armour and troops. By such magnificent acts of selfless bravery, Raoul Wallenberg personally saved more than 30,000 Hungarian-Jewish lives directly, and possibly, many

---

[1] *In May, 1960, Lieutenant-Colonel Adolf Eichmann was captured in Argentina by the Israeli secret service, the Mossad. He was smuggled to Israel and tried for war crimes and crimes against humanity, in Jerusalem. Found guilty, he expressed no regret for his actions and was hanged at Ramle, May 31, 1962.*

[2] *Today, I wonder if Hilter's* schema *for world domination wasn't motivated by a pathological obsession to exterminate the world's Jewry along with the Slavic race, given the continuing transports, which wasted troops in the face of the advancing Russians. A reading of the minutes of the infamous Wannsee Conference on January 20, 1942, chaired by* SD *Chief Heydrich, wherein the Final Solution was endorsed, six months before Germany invaded Russia, would suggest this might have been the case.*

thousands more, indirectly. Adolf Eichmann and Raoul Wallenberg actually met in Budapest, just before Andras and I visited with Raoul on Christmas Eve, 1944. Raoul's efforts to convince the fanatical Eichmann to end the senseless slaughter were ignored. Knowing that he was in all certainty, a marked man, Raoul nevertheless continued his campaign, staying constantly on the move, to evade Eichmann's henchmen.

The inspections of our apartment continued almost every other day, for a week. Although these were not something about which I ever became blasé, thanks to Andras' intelligence, we usually had a half-day's advance notice, although there were one or two occasions when we had less than an hour. We endured six agonisingly thorough searches, which seemed obsessive, even by SD standards, given the lack of any new 'finds' in our unit since Mitzi's abduction. What did they want with us? Karola, Andras, and I canvassed the apartment buildings door to door, whenever we could, to warn the few remaining Jews, mostly partners in mixed marriages, urging them to make themselves scarce. The majority did not heed us, believing that the murky German racial laws would somehow protect them. Tragically, they were mistaken.

Karola and I developed a system to prepare for searches that worked beautifully. On Andras' cue, we took turns keeping a lookout through the slits in the front window shutter. When we saw the search party arrive, we went into action. As they approached our front door, I was on my way to the bathroom. Scrambling across the obstacle course of the toilet and sink, I crawled through the open window, dropped into the airshaft, and pulled the window three-quarters shut. We rehearsed the drill until I could do it in twenty seconds, from living room sofa to ventilation shaft. Karola was usually able to buy me a few precious moments, with clever delays and distractions.

Nonetheless, I was never able to completely overcome my deep-seated fear of discovery. No matter that we had practised thoroughly and I was prepared mentally, the incidents took on an almost surreal existence of their own, where time and space were suspended. When I went out the window, it was as though, like Alice, I was passing from present reality into a new dimension; the vertical concrete bunker became a time machine. Although common sense and my wristwatch testified otherwise, every fifteen-minute episode became an endless, waking nightmare of horrors, a terrifying drama in which I both played the lead and was also an observer. The fear was so real that I could taste it. The image of my being discovered, my private phobias, and the pervading sense of foreboding and gloom often ended abruptly in a flourish of gallows comedy. On the second to last occasion, an *SD* man methodically surveyed my lair.

Apparently satisfied with the absence of Bolsheviks, Allied secret agents, and Jews, he pulled a partially consumed cigar from his breast pocket, lit it, and tossed away the wooden matchstick. It landed, a glowing ember, on my sleeve. I was paralysed with indecision. If I moved a muscle to blow it out, I was dead. On the other hand, if the wool started to smoulder… He smoked casually, elbows on the window ledge, savouring each inhalation, and inspecting the damn thing lovingly, it as if was about to give birth. As a sometime habitué of downtown Toronto's nightspots, I had become more or less resigned, even accustomed, to surviving beer spills and cigarette smoke. This stogie was a doozy, a foul stinker! It combined the stale odour of an army barracks mixed with the distinctive aroma of the Horse Palace. The rank odour drifted in swirls around my head, insinuating its way into my nostrils. If I gagged… Between puffs, he hummed the wedding march by Wagner. Perhaps he was going soon to the altar. Good luck to his bride! My head was spinning so much that thought I would faint. The match, by now, had dropped harmlessly to the bunker floor.

'*Thank God for small mercies! Stop breathing, Joe lad! You're a good swimmer. You know you can do it!*'

He rounded out his interlude by simultaneously spitting heartily and flicking the butt at my head. I ducked as the red-orange tracer flew past my face, hitting the wall. He disappeared. Seconds after he had flushed the toilet, I bailed through the window, closed it, and shut the bathroom door, then sat down on the tile floor, until the waves of nausea passed.

Visit number six solved the mystery. The Russians were coming. Each day, the blasts of bombs and artillery barrages grew louder as the battle for Budapest advanced inexorably toward the city's bridges. Karola had remarked to me that the Germans had recently paid unusual attention to the kitchen area. Another clue was the presence of at least one German wearing a Signals shoulder patch, on the last three visitations. On visit six, following the *de rigeur* poking under beds and inside cupboards and closets, topped off with an examination of my cooler, the senior German officer curtly dismissed his men and summoned Karola into the kitchen. Then, the *Obersturmbannführer*[3] made a declaration. Karola recounted it to me.

"*Fraülein* Koschwitz, my Commander has authorised me, under the provisions of the code of military law of the Greater Reich, to execute this warrant which, you can see, is properly signed, giving me the right to take possession of your apartment for strategic purposes. You will be permitted to remain, and will be compensated modestly, by me, for

[3] *Lieutenant-Colonel*

your co-operation and inconvenience, *if you do not interfere*." She felt that his steely-grey eyes were drilling into her skull.

"For what purpose, Colonel?"

"That information is classified, *Fraülein*"

"Tell your General that I do not find that satisfactory, and do not give my consent."

"Very well, *Fraülein*. However, I must let you know that the *Obergruppenführer*[4] has given me full authority to have you arrested and summarily executed for subversive resistance, under a state of martial law. In case you have not noticed, the Bolsheviks are storming the gates."

"Please, spare me the dramatics, *Obersturmbannführer*. So, shoot me, if it makes your *Obergruppenführer* happy. I still insist on the right to know your purpose. I'd like to know if you intend to turn my building into a heap of rubble as your last bastion of defence."

"Very well, but if you repeat this, I personally will shoot you, *Fräulein*. Your apartment has been selected from several possible sites, as it is ideally laid out and well-situated to serve as a W/T, that is, radio communications sub-station."

"So that the Russians can detect it and blow us to bits, or will you be too busy overseeing the activities down at the river to notice?"

"Yes, the first is a distinct possibility. The other is of not my area of responsibility. I speak as a field officer of the *Waffen SS*, W/T *Dienst*, not the *Einsatzgruppe*!"[5] Do be careful of what you say. People are being shot out of hand for much less out there."

"As I've seen. Why don't you do something to stop it? You appear to be a decent man. And just how much space will your radio base take up?"

"All but your sleeping quarters."

"Absolutely not!"

Karola said that a fierce argument ensued with accusations and counter-accusations flying. She admitted that she had pushed him hard with her demands and sarcasm but toned it down when he implied that he didn't care if she agreed or not and that her lifeless body would end up in the Danube, to join those of her neighbours. Then, for some inexplicable reason, he relented, admitting that the short wave equipment and space for the operators could be made to fit into the kitchen and spare bedroom. I had been incommunicado in 'the cooler' for three-quarters of an hour, shivering, at first concerned for Karola's safety and then thoroughly annoyed that she had likely forgotten about me. I was unable to hear the

[4] *General*

[5] Waffen-SS *Special Action death squads were mobile killing units which were used extensively in the East.*

brouhaha; the soldier, having finished his search, thoughtlessly shut the bathroom door.

I offered the opinion that the Lieutenant-Colonel's about-face was due to her good looks and well-earned reputation as a *cordon bleu* chef.

"I does what I can, milord." She winked. She had acquired an uncanny ability to mimic in English, her third language, as a teenaged fan of English movies.

Karola's ability to influence and persuade through her mystic power to interpret another's mood and motives, combined with her intelligence, stubbornly persistent logic, charm, and *chutzpah*, was astonishing. I tried to imagine her in full flight, alternately battering and cajoling the *SS* Lieutenant-Colonel, a truly indomitable force of nature. Again, I owed her my life.

Our first need, however, was to regroup so that I could lie low, out of sight, before the first shipment of equipment and men arrived at 7:00 a.m.

"Well, Joe, here's another fine mess. How are your survival skills?"

"Thank you for your concern, *Fraülein* Koschwitz, but I'd rather risk living in the streets or better yet, shack up with Raoul's stunning Swedish assistant, than be stuck here in the cooler twenty-four hours a day, seven days a week." I looked at her slyly, waiting for a reaction.

She ignored my unsubtle barb. "Don't worry, my boy. You won't be sleeping in the gutter. I have already worked it out. Trust me!"

As in Mitzi's time of need, Karola's natural talents for what was known in late twentieth century parlance as "crisis management," came to the rescue. The radio 'base', she determined, would be situated in, and restricted to, the kitchen and spare bedroom, as the officer had agreed. That was a larger area than she had wished; she was adamant that she would only give up another "…hair's breadth, over my dead body!"

She looked through me, reading my mind. "Yes, yes, you're staying in here, not in that smelly rat hole."

"Where?"

"Right here, in the master bed room and the parlour! Eat, sleep, and dine, Joszi." An explosion rattled the china plates in the pantry.

"Karola, I trust you, you know that, but I don't see how it could possibly work!"

She explained her plan; it was elegantly simple. When she had finished, I knew that it was not only a possibility, it was the only possibility.

We ducked when we heard the angry whine of shrapnel. It spattered like hailstones on the shutters.

"Nasty stuff, shrapnel. Napoleon Bonaparte was a young Captain of Artillery when he fired a 'whiff of grapeshot' over the heads of the Parisian Mob, at the start of the French Revolution. It got him promoted. Any poor devil caught in its pathway would be halved and quartered by assorted chunks and shards of white-hot, cast iron. If it doesn't kill or maim you, the blood poisoning will finish you off! Either way, it's curtains." I tried my best in broken German, and English.

"What is 'blood poisoning', Jozsi?" she queried.

"A slow, ugly and very painful death. The shreds of metal are embedded in your flesh and cause gangrene, a serious infection, unless you're lucky enough to get immediate treatment. Even then, it's unlikely that a surgeon working in a field hospital without an x-ray machine handy could possibly find and remove every single fragment."

"But, if the fragments are white hot, as you said, wouldn't they be clean?"

"A very good question." I was in over my head, because of my limited ability in German. It would have been so much easier in Hungarian. I repressed the urge and continued, "You're right, except when the shrapnel hits, it goes through your clothing and buries itself along with the dirty fibres in the tissue. That's what causes the infection."

"Ugh!" Karola shivered, squeezing my hand, for an instant. "I'm sure a Swedish beauty could pick out every bit, with her slim, talented fingers."

'*Touché!*'

I went into the master bedroom to organise my books and clothes. It was late afternoon and I felt like relaxing with my secret vice, a juicy and thick Hungarian whodunit novel which I always replaced in the bookshelf to avoid arousing her curiosity. I had settled comfortably into the armchair beside the front window to take advantage of the remaining hour of natural light when a violent explosion threw me out of the chair. Possibly, I may have jumped but, whichever the reason, I landed tailbone-over-teakettle on the floor, ear-ringing deaf, eyeglasses bent like a pretzel, but miraculously, uncut. Cautiously, I raised my head to vaguely see sunlight streaming through a dozen new pockmarks in the shutters. Fragments of glass lay scattered on the floor. The hours of lectures, films, demonstrations and explosives training at Camp X and Beaulieu told me that I had narrowly escaped death. If the shell had detonated even ten metres closer, its force would have driven a load of shrapnel through the wooden shutters and shattered the window, with the net effect of decapitating me instantly.

Karola rushed in, fearing a messy show, she later recounted. She was relieved to find only broken glass, which she hastily brushed into a heap. She sat on the rug cradling my head in her lap, consoling me, while wiping my forehead with a lavender-scented handkerchief. I took my time to recover, relishing every second of her attention. Eventually, the spell was broken; Karola helped me up and led me to the sofa. If she noticed the Hungarian paperback thriller, flung against the wall, she chose not to mention it. After covering me with a blanket, she brought some tea, and bid me go to sleep. As she was leaving, she bent over me in a motherly way, to adjust my blanket. Our eyes met for an instant, as if she was reading my mind.

"Go to sleep, Jozsi. Sweet dreams!"

The next morning, at 5:30, Karola was already organising the kitchen and spare bedroom while I puttered around in the parlour, arranging my makeshift digs. I pulled the armchair well back from the window. My ears were still humming, when a burst of mortar and shrapnel explosions rocked the building like Olympian thunderbolts. She rushed into the living room and together we looked through the shutter's peepholes. It was precisely 7:00 when two grey, unmarked trucks, the size of small moving vans drove to the entrance. Six German uniforms leapt out, led by the dashing *Obersturmbannführer*, who bounded with enthusiasm up the front steps.

"Off you go now, mate, into the vent shaft. I'll knock you up when I've sorted out this lot."

"*Fraülein* Koschwitz, *Obersturmbannführer* Bruckner here. Open up, please!"

I chuckled at her Magyar-inflected music hall patter as I grabbed Jan's heavy coat and sped to the cooler. 'Amazing Karola', the unflappable, had everything under control.

Isolated in my refuge, I could hear occasional, muffled thumps and cursing which I assumed was the sound of the men carting in their gear. With nothing to do, I sat, leaning against the wall, staring up the clouds through the skylight. For the first time, there were no inquisitive visitors to inspect my hideaway. I was dozing when Karola's head poked through the window,

"All clear. Come out; come out, wherever you are! Quietly now, mind!"

She assured me that the living room door was locked securely. It was now 9:00: two hours! This was my all-time record in solitary. She told me about the morning's events, both indoor and out.

"Did Bruckner happen to say how long he expects to be holed up here, Karola?"

"Oh, he's no fool, Joe. *Obersturmbannführer* Bruckner won't be here much. I doubt we'll see him anytime soon. Army business will keep him busy elsewhere, *natür-*

lich."

The remaining windows were vibrating so much that I expected them to fall out of their frames. I chanced a peek through the cracks in the shutters. "Karola, Come here! Look, out the window…higher up… at twelve o'clock. It's snowing Russians!"

"Oh, my God. It's an invasion!" she exclaimed in Hungarian, which I pretended not to understand; she repeated something similar in German.

In the distance, hundreds of parachutes with jumpers dangling like rag-dolls descended like avenging angels, the heavens filled with twin-engine *Ilyushin* 11 bombers, spewing out a continuous stream of bodies. For a moment I was envious as I relived my first unforgettable view of Rolly's bonfires spread out in candle formation, beneath the wing of the Stirling, as we circled the clearing at Papuk.

"Judging by this activity, I don't think Fritz be with us for long," I observed.

The first Russian paratroopers were touching down, swarming like flies buzzing above a carcass. Angry, greyish bursts of flak from German radar-controlled '88's' and '10-0-5's' artillery batteries 'walked' upward, seeking, and locking with precision, onto the *Ilyushins*' altitude. Once the anti-aircraft fire had found the range, it was decimating the huge aircraft. Some planes staggered mid-air, like toy gliders hitting a wall, as they burst apart, consumed in huge, oily orange-black fireballs. Others exploded and flew on, disintegrating in slow motion into fiery fragments, pinwheeling earthward. Scores of hapless jumpers who had bailed from the flying coffins, their canopies ablaze, hurtled hundreds of metres like fiery comet trails, free falling to instant obliteration. Other chutes, their harnesses emptied of human cargo, were drifting haphazardly, wandering like ghostly, giant white jellyfish. Karola and I watched this surreal scene with astonishment. Hundreds of jumpers who had survived the fireballs and flak were landing unscathed, discarding their silk, and mobilising swiftly for combat. Immediately, the German mortars and machine guns opened fire with murderous effect as soon as the airborne troops touched down. Yet, they continued to come in, in waves. Were the Soviet hordes truly invincible, or were they simply so numerically superior that their commanders used them as limitlessly expendable cannon fodder? Either way, they appeared to be unstoppable.

"It's sickening, Joe! The Nazis are machine-gunning them. They've barely landed."

It would have been unwise to try to rationalise these tactics, so I didn't. At least the Germans were giving the jumpers a chance to land and get mobile, even though Hitler had ordered that Budapest be defended to the last man and bullet. After a few minutes, Karola broke the silence, "So, you think Germany's done for here, Joe? I hope so. But, what if the Russians are worse?"

"Hard to imagine, but anything's possible...."

A short while later, Karola left her place at the window. "I must get back. The 'boys' in the back room want lunch at twelve and the arsenic soup's very tasty today. I'll bring you some. Andras is coming sometime after dinner. I think it will be okay, if he's not in uniform, don't you?"

"I'm not so sure. How will he get past the guard dogs outside? They're patrolling the entrance and demanding papers from everyone, coming and going."

"Colonel Bruckner gave me his word that I can pretty much do as I please. He even gave permission to contact him directly, through the operators, if I encounter any...problems. I'll say that Andras is an old lover, etcetera, etcetera." Her excitement and pleasure in so easily outfoxing the *Obersturmbannführer*, was obvious.

"I'm sure glad you're on my side!"

"*Viszont Latasra, Jozsi*!"

"Same to you, Karola, I guess."

"*Vis...zont...Lat...asra*: See...you...soon!" She enunciated slowly. "I'll teach you Magyar!"

"I'm looking forward to that!"

Andras arrived that evening accompanied by Matyas Pirithy. Both were in good spirits, although they confided they were very worried for their families' safety. The streets, they said, were strewn with decaying corpses: Russian, German, and non-combatant Hungarians, including women and children, many of whom had been dismembered and mutilated. Civilian casualties from shrapnel wounds and napalm burns caused by *Panzerfaust* flame-throwers were clogging the over-extended hospital wards, their corridors were choked with the wounded and dying. Matyas, ever the scholar, observed that the city resembled a medieval woodcut engraving of the Black Death, maybe worse. The rotten stench of decay permeated everywhere.

The majority of Arrow Cross stalwarts had prudently burned their uniforms and gone into hiding, Andras remarked wryly. I inquired about Raoul, and Andras confirmed that he was working non-stop to end the German atrocities, through his office in the Swedish legation. Karola spoke for us all, "The man is truly one of God's angels. I pray that you, or someone, can convince him to get out of Hungary, now, before it's too late."

"It's getting worse by the minute. We've learned that the Russians would love to snatch him; for what reason, I don't know" Matyas said, gravely. "The underground has learned that he's accused of being a tool of American subversion, an anti-Soviet conspirator sent by Allen Dulles and the OSS to spy. That's all just a cover for something. His humanitarian efforts are supposedly only a front for American newspaper propaganda. It's outrageous!"

"Hitler used The Big Lie to get what he wanted," I offered.

"You're right about that. We have new evidence showing that German Intelligence is playing dirty games to discredit and ruin him. They couldn't do it themselves, so they feed Stalin and his cronies this crap. I personally suspect it's not the *Abwehr*. It smacks of a more sophisticated mind at work; the *Abwehr's* Wilhelm Canaris is a clever one, but he's not that devious. I'd love to know who the mastermind is. I'd strangle the bastard with my own hands!," stated Andras emotionally. "Uncle Joe Stalin will use it, if it suits his bloody-minded purposes. What's one more life to that old hoodlum, along with what, nineteen million, plus or minus a million? The rumours are flying thick and fast."

"Can you imagine Raoul Gustav Wallenberg setting up an anti-Russian counter-intelligence mission here? How could he even have had the time, much less the inclination? It's despicable!" Matyas was nearly shouting. Karola calmed him, gently.

After they had left, she and I sat and talked quietly, with the war's not-too-distant rumblings for ambience. Excusing herself, Karola went to check on the radio crew, and soon returned "All's quiet on the eastern front."

As if in contradiction, a violent explosion showered us with clouds of plaster and dust. The building vibrated like a tuning fork. The shock knocked Karola off balance, throwing her into my arms. I held her trembling body as we fell to the rug together, Karola sprawled on top of me. I remember looking up to see if the ceiling was still intact; it had been slightly cracked and buckled in several places by the tremors, but appeared as though it would hold up, at least for the next five minutes... Then I realised that Karola's warmth had aroused me and I kissed her lightly, softly, and tenderly. She responded, tentatively.

Suddenly, there was a knock on the parlour door. We froze. Karola raised her head, finger to her lips.

"*Wer ist da*?" Her heart was pounding against my chest.

"*Fraülein* Koschwitz, are you alright?"

"*Ja, mir gehts gut, danke. Gute nacht!*

"*Gute nacht, Fraülein.*"

"Which one was that?" I whispered.

"Harald, the head technician; he's the friendliest of the group. I think he has, how do you say, a crush on me."

"How nice for you both!"

"Oh, really? Do I sense the green-eyed monster here? Joszi, he's young enough to be my son and he is the enemy, for heaven's sake! Silly man…come here!"

The depth and range of Karola's fervour in our dark haven was extraordinary: passionate, tender, and intensely stimulating. I felt my body's arousal as I was consumed with an overwhelming desire, an obsession, to possess her, immediately. I realised how much and for how long I had wanted her. Maybe, it began at Christmas dinner or after the party. I wasn't sure. It didn't really matter. We wanted and needed each other, now, desperately; there was no guarantee of tomorrow. We were here, consumed with the hunger of new lovers in our desire to possess, to explore, to seek, and to delight in one another, if only for a brief instant, which was, after all, all of the time there ever was or would be.

Within seconds, Karola had taken command as she unfastened the buttons of her blouse, then leaning forward, found me and gently took me inside her body. The sweet, heady scent and delight of her secret warmth cascaded over me, her body a wonder of pale, white skin, soft as cashmere. I was lost: a stranger in her paradise of ecstasy. She guided me, sweetly, on a voyage of discovery, savouring her secret delights that knew no limits or boundaries.

We collapsed, utterly spent.

"That was some Hungarian lesson, Miss Koschwitz!" I sighed.

"You don't need lessons, Joszi," she replied, kissing me wetly. "You already make love like a Magyar!"

"That's good?" I asked.

"That's good!

"Can I tell you something, Karola?"

"That depends…if it's nice, of course. But if you're going to get all weepy about some sweet little Miss Canada at home, no, I don't want to know."

"I just wanted to tell you that you are a truly magnificent lover and a dear, sweet, and courageous lady."

"Thank you. But that fits the description of someone's nice old auntie" she whispered, nuzzling me. "Show me!"

"With pleasure."

Occasional explosions accompanied our lovemaking, punctuating the night with unpleasant reminders of the real world that we were doing our utmost to pretend did not exist. The street was in darkness as mortar fire had knocked out an electrical substation the previous day. We still had hydro in the apartment; I was certain that our German guests would have brought a portable generator, as emergency backup. I wandered over to the shutters to see if there was any new excitement on the streets.

"Karola, you've got to see this!"

A Soviet tank, Type T-34, with its treads torn loose, was in flames, 'brewing up', burning furiously. In its death throes, it had lurched into and snapped off a water hydrant that was spewing a geyser of steam and water with little effect on the raging conflagration. The crew, three human torches, managed to exit from the inferno through the jagged hole where the gun turret had been sheared off. In a desperate attempt to extinguish the flames, they were flinging themselves into the overflowing gutters, their limbs thrashing wildly as they rolled and writhed in agony until all that remained were charred, foetal mummies. As a finale, the tank's fuel and ammunition exploded, tossing the vehicle upward at least one metre. It landed on its port side, delivering the coup de grâce by crushing the incinerated remnants of the crewmembers.

"How awful! Oh, Joe, if only they could have been SS instead!"

A familiar voice called through the door. "*Fräulein* Koschwitz! *Panzerfaust!* "

"What's a *Panzerfaust*, Joe?" she whispered.

"He must mean a flame thrower, or bazooka: some kind of tank killer."

"*Ja, wunderbar. Guten nacht, Corporal!*"

"*Guten nacht, Fräulein*"

"Harald?"

"Ssshh. Come here." She pulled me down onto her warm body, on the sofa bed.

New Year's Day, 1945, was, for the most part, uneventful, although I witnessed the shooting of a guard, by sniper fire, at our building's entrance. I was idly watching the street through the shutter's shrapnel holes and the sentry, a heavy-set middle-aged sergeant, was standing at ease, the butt of his rifle resting on the ground exactly where Karola's china cup had been placed by the departing German, only nine days before. He suddenly crumpled, falling sideways to the pavement. Blood from an exit wound was matting the hair behind his left temple. Within thirty minutes, an SS armoured carrier arrived, and four non-coms, with an *Untersturmführer* [6] alighted. Two privates hastily retrieved their comrade's body, placing it in the vehicle's rear compartment. The *Untersturmführer* appointed a corporal to take over sentry duty and, revolver drawn, led the two-man squad up the street, out of my range,

[6] *Junior lieutenant*

in the probable direction of the shooter. Fifteen minutes later, they returned, prodding a youthful Russian paratrooper at bayonet point; his hands tightly clasped behind his head as he stumbled to keep pace. His Slavic-featured face was a mass of bloody gashes. At this distance, I could see that one eye was swollen and tightly shut, with a large oval red patch surrounding it, the perfect imprint of a rifle butt. The lieutenant halted, presumably to brief the guard and driver, then continued with his *Truppe*, across the street, and into the basement of a derelict building. After ten minutes, only the three Germans emerged. The sentry saluted the *Untersturmführer* as he boarded the half-track.

By the first week of January, the street battles had escalated to such a level of intensity and ferocity that any civilian who dared venture outside was in mortal peril of being caught in the indiscriminate crossfire. Hitler's maniacal *Führer befehl*[7] was being executed at enormous cost by a still loyal and capable officer cadre for whom surrender or lack of zeal was tantamount to suicide or summary execution by roving bands of grim *SS Feldpoleizi*. The resulting sacrifice of experienced, battle-seasoned *Wehrmacht* and *Waffen SS* troops could only hasten a Soviet victory in The Fatherland.

Our resident W/T technicians' stock of rations was nearly depleted, as was Karola's hoard of black market goods. The operators' frantic requests to HQ for replacements were futile. German supply transports could not penetrate our sector, they were told. We were more fortunate than most of our neighbours to still have a few staples such as flour and dried lentils, but Karola's obligation to feed the W/T crew and guards was taxing her ingenuity. She had hidden her sparse supplies, refusing to share with the Germans.

She decided to go to the market. I stated my strong opposition unless I could go along with her, but she refused. Her plan was boldly audacious; she would bring the *SS* sentries as her guards and drudges. I thought she was utterly mad. But we were living in cloud cuckooland.

"I…I'm more than capable of protecting you! The Germans will be easy targets for any Russian sharpshooter."

"Joe, listen to me. My answer is no! I don't doubt your abilities in the least, but you'll be risking not only your safety and mine, but my friends' too! Everyone is jumpy. So far, no one except Andras, Matyas and some of my most trusted associates know you or your whereabouts. It stays that way. End of discussion."

[7] *Orders issued directly by Führer Adolf Hitler, who, at the close of the war, was the self-appointed Supreme Commander of Germany's Armed Forces. It was treasonable to countermand, modify, or simply question a* Führer befehl.

I insisted upon underwriting this crazy venture and gave her some of the dwindling DIBBLER money from my cache, which she accepted. She claimed that the guards had obtained *Obersturmbannführer* Bruckner's permission to go with her, via the W/T.

"But then I suppose it was easier for him than arguing with you!"

"Do you want to starve or survive? A little hug and a kiss for luck?"

"Nothing more?"

"No time, you beast. When I get back!"

During a lull in the fighting, in the mid-afternoon, she set off, slogging determinedly through the fresh snow, to God knows where; the two soldiers, with rifles at port, warily covered their front, rear, and flanks. I watched until they had disappeared into the blizzard.

Two hours later, they re-appeared like three wraiths, out of the storm's impenetrable whiteness. She had dragooned her escorts into toting the booty. They were trailing her by at least five paces, as she ploughed majestically through the knee-deep snowdrifts that had buried the front steps.

"You're a sight for sore eyes," I said.

"Pardon me?"

"It means 'welcome back'. How did you make out?"

"Well enough. Nevertheless, there's very little meat left and what is there....*oy vay*!"

"I haven't heard that expression since high school. Are you Jewish?"

"Not that I know of, but as they say in America, isn't everyone? We'll be slimming down over the week or two, but I'll make certain that we have one meal per day. German HQ sent a message that they're going to make a run tonight with a shipment of supplies so we can scrounge from that, which should not be a problem, since I do the cooking. They'll never notice and if they do...."

A grenade, lobbed from a passing motorcycle blew up one of her two SS bodyguards at 9: 00 the next morning. The blast blew away large chunks of the front brickwork and peppered our Swiss cheese shutters with some fifty more holes. The man's blood-soaked boots remained upright, curiously untouched, while his torso and fragmented body parts lay in disarray, staining the snow. The W/T technicians notified their HQ. The ravens of Budapest, already plump from the leavings of the savage carnage, were quick to find and feast upon this newest windfall. From a distance, an onlooker might have thought that the body was somehow alive, as the birds burrowed for delicacies under the uniform. A Russian sniper, clearly visible in a window across the street, used the cadaver as bait, and shot the first curious German through the eye. He also shot a raven, for good measure, then withdrew for fresher pickings. Sometime that night, a German supply truck delivered the rations and retrieved the grisly remains that the birds had rejected.

Forced to remain undercover in my room for too long, much as I enjoyed Karola's company, I had acquired an acute case of cabin fever. I was itching to go outside to do something useful. Half-seriously, I told Karola that I wanted to join up with the Russians. Andras, for whom Karola had somehow obtained blanket permission to visit the apartment, came over in the evening, wearing civvies. He explained ruefully that he had retired his uniform to avoid being shot by twitchy Russian snipers. He convinced Karola to let me accompany him on another mission for Raoul.

"It's routine, though I can't guarantee it will be completely safe; basically, we must exchange this envelope for another."

"Payment for safe papers, I assume. A dead drop, is it then, Andras?"

"More or less."

"Give me the envelope. I'll keep it inside my jacket."

It was moonless and snowing lightly when we set out at 9:00 that night. It was exciting to be living on the edge again, and I enjoyed the best workout I had had in many months. Andras was in first class condition although I felt I acquitted myself rather proudly as a Camp X and Beaulieu graduate. Like street urchins, we ducked up and down alleys, scaled walls, climbed fences, and cut through burned or bombed-out shells of buildings to avoid any meeting with Russian or German patrols. Had we known of the German military's inclination to lay elaborate booby traps when retreating, we might have been a little less fearless. Perhaps Andras knew where the tripwires and other such mantraps were hidden, but he appeared unconcerned as we darted from one possible disaster to the next. It was more like a schoolboy lark than a life-or-death errand of mercy as we scrambled to evade the Soviet security checkpoints. Except for sporadic bursts of automatic weapons and machine gun fire, or the occasional stray bullet whining over our heads, occasionally punctuated by the intermittent *whump* of incoming mortars, German resistance seemed at most, dutiful, to downright futile.

Then our luck ran out. We scaled a fence, and hit the ground simultaneously. Ten metres down a blind alley, where it opened onto the street, two *Waffen-SS* men had set up a *Schmausser* machine gun on a tripod and were engaged in loading loops of cartridge belt. Fortunately, they were facing the street.

"Options, Lieutenant?" Andras

whispered.

"Number 1. Back up over the fence behind us: tricky, maybe impossible. They'd stitch us before we're half-way up." I offered.

"Number 2?"

"It's all yours, Captain."

"Lie low and freeze our knackers?"

"No thanks, Andras…Three?"

"Follow me." We crawled, retreating backwards up the passageway. Halfway, we stopped to parley.

"I can handle the gunner if you can take his mate," I stated.

"Roger!"

"Good. We go back, ten feet away, stop at the drainpipe. One damn good twist to break his neck. Then run back, over the fence. Can you handle that, Captain?"

"Lieutenant, I'm a soldier, damn it, in case you forget!"

"Sorry, Captain. Up to the downspout, silently! Then we go, hell for leather, whammo, on three."

Andras shot me a puzzled look. We halted when we reached the position. Up ahead, the soldiers were bent over the gun, muttering, examining the ammo clip. The sergeant was standing up, adjusting, and positioning the gun.

"Runter!" (Get down)

We saw two muzzle flashes at eleven o'clock, then heard the gunshots in rapid succession. The ammo sergeant's head exploded from under his helmet as if it were an overripe melon. He crumpled heavily backward onto the sandbags where he lay sprawled, toes and fingers twitching. The gunner sat staring down at his greatcoat, where blood-speckled grey matter, once the contents of his companion's skull, had been sprayed. To his obvious horror, and ours, a small object was lobbed into the nest. Without second thoughts, Andras and I stood up, ran pell-mell then dove for the ground just as the grenade detonated.

We looked up to see the gunner's body rise and disintegrate mid air, as the emplacement was consumed in a raging, red-orange corona. The magazine exploded in a spectacular 24th of May fireworks extravaganza. Phosphorus and cordite Roman candles sprayed a lethal fountain of live fifty-calibre rounds and shrapnel, sending hot steel, wood, and brick debris buzzing like hornets. The cannonades were caroming randomly. I remembered a history teacher stating that more of the gunnery crews on the wooden men o' war at Trafalgar were maimed, mutilated or decapitated by flying splinters of Douglas Fir, than by the French twelve-pounder cannon balls. It was a bleak fact of a sailor's life, or death, he concluded.

Ten minutes later, the raging firestorm had reduced itself to a cremation pyre.

"*Götterdämmerung*." Andras intoned. "The twilight of the gods..." He paused. Voices were approaching, shouting jubilantly in Russian. Their blood up, the hunters were coming to inspect their kill.

"We're in trouble again, Captain," I whispered.

I pulled on his sleeve as I started to crawl backwards. He followed. I didn't stop until my soles were indenting the wooden fence boards

'*Now what?*'

'*You're trapped, mate. Either hope you fade into the woodwork or come out walking, calmly, and slowly, hands up, and smile, smile, smile.*'

A Russian paratroop lieutenant, wearing a fur hat the size of a beaver with a prominent red star like a third eye, approached the smouldering remains and poked at them with his bayonet, as though stoking a dying campfire. His comrades applauded his running commentary.

As we lay flat out, breathing snow, I tried desperately to dredge up something useful to say in Russian. I came up with two swear words which were extremely insulting, as well as a toast, *Nazdarovia*, and *Tovarisch*. '*John Coates, where are you? Best to shut up and leave the international diplomacy to Andras. No, kill or be killed, remember? Okay. Let's go for broke.*'

Using the butts of their rifles, Lieutenant Beaver's two comrades-in-arms pushed over the burnt-out machine gun and one of them commented as they turned to walk away. An unexploded round suddenly burst, sending a bullet between the Beaver and his sidekicks. They roared, obviously amused.

"What did he say before that?"

"He asked if either one had a camera."

"A memento. 'Dear Momma, This is me, your son. I am in beautiful bombed-out Budapest with my two faithful comrades. That's Ivan Ivanovitch on my right and Valery Issovitch, your long-lost cousin, is the stupid-looking one on my left. The other two are roast fascist pigs.' "

Andras suppressed a chuckle. "Let's get out of here before they come back with the whole battalion for dinner."

After more dodges and detours, Andras finally led me to a dilapidated wooden shed at the rear of a run-down printing establishment. It was padlocked; the door and frame looked sturdy.

"The key?" I asked.

"Right here. Huh, it's not there. That's strange! It should be under this log."

There was at least one bush cord

of firewood stacked high against the shed's left wall.

"Maybe they forgot it or else it fell down and it's long gone, buried deep in the snow. Give me a second." I had kept my trusty, rusted Pécs safety pin fastened inside the lining of my jacket; the tumblers yielded readily. I smiled, handing Andras the opened lock.

"After you, Captain!"

"You're good. Where did you learn to do that?"

"From a kindly English squire who was also a master of the gentlemanly arts of break and enter."

"Were you in jail with him?"

"Not exactly, he was my instructor at an SOE training school, called Beaulieu. You may have heard of it?"

"Oh yes, indeed. When I was a student at the military academy, my parents sent me off on the grand European tour, to teach me about the world, I suppose. I was a guest in the Beaulieu manor house for one glorious August weekend. My travelling companion, a Frenchman had, what do you say…family connections? I wonder if Wanda the Viennese chambermaid…?"

"Vanda? Wiennese?"

"Very amusing. How's your Hungarian?"

The shed reeked of pigeon droppings, damp paper, and dry rot, much like the airshaft. Stepping with care between haphazard stacks of discoloured paper that threatened to topple over and crush us, we clambered over and around clusters of cast off office furniture, and a large manual press, as well as an assortment of wreckage particular to the proprietor's trade.

We joked and swore as we picked our way through the hotchpotch to reach an oak filing cabinet which was facing inward, pushed flush against the back wall. Andras attempted to dislodge it. "Don't stand there laughing. Help me pull this out!"

"Damn, it's locked too! Let's see just how good you are now, Mr. Beaulieu safe-cracker…"

"A piece of cake for this master. Step aside, Captain, if you don't mind…."

We wrenched open the obstinate bottom drawer and knelt to examine a quarter century's accrual of invoices and receipts, neatly tied in annual bundles, with coloured ribbons. There was no envelope.

"It's here, Joe, I know it is. "

"Maybe, if we empty the drawer, it's hidden underneath."

"*Wunderbar!* Behold! Fifty Swedish permits!"

"Let's hope they're all there. I'd love to see one, but, maybe it's not such a good idea." The manila mailer was carefully sealed with bookbinding tape. I produced Raoul's somewhat crumpled envelope from my jacket. "The gelt!"

"What else have you tucked away in there? Give me those pieces of tape…carefully, don't tear the package…. Would you please help me pack this drawer and slide it back in?

"What time is it?" he queried, as he placed the packet inside a waterproof pouch.

"Half-past midnight."

"As soon as you've pushed this monster back, we're gone."

"It's kinda creepy here, isn't it? By the way, Captain, have you thought about covering our tracks? Anyone who can see lightning and hear thunder could trace us here!"

"*Certainement, monsieur.* You underestimate the healing powers of ze nature. Ze leetle grey cells, zeh tell me that eet is making *beacoup de neige*. Soon ze tracks zey will all disappear, et voilà. 'ave a look out ze window, Inspector."

His monologue was suddenly interrupted by a loud thud on the door. I pulled Andras down with me onto the floor.

"Rifle butt!" he whispered.

"Sssh."

"Do you hear voices?"

"Not if you keep talking!" Five minutes passed in silence. From somewhere up in the overhead rafters, a pigeon cooed. "I'm taking a look. Stay low." Warily, I crawled toward the small window that was positioned beside the door. I raised my head slowly to peer through the frost and grime-covered glass, and managed to clear a postage stamp-sized patch with my sleeve. I could see only snowflakes swirling past. "It's nothin'. Maybe a branch fell against it or…."

Something was scratching at the door. "Did you hear that, Joe?" The scraping was now accompanied by low moans, and whining.

"If it's a Russian or a German, he's doing a good imitation of a dog, Andras!"

"Then let's go before his howling brings the whole pack here!"

"I can see the tail. It's a big one. Hope it's not hungry!"

"Fee,fi, fo, fum, I smell the blood of an Englishman."

As I had not had the best of luck with dogs in Hungary, I quickly cleared out of the shed, leaving it to Andras to calm the beast and lock the door.

The trip back home took less than a half-hour. Before we separated, I thought it worth asking, "Andras, old boy, I've been wondering..."

"Yes, old friend?"

"Well don't be offended, but Jan

Wolzlieger insisted that John and I spend days memorising maps of Budapest. I seem to recall that the printer's shop was less than fifteen blocks from Karola's apartment. Why did we take such an infernally round-about route to get there?"

"No offence taken. To avoid German machine gun nests and Russian tourists. By the way, thank you, on Raoul's behalf. Your companionship gave me comfort and the courage to do it."

"Maybe we've helped Raoul short-circuit some of this insanity, Andras. Please give Raoul and his lovely assistant, Sonja, my very best regards and Karola's also, to Raoul, of course. Good night."

"Good night. Oh, Joe, I'm curious. What's a 'whammo?' "

"Sorry, that's highly classified Secret Agent lingo."

"Are all Canadians as full of it as you? Good night."

Although the Germans had abandoned any attempt to patrol our entranceway because of the rapid attrition of guards, I skulked into the small foyer. At Karola's door, I hesitated, listening intently. The interior was silent: no talking, no clatter of teletypes, and no Morse repeaters. As I reached to turn the handle, the door opened. Karola was smiling. She had been waiting up, in case I had encountered problems. We slipped into the front room without being noticed by the W/T crewmen. She locked the door.

"You are a sight for eyesores!"

Desire overcame grammatical correctness.

Over the course of the following week, several near-miss mortars and rockets, as well as two nighttime bombings rocked the building. Russian Counter Intelligence had obviously located the radio base and we were very close to German defensive positions. It was extremely nerve-racking to have to 'sit and take it' during the daytime attacks, but the night bombings were sinister, more malevolent, perhaps because the enemy was invisible. The thunder of the aircraft, which, as we were all too mindful, had been loaded with tonnes of high explosives and dispatched expressly to blow us to smithereens, was demoralising. Nothing in my training had prepared me for the mind-numbing intimidation and terror of being at the epicentre of a bomber raid. I was able to relate with admiration to the dreadful ordeals of the British people during the 'blitz'. Amazingly, the Soviets never attempted a commando raid against the W/T station. Nor did the mortars, rockets, or bombs ever score a direct hit. One well-aimed Russian *Katushka* rocket fired directly through the front window would have ended it all. During the bombardments, whether at day or night,

Karola and I lay huddled in each another's arms on the couch. The ceiling and walls were still more or less intact. Another concern, apart from the two of us being pulverised or buried alive was that an explosion would blow our safe room door off its hinges.

As if this wasn't enough excitement, early in February, a street battle erupted diagonally-across from our building. We could watch and hear the action from our vantagepoint, through the cracks and the myriad shrapnel holes in the shutters. It was a very exciting time. We saw three tanks blown up; two of which were German. The crewmembers that were not incinerated were machine-gunned, as they bailed out. On another occasion, the Germans ambushed and hijacked a horse-drawn wagon that was hauling supplies to the Russian position. All that remained on the road after the skirmish was the empty, overturned wagon and the unfortunate draught horse, lying dead in its traces.

This was manna! For the locals, including us, it was far too tempting a 'gift horse' to pass up. To me, the problem was how to get at it, before the meat rotted, without being an easy target for sharpshooters of either side.

Karola's solution was bold, plucky, and slightly wacky. Armed with two large butcher knives, with a thick sheaf of newspapers folded under her arm, she simply walked outside and knelt in the centre of the road, at the side of the carcass. She proceeded to cut off slabs from the choicest parts, setting each out meticulously to drain, on outstretched layers of paper. Suddenly, all firing and fighting stopped, as the dumfounded men and officers on both sides stood transfixed by the spectacle. When she had wrapped the filets, and thoroughly wiped the knives on the remaining paper, she stood up, a parcel under each arm, and, without a glance at the awe-struck troops, walked to the building's entrance. Throaty cheers and whistles broke out, first from the Russians, then the Germans. Karola did what only she would have dared to complete this audacious piece of street theatre. She set down her packages on the front step, then Diva-like, she waved graciously, acknowledging the accolades. She then scooped up her treasures, as though they were bouquets, and stepped inside. The drama ended, the troops resumed battling. Many women in the apartments followed her lead over the next few days. The novelty had worn off for the troops who paid scant attention. The carcass soon became well picked-over as humans, ravens, dogs, feral cats and rats competed for the ever-diminishing edible morsels.

The gods of war, if not of draught horses, ordained that another Russian supply wagon would be captured, further up the street. This time, Karola was caught off guard.

Several knife-bearing neighbours descended on the horse almost as it toppled over. The carcass was reduced to a skeleton with hoofs and a tail, within hours of its demise. Undeterred, Karola bartered some of the W/T operators' rations of flour and milk powder for chunks of meat. We ate one decent meal daily, thanks to her foresight, until the Germans went away.

Columns of Russian armour now wheeled over the Danube *en masse*, threatening to overwhelm the German defences. We watched as German sappers dynamited bridges in futile attempts to halt the Soviet juggernaut. The Russian engineers rapidly threw pre-constructed sections into the river to make floating bridges, allowing the onslaught to advance into the city centre. The Red Army's brilliantly flexible and opportunistic deployment tactics were breath taking to watch. Stalin's generals had obviously learned well from the invaders while defending their Motherland, the *Rodina* and had skilfully adapted the principles of *blitzkreig* to their objectives.

It became commonplace to peer out our window and count how many bridges remained. Karola would comment, "Oh look, there's another one gone."

The Erzsebet Bridge, which was not far distant, simply ceased to exist as we watched. The sudden, violent shock waves shattered a rear window, which, Karola said, had injured Harald with a large chunk of flying glass. It reminded me of a night exercise at Camp X when the lads were a little too generous with the gelignite, creating some havoc in Whitby and Oshawa. Within two hours, the Russian armoured brigades resumed their crossing. Karola avoided the radioman's pleas for help, by retreating behind our locked door. We heard the technicians quit the apartment and watched as they wove and dodged towards the German outpost, ducking the Russian sharpshooters. One later returned; it wasn't Harald.

A week later, to the day, the radio operators, assistants, and the sole remaining guard destroyed their wireless equipment, abandoned the apartment, and walked out. Alarmed, Karola had rushed out to the kitchen to investigate the commotion. I couldn't wait to have a look at their W/T apparatus, but the destruction had been thorough; nothing remained for the Russians but a tangled mass of wire, smashed metal casings, and crushed vacuum tubes lying scattered over the kitchen floor. I surmised that the installation was less elaborate than I had guessed.

The next day, February 13, 1945, we took Karola's short-wave radio from its hiding place inside the Victrola to hear Radio Moscow announce the victorious end of the fifty-day siege of Budapest. The unconditional surrender of all German forces was effective immediately. Now that the last obstacle on the road to Vienna had been removed, the announcer intoned through the static, the fall of the Reich was assured. The German's last desperate hope, a relief column, General Gilles' 4th Panzer Corps, had been stopped in its tracks twelve kilometres outside the city. Rumour was that the Supreme Commander of German Forces, Budapest, General Pfeffer-Wildenbruch, was captured hiding in a sewer.

Russian soldiers were wandering everywhere, firing helter-skelter at street signs and traffic signals, shop windows and the crosses on church steeples. There was no sign anywhere of military authority. The liberators of Budapest were out of control. I reached for Karola's hand,

"*Gere Ide*!"[8]

"Say again?"

"*Gere Ide*! *Szabad Magyar Orszag*. Long live a free Hungary!"

Clichéd as it seems, there was a stunned silence. I could hear the mantle clock ticking and then chiming 11:00 a.m. Karola looked at me in stunned disbelief, fading to bewilderment, and finally pained distress. Her next words will be forever in my memory.

"Why, Joe, tell me why?"

I shrugged.

[8] *Come here.*

"You mean that you understood everything…everything? The party, my conversations with Andras…."

"Yes. Why? Does it matter?"

Her eyes welled with tears.

"You have to ask me why? Because, I thought I knew you! When did I ever ask about your background? Your military experiences…are you married…do you have a sweetheart waiting in Winnipeg or Toronto or wherever you call home? I believed that I cared for you, and you me! I trusted you. Now, I don't know….

"I confided so much in you, Joseph Gordon. Is that name part of your cover, too? No, don't bother. I just don't care."

"It's a name I have been ordered to use. Joseph is really my first name. I swear, Karola!"

"Thank you. It's so nice to know your lover's name."

I was stunned and embarrassed. I could not recall a single moment when she had been depressed, cynical, or indecisive. Had my elaborate con job ruined a beautiful friendship? Was I so deeply immersed in and accustomed to elaborate half-truths that I was incapable of a relationship that didn't feed on self-serving deception? I knew that I must level with her, there and then, or leave. I owed her deeply for her loving care.

I told her that the deception was

entirely my decision, seconded by John, on our first night together in Hadik. I explained our reasoning. Eventually, after a very long and strained silence, she quietly stated that Karola the realist, understood. As a woman, however, "You could have trusted me, Joe, that's all...

"Now, my Lieutenant Joseph G., let's celebrate what we have been through…together. Long live love, Hungary and Canada!"

Our idyllic mood was interrupted, but not entirely unpleasantly, by a rap on the door. We hastily sorted ourselves out before Karola went to answer it. It was the goddess, Madeleine, my chauffeur from Christmas Eve, with the disturbing news that the dreaded NKVD[9] was hunting down and carrying out wholesale arrests of persons deemed a threat to state security. Their dragnet was indiscriminate, reaching into all strata of society.

"Neighbours are getting back at neighbours, settling old scores. Relatives are ratting on kinfolk, for a few pengös, loose change. Kids are getting even, accusing their parents of anti-Marxist tendencies, for a spanking or withholding their allowance. You can go into any police station and give the NKVD a name, or a list. Down it goes on the directory, without questions. It's another reign of terror. Nothing has changed."

The horrors of Stalin's regime with its mass executions and starvation of millions, the brutal labour camps and state-sanctioned psychological torture, brain washing carried on in the name of science in the Gulag hospitals, have been extensively documented.

"Raoul Wallenberg and Andras Hegedus are wanted men. There may be a bounty for turning them in. Please do something to help find them before it's too late. The only difference between the Russians and Nazis in Budapest is that the NKVD carry out their executions in prison basements or the back seats of automobiles!"

Madeleine's heavenly dark eyes were glistening with tears. We offered her a glass of brandy, which she declined. I promised to act immediately. We shook hands and she left. I never saw her again.

With my knowledge of Magyar

---

[9] *NKVD, the Russian* Narodny Komisariat Vnutrennykh *Del, People's Commissariat of Internal Affairs.*

---

[10] *Karola's outstanding courage and resourcefulness under extremely perilous circumstances were recognised by His Majesty's Government, when in 1945, she was cited as follows (abridged). "…You concealed in your apartment two escaped British Army officers. Major Coates you hid from 12 to 17 December; Lieutenant Gordon from 12 December 1944, until the arrival of the Russian liberating army. You continued to hide the latter, even after your apartment had been taken over as a German HQ. You took exceptional risks to save his life. It is desired to commend your courageous action in the highest possible terms. As a small token of recognition…(you are to receive)…a payment of 125,00 pengös. It is not desired in any sense to make a comparison between the above amount and the invaluable and inestimable services, which you have rendered in saving the life of a British Officer. You are asked to receive this sum as a symbol of the gratitude of the British people."*

no longer a liability, Karola[10] and I reckoned that I could pose convincingly as an anonymous Budapest native and scour the city freely in pursuit of Raoul and Andras. Time was not on my side; I had to get started right away. Where better to begin, than at Andras' home?

1945.

KOSCHWITZ, Karola,
Krusper utca 1.c.(3),
BUDAPEST.

KOSCHWITZ
Karola

1. It has been brought to the notice of His Majesty's Government and of His Official Missions in HUNGARY that during the German occupation of Hungary and under the Szallasi regime you concealed in your apartment two escaped British Army officers. Major Coates you hid from 12 to 17 December, Lieutenant Gordon from the 12 December 1944 until the arrival of the Russian liberating armies. You continued to hide the latter even after two rooms of your flat had been taken over as a German headquarters. You took exceptional risks to save his life, such that even after three police and Nyilas searches he was not discovered.

2. It is fully realised that in so doing you were placing in extreme danger your own life and the lives of your nearest and dearest. It is desired to commend your courageous action in the highest possible terms, together with your devotion to the cause for which the United Nations have fought this war.

3. As a small token of recognition I am instructed to make to you a payment of 125,000 Pengo. It is not desired in any sense to make a comparison between the above amount and the invaluable and inestimable services which you have rendered in saving the life of a British Officer. You are asked to receive this sum as a symbol of the gratitude of the British people.

Major-General,
Commissioner.

Citation from British Government 1945, for Karola Koschwitz

CHAPTER 11
Miles to Go and Promises to Keep

When I knocked at her apartment, Ilona, red-eyed and wan, came to the door.

"Joe! Come in! I am so glad that you're here! Would you care for some tea?"

Her patrician features showed the strain of her ordeal; she admitted that she had stayed up all night, keeping vigil. I followed her into the small kitchen where the kettle was boiling on the gas range. As she was pouring water to heat the teapot, I gathered my courage and took the plunge, admitting that my first language was Magyar. She shrugged and responded in Hungarian, "Thanks for telling me. It's wartime, you're a soldier and an escaped PoW. You have your reasons, I'm sure. No sugar, sorry. Come, sit down." As she gave me the cup and saucer, her hand was trembling.

"Joe, I'm worried sick. Andras went out more than twelve hours ago, and he hasn't returned."

"Did he give you any hints or clues before he left?"

"No. If his work involved direct contact with Raoul, he rarely told me where, when or what, until afterward. It was his way of protecting me. He usually confided in most other matters, and often asked for my advice."

"Ilona, I don't want to alarm you, but from what you say, maybe Andras' absence is connected with Raoul's disappearance. Andras might be helping Raoul to go to ground."

"I've been afraid to admit it, Joe, but I suspect that someone, maybe an acquaintance, even a trusted ally, has turned them both over to the Russians for a large reward. Andras had to rub shoulders with some very shady types to get things done. It would take a lot of character to resist blood money these days!"

"On the other hand, they might have both gone temporarily into hiding," I lied, knowing that her explanation was more plausible. "I'm on my way now to find out whatever I can. I give you my word that I'll let you know if I turn up anything, anything at all." It was well known that Andras was fervently anti-Communist; his advocacy for a democratic, neutral Hungary was his personal *raison d'être*, as was his support for Raoul's crusade. Privately, I feared for them both.

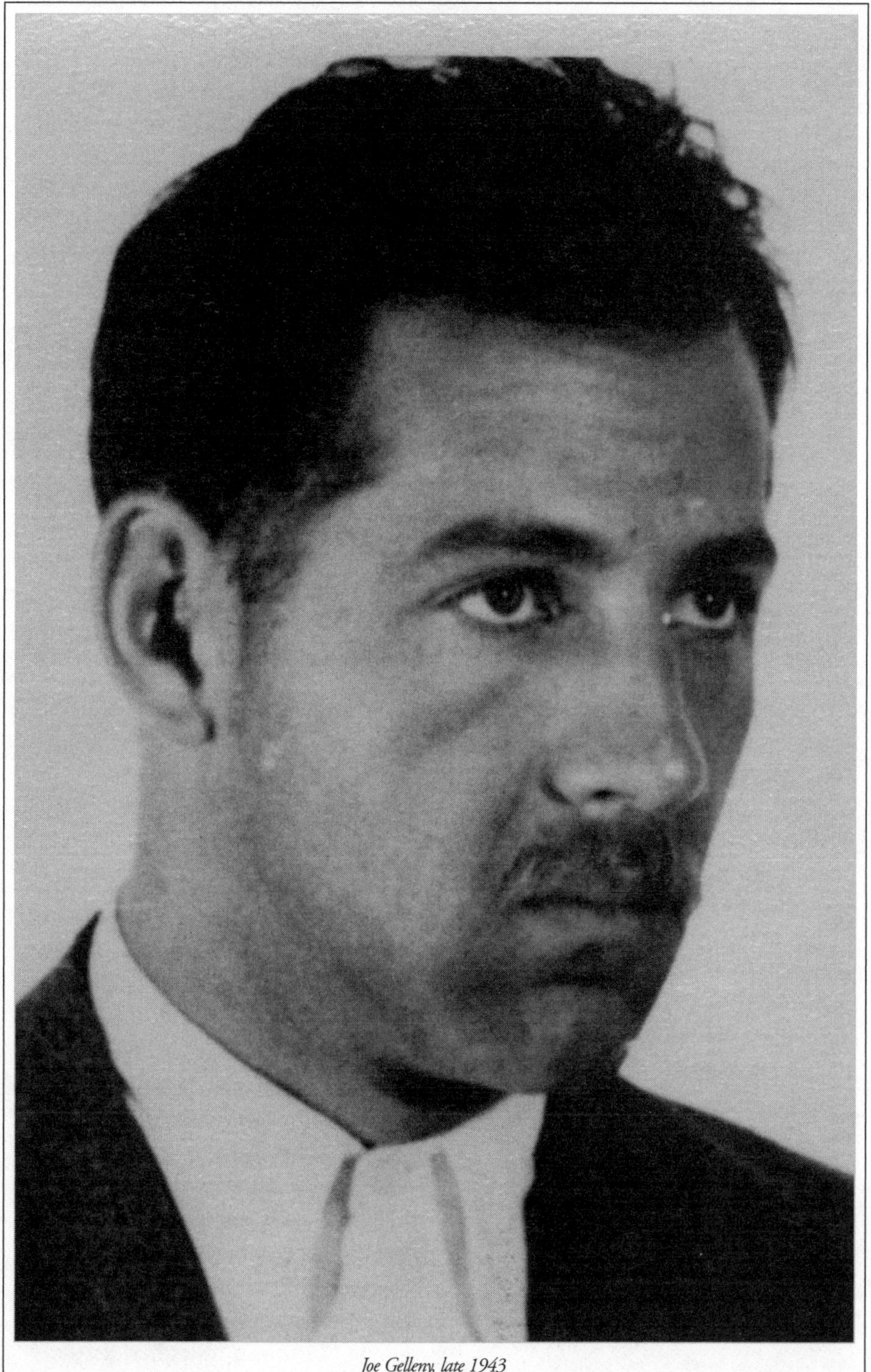

Joe Gelleny, late 1943

The rape of Budapest was in progress. The city's streets were in utter chaos; the thousands of Red Army soldiers who had been assigned, presumably, to prevent a general uprising, had, in effect, been awarded a two-week victory spree, *carte blanche*, an unrestricted license to pillage and plunder. Their senior officers, as well as the military police cadres and the NKVD, were preoccupied with the round-up of suspected Hungarian fascists, anti-Communists, or anyone whom the Commissars, the Army's political bosses, decreed an enemy of the regime. In the absence of any military or civil controls, the rank and file swaggered and rampaged like *berserker* Vikings.

It was open season on female inhabitants of Budapest. No woman, regardless of age or physical condition, was safe from the posses of bullyboys, neither in the streets, nor even in her home. Scores of school-aged girls and young women committed suicide by jumping from the windows and balconies of their office buildings and apartments, preferring a horrible but almost instantaneous death to degradation and rape by the gangs of ruffians. I witnessed two acts of desperation by women who were compelled to jump from their apartment balconies with their half-dressed attackers in close pursuit. This quickly became a popular spectator sport for the jeering crowds of soldiers who made wagers while hurling obscene taunts at the terrified women to encourage them.

On another occasion, I watched in horror and revulsion as a soldier picked up his prey, a naked female of perhaps eighteen, and hoisted her over his head, to display her pathetically struggling form, King Kong-like, to the appreciative gladiators below. He then heaved her over the edge of the balcony railing. The body plunged six stories, bounced off the roof of a burnt-out automobile, and rolled lifelessly onto the pavement, her grisly remains forming a pitiful collage of blood, bone, and tissue. His comrades applauded this act of martial bravado with hoots, wild gunfire, and exuberant demands for an encore. In appreciation, he bowed deeply as wagers were paid off and fresh ones made. Many warriors, flush with their success, stuffed their winnings under their hatbands and belts, for ease of access at the next performance.

Fuelled by alcohol and the arrogant self-righteousness of unquestioned supremacy, these conquistadors staggered and swaggered though the streets of the city in a continuous quest for new victims and fresh booze to slake their thirsts. When the stock of wine and liquor in restaurants and hotels had been exhausted, the bleary-eyed boys from the Caucasus used their jackboots and rifle butts to demolish the doors and windows of pharmacies, hair salons, and barbershops, in quest of any alcoholic fluids. The resulting scrambles frequently produced uncomradely mêlées for bragging rights to any containers of hair tonics and rinses, colognes, perfumes, and the old reliable rubbing alcohol.

Any woman who was unfortunate enough to be found inside these establishments was viciously raped, after which her battered body was abandoned. Well-intentioned female Samaritans, who ventured to come to the aid of the victims, did so at great personal risk. I witnessed such selfless acts of bravery and participated in one successful rescue.

These unbuttoned heroes of the Red Star lurched onward, guzzling assorted bottles of rotgut, trailed by their entourage, with rifles firing indiscriminately, spoiling for new conquests.

Walking was an exercise in self-preservation. It was decidedly reckless, if not masochistic, not to yield the sidewalk promptly to any oncoming phalanx of hardy revellers, many of whom sported necklaces of garlic, perhaps as amulets to ward off malignant Magyar spirits. Failure to show due deference could result in being elbowed into the gutter to receive a corrective dose of blows and kicks. It was an even graver breech of street etiquette to step anywhere close to the comatose body of an alcohol-sodden fallen warrior. With these rules firmly entrenched, I amused myself by making believe that I was shaking a tail as Blokey, Rolly and I had done in Bournemouth and Southampton.

For the most part, the Russian hooligans were youthful, peach-fuzz farm boys, like Jonas, the sobbing, trembling Lithuanian conscript, who might well have been one of these, but for the fortunes of war. I thought of the goddess' accounts of domestic accusations and bitter betrayals that were tearing families apart. War's evil, I decided, was its seductive power to brutalise the conqueror as well as the vanquished. I wanted no more to do with it.

My melancholy meandering led me to Andras' haunts. All offices, including that at Raoul's factory near the Jewish ghetto, had been vacated, gutted by artillery, and burnt out. Homeless wretches roamed the ruins of the moonscape, scavenging for paper and wooden furniture for fuel. They huddled, silently clustered around their meagre bonfires. The forger's shop and shed had been razed, and its contents torched. Had some astonished nomad discovered Raoul's envelope? I tried to visualise what might have ensued: a minor riot, a charitable distribution of the wealth...? Perhaps the shop owner had retrieved it. Taking a few of my remaining coins and pengös from my trouser pocket, I handed them to a grizzled, middle-aged man, whose upper right arm was poorly bandaged with a filthy rag. He rose and saluted me with his left arm, while his woman smiled and three beautiful waifs looked on. I asked in

Hungarian if he knew Captain Andras Hegedus. He nodded, replying that he did, but he hadn't seen him recently. I thanked them as I walked away. Perhaps the man was a veteran of the *Nyilasok*, or the *Honved*, perhaps not. I didn't care anymore.

I went to a small café where Andras had taken me after we had watched the prisoners disposing of corpses on the banks of the Danube. The proprietor whispered that he had not seen Captain Hegedus for a week. There was one last hope…the Swedish Legation.

The young male receptionist's nameplate indicated that he was Swedish; in the best tradition of the diplomatic services, he spoke idiomatic Hungarian fluently. "I'm sorry, sir, Mr. Wallenberg is presently unavailable."

"Do you know when he is expected to return?"

"His personal secretary, who would have that information, has been called away."

"Do you happen to know Captain Andras Hegedus"?

He indicated he did not, adding, "Would you care to leave a message for Mr. Wallenberg?"

"Please let him know that Joseph Gordon, a friend of Captain Hegedus, was inquiring."

He smiled and assured me that my will would be done.

Now, to break it to Ilona, but how? I knew that I could count on Karola's intuitive sense and went to ask her advice. It was not necessary to tell her that my inquiries had drawn a blank.

"You don't have to tell me. I can see it in your expression. They're gone, aren't they?"

"I don't know if that's certain, but it's not looking very promising, Karola."

She wept as we sat on the sofa, holding hands. Eventually, Karola suggested that Ilona needed to hear the truth from a friend and that I should go and stay at her apartment for a few days.

"What about you? Won't you come too? I can't abandon you here with all the craziness that's going on. It's ugly out there and only getting worse by the minute."

"I can handle it. See this?" She produced a 9mm Luger. "The last German guard thoughtfully left it under the mattress, with three full clips of bullets. If things get too nasty, there are one or two places where I can disappear, safely, only minutes away."

Based on my odyssey, I argued that there was no place in the city safe from soldiers running amok, or the tentacles of the NKVD. She assured me that she would be cautious, and would come to see us in a few days. With a promise to visit her daily, I put my few belongings into a paper bag and was preparing to leave.

"Aren't you forgetting something, Jozsi?"

"Of course!" We embraced.

"Something else." Smiling, she produced from behind her back the Hungarian detective novel. "Don't tell me who did it!"

"I have six pages to finish. So you did know!"

"Not really. I actually thought you were trying to learn Magyar. Silly me!"

Ilona was extremely distressed when I arrived at her apartment. She introduced me to two male associates of Andras', who had informed her moments earlier that Russian secret police had apparently abducted both Raoul, and Andras, and other members of the group. The men admitted that their information had been pieced together, based upon hearsay, although a well-placed mole inside Russian Intelligence would neither confirm nor deny the possibility.

"Maybe it's Soviet disinformation, a plant designed to trick us into revealing where they are hiding," I offered.

"Maybe so," one replied. "But not a single person inside or outside of the organisation has offered us definite proof that they have sighted either one. We've combed the entire city, including all of their usual hangouts and safe houses...."

"The Swedish Legation of course is co-operating fully and we're in close touch," added the other. "They did put up a considerable sum so that we could post a reward through the network, but so far, we've been unable to turn up anyone with solid evidence to verify the more than fifty reported 'sightings.' "

"Rumours, red herrings, nothing reliable, *nyet*, unfortunately, Mrs. Hegedus", commented the first speaker.

"Incidentally, Joe, a male fitting your description made inquiries of young Lars at the Legation's front desk this afternoon" offered one of the men.

'*So, that was the lucky Lars*!'

I described my relationship with Andras, including my one meeting with Raoul, to explain my activities. They thanked me.

"We're sorry, Mrs. Hegedus. We won't give up."

When she had shown them out, Ilona asked to me to sit down beside her. Taking my hands, she looked at me directly. "You're a smart man, and I know how much Andras values your opinion. You've heard these men and you yourself have been out searching. I want your candid opinion, Joseph. Please don't patronise me.

Is…Andras…likely…gone?"

"I honestly don't know…the longer he, they're…If I was a betting man, Ilona, I'd venture that the odds are three to one that Andras and Raoul have been detained."

"Arrested…thank you for your frankness. I'll have to ask your forgiveness, but I must retire to me bedroom for a while. Please help yourself to the tea, while it's still hot."

I felt increasingly uncomfortable, as though I were an intruder, sipping her tea while her sobs were clearly audible through the bedroom door. At last, deciding it would be best to leave despite Karola's admonition, I tiptoed to the bedroom door and rapped softly.

"Ilona, Joe here. Is there anything I can do? I thought I'd pop back tonight to see how…."

From inside the bedroom, Ilona spoke quietly, "Please don't go." I opened the door. Ilona was standing at her dresser, brushing her golden hair. "Forgive me for abandoning you, Joe. I do appreciate your concern and company. You are welcome to stay if Karola doesn't mind… if you want to."

Over the next three days, Ilona's apartment became a haven for six young female friends who had either been harassed or attacked by Russian servicemen. They were charming, cheerfully amusing and pitched in enthusiastically to help Ilona cope.

Each morning, Ilona and I sat with large map of Budapest spread over her dining room table to plan my daily excursions to look into Andras' more obscure watering holes and hangouts in the outskirts of Budapest. By mid week, military police were visibly restoring a semblance of social order while work crews began clearing up the post-rampage tonnes of broken plate glass and pieces of military hardware. Giant cranes with buckets mounted on huge trucks scooped up, and carted away the charred hulks of German and Russian tanks, crushed mobile artillery pieces, and assorted misshapen masses of armour. A few bakeries, delis, and butcher shops had reopened to line-ups that began before dawn. All of the would-be customers with whom I stopped to chat expressed the hope that the Western powers would use their influence to intervene and obtain Moscow's consent to permit the distribution of food and medicine, to prevent a national calamity. I kept my reservations about the likelihood of such a miracle to myself.

Karola and I spent enjoyable time together every day. In spite of increasing shortages and the strain of worrying about Andras, Raoul, and her colleagues, she was managing well. She had not encountered a single problem with the Russian servicemen, she said, because, "I've made friends with two Ukrainian women from the local security patrol who are my guardian angels every time I go out."

Several times, while making my daily forays in search of clues about Andras and Raoul, my instincts telegraphed a warning that I was under surveillance. It was not a simple matter of pride or bravado to shake an amateur sleuth or two by pulling off dazzling diversionary tactics. These were almost certainly *NKVD* professionals, counter intelligence thugs in trench coats and fedoras, who would just as soon slip a knife under my ribs as waste their breath tracking my wanderings. I was putting the security of my dear friends at stake, simply by being on the loose. I resolved to reach deeper into my bag of tricks and get a good look at my pursuers. My stereotypes of *NKVD* 'watchers' went up in smoke. The Soviet secret service had apparently embraced gender equity, as my bloodhounds were invariably the same male and female duo whom I christened Sacha and Svetlana. They were young and distinctly unthug-like; she was an attractive, well-dressed, slim brunette. Sacha was lean and hungry like a marathon runner, and they blended almost perfectly into the cityscape. Neither had on a gabardine overcoat although Svetlana usually wore a red and white kerchief. They were very good at the game, but fortunately I had spotted them early on and was convinced that I was playing them like fish-on-a-line.

Evenings at the apartment with Ilona and her charming friends were delightfully relaxing, despite our concern about Andras' and Raoul's whereabouts. All of the women were trusted associates from Andras' group, under thirty, good-looking, either single or widowed, and apparently pleased to have discovered a friendly, non-Russian male under fifty. They had brought enough food and wine to eke out one meal a day for two weeks. We usually entertained ourselves in the evenings by playing card games, beginning with hearts and euchre. I taught the women craps and stud poker, which they adored and soon surpassed me in skill and winnings. When they had relieved me of my pocket change, we often indulged in serial erotic storytelling, which we called *Scheherezade*. Without putting too fine a point on it, the first narrator would spin an elaborate sensual fantasy, to which the next person had to add, and so on. Though not highly original, the effects of the wine and close camaraderie conspired to produce some extraordinarily intricate libidinous tales, worthy of Chaucer, and the *Decameron*. Our den mother, Ilona, was amused by our carryings-on, but never joined directly in the fun and games.

Each night, one of these wonderful, free-spirited women and I slept together. Our one-thousand-and-one-night fantasy ended drastically short of that blissful mark, however, after only five when our idyll went up in smoke.

While returning late one afternoon, and still relishing the afterglow of an ardent encounter with Karola, I knew that Sacha and Svetlana were on to me. Checking for their reflection in a newly reglazed florist's window, I was alarmed to see not the usual suspects, but two archetypal *NKVD* louts actually wearing dark raincoats, and Al Capone-style fedoras. It took half an hour of my best tactical manoeuvres to give these two the slip. When I finally reached Ilona's building, I glanced quickly up and down the street, before going into the entranceway. The spare key was missing from her secret hiding place…not a good sign. I tried the door; it was unlocked. Alarms went off in my head. Had there been a break-in? I opened the door a crack and heard Ilona's distinctive, soft voice. The quality was conversational.

'*She has some unexpected visitors and forgot to lock the door.*'

I reached into the closet to hang up my jacket and was stopped cold. A green *NKVD* tunic, complete with colonel's pips on the shoulder boards and clusters of service spaghetti and medals on the breast pockets, was squarely draped from a hanger.

"Joseph, is that you?"

'*Good Lord! Now what?*'

Ilona met me in the hallway and shook her head, then brought me to the living room. She introduced her new billet, Colonel Sergei Sergeivitch Kovnick, of the *NKVD*. He neither rose to shake my hand, nor smiled. This *boychik* was a piece of work.

Short, plump and balding, his cratered face positively bloomed with a pockmarked beak, creating a resemblance to W. C. Fields. Unlike the comic Mr. Fields, he was transparently humourless. His sour demeanour was that of a man permanently resigned to the predictable failure of others to rise anywhere close to his expectations. His shifty, ferret-like eyes appraised me, as if sizing me up for a noose; shades of the farm boys at Abaliget!

Three of the women sat in a row on the sofa, sad and downcast, like birds on a wire. They realised that our dance cards had been revoked. I knew that my goose was cooked, carved, and about to be served on a platter. At least the sanctimonious fellow had brought along some provisions which Ilona and the six beauties had whipped into a respectable vegetarian supper.

The Colonel spoke only Russian, with which Ilona had some familiarity while the women and I understood little to none. He proceeded to deliver an oral essay on the rebirth of church architecture in sixteenth century Budapest. I understood Ilona to say this was the thesis of an unfinished doctoral dissertation; like his comrade boss and fellow Georgian, Iosif Vissarionovich Dzhugashvili, a.k.a. Joseph Stalin, he had abandoned holy orders of the monastic life for the worldly rewards of Marxism.

After supper, while Ilona and the other women cleared away the dishes, Colonel Kovnick produced two vodka bottles from his kit bag. He generously poured four fingers' worth into each person's wine glass and bid us join him in saluting the *Rodina*, his Motherland, Joseph Stalin, the new Peoples' Republic of Hungary, Winston Churchill, F. D. Roosevelt, and for all I knew, international soccer. His cup, which was very nearly overflowing, was drained in one gargantuan gulp. I took one sip to be polite and I knew that I detested the stuff even more than Scotch. It had already been a long night by 7:00 p.m. and would, apparently, only get longer. Four of Ilona's six friends had quietly and wisely vanished into the kitchen. The remaining two, Anna and Andrea, had obviously acquired the happy faculty of sleeping with their eyes wide open, or so I surmised, until I felt my feet engaged in a tantalising tripleheader game of footsie. I hoped that the Colonel wasn't one of the players.

By 8:00, although he had almost polished off the first bottle, the Colonel was distressingly sober, coherent, and had not once used the bathroom. I attempted to catch Ilona's eye as she struggled valiantly to relay his rambling monologue. Neither she nor I had consumed more than a thimbleful of his elixir. I was considering the possibility of strangling him, slowly, with his red suspenders, to end the unbearable tedium.

Ilona suddenly coughed, stood up unsteadily, and excused herself. Hearing water running in the bathroom, I thought it a friendly gesture to knock and inquire about her condition. As I stood, the Colonel laid a liver-spotted, ham-like fist on my arm.

"*Nyet! Nyet!*"

I wasn't going anywhere. "Am I a prisoner?"

He didn't reply, but stood up with alarming agility, threw down his napkin, and walked gyroscope-steady to the apartment entrance, then flung it open to reveal a robust Red Army corporal filling most of the doorway. My heart sank. Ilona returned and the Colonel's treatise resumed. By now, he was holding forth on something to do with a collection of jewelled Easter eggs at St. Petersburg's Hermitage Museum. The remainder of the evening was more of the same endurance contest, alleviated only by pleasurably furtive under-table canoodling.

He decreed it was our collective bedtime at 10:30, sharp. As we rose wearily but ever so gratefully from the table, Ann and Andrea gave me what could be best characterised as sly and very sexy come-hither glances. I didn't need any further enticement. The Colonel summoned his corporal from the hallway to make up the mattress which had been appropriated from the girls' bedroom. Eventually, we all were settled in. Typical of many 'professional' drinkers, the Colonel was already dead to the world; his lugubrious snoring was resonating throughout the apartment.

Sometime after midnight, I awoke. My two dinner companions were fast asleep. I debated what I should do. I tiptoed into the next room. The Colonel was lying open-mouthed on his back, with the holster of his gun tucked under the pillow at his head, Stirling Hayden-style. He would be an easy mark, but the armed guard planted outside, facing the door, was a considerable obstacle to overcome. Escape from a window was not an option as we were on the fourth floor with a straight drop down as there were neither balconies nor fire escape ladders. I wasn't a Hollywood stuntman or Johnny Canuck. The *NKVD* would be merciless in their retribution, regardless of whether or not I succeeded. As a survivor of the tender mercies meted out by the Second Bureau and the SD, it was a gamble that I was prepared to face, but not at the risk of SMERSH[1] taking cruel vengeance on Ilona and our friends. Escape from here was certain suicide, a definite 'non starter'. It didn't require a great deal of political *savoir-faire* to figure out that I was the Colonel's number one target and Ilona was a marked woman.

Next morning, a chipper and sober Colonel Kovnick confirmed what I had already deduced when he announced that I would accompany him to *NKVD* HQ. Through Ilona, he insisted that I was not a prisoner and promised that I would be back by nightfall. I had heard that tune before at Zugliget and went to pack up my scant belongings. Ilona was similarly convinced and begged the Colonel's indulgence for a half-hour's respite. Surprisingly, he agreed. Our farewell was bittersweet. I had wanted so much to locate Andras and Raoul. Ilona was fragile and vulnerable. As with Mitzi, I felt a deep sense of compassion for her. We sat in silence on the edge of her bed, holding hands, until the Colonel knocked on the door. Our time was up. As I came out of the bedroom,

'If looks could kill...'

The Colonel was understandably envious. Ilona Hegedus was strikingly beautiful in a Nordic sense, classically patrician, sophisticated, and well educated, the cultured product of another world of exclusive clubs, five star restaurants and box seats, with privileged access to the finest luxuries. She radiated refinement, aristocrat breeding, and subtle depths, which few men would ever know. It was not easy to leave her there.

It was a cold but brilliantly sunny morning when the Colonel, the hallway watchdog, and I walked down-

[1] Smyert'shpionam or *"Death to Spies," was the Russian military's counter-intelligence agency, 1942-46. Its name catches the flavour of its corporate vision, mission, and grim achievements.*

town to their HQ. When the institutional odour of carbolic acid hit my nostrils, it was *déja vu* all over again, as Louie would have said; I was transported back to the little rural railway station at Abaliget. The interrogation was low key, more like a job interview. There were no rope restraints or handcuffs. I wasn't threatened, smacked, kicked, or electrocuted. The interpreter was polite, patient and spoke upper class Hungarian. They confiscated the few Hungarian books and my precious notebook that I had packed. I listened carefully to each question and answered as fully and truthfully as I could. Unlike my many previous cross-examinations, this time I didn't have the advantage of understanding this interrogator's Russian questions. The primary case officer, an *NKVD* second lieutenant received high marks for consistency, by responding to all of my answers with "*Da, da*" or, most frequently, "*Nyet, nyet.*" He conferred regularly with Colonel Kovnick, who was otherwise mute. When I asked if they had finished with me, the lieutenant's reply was simple: *"Nyet."* Similarly, when I asked to be allowed to go back to Ilona's, after they were done, "*Nyet*!" When I asked to be released to the British legation, he responded, "*Nyet, nyet*!" to underscore their general reluctance.

After two hours of repetitive grilling, it was apparent that my credibility was severely strained. The interpreter made this clear when he stated that his superiors did not for one minute believe that I was a) Canadian, b) British or c) a soldier of either country. My use of Hungarian was suspect. I believe they assumed that I was a Hungarian *Nyilas*, or, by some stretch of fancy, a German deserter, as I was unable to satisfactorily explain to whom I reported. They said I would be required to undergo further "tests." Naturally, I asked what that implied. Had the prestigious Pavlov Academy in Moscow developed a psychological litmus test of nationality? The thought of facing more inane inkblots and drawings of two-faced witches in big hats was depressing, but a far, far better prospect than Ference Csongor's ministrations.

I was taken and locked away in a clean ground floor cell with a heated radiator, fresh sheets, a stainless steel washbasin, flush toilet and a high, small, barred window. There was a notable absence of lice, cockroaches, and nocturnal mice. I prayed that Andras and Raoul, if indeed they were prisoners, shared my relatively good fortune.

The next day was the same: more relentlessly stupid interrogations alleviated only by relentlessly boring cell time.

On the third day, a severely coifed female *NKVD* jailer awakened me at 6:00 in the morning with a breakfast tray and terse instructions that I must be ready to move out at

7:00. In the exercise yard, about a dozen prisoners had been marshalled, waiting for something to happen. Three trucks were idling, in the eternal 'hurry up and wait' army fashion. We waited.

A dauntingly robust Red Army private approached. With his burp gun, which was aimed directly at my belly button, he gestured that I should climb promptly into the back of the lead truck. I complied.

The truck laboured in low gear as it pulled out of the compound. I sat down on a low steel bench between two companions while the guard sat opposite, staring stonily. The burp gun's muzzle tracked our every motion like radar as the truck bounced and pitched.

I checked the time on my gold-plated Bulova wristwatch. It was 7:45. The Russian private reached out his left hand.

'*Ivan wants to have a closer peek*.' I pushed up my sleeve to show it to him.

"Da, da!" he muttered, wiggling his outstretched fingers impatiently. It dawned on me that he didn't want to look at my watch; he wanted to take it, my high school graduation present.

"Nyet!" I exclaimed.

"Da, Da!" he replied.

Two '*da's*' with a burp gun beat one '*nyet*'. Reluctantly, I slipped off the shiny expansion bracelet, which he slid onto his left wrist, beaming approvingly. I had made a friend.

'*Where in the hell are we going?*'

We were going straight into hell, hell on earth: a combat zone!

'T*his is just great. I've been conscripted into Uncle Joe's army!*'

The truck jerked to a stop short of the front line where a massed tank and artillery engagement was raging. The sound of fury and thunder of rocket salvos and heavy artillery rising from the battleground was deafening, shaking and vibrating the ground as though the world was flying apart. It was as if the siege of mortars and bombings at Karola's had been magnified one thousand times. All around us was death and wreckage. The husks of derelict artillery pieces and the shells of armoured behemoths were overturned, smashed, and burning. Spent shell casings of every model and type known to military ordnance littered the fields. Scorched corpses and severed fragments of thousands, or tens of thousands of Red Army, *Wehrmacht* and *Waffen-SS* tank crews and infantrymen sprawled where they had been cut down or blown to pieces and flung into the mud.

The guard pointed to 'our' wristwatch and held up five fingers. We were taking a pee break. It was difficult enough to walk without stumbling over some grisly cadaver, much less find a suitably clear, private spot of ground where I could relieve myself. Perhaps I was overtired or hallucinating, but in the grinning rictus of death, it seemed that the corpses lying face up were reaching up to grasp and pull me with them into eternity. The stench of death was one thousand times more disgusting than I remembered from the Partisan killing grounds of Vocin and Slat in Yugoslavia. Contingents of Russian medical corpsmen walked the fields doing battlefield triage, prodding the bodies to distinguish the quick from the dead. One of them stepped on or poked an anti-tank mine. The deafening blast ripped off his legs like matchsticks. His body arced skyward and landed heavily several metres away. A burying detail stopped long enough to note the points of impact, then continued with its gruesome, methodical work of gathering ID tags and compiling matching body parts in Frankenstein heaps. German dying and dead were prodded and then ignored.

The ground was deeply furrowed and channelled with trenches and snakelike ditches where armoured treads and tracks had only recently charged and parried and thrust. A cold rain began to fall, and soon had overflowed the shell holes and ruts, making obscene rivulets of bloody runoff.

Legions of rats had already begun their macabre feast. I reflected on the valour of our Canadian boys in the muddy horrors of Mons, Passchendale, Ypres and Vimy, less than thirty years ago. It had been proclaimed by our leaders as the war to end all wars. We knew everything and had learned nothing.

After relieving ourselves, the two miserable captives and I were herded back onto the truck. They each wore the ragtag remnants of Soviet Army uniforms. Unlike Jonas, they wore their issue boots. Perhaps they had behaved extremely badly in Budapest or were deserters, as they were handcuffed and chained together. One of them ventured to ask the guard a question. He shrugged as if he didn't have the remotest idea as to what we were doing here, or why, then turned up the fur collar of his greatcoat and rapped the roof of the cab with his stubby gun barrel. The truck lurched forward; we prisoners huddled together, shielding ourselves from what was now driving sleet. Whether from the rigors of vigorous interrogations or recent excesses in Budapest, my two companions had the morose faces of death row inmates. The truck pulled up to a mobile Russian command post. On the horizon, the muzzle flashes of artillery flickered with the effect of a spectacular display of sheet lightning, revealing the ghostly clouds. With knowledge of physics and some mental math, I estimated that we were less than five kilometres from the action.

We were locked in a small, unheated shack for two days, allowed supervised use of a foul latrine, and fed field rations twice daily. An *SS-Mann* was thrown in. Though scruffy and unkempt, he was a poster boy for the Nazi's *Strength Through Joy* physical-fitness movement. Klaus, or so he said he was named, swore to me that his father was a pro-Communist industrialist from Düsselldorf, who would gladly fork over a huge reward to the Party if his son were released. He vehemently denied that he had ever seen action in Russia. The *NKVD* likely found the central paradox of the first part doubtful and refused to accept the second, given the torn but still decipherable remnant of a *Leibstandarte SS-Das Reich* armband. My two Russian companions were scheming to do him in, so Klaus requested a transfer to relative safety in a segregated hut for German undesirables. I was interrogated twice more, without mistreatment, but scored no points on their credibility scale. Therefore, it was moving time again.

My next port of call was a forward post, which, for reasons unknown, was even closer to the battle zone. It consisted of two utilitarian wood buildings, reminiscent of the mess hall at Camp X. My fellow inmates were a cosmopolitan mix of Hungarians, Germans, Russians, and other assorted Slavs.

The officers and guards were obviously recruited from a Siberian village of Brobdingnagians; not one was less than six feet two inches tall. Our nursemaid was a colonel who towered a hand over six feet six. He was indeed a native Siberian and a direct descendant of a horseman with Ghengis Khan's rapacious Golden Horde, the scourge of the steppes, as I was to discover.

We were ordered to strip to the skin as water hoses deloused us in shivering parties of six; then we donned clean towel swaddling while our clothes were boiled in large steaming vats. The odour was foul, but the hearty women stirring the brew with wooden ladles the size of canoe paddles, smiled at us continuously. Meanwhile, we were shown a tub of brown, smelly goop and instructed by hand motions to rub it into our hair and scalp. It had the pungent odour of coal tar dissolved in kerosene, which it was. We rinsed, dutifully applied another dose of louse liniment, and then rinsed again.

While sitting in the waiting room for my clothes to dry, I had an insane impulse.

'I'm going to speak in Russian to Goliath and try to make friends. He's in charge around here, and I've nothing to lose! What's the worst he can do, shoot me for lousy (ha! ha!) grammar?'

I blurted out a standard phrase of greeting. Then, stupidly, I stood up and offered him my hand; my towel slid down to my ankles, onto the concrete floor. The interpreter's expression was shocked disbelief.

To my utter amazement, the colonel replied, in English.

"Never mind. I get your towel Lieutenant," which he promptly did.

When I had once again girded my loins and regained my composure, I thanked him in Hungarian, Russian and for good measure, English

He chuckled and through the interpreter asked, "Which of these is your native tongue, Hungarian or English? I think it is not Russian."

"Both are, sir. I was born in Hungary but came to Canada with my family as a young boy. I am now a citizen of Canada, though I am presently serving in the British Army."

This seemed to have piqued his interest. "This is very confusing. What is your name, please? Tell me about your life in Canada."

I briefly told him my life story, beginning with my early childhood in Hungary, and my new life in Canada. I included the fact that I had joined the Canadian Army and transferred to serve with the British military. When I finished, he excused himself, went into his office, and closed the door. With nothing to do but wait for the outcome, I struggled to appear composed but images of the prisons I had known flashed like neon signs. Thirty minutes later he returned with a blue file, which had my name, Gordon, Joseph, on the tab. I was thankful that it wasn't Csongor's report. I arose.

He spoke rapidly; the interpreter addressed me in English. "My Colonel's name is Valery Grozny. He wishes me to say: Lieutenant, in wartime there will always be questions about those individuals, who for whatever reasons, do not appear to be, you might say, credible. We Soviets are certainly vigilant, indeed concerned, as we should be, with the possibility of overlooking, if not welcoming, persons who mean to do us harm."

The interpreter paused, to digest the Colonel's next words. Then he nodded and continued, "I have read your file very carefully; the interviewers have not found any evidence to cast doubt or suspicion on your authenticity. Any further attempt to establish your credibility is an obvious waste of our time and yours. I believe that you are who you say you are, Lieutenant Gordon, and I am recommending to *NKVD* Budapest that you be set free, immediately!" Both of them were smiling broadly.

I felt I was going to keel over; was I trembling with the surge of adrenaline, or with the cold? I could barely manage to squeak: "Col...Colonel Grozny, I can't begin to tell you how... deeply... grateful...I am. Thank you, Sir! Thank you very, very much."

A depressing thought occurred. '*As a garden-variety army Colonel, how much clout could Grozny actually have with the omnipotent*

NKVD?'

"You can't go anywhere like that, Lieutenant. Get dressed, and I'll take you to the canteen for a decent bite then you can sleep here on the couch in my office. It's quite comfortable and quiet.

"Fortunately, there's a clerk working late in the office. She'll type your release papers, etcetera, then I'll have to send a teletype to the NKVD station in Budapest for confirmation, of course. I can foresee no problems except for the lateness of the hour. If I have to patch through a call to have a dispatch rider go to Colonel Kovnick's billet, so be it."

"Excuse me Colonel, could that by any chance be Colonel Sergei Kovnick?"

"As a matter of fact, yes. You know of him?"

"Yes...but, I don't think he likes me very much." I told him some of our brief, recent encounter.

"He does now. Colonel Sergei Sergeivitch Kovnick is my father-in-law and, it just so happens that the chief of the security service appointed him as my prime referee and mentor for my transfer next month."

'*There's my answer. He's married to the old bore's daughter. Sure hope she got her mother's looks*!'

"He won't turn me down, Lieutenant. You know, I'm sure how these things work. It would be the kiss of death to our career plans...his and mine. Marika and I just made him a very proud grandpa, for good measure. Here's their picture!"

She was a real doll; baby looked a little bit like Grandpa Sergei Sergeivitch, but might grow out of it.

"Congratulations, Colonel. I envy you your beautiful family."

"Thank you. Go home and make some Canadian ice hockey players with that sweetheart of yours. I'll line up an escort and supplies at first light and with luck, you'll be on your way after breakfast. Is this satisfactory?"

'*Satisfactory?'* I could scarcely believe this astonishing change of fortune. It was almost too incredible to be true. '*What if I hadn't screwed up the courage to make that asinine Russian overture to him*?'

'*You'll never know, laddie. You seized the moment and here you are,* almost *free!'*

Yet, I couldn't live with myself if I didn't make one last attempt.

"Colonel, please forgive me, but I have two friends in Budapest who have not been seen for many days. Could you perhaps make inquiries through your channels?"

"That all depends. What are your friends' names?"

"One is a Swedish citizen, Mr. Raoul Wallenberg and the other is

Captain Andras Hegedus, a Hungarian Army officer."

As the translator spoke, the Colonel's smile froze; his manner became icily remote. "*Nyet.* Such information is not available, Lieutenant. Do not ask this again."

In every other way, Colonel Grozny was as good as his word. The escort, none other than cheery burp gun Boris, embraced me with a warm hug. My Bulova glinted on his wrist, but no matter. It was more than a fair trade. What a difference a day and a friend with excellent connections could make, even in this brave new, classless society. I was issued a pair of combat boots with warm wool socks, gloves and a scarf, a larger-than-life Army greatcoat, and a Red Army fur hat, without the red star. Boris and Valery grinned at the sight of me, apparently almost disappearing inside the capacious folds of the long, heavy coat; they said that I resembled a Don Cossack, minus the horse. I had dropped a great deal of weight since Pécs and was down to forty-nine kg, soaking wet, literally, as verified during the delousing episode.

Grozny briefed Boris, instructing him to head directly toward Debrecen. With the warmest of wishes for our mutual success, the Colonel, his interpreter, and I bid farewell. Boris proved to be a resourceful and responsible guide, although he lacked the usual jeep. He avoided the rural roads, which twisted and meandered with unmilitary inefficiency and we made good time, taking a beeline across the ice-locked ponds and fields. The sky was crystal clear, the air fresh and brisk, but not bitter. The creeks and streams were beginning to burst their icy bonds of winter; it was as though spring, the magic season of rebirth of all things bright and beautiful, had waited for this day to preview its wonders. I wanted to sing with joy and was about to, when an American Army Airforce Thunderbolt and a Russian Stormovik fighter swooped down in tandem to eyeball us, dipped their wings in approval, then soared into the early March sun. A fanciful thought occurred: might my friend Louie have been in the cockpit of one of those T-Bolt birds? We were heading directly away from the front, so there was no sign or sound of battle to spoil my optimistic mood.

We walked onward to a small Russian outpost, where four newly released American USAF aircrew joined us. We shared our supply of wonderful sausage and bread that Colonel Grozny had thoughtfully provided. The fliers were friendly, easy-going lads and as pleased and excited to be trekking to freedom as I was. Our growing band took on another member, a British officer, and together we hitched an early morning truck ride into Badaörs, which had been taken over as a provisional Russian fighter airbase.

Our Russian hosts at Badaörs

kindly invited us to eat with them in the regular officers' mess. This was wonderful until we found out that the Russian fighter pilots dined in a reserved mess, which served much better fare. We pushed our hosts hard for admission into the élite club, through a Russian-speaking American. The Base CO finally caved in and agreed to admit us to the true Soviet warriors' mess, where we joined him and his squadron in considerable luxury and immediate acceptance. Our Soviet cousins certainly knew how to reward their folk heroes. Vodka, beer, and wine flowed like the Volga as we toasted Stalin, Roosevelt, Churchill, and eternal Allied brotherhood many, many times and rowdily sang bawdy Russian drinking songs. We likely spilled more than we drank at the final blowout. When it was my turn, *Mademoiselle from Amentières* was the only English pub tune whose words I could remember; it was an instant hit. "*Inky dinky parlez-vous*" reverberated majestically in their superb bass and baritone two-part harmony. I couldn't help but notice as we hoisted our drinks that many of the fighter pilots' hands bore scarring and abrasions. Curious, I asked our resident Russian-speaker to find out the reason.

"*Stormovik*!" The Russian flier made the motions of a pilot pushing an aircraft joystick.

When pressed, the airman explained that the sheet metal in the cockpit of the earliest *Stormovik* models usually had ragged edges, which were left unrolled by the factory, in an effort to cut down production time. The scarring was the proud mark of long and distinguished service, they said, since in later versions of the fighter, the design flaw had been corrected.

Immediately upon our arrival at Badaörs, Boris had disappeared. An hour later, he showed up and reported that he had commandeered a civilian house, only minutes from the base. He waved away our questions when we asked him to enlighten us about the arrangements he had made to compensate the owner. The two aged inhabitants hovered, but left us to ourselves. Our farewell party in the fliers' mess had run out steam, or more precisely, vodka, which I had shunned like the plague. Feeling no pain, we tottered unsteadily down the mess hall's wooden steps, crooning *Don't Sit Underneath the Apple Tree*, and were proceeding towards our billet when I heard my name shouted loudly in Magyar, "Joe! Joe! Joseph Gordon! It's Andy, Andy Daniel! Come back! Get me the hell out of here!"

There stood a forlorn Andrew Durovecz, late of SOE Mission WINDPROOF, and my Camp X colleague. Andy was in a compound, which was enclosed by a forbiddingly high barbed-wire fence. I asked him what was going on. He shook his head. I came closer and tried again.

He said he was being "detained." His hearing had not completely recovered from the damage done by the *SD*, so we shouted, "How did you get here, Joe? Can you get me released, too? These bastards think I'm an anti-Communist or some kind of half-assed Trotskyite counter revolutionary. What a bloody joke, Joe…me, Andrew Durovecz, an anti-Bolshevik!" He was very agitated and upset. My dinner companions, including some Russian officers were approaching.

"Take it easy, buddy. I'll speak with the CO first thing in the morning and try to get you sprung. This group's heading out to Debrecen tomorrow morning. You can join us!"

When I requested a meeting with the Base Commandant in the morning, the interpreter/clerk stated that his Chief had the flu, "vodka flu," he muttered, under his breath, and was extremely busy. I promised him that all I needed was ten minutes, tops.

"It's my ass if you upset him and I'll see that it's yours too if you do. Hold on." He spoke into the intercom. "Go in, but knock first, gently! I'll be there in a moment. Oh, shut up!" he hissed, glaring at the telephone resentfully. He answered it, deferentially, his voice brimming with the milk and honey of petty smarminess peculiar to minor bureaucrats.

The drapes in the colonel's office were drawn. By the dim light of his desk lamp, he appeared as if he had been broadsided by a freight locomotive. He was definitely not in the drinkers' hall of fame, alongside Colonel K. I hoped that I looked less of a mess. The interpreter arrived with tea, and served it fussily while his boss searched for his eyeglasses, which were pushed up and resting on his head. All the while, the Commandant complained about the paper overload from Moscow which threatened to ground the entire Russian Airforce. For proof, he motioned toward his overflowing in-basket. I shook my head and clucked sympathetically, to signal total agreement with his sentiments. This man was severely hungover, thoroughly frazzled, and likely to have his bitchy assistant call in the guards to throw me out on my ear without much provocation.

Suffice to say that El Supremo had found Andy's written account of his escape from Zugliget a bit thin. Realising that I had one minute to make a pitch, I described the Camp's country club atmosphere, and then briefly told my version of Andy's and my own breakout, without mentioning John. He was beginning to come around, I thought, until unexpectedly, he expressed some reservations about my *bona fides*. The interpreter clicked his pencil rapidly against his front teeth, waiting to see me self-destruct. My armpits were suddenly soggy.

"May I suggest that the Colonel contact Colonel Grozny for a reference?"

The clerk looked as though he would positively have a bird. "Russian Airforce Colonels do not telephone Army Lieutenant-Colonels!" he hissed.

"Well, in this case it might be acceptable. He's with the *NKVD*." '*Almost*.'

I finished him off with an embroidered fairy tale about Andy and I as inseparable Hungarian-speaking childhood chums in Toronto, ending on a truthful note by endorsing Andy's claim to charter membership of the Canadian Communist Party.

My bluff had either worked or the Colonel wished wholeheartedly to get rid of me at that moment. He agreed, somewhat testily, to release Lieutenant Daniels, if I would solemnly accept full responsibility. I wasn't sure what that meant, but, nevertheless signed some indecipherable official papers in order to placate him and get going before he or his helpmate thought up any more technical hitches. Within twenty minutes, Andy was waiting in the front yard, a free man.

In my absence, the group had appointed me as their leader. Half-jokingly, I demanded a recount, but they insisted, explaining that I was best qualified as I held the highest rank, spoke English and Hungarian, as well as a smattering of Russian. Off we went, gathering new members, mainly Americans, who were out for a good time, as were we all. We were now ten and growing. We walked, hitched rides on farm trucks, and army lorries, walked some more, ate country fare, and consorted with the local women whenever possible until all nineteen of us, fifteen Americans, one Englishman, Boris, Andrew and I, waltzed into Debrecen. Boris led us directly to the American Embassy. He had confided to Alex, our Russian-speaking Marine from Pittsburgh, and anyone else who would listen, that he was so captivated by 'Amerika' that he wanted to apply for a visa. We never saw him again; he simply vanished. The Embassy clerks and officials said they had no record of his application. I now believe that his open admiration for the bastion of capitalism, which he stated indiscreetly and frequently, was reported to the secret police.

The wonderful Embassy staff had actually rolled out the red carpet for a heroes' welcome and offered us anything we wanted. To a man, we chose a shower with unlimited hot water, foaming shampoo, huge bars of soap, and towels bigger than a football field. Waiting on my bed, an attendant had laid out a grooming kit, pyjamas, and a luxurious white terry cloth dressing gown, embossed with the American eagle. After a nap, we were *fêted* at a lavish banquet, then each sent to his own, unimaginably comfortable, warm bed, with king-sized mattress and down pillows.

The next morning, following a massive ham and eggs breakfast rounded off with litres of hot American coffee, country cream, and sugar, my hosts politely inquired whether I wished to make a statement. I agreed to an interview, which was mercifully brief, congenial, and non-invasive. At the conclusion, when an aide asked if I had any requests, I mentioned that I would appreciate being put in contact with their British counterparts. He picked up his phone and within a half-hour, Andy and I were being driven in the Embassy's Lincoln to the British Military Mission. The driver, a personable, courteous young black man, drove sedately and chatted in Magyar, pointing out Debrecen's main attractions.

The British were equally warm and welcoming. Naturally, Andy and I were asked to give separate depositions, "…just for the record, chaps, if you would both be so kind."

I summarised DIBBLER and outlined my experiences from Orfü to the present, supplying as many dates, locations and names as I could recall, or thought relevant, while a male stenographer recorded my statement. There were few interruptions. At the end of two hours, the Major asked if I had any questions. I did.

"I'm curious Major. As I stated in my deposition, I sent two sets of W/T messages, one to HQ and one to Captain Rolly Young at Papuk for good measure, and received confirmations, before Admiral Horthy's radio address on the fifteenth of October. I copied to Istanbul, as well. Did they actually arrive?"

"Yes, we did receive the first set." End of interview. He told me that Andy and I would be put on a flight to Sienna. The following morning, the major accosted me at Debrecen airbase.

"Oh, Lieutenant Gordon, one moment, if you don't mind."

"Major?"

"Apropos of our discussion yesterday, at the end…"

I wasn't going to make it easy for him, as I knew what was coming. "Sir?"

"I'm afraid I was quite wide of the mark in my facts, Lieutenant. Actually, the logs have no record of any messages being received with your call sign on those dates. Have a safe flight and good luck." That was that.

Medieval Sienna was picturesque and unbelievably quaint; with the surrounding Tuscan hills as backdrop, it was enough to inspire me to want to learn to paint landscapes. Fortunately for the world of art, we had to hurry or miss the boat in Naples. The voyage to Southampton was a pleasure cruise. With only a handful of Americans on board to create some diversions, there was little else to do

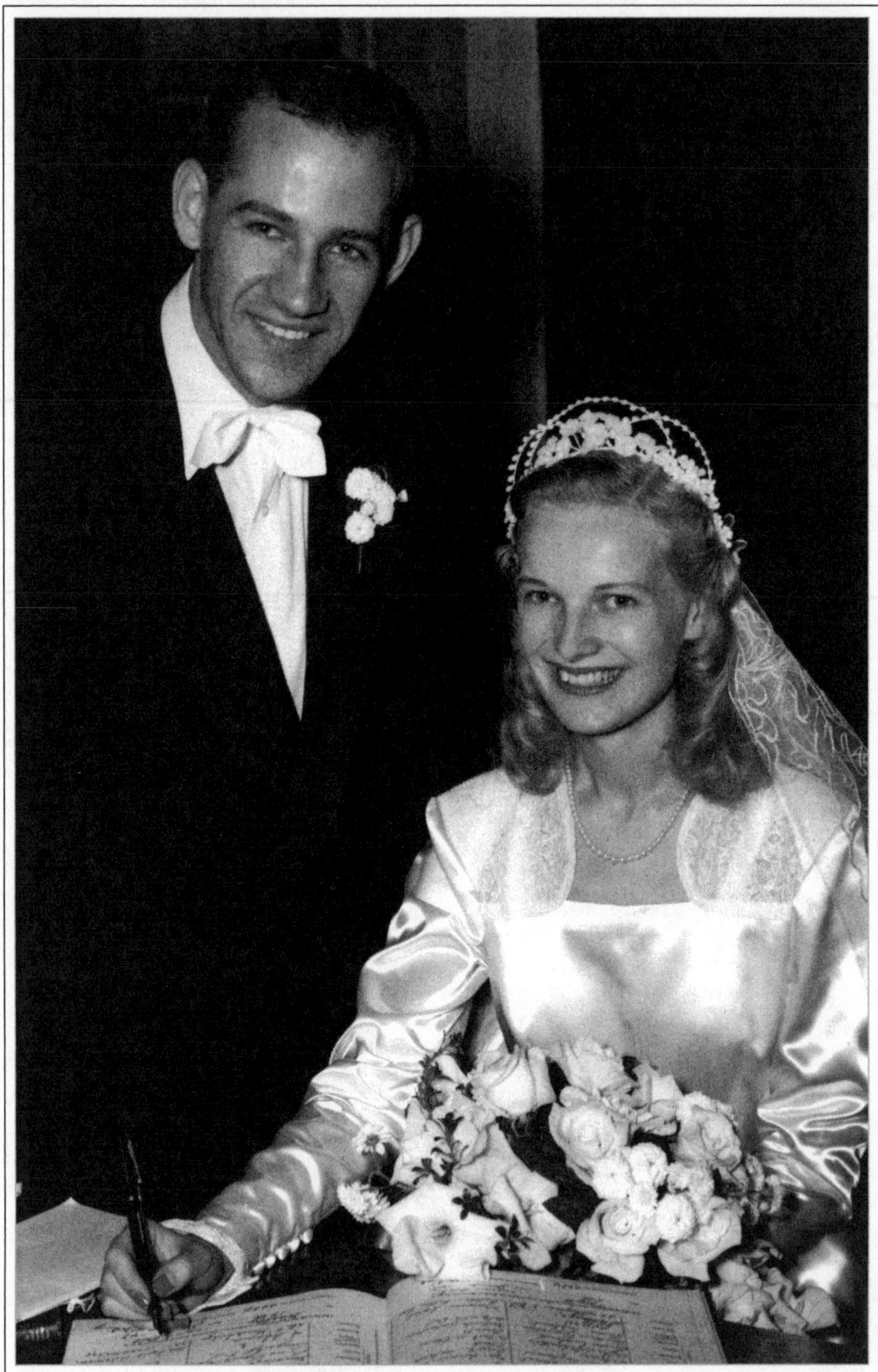

Joe and Helen, happy at last, the "almost" bride and groom signing the wedding register

but read, sunbathe, shoot the breeze, eat and sleep, but that was more than enough. When we docked in Southhampton, SOE staff picked us up, and we were chauffeured to a first-class London hotel where 'anything goes' was the byword. Andy and I were separated and filed individual reports. These three reports which I made have never been unearthed.... Were they lost, misfiled or ...?

I was looking forward to returning home to Canada to see Helen and Dad and jumped at the opportunity to sail by myself to Halifax. Andy and I did not meet up again until later, in Canada.

The Halifax railway station was mobbed with thousands of fellow Canadian servicemen and women. I boarded the Toronto-bound CN train, and settled down to read about how we had saved the world in *Maclean's* and *New Liberty Magazine,* and *The Toronto Telegram*, where I was delighted to find that *Major Hoople's Boarding House,* as well as *Mutt and Jeff* were survivors, too. I slept sitting up for most of the trip to Toronto, where Major Art Bushell, of Camp X, met the train and took me under his wing for a day.

'Here Comes the Bride? What's going on?' My beautiful Helen smiled radiantly as her brother brought her ever so majestically down the aisle, toward me.

'Looks like you're almost *married, laddie, so for heaven's sake, wake up and pay attention.'*

Afterword

Years later, my beloved wife Helen reminisced about her recollections of that day.

All the weddings that I can remember have been beautiful occasions. The bride was always radiant and serene and the ceremony flawless. What events must have preceded these perfect nuptials? Did pure harmony always reign supreme? In my case, it was not to be.

In my house, pandemonium was the order on that sun-filled morning. The cake had yet to be delivered to the Old Mill, the site of the reception. There was a delay in the arrival of the corsages and bouquets and the members of the bridal party had to rush to appointments at the beauty salon. Our house was the main staging point for scads of out-of-town relatives and friends, who milled about, adding to the confusion. There were line-ups for the bathrooms and guests had commandeered the bedrooms where they readied themselves for the festive affair.

Joe and Helen walking down the aisle

By one-thirty, all and sundry, including Mom and Poppa, had departed for the church. Emily, my sister and bridesmaid, had stayed behind to help make the final adjustments to my gown. We checked our 'faces' one final time and then hastened downstairs. The house was unnaturally quiet. Where was everyone? At the church, of course! The kitchen clock read one forty p.m. I assumed that my driver was waiting impatiently in the front room or outside. I was wrong; the old home-stead was empty and so was the driveway. Emily and I had been stranded. The clock showed one fifty p.m., and it was a ten-minute drive to the church.

Tears welled up; how could a bride be so neglected and aban-doned? I had waited so patiently for this day, only to be spurned, by my family and fiancé. I decided that I would not go through with the mar-riage, even if they came for me now in the King of England's royal coach.

Emily pleaded with me, while drying my tears. She convinced me that it was all a unintentional blun-der created by the general last-minute chaos. Further-more, Joe would be waiting at the altar, for-saken and distraught that his bride had not appeared. Then, the absurdity of the situation struck me, and we started laughing, hysterically. I regained control sufficiently to devise a rescue plan.

"Emily, call a taxi and tell them we were due at my wedding five minutes ago."

We patched our makeup and dried our sniffles. The cab pulled up at the door within fifteen minutes. We snatched up our bouquets and darted out the door. The driver stared in shocked disbelief at the sight of a bride in full regalia fol-lowed by a bridesmaid, holding the wedding gown's train.

"Weston United Church. I'll pay for any speeding ticket!"

"Hell, I didn't know I would be driving a bride and her lady-in-waiting to a fancy wedding! If they had told me beforehand, I'd have worn a clean shirt and washed this old buggy…and decorated her up, real nice, too!"

The "abandoned bride" was late for her wedding, but courageously smiled, took her brother Vic's arm and proceeded towards her "almost abandoned" groom.

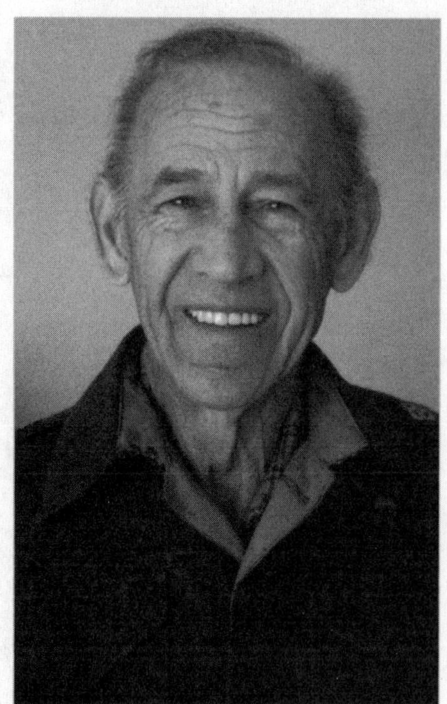

"It still fits!" Joe in his WWII uniform, May, 2000

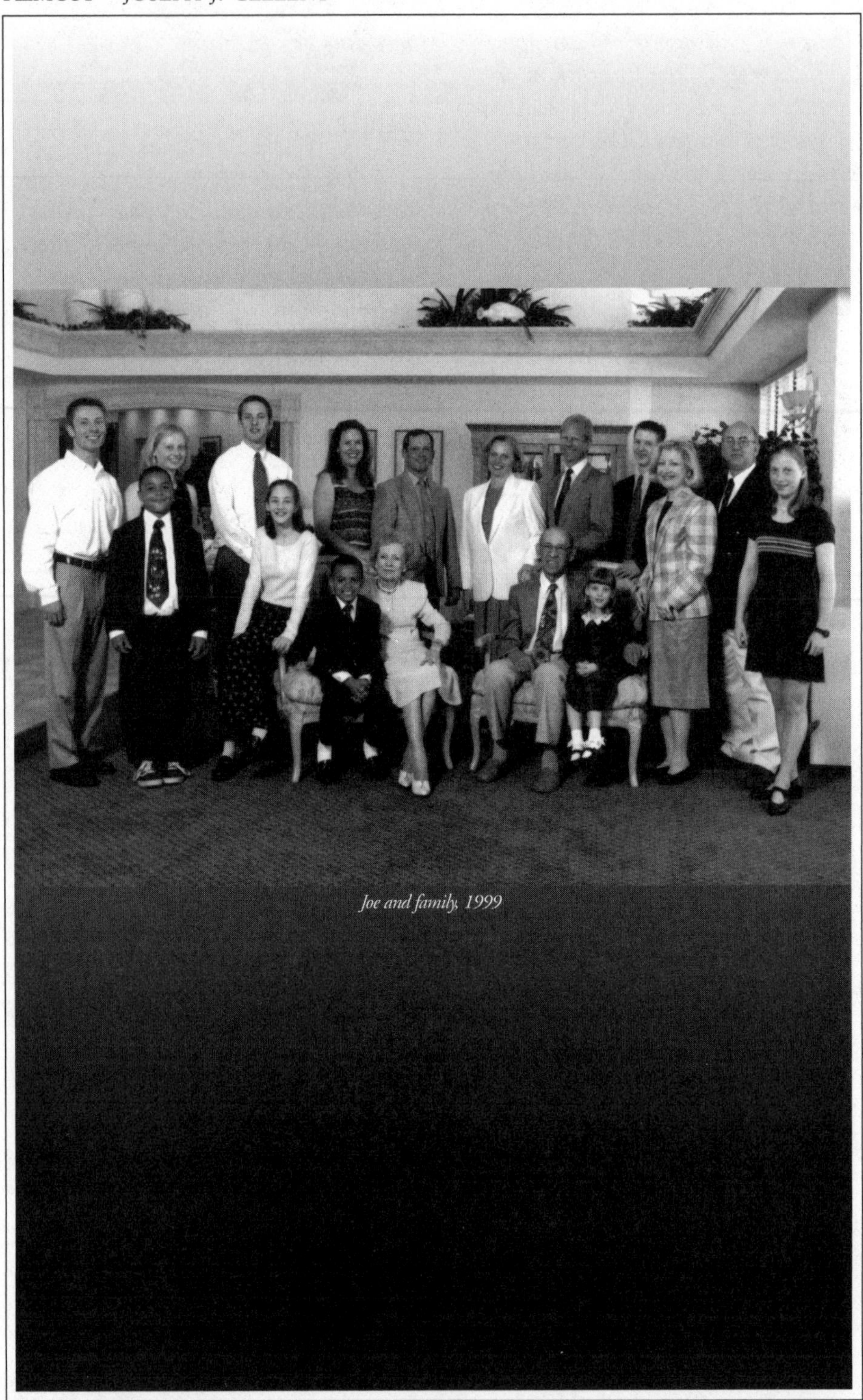

Joe and family, 1999

(1)

N.T. 1/4

Subject: Operational Personnel - HUNGARY.

CONFIDENTIAL.

HQ SOM,
CMF.

G/114.

1 April 1945.

To: M-3 (3 copies).
HQ SOM.

The following personnel were interviewed by the Commander on the 31st of March who has given instructions that your Section is to make the following arrangements for their immediate future and ultimate disposal:-

1. Lieut. J. GORDON.

(a) It is understood that this officer was enlisted in the Canadian Army in Feb. 43 as an O.R. and joined the organisation in July 43. M.S. state he was commissioned on the 18th of March 44 and posted to Mil. Est. 76.

In view of the above his ultimate discharge and any gratuity payable is a matter for the Canadian authorities.

(b) Report to be completed by Tuesday 3 April 45.

(c) To proceed on one week's leave to ROME on Wednesday 4 April. ✓

(d) Transport to be arranged and also hotel accommodation as part of the SOM allotment. ✓

(e) To draw money for leave purposes through Finance. ✓

(f) To be photographed for record purposes if not already done. ✓

(g) Sea passage to CANADA to be arranged prior to

(1190) Wt45451/225 110m 1/44 FHD Gp38/10.

Army Form W.3121

Date recommendation passed forward

	Received	Passed
Brigade		
Division		
Corps		
Army		

........Brigade........Division........Corps

Schedule No........ Unit H.Q. S.O.(M).
(To be left blank)

Rank and Army or Personal No. Lieutenant (Provisional rank).

Name Joseph GORDON.
(Christian names must be stated)

Action for which commended (Date and place of action must be stated)	Recommended by	Honour or Reward	(To be left blank)
Lieut. Gordon was a member of a small British party which dropped by parachute into HUNGARY in September 1944 with a special mission. When captured Lieut. Gordon showed great physical courage under continuous and brutal interrogation and by his cleverness and resource he was able to hide the real purpose of his mission from the Germans and to mislead them completely. Through a trying period of several months captivity he was the main standby of the leader of the mission, who says of him "Neither lengthy interrogation nor tedious nor trying imprisonment could damp his spirits. In dealing with interrogaters he showed toughness, reliance, and dexterity of mind. He did in fact outwit them." After helping to arrange the escape of another officer from imprisonment, Lieut.	Colonel FRANCK, Comd. HQ SOM.	M.B.E. (Civil)	

P.T.O.

Gordon made a hazardous but brilliant escape of his own. He succeeded in remaining in hiding under the most dangerous circumstances throughout constant searches and finally crossed the Russian lines into safety, bringing valuable information with him.

If a casualty as under, fill in date.

Nature of Casualty	Date
Killed in action	
Died of Wounds	
Died	
Missing	
Prisoner of War	

P.T.O.

Regent Miklós Horthy's Radio Proclamation, October 15, 1944 (abridged)

Ever since the will of the nation put me at the helm of the country, the most important aim of Hungarian foreign policy was, through peaceful revision, to repair, at least partly, the injustices of the peace Treaty of Trianon. Our hopes in the League of Nations in this regard remained unfulfilled.

Hungary was forced into war against the Allies by German pressure, which weighed upon us owing to our geographical location. But, even so, we were not guided by any ambition our increase our own power and had no intention to snatch as much as a square metre of territory from anyone.

Today, it is obvious to any sober-minded person that the Reich has lost the war. All governments responsible for the destiny of their countries must draw pertinent conclusions from this fact, for, as a great German statesman, Bismarck, once said: 'No nation ought to sacrifice itself on the altar of an alliance.' Conscious of my historic responsibility, I have the obligation to undertake every step directed to avoiding further unnecessary, bloodshed. A nation that would allow the soil inherited from its forefathers to be turned into a theatre of rearguard actions in an already lost war, defending alien interests in a serf-like spirit, would lose the esteem of public opinion throughout the world.

With grief, I am forced to state that the German Reich, on its part, broke the loyalty of an ally toward our country, long ago. For a considerable time, it has launched ever-new formations of Hungarian armed forces into the fight outside the frontiers of the country, against my wish and will.

In March of this year, however, the Führer of the German Reich invited me to negotiation in consequence of my urgent demand for the repatriation of Hungary's armed forces. There, he informed me that German forces would occupy Hungary, and ordered this to be carried out in spite of my protests, even while I was restrained abroad. Simultaneously, German political police invaded the country and arrested Hungarian citizens…."

The Germans do not keep their promises. In the shelter of German occupation, the SS tackled the Jewish question in a manner incompatible with the demands of humanity, applying methods it had already employed elsewhere. When war drew near the frontiers, and even passed them, the Germans repeatedly promised assistance, yet again, they failed to honour their promise.

I have decided to safeguard Hungary's honour even in relation to her former ally, although this ally, instead of supplying the military help (which) he promised, meant to rob Hungary of its greatest treasure-its freedom and independence.

I informed a representative of the German Reich that we were about to conclude a military armistice with our previous enemies and to cease all hostilities against them.

Trusting your love of truth, I hope to secure in accord with you, the continuity of our nation's life in the future and the realisation of our peaceful aims.

Commanders of the Hungarian army have received corresponding orders from me. Accordingly, the troops, loyal to their oath and following an order of the day issued simultaneously, must obey the commanders appointed by me. I appeal to every honest Hungarian to follow me on the path beset by sacrifices that will lead to Hungary's salvation.

Soot from inside a water heater or almost any stove pipe can be used to darken the eyebrows and the hair. With careful use of soot, coal dust, charcoal, charred wood, burned matches, black ashes of paper, a burned cork or even shoeblack, the eyes can be faintly shadowed on the top and bottom lids to add to the swarthy effect. Be careful not to overdo the effect and to blend all edges out to nothing. Try using a little of the black mixed with the rust color to accentuate "bags" under the eyes, hollows in cheeks or even a broken nose effect, which is achieved by adding faint shadows high on one side of the nose and near the tip on the other side, and rubbing the color off on the opposite side, so that your own lighter skin forms a highlight. Cheek bones can be heightened in the same way.

The sharp point of a burned match can serve as a pencil to thicken eyebrows. *Draw* hairs on the brow rather than smudge them on. Try drawing a few hairs on the nose bridge and note the "heavy" effect. Applying shadows high on both sides of the bridge of the nose adds age.

A mechanic's face, with ingrained grease, can be effected by rubbing in black grease from an engine or hub-cap, or even plain soot in a drop or two of oil, and then rubbing some of it off. A fine crop of synthetic blackheads can also be achieved this way. Shoeblack rubbed very thin on the face gives a gray, unhealthy, almost dead look to the skin.

Shoeblack brushed into the nap of clothes, hats, caps, around the collar, etc., and a damp soap bar rubbed into that, give a good imitation of shiny, crusted dirt and grease. It should be done while the clothes are naturally wrinkled to the body, since the top of wrinkles catch most of the dirt.

Try the following effects for greying hair, mustache or eyebrows. The results will vary with the materials as well as with the texture and greasiness of the student's hair. Try grey ashes, both wood and paper, powdered down by rubbing them in the palm of the hand; try talcum powder, flour or shoe-white greyed down a bit with one of the blacks. Comb this in well and add more until you get the effect you want. Try not to get it on the skin at the hair line or in the thin hair above the ears or back of the head. If you do, remove it. When you have succeeded in making the body of the hair grey, take some of the whitest hair in one palm, rub the hands together, and go over the area lightly, just touching the top hairs. Comb it carefully or rumple it up to fit the character you are assuming.

The effect of a stubble beard of one or two days' growth is best put on by using a dark thick grease and a rough sponge; certain brushes or a coarse napped material will serve. Stipple or pat the grease on the natural beard area, being careful not to make it too dark or heavy. Try for evenness and thin it out on the top edges.

Don't forget the hands. They too must match. Treat them with the same coloring as the face and to the same degree. Check up on your nails. Should they be clean or dirty?

Remember, if you are not too sure of some effect, use it only at night. In the daytime use only the few selected, simple, most effective disguises you are sure of from practice and know you have time to complete. Time yourself. Wear the effects and time *them* to see how long you can count on each one.

A page from the SOE Training Syllabus

Almost..., written by Camp X Historical Society President, Alan Paul Longfield, is the second in the Inside-Camp X series of books relative to the world of clandestine warfare, detailing Canada's role in the WWII 'secret war' and 'STS 103' (Camp X).

Until recently, little had been known to the public about Camp X, the top secret SOE training school, located in what was then, the small, rural town of Whitby, Ontario, Canada. Through the success of Inside-Camp X, the extremely important role that Canadians played in the Allies' covert war has now been documented for all time.

Almost...is Joe Gelleny's gripping personal account of his training as a secret agent in Canada and overseas, and his two secret missions behind enemy lines, during World War Two.

Alan and I will continue in our mission to bring this message to the public by producing additional books on the subject of Canadians' participation in the Second World War. Nevertheless, we have always had a higher priority, namely, to see the only original building in existence, returned to the site of Camp X. This structure would be converted into a living museum dedicated to the men and women of STS 103. Lest we forget.

To meet this end, the Camp X Historical Society, which is a registered not-for-profit organisation, has established the Camp X Building Acquisition Fund which will be used solely for the purpose of moving the building onto the original site. Once re-located on the Camp X property, the Society will require considerable funding in order to meet present standards and local By-laws, to operate as a public museum. Your donations of \$5.00, \$10.00, or \$50.00, payable to: Camp X Building Acquisition Fund, will be greatly appreciated and can be forwarded to:

Camp X
Building Acquisition Fund
467 Fralick's Beach Road
Port Perry, Ontario, Canada
L9L 1B6

Thank you very much.

Sincerely,

Lynn-Philip Hodgson
Vice President and Director, Camp X Historical Society
Author, Inside-Camp X.

Photographs Credits

Photo	Location	Credit
# 1	Acknowledgement	J. J. Gelleny
# 2	Foreword	J. J. Gelleny
# 3	Chapter 1	William Hardcastle
# 4	Chapter 1	Robert Stuart
# 5	Chapter 1	Robert Stuart
# 6	Chapter 1	Hamish Pelham Burn
# 7	Chapter 1	Lynn-Philip Hodgson
# 8	Chapter 1	Lynn-Philip Hodgson
# 9	Chapter 1	Lynn-Philip Hodgson
# 10	Chapter 1	William Hardcastle
# 11	Chapter 2	J. J. Gelleny
# 12	Chapter 2	J. J. Gelleny
# 13	Chapter 2	J. J. Gelleny
# 14	Chapter 3	Inside – Camp X
# 15	Chapter 3	Jack C. Stainaker
# 16	Chapter 4	J. J. Gelleny
# 17	Chapter 4	Ian D. Foster, Handley-Page 57 (Halifax) 'Rescue'
# 18	Chapter 4	J. J. Gelleny
# 19	Chapter 4	J. J. Gelleny
# 20	Chapter 4	J. J. Gelleny
# 21	Chapter 4	J. J. Gelleny
# 22	Chapter 5	J. J. Gelleny
# 23	Chapter 5	J. J. Gelleny
# 24	Chapter 5	J. J. Gelleny
# 25	Chapter 7	J. J. Gelleny
# 26	Chapter 7	J. J. Gelleny
# 27	Chapter 8	Inside – Camp X
# 28	Chapter 8	J. J. Gelleny
# 29	Chapter 8	J. J. Gelleny
# 30	Chapter 8	J. J. Gelleny
# 31	Chapter 9	J. J. Gelleny
# 32	Chapter 10	J. J. Gelleny
# 33	Chapter 11	J. J. Gelleny
# 34	Chapter 11	J. J. Gelleny
# 35	Afterword	J. J. Gelleny
# 36	Afterword	J. J. Gelleny
# 37	Afterword	J. J. Gelleny
# 38	Appendices	J. J. Gelleny
# 39	Appendices	J. J. Gelleny
# 40	Appendices	J. J. Gelleny
# 41	Appendices	J. J. Gelleny

Index
The Players